LOCHS AND LOCH FISHING

BY

HAMISH STUART, M.A., LL.B.

British Library Cataloguing-in-Publication Data
A catalogue record for this book is available from
the British Library

A Short History of Fishing

Fishing, in its broadest sense – is the activity of catching fish. It is an ancient practice dating back at least 40,000 years. Since the sixteenth century fishing vessels have been able to cross oceans in pursuit of fish and since the nineteenth century it has been possible to use larger vessels and in some cases process the fish on board. Techniques for catching fish include varied methods such as hand gathering, spearing, netting, angling and trapping.

Isotopic analysis of the skeletal remains of **Tianyuan man**, a 40,000 year old modern human from eastern Asia, has shown that he regularly consumed freshwater fish. As well as this, archaeological features such as shell middens, discarded fish-bones and cave paintings show that sea foods were important for early man's survival and were consumed in significant quantities. The first civilisation to practice organised fishing was the Egyptians however, as the River Nile was so full of fish. The **Egyptians** invented various implements and methods for fishing and these are clearly illustrated in tomb scenes, drawings and papyrus documents. Simple **reed boats** served for fishing. Woven nets, weir baskets made from willow branches, harpoons and hook and line (the hooks having a length of between eight millimetres and eighteen centimetres) were all being used. By the twelfth dynasty, metal hooks with barbs were also utilised.

Despite the Egyptian's strong history of fishing, later Greek cultures rarely depicted the trade, due to its perceived low social status. There is a wine cup however, dating from c.500 BC, that shows a boy crouched on a rock with a fishing-rod in his right hand and a basket in his left. In the water below there is a rounded object of the same material with an opening on the top. This has been identified as a fish-cage used for keeping live fish, or as a fish-trap. One of the other major Grecian sources on fishing is Oppian of Corycus, who wrote a major treatise on sea fishing, the *Halieulica* or *Halieutika*, composed between 177 and 180. This is the earliest such work to have survived intact to the modern day. Oppian describes various means of fishing including the use of nets cast from boats, scoop nets held open by a hoop, spears and tridents, and various traps 'which work while their masters sleep.' Oppian's description of fishing with a 'motionless' net is also very interesting:

> *The fishers set up very light nets of buoyant flax and wheel in a circle round about while they violently strike the surface of the sea with their oars and make a din with sweeping blow of poles. At the*

flashing of the swift oars and the noise the fish bound in terror and rush into the bosom of the net which stands at rest, thinking it to be a shelter: foolish fishes which, frightened by a noise, enter the gates of doom. Then the fishers on either side hasten with the ropes to draw the net ashore...

The earliest English essay on recreational fishing was published in 1496, shortly after the invention of the printing press! Unusually for the time, its author was a woman; Dame Juliana Berners, the prioress of the Benedictine Sopwell Nunnery (Hertforshire). The essay was titled *Treatyse of Fysshynge with an Angle* and was published in a larger book, forming part of a treatise on hawking, hunting and heraldry. These were major interests of the nobility, and the publisher, Wynkyn der Worde was concerned that the book should be kept from those who were not gentlemen, since their immoderation in angling might 'utterly destroye it.' The roots of recreational fishing itself go much further back however, and the earliest evidence of the fishing reel comes from a fourth century AD work entitled *Lives of Famous Mortals*.

Many credit the first recorded use of an artificial fly (fly fishing) to an even earlier source - to the Roman Claudius Aelianus near the end of the second century.

He described the practice of Macedonian anglers on the Astraeus River, '...they have planned a snare for the fish, and get the better of them by their fisherman's craft. . . . They fasten red wool round a hook, and fit on to the wool two feathers which grow under a cock's wattles, and which in colour are like wax.' Recreational fishing for sport or leisure only really took off during the sixteenth and seventeenth centuries though, and coincides with the publication of Izaak Walton's *The Compleat Angler* in 1653. This is seen as the definitive work that champions the position of the angler who loves fishing for the sake of fishing itself. More than 300 editions have since been published, demonstrating its unstoppable popularity.

Big-game fishing only started as a sport after the invention of the motorised boat. In 1898, Dr. Charles Frederick Holder, a marine biologist and early conservationist, virtually invented this sport and went on to publish many articles and books on the subject. His works were especially noted for their combination of accurate scientific detail with exciting narratives. Big-game fishing is also a recreational pastime, though requires a largely purpose built boat for the hunting of large fish such as the billfish (swordfish, marlin and sailfish), larger tunas (bluefin, yellowfin and bigeye), and sharks (mako, great white, tiger and hammerhead). Such developments have only really gained prominence in the twentieth century. The motorised boat has also meant that commercial fishing, as well as fish farming has emerged on a massive scale. Large trawling ships are common and one of the strongest markets in the world is the cod trade which fishes roughly 23,000 tons from the Northwest Atlantic, 475,000 tons from the Northeast Atlantic and 260,000 tons from the Pacific.

These truly staggering amounts show just how much fishing has changed; from its early hunter-gatherer beginnings, to a small and specialised trade in Egyptian and Grecian societies, to a gentleman's pastime in fifteenth century England right up to the present day. We hope that the reader enjoys this book, and is inspired by fishing's long and intriguing past to find out more about this truly fascinating subject. Enjoy.

PREFACE.

MYSTERY, romance, the freedom of the larger heaven, these are the possessions of the lake, so long as a tarn gleams like a blue jewel set in the swart hills, so long as a legend runs, so long as the commoner of air has a heritage.

Of the mystery the kelpie is not alone the overlord; he shares the kingdom with many creations of the fancy born of the grey silence under ghostly hills, of the crested wave, white-gleaming above the dark depths, of the ominous calm of the amber-surface fading into the blackness of the inner places, home of the demon trout, that ·haunts every lake retaining its legacy of the Wilderness, as an heir of the unknown that may be terrible. Each cast or any cast may bring up this demon trout. The fancy is always raising, hooking and playing him for doom and the breaking of the spell of ʋld enchantment.

Nor is the realism of angling wholly able to check the fancy or lull to sleep the ambitious pleasures of hope. Each lake must be a Loch-na-Breack Mohr and hold its big fish, which, for the most part, are unknown to fame. The Thames angler has his ambitions; but they are ambitions set on a fixed fish known of some men and capable of being known of all. The salmon angler knows the limitations of his most optimistic hopes. Rivers can become low, their area is confined, and salmon will show. The prose of the net deals with figures, and pounds, and ounces. Its arguments are facts, destructive of all mystery.

Least of all can the dry fly angler enter the lists. His feeding fish, his "smutters," his "tailers," his "bulgers," and "genuine risers," they are catalogued and tabulated, and their chronicles are writ in the transparency of limpid water and sun-dried shallows.

Of the lake alone is the mystery.

And old romance sits ever by its shores. Even prosaic Loch Leven, where one pays half-a-crown an hour to angle in a fish-pond peopled by a masterful race of civilised fish of lithe activity, has its Lady of the Mere—superior to good days and bad—a possession for ever, set above the bringing down of trout to the grave with blood. East, West, North, and South, over lakes large and small, famous and mutely glorious, the same old romance lingers. The shade of Cormac Doil is with you as you angle in Loch Coruisk; the mountain breeze from every Ben-na-Darch that carries out your line pipes a thousand legends; in the ghostly silence of the evening the boat song of dead clansmen comes across every Hebridean lake, and the air is vocal with the sound of voices long since still; every dismantled ruin is restored; every greener spot on the hillside has its history that is a romance, its legend that is tragic, comic, pathetic, human, but ever dramatic and always interesting.

Of the lake are the mystery and old romance.

And the larger air, the glorious heritage of its commoner? It is the very elixir of life itself, the intoxicant which inebriates in its free sweep when we breathe the same air, live the life of Nature herself, think her thoughts in a glorious union that is of the very essence of the higher and truer Pantheism. In a single week the breathing of such an atmosphere and the living of such a life should send one swinging over moor and fell, over rocks and stones, in the exuberance of new-found life and the paradise regained of super-abundant vigour until the old, fierce fire of the lost youth of the world thrills through every vein, makes each muscle grow instant young, each nerve become a servant of the will and the heart bowed down leap to the rainbow in the sky and catch the music of the shrill, free wind amongst the listening rocks and the dancing reeds.

Of the lake are the mystery, old romance and the larger air.

These attributes alone are sufficient to justify the writing of a book devoted to the charms of loch-fishing and the joys of wandering in lakeland.

But lakeland had a further claim upon the consideration of the angling writer. It has received but scant justice, and there is no book exclusively devoted to loch-fishing. It was this consideration which tempted me to essay the task of filling up the blank in our angling literature. That I have filled the blank, I neither hope, nor expect, nor pretend. The volume now submitted is the hasty product of thirty evenings' work after days of such toil as modern "evening paper" journalism necessitates. In many respects, it is an incomplete treatise, and in no sense can it be claimed that it exhausts lakeland. Possibly some of its defects in this respect are due to the progressive nature of angling knowledge, and the insoluble, or at least, difficult character of many of the problems of fish-life, fenced as it is with an inviolable, elemental barrier. In any case, if I have succeeded in indicating the kind of thoughts angling compels the angler to think, and have, in their stating, succeeded in vindicating the claim of angling to be not only the contemplative man's recreation, but also the best and most brain-resting of sports for the mind fore-done with the storm and stress of modern life, I shall be amply rewarded.

I may, venture to claim for "Lochs and Loch Fishing," that a consistent theory of fish-life—the Sensational theory—runs through all its pages, that the facts stated are the result of personal observation, and that both the facts and the inferences drawn from them are for the most part original, even if they are not accepted as satisfactory.

With regard to the chapters on the future of our lakes I may mention that, since this volume was in the Press, the facts of some instructive cases have reached my hands, entirely corroborating the theories advanced, which, I now regret, not having put in more dogmatic form. That our lakes yield but a poor harvest compared with the yield of thirty years ago, and that there is no comparison possible between their present productivity and their sport-giving capacity both in the days of Franck and of Thornton, are facts beyond dispute. Franck can be thoroughly relied upon as a witness on this point, while those who doubt that Thornton could kill, inter alia, six trout, weighing 32lbs., in a morning, on Loch Tay, may be doing the memory of that gallant officer an injustice. That the glories of those days can be restored I do not doubt, but the difficulties attending the restoration are great, and are, I venture to think, stated with fairness, if not with clearness, in the following pages. I may add to what is stated therein that both in the case of salmon rivers and of our lakes, the restoration of natural conditions must be the chief object of all amelioration and reform. As to the former, in the old days when "baggits" and "kelts" could be freely come by, the "spawners" were spared. In these days, the "spawners" are sacrificed and the spawning beds, which should be the chief care of conservators, are shamefully neglected in order that a greater appearance of active interest may be secured by ostentatious and mostly useless stocking with fish purchased with wasted money, which could be far more profitably employed in watching and improving the "redds." One hundred spawners, who make an average success of what is too often the last duty of a salmon, mean an addition of 1,000 fish to the river or loch, or both. The fact speaks for itself. What is true of rivers, is true of lakes, and in dealing with the future of the latter, I have urged the importance of aiding and imitating nature, of making all ameliorations in accordance with her laws, and of constructing our fish-farms and improving existing environments on the lines of her best and most instructive models.

For such errors and blemishes as the volume contains, I need scarcely offer any special apology, though it is perhaps necessary to explain, that here and there, I adopt my own nomenclature, as when for example, I prefer to call a "bob" fly a "first dropper," and to disregard custom. It may also be mentioned that my "hook numbers" refer to the "Pennell-Limerick" old scale, in which No. 12, corresponds to No. 3, new scale.

"Lochs and Loch Fishing" has been almost entirely written; here and there occur a few excerpts from articles which I have contributed to the sporting and daily papers. These excerpts have been sub-edited and adapted to my purpose. For permission to utilize them I am indebted to the kindness of the Editors of "The Field," "The Angler," "The Fishing Gazette," "Westminster Gazette," "Globe," "Bradford Daily Telegraph," and other papers.

The plates have been specially prepared for this work, and I am indebted for the original "pictures" to, amongst others, Mr. Thomas Wilson of Harris, Mr. Hill of South Uist, Mr. Leopold Layard Budleigh-Salterton, and Mrs. Collingwood of Lilburn Tower, Northumberland, whose very clever snap-shots of leaping salmon were taken, with the assistance of Mr. A. B. Collingwood, on the Mingan River, Labrador. I regret that a series of plates which I had designed to illustrate the evening rise and loch-fishing in a calm do not appear in the present edition. If the book is ever reproduced, the omission will be rectified. There is nothing more difficult to obtain than pictures of fish and fishing. When you have the subjects, the camera is absent, and when you have the camera, it kills the subjects. Anyone who has ever been followed the livelong day, when angling, by a photographer, will appreciate the difficulty.

In conclusion, if "Lochs and Loch Fishing" has only touched the fringe of the subject and left much to be said, I trust that it will be accepted in the spirit in which it was written by one who, "if no fisher, is a well-wisher to the game" and to all who follow it by stream, loch, canal, pond or sea, North, South, East or West.

HAMISH STUART.

LEEDS, *1st August, 1899.*

CONTENTS.

PART I.—LOCHS AND LOCH FISHING.

PART II.—PRACTICAL LOCH FISHING.

CONTENTS.

ILLUSTRATIONS.

PART I.

LOCHS AND LOCH FISHING.

CHAPTER I.

THE DUFFER'S PARADISE.

"Those fish of simple faith and ready rise,
Trout of the lake, the Duffer's Paradise."—*Anon.*

Pompey's Pillar as the most famous of all possible misnomers has a serious rival in the phrase "The Duffer's Paradise," with which certain angling critics, whose knowledge of the art of loch fishing is in inverse proportion to their self-sufficiency, have chosen to dismiss this department of angling. The purist, whose contributions to the entomology of angling cannot be overvalued, goes even further than the careless critics referred to, and classifies loch fishing as unworthy of serious consideration as a candidate for a position amongst the angling arts. While condemning loch-fishing as a mere off-shoot of the "chuck and chance it" school, he damns it as the worst possible development of that degenerate and out of date system of fishing with the fly.

The careless dictum of the casual critic may safely be ignored. He is generally an all-round angler open to conviction and ready to admit, if only on the evidence of the difference in results secured by difference in methods in loch fishing, that there is far more art in the apparently mechanical casting than meets the eye. In all probability he has seen but one style of loch fishing—the steady, monotonous drift before the wind, the dual control of a certain portion of an ascertained stretch of water thrashed with methodical precision by one angler in the right of the bow, and by another angler in the right of the stern. He has been educated in the belief that there is no possible evolution from this style which, for aught he knows to the contrary or perhaps cares, may have been, and most probably was, the method of Simon Glover when he angled in Loch Tay, and will be the style of his own descendants to the tenth generation when he resigns the rod to other hands and crosses the Styx in the craziest of immortal boats. He has heard from his youth upwards that to fish with the fly for loch trout in a glassy calm is to essay the impossible, and it is part of his inherited faith that lack of wind is the best possible excuse for hours of idleness and superlative indulgence in the dolce far niente by the loch side. Nay more. He will tell you with all the assurance of a Trentsider waking axiomatic as to the rooted aversion of the salmon of the Midland river to the fly, that a good ripple is a condition precedent to good sport, and if a river fisher with some skill in the special art of the stream will grow equally dogmatic in assuring you against the evidence of your own experience, that when the breeze comes and the ripple curls shorewards the art of loch fishing is reduced to one of merely mechanical skill, while results differ not by reason of any exercise of the head, but in precisely the same degree and from precisely the same cause as does the head of game killed by a good shot in a good position from that killed by a bad shot indifferently stationed on a "cover" or "driving" day. Just as one wild-goose, he may tell you, arguing through the suggestion of this shooting analogy, successfully stalked by the solitary shooter, bringing guile and wile to bear on guile and wile, is worth a hundred "rocketers" sent on to a well-planted gunner by an army of well-arranged beaters, so one river trout successfully circumvented and taken in clear water with a cunning worthy of the Red Indian, is worth a whole cartload of loch trout taken by promiscuous casting by guile that is wholly un-ambushed. There is in his argument such a measure of plausibility, that ex hypothesi, it may be admitted that he states a half-truth. There is, on the other hand, a fallacy—the fallacy that he begs the question and assumes that it is an accepted axiom that the loch reduces all ang-lers of average skill to the same level, and is, therefore, by parity of as-sumption, rather than by parity of reasoning, "The Duffer's Paradise."

Even admitting, however, that success in loch-fishing is dependent absolutely upon difference in mechanical skill, it is obvious that the degree of that skill must vary, and equally clear that if the skill varies, it is capable of being developed and is therefore at once an acquired and a "natural" art—acquired, that is to say, because capable of ac-quisition by practice, and natural because some loch fishers, sharing the great characteristic of all sportsmen, seem, apart from training and practice, to be more richly endowed with natural aptitudes than are others.

Of anglers, and of the loch fisher as a member of the family, it may with truth be said that the best are born and made, the inferior samples are made only. And it is quite immaterial whether we speak of the combination of head, eye and hand which together, and by the strength of their unity when lodged in an active frame, physically and mentally well-equipped, make the expert at any sport what he is, or merely assume the quick and accurate eye, the responsive hand that is never in front of the optical sense, which constitute mechanical precision at a sport, ignore the intelligence—the brain of ice deep-seated in its own thick-ribbed tenacity of reasoned purpose—and reduce true genius in one of its manifestations to the dull level of a merely perfect contrivance of unimpeachable parts and immaculate whole.

Assuming this last and lowest form of skill to be the only attribute of the successful loch fisher, even on that assumption the possessor of mechanical ability must necessarily conquer his less richly endowed rival. From the mere fact of this difference in skill, there follows, moreover, the inevitable conclusion that in this mechanical exercise of inherent talent the prima facie vindication of loch fishing as an angling art is to be found. It follows further that when this mechanical skill is absent, or even when it is present, practice can in the one case create it and in the other develop it, until a mastery over all the intracies of the art, in this its lowest form, can be obtained, which proves when in exercise and by the results achieved, that though almost any duffer can hail the loch as his paradise, under favourable conditions, there are open to him higher paths which experience will teach him how to tread.

Even the most rigid disciple of Lochlevenism cannot fail to be struck with certain facts when fishing any lake, that had he caught their inspiration and learned their lesson would have raised him above the merely empirical and traditional methods of the older school.

The first principle of scientific loch fishing is to treat the loch as a large pool in a very slow-running river, or if the apparent bull be permissible, to treat it as a large pool in a currentless river.

The stating of this as the postulate or first principle of the science of loch fishing naturally leads to a consideration of the attitude of the purist. His creed may be briefly summed up in the dogma, that no fish is worth killing which can be killed with any fly not an exact reproduction of a natural fly or by any fly, whether an exact imitation or otherwise,

not acting in a natural manner. This one and only article of his angling constitution proceeds on the assumption that the trout of certain
rivers are so highly educated that they can at once detect the very slightest and apparently most immaterial divergence from the natural fly, so
that a leg too many or a shade of colouring accentuated is sufficient to
make them decline with reasoned scorn the most deftly placed imitation of the real Simon Pure. Certain sorts of river flies used by the
" wet " fly fishers, he admits, do resemble the natural article, but this
partial holding of the mirror up to nature is, he maintains, rendered
wholly valueless in practice, when the fly is made to behave in a manner in which no fly ever does behave. This being so, it is only natural
that loch fishing with the fly is pronounced by the purist to be not fly-
fishing, but a sort of surface-spinning with the fly. He declares with
all the dogmatic fervour of the exclusivist that loch flies are mere abor-
tions, and that qua fly-fishing, loch fishing cannot be a science, because
its lures are lusus nature and never deceive trout to their doom by an
imitation of nature.

The purists thus fall into one of the most common of all fallacies. They
assume that because all asses are animals and all men animals, that,
therefore, all men are asses, a position which may be true but is certainly
not a logical sequence from the two initial premises. It may be, and
indeed is, perfectly true that the trout most worth catching are wary
trout deceived to their doom by presenting to them apparently natural
food that is really artificial. But it is surely a begging of the question
to assume that the natural food of trout does not vary with the environment of the fish, ignoring the well-established fact that the trout
is omniverous and a most materialistic optimist in the matter of food
possessed of only one dietetic axiom : " Whatever is, is good to eat."
It may, perhaps, surprise the purists to be told that on certain lochs the
trout, unlike the highly educated trout of the south, who have forgotten that Colonel Hawker ever killed their ancestors from horseback, are no more excited by the rise of a perfect fluttering yellow snowstorm of May flies, than they are by the millions of ephemerids that each
summer day dance their brief hour of life away in the fretted shadows
and shafts of sunlight beneath the overhanging boughs that weep and
wave over the shores of their wide-spreading home. It may still more
astonish them to hear the axiom enunciated that loch fishing, when

scientifically pursued, both in the matter of flies and in the methods of using them, is as much a faithful adherence to what may be vaguely termed natural law in the angling world as is dry-fly fishing itself in its very highest development.

The laws of angling when justly stated are as truly non-arbitrary and as wholly declaratory as are the laws which perfect justice would emanciate. The latter would recognise that though principles alone are constant, the circumstances of their realisation so modify them as to give them an appearance of difference that is most deceptive when synthesis usurps the place of analysis.

It is in this very confusing of the science with the art of fishing, or to speak by the card, this confusing of the science and art of dry fly-fishing with the science and art of loch fishing, and in the consequent ignoring of the fact that both rest on the same broad basis of fundamental principle, that the purists have with the ignorance of little experience condemned loch fishing, and with a vehemence, begot of that exclusivism to which I have already referred, have described the loch as " The Duffer's Paradise." I hope in the succeeding chapters to show that the loch-fisher, like all fishers and all students of fish and their ways, stands like Newton on the shores of an undiscovered and certainly but half-explored sea. For him the great book of nature holds chapters that have never been read, or when read, have been imperfectly understood-chapters, on which the light of truth may never shine save through that darkness, dreaded by the life of thought, the sleep of reason that knows no waking—the utter night of old oblivion in which the heirs of all the ages inherit but the deep-dug dust.

I hope in these pages to be able to show that the loch fisher is not the mere machine he is so often represented to be, but an angler who not only adheres pretty closely to the accredited axioms of angling deception by appealing to nature, and that, too, in no narrow and restricted sense of the phrase, but also that he angles as truly with his head and not merely with his hand as does the most up-to-date of dry fly-fishers in the most difficult and consequently ideal of chalk-streams or other southern rivers whose clear waters the " all-seeing cycle of the sun " lights up with a splendour that is a challenge to human skill.

Presuppose the raising and hooking process finished and that the loch fisher is using, as he will and should often use, tackle as fine and general " gear " as delicate as that of the " dry fly " man, or the " far and fine " exponent of the river, and the playing of a big, or even a decent, fish is quite as difficult in some lochs and far more difficult in others than it is in any river. In certain weed and reed-haunted Hebridean lochs the expert river fisher will find himself completely beaten time after time, until he learns the art of playing a big fish—I mean a fish of from 4 to 8lbs.—from and with a boat. Even comparatively small trout, if he adopts the ordinary method of playing a fish, may give him infinite trouble and by their rushes to windward while the boat goes to leeward may introduce him to difficulties equivalent to those in which he has found himself when a river trout has passed beyond control and gone where he cannot be followed.

If the raising and hooking have to be done in a glassy calm or in a half or whole gale of wind new difficulties arise.

In a calm, whether the fish be rising or not a single boil breaks the surface of the lake from shore to shore, he will have to exercise not only the utmost patience, but the greatest possible measure of delicacy. His " fishy " eye must be of the keenest searching for likely spots—a space between the weeds, a likely hold beside some friendly stone, a taking bit of dark water beneath the boughs, a round bit of grass-covered turf on the bottom, beside, or in, all of which some great trout may lurk. There must be nothing and yet something of the " chuck and chance it " about his methods, but a reasoned purpose carried out with indomitable will. The cast must sweep with the softness of an inspired web to fall with a gentle kiss on the calm surface ; it must be sunk to the proper depth and move with the steady precision which an assured plan of campaign can alone give it ; if a fish shows he must be watched and only struck at the proper " psychological " moment when intuition and the sense of touch that practice gives, if it does not create, tells him that the fly has been sucked in.

Yet must he in the best sense " chuck and chance it," too. His flies must never be out of the water. Fish lurk or travel in strange and unexpected places, and the mad hermits or tourists of the lake are generally worth catching. A fish will move from deep to deep, from shallow to shallow, and in the mere fact that when moving he travels high and may be killed, not because he is feeding, but because he is in motion, is found not only the justification of continuous casting even on unlikely water, but also one of those lessons which experience and observation teach.

If fish are rising to the natural fly and feeding, then comes the angler's opportunity, and in calm, bright, fine weather without a ripple from shore to shore, loch fishing then becomes a positive art, and is as truly scientific fishing, even from the entomological and imitative point of view, as is dry fly fishing in its highest development with this exception—and it may be frankly admitted, that the angler is not under the same necessity of concealing himself by ambushed guile of a personal kind. He has simply to keep the boat still, move noiselessly when he does move, cast far and fine, judge and time the rise, often long-drawn out, deliberate and slow, and, when the fish is hooked, play him quietly and effectively.

If when the garish day is done, he has to angle in the dusk or play fish in the pale moon's most uncertain and deceptive light, he will find that a new charm has been added to angling's long list of joys because a new difficulty has to be overcome and a new kind of visual power, dependent to some extent on the sense of touch has to be cultivated.

Before passing, however to practical details, I must—with the apology that angling is essentially the most egotistical of sports and that, therefore, the angling writer is necessarily a person privileged, indeed compelled, to blow the trumpet of apparent self-laudation if he would prove the right to say experto crede—here set forth in support of my theoretical contention that the loch is not the "Duffer's Paradise," certain facts which show a marked difference, if not in the degree of skill possessed by some anglers, then assuredly in the efficacy of their methods.

I confess to be at some loss as to what statistics to quote from amidst a bewildering plethora of choice. However, as all the figures at my command seem to prove the same truth, I choose my results in a particular lake—perhaps the most difficult and "sporting" loch in Scotland as proof of my contention so far as an individual sheet of water is concerned, while I quote the results of my South Uist season of 1890 with a view to the same end in the case of many waters, a greater variety of days and a larger company of brethren "in rods" but rivals in renown.

As to the first, I find that on the loch in question, which is a lovely tree-crowned Argyleshire lake, I killed in eight days 64 trout, weighing 97½lbs., against the average basket of from none to two fish killed by the other anglers who fished the loch during the same season. This result was achieved not by special skill, but by the steady adherence to particular methods, by an obstinate tenacity of purpose that unrewarded hours of labour could not daunt, and by the use of the head as well as of the hand.   The loch in question is a peculiar one, and in a later chapter Ishall revert to its idiosyncrasies as the most educative and difficult sheet of water in Scotland, or perhaps out of it.

As to the second, my statistics cover a wider range of days, include by way of comparison the takes of a larger body of anglers, dry fly men and wet fly men, loch and river anglers, salmon slayers and trout fishers, and naturally embrace a greater variety of waters.

The figures are those of the South Uist season of 1890, and the fish were caught entirely with the fly in the very excellent waters of the Lochboisdale Hotel, waters of which I have a very high opinion and many happy angling memories.   During twenty-four particularly bad days (some of which were only an hour or so of angling duration), I killed, fishing alone in my own way, 99 sea trout, 130½lbs.; and 224 brown trout, 124¾lbs.; or 325 trout, 255¼lbs.—an average of about 14 fish, 10½lbs., per occasion; whereas a daily average over the same period of fourteen other rods fishing in pairs took, per diem, 68 trout, 31¼lbs.; or about 5 fish, 2¼lbs., per rod.   Throughout that season, which was a very fair one. I fished in this district on thirty-six occasions, and secured 110 sea-trout, 140½lbs.; and 358 brown trout, 224¾lbs.—an aggregate of 468 trout, 365¼lbs. (an average of 13 trout 10lbs.) out of a total aggregate for the season in the hotel lochs of 1,036 sea-trout, 1,113¾lbs.; and 3,817 brown trout, 1,693¼lbs.; or, in all, 4,853 trout, 2,807lbs., my proportion of weight being thus over one-eight, and the average (on calculation) per rod of those fishing together just over 3lb.

I have already apologised for quoting these figures in support of my theoretical arguments.   They may be left to tell their own story greatly and are " stubborn chiels," which seem to emphasise the conclusion that though the loch may be " the duffer's paradise," in so far as an indifferent angler has a better chance of killing fish in some days on certain lochs than on a river, yet so far from the loch being merely " the duffer's paradise " it affords as wide a field for the exercise of reasoned and mechanical skill as does the river.   Nor do lochs yield pride of place in infinite variety to rivers and there is just as great differences between lakes as there is between streams—some lochs being as much more difficult to fish as a clear running trout stream meandering through an English meadow is than some dark hill-fed torrent that leaps " from the mountain's crown " in the untrodden places of the lonely North or West. The truism, that success in every department of angling, even the simplest, is differentiated by the degree of skill, experience, and intuition possessed by the angler I have specialised and applied to the loch. I should use precisely similar arguments, but different facts, to show that even angling for small roach and confiding gudgeon in the beautiful canals of England is, in the matter of results, equally a question of skill, simple though it looks when one observes an expert professional bait-catcher taking fish by the hundred. An hour afterwards one's opinion as to the simplicity of this kind of fishing would be considerably modified if one met the average amateur with his beer-jar essaying to wile the companions of the same fish to their doom at the same spot and with precisely the same lures. He would catch fish, it is true, but the number of his victims would be as one to ten. So is it with loch fishing. The duffer in most lochs will find a limited sort of paradise when he angles under favourable conditions, or when the fish are small, unsophisticated and hungry. Loch trout, like salmon, will rise to a very badly thrown fly, just as birds will sometimes fly into the shot of the most inexpert of shooters. The triumphs of the duffer on the loch are, however, only duffer's triumphs. Under the same conditions the experienced angler will kill far more fish, while under difficult and " sporting " conditions, the loch may prove the duffer's inferno and the very antithesis of his so-called paradise.

Before, however, I deal with practical loch fishing, there are very many problems to be discussed, which experience on many lakes has suggested and which must be stated for obvious reasons. The problem of the future of our lakes is of such importance to all loch fishers that I make no apology for the many chapters dealing with it and with kindred questions, while it is impossible to state the art and science of loch fishing and to justify the claim of loch fishing to be regarded as both a science and an art and a sharer in the vindication of angling as the contemplative man's recreation without regarding the lake for many other aspects than the narrowest of all—a place in which one can kill fish by certain methods.

CHAPTER II.

"And the lake her lone bosom expands to the sky."

From Land's End to John o'Groats and from Loch Leven in the east to the loneliest lake in the wilds of Connemara that resigns the setting sun to Indian worlds, Great Britain and Ireland possess lakes that illustrate every variety of freshwater sea found in the temperate zone. It is true that the United Kingdom boasts no great lakes like those to be found on the Continent or in North America, but relatively to the land area Great Britain and Ireland possess lakes that, on a small scale, are the same in all essential features as the different varieties of lakes of which the "temperate" world can boast. Of the Scottish lakes themselves it may almost be said that they epitonize the lake-life and physical character of the temperate zone, though naturally their fauna and flora are for the most part peculiar to themselves, while certain species of fish and plants are common to both hemispheres.

From the narrower point of view of the oceanographer or lacugrapher to invent a new word, the Scottish lakes form, however, a perfect epitome of all the lakes of the world, and when Sir John Murray has completed his survey of them and published his charts, this fact will be more abundantly established. In the meantime it will suffice to say that in such spreading waters as Loch Lomond, the great chain of lakes running from Loch Ness to the head of Loch Linnhe, Loch Awe, Loch Rannoch, Loch Errochd, and other lakes too numerous to mention in detail, we have samples of the true inland sea in miniature. Smaller lakes of the Loch Vennachar, Loch Lubnaig and Loch Ard type, to name three only of the better known examples, scarcely attain to this dignity, while Lochs Earn and Tay, though deep lakes, occupy a sort of middle position. Shallow lakes like Loch Leven are almost peculiar to the country, while the thousand lakes of the Western Islands, though lacking something of the mystery with which the waters of lakes of great depth are always shrouded are, nevertheless, equally characteristic and relatively to the other lochs of Scotland, are by far the most interesting to the curious student of fish, if only because they afford him opportunities of studying fish life under circumstances and conditions that very closely approach the primeval order. In other words, the Hebridean lakes are so numerous and so mixed in their physical character, that, on the one hand, the whole of certain islands become in times of deluge practically one vast lake or series of connected lakes in which the fish migratory and non-migratory enjoy a perfect jus spatiandi to the confusion of acknowledged habits, while, on the other hand, certain lakes become of indeterminate character and are neither salt water nor fresh, nor yet brackish, but assume one of those characters to the temporary exclusion of the other two to a degree varying according to the rainfall or the state of the tides or both, and sometimes the strength or direction of the wind. As a result of this peculiar condition of affairs, exceptional opportunities are afforded of tracing the actavic connection between the sea-trout and the common trout. It is indeed natural that in a land where one acre of water occurs to every seven or ten of land (these are the respective proportions of Benbecula and South Uist) and where salt water rivers are found and tidal pools, lochs and ditches abound, the facilities for observing how readily the common trout becomes nomadic and passes from the accredited position of a non-migrant to that of an occasional migrant should be numerous, that afford clear proof the migratory tendency is a pure creation of the necessities of environment.

It may serve a double purpose to here emphasise by an example from these Western lakes the educative aspect of the loch as a guide to the habits of fish.

That all trout are migratory is a proposition whose general accuracy few or no persons who have given the fish any consideration will dispute. The migratory tendency, or, to give it a somewhat misleading title, the migratory instinct, may vary in the degree of intensity with which it manifests itself; but it is always present, and may, for purposes of generalisation, be said to depend for its development far more upon circumstances than upon heredity, it being an almost axiomatic proposition that the strongest traits in " short-generationed " animals, as the results of environment, may vanish under its influence.

If it be accepted that the conditions of existence mould the habits of life, it becomes at once clear that the search for "the necessities," as we term them, is the ruling motive of animal existence. A fish, therefore, if it cannot obtain the necessities in the water in which it finds itself, will migrate, if it can do so, to other water which cannot be less unkind and may well prove more generous in the matter of food. At one season of the year food may be scarce in a particular section of a river and plentiful in its lower and tidal reaches. When such a state of affairs exists necessity will compel the fish to become a rover. When it discovers that roving pays, and has battened on the rich feeding of the estuary, the migration of necessity becomes the migration of choice, and a priori you have the migratory habit established.

That the fish of certain streams pass through these stages can be judged from what has occurred in New Zealand in the case of virgin waters that have been stocked with English trout. In certain of the rivers of that colony food appears to be scarce at some seasons. The consequence was that the fish moved down to the estuary, and thence to the sea, in both of which they found such abundance of food that they have become essentially as migratory fish as the salmon, though descended from so-called non-migratory trout, and have in fact become "salmon trout" in the applied sense of the phrase construed in relation to their habits. Here environment has evidently triumphed over heredity. Nor is there anything unnatural in the victory, for heredity is merely a legacy of habit, which in this sense is not doing what one's ancestors did, but what one's ancestors would have done under similar circumstances.

Viewed in this light, the migratory tendency of the trout is obviously not so much a vice of any particular species of trout as a characteristic of all trout. Though the scientist may insist that certain trout display the migratory tendency in a more marked degree than others, he can only do so at the risk of being involved in contradictions and being brought face to face with practical examples of the same species of trout displaying far different tendencies under far different conditions of existence. While I should be prepared to admit that the tendency of that so-called distinct species of trout the salmo levenensis is to descend, yet cases are on record of its ascending, at seasons other than the spawning season, during which, of course, the tendency of all the sal-monidæ is to ascend.*

Such isolated cases are, however, of no great moment, unless the whole circumstances attending them are proved, in seeking to demon-strate that the migratory tendency is dependent for its development upon environment.

These generalisations lead me to now to consider the speical lesson of certain Hebridean lakes on this point. I take a South Uist case, though I am under no necessity to do so.

On the western side of that island there are amongst many lakes five that are connected in a peculiar kind of way with the sea and with one another. The common outlet to the sea is a ditch some ten to fifteen yards wide, which finally passes through a pipe led out into the Atlantic. Some distance up this ditch another ditch branches off to one of the lochs, into which a small drain falls from yet another of them. In the first of these two lakes bull trout and sea trout abound, and there are great quantities of trout—mostly of a small size, but all, or nearly all, of them presenting the silvery appearance of the trout of the ditch—an appearance which indicates an occasional marine bath, and of which the tangible outward signs are the looseness with which the silver scales adhere to the fish and their liability to rub off and stick to the hands or anything coming in contact with them.

It is important here to note that the conditions of existence in this loch are not of the best, that that its feeding is poor, in fact, just suf-ficiently irregular in quantity and quality to furnish the necessity which prompts migration, not, however, of the established and habitual, but of the occasional and opportune variety. In the other loch, from which there is a clear passage to the one just referred to, and from it, of course, to the sea, the feeding is probably of the richest and rarest kind to be found in any water of the United Kingdom. The bed of the loch is almost entirely covered with a soft green mossy weed, while its waters are a mass of vegetation, with stretches of sand and fine clean stone be-tween the beds. The lake, as may be supposed, abounds in food of

---

*An instructive example of this ascending tendency is afforded by trout confined in a reservoir where there are no spawning facilities. If a pipe be led out of the loch from a trough at a lower level than the loch, the fish will ascend the pipe and fall into the trough where they may be secured and the reproductive process completed. The hint and the use to which it is put are of value to corporations.

every kind. Were it not for the fact that is carries an incredible number of lusty fish, the average size of these, at present about ¾lb., would
be largely increased. The loch, however, is full of fish, as may be
gathered from the fact that I once killed in it 74 trout, weighing 46½lb.,
in a very short space of time. Here the fish are under no necessity to
wander, and they never do wander, though the road to the sea is as open
to them as it is to the fish in the lake below, which is much less bounti-
fully supplied with food.

If we now revert to the main ditch, and investigate the conditions prevailing in the three other lakes, whose road to the sea it forms, we will
find a still stronger confirmation of the truth that the tendency to migrate
is not a predisposition, but the result of predisposing causes operating
through necessity upon what we term an instinct, though it may more
truly be called an appetite. The lower two of the three lakes are in
reality one lake, which has been artificially divided into an upper and
a lower lake by a road built through the original lake. At a certain point
in this road a breach (bridged over) some five feet wide has been made,
so that the two lakes are connected by a small channel of the width just
mentioned, and sufficiently deep to allow the passage of a small boat.
The lower lake was, as it happens, a portion of the original single lake,
which afforded but poor feeding, feeding, in fact, equal in quantity and
quality, to that of first of the five lakes mentioned, from which necessity
compels and opportunity permits the trout to migrate. This lake abounds
in large sea trout, which rarely enter the upper lake in any number, while
its ordinary trout are of a small average size, and when large display most
markedly all the appearnces usually shown by fish that have had a trip
to the sea, and rarely, if ever, that richness and depth of colouring,
which, together with their size, would declare them migrants from the
upper portion of the divided lake.

That upper portion is rich in feeding, which grows richer the nearer
one approaches to its further end, where it is united with the last of
the five lakes under notice. It abounds in fine trout of about 1lb. in
weight, which never show any tendency to migrate nor any of the signs
of ocean sojourn, though the road to the sea is both short and easy.
Here again they are not under the necessity of migrating, and the predisposing causes towards migration are more than counterbalanced by the
inducements of environment, in the shape of a good and abundant supply

of nourishing and suitable food. Migration would, in fact, be an absolutely superfluous waste of energy and enterprise.

In the last lake of all connected with the one just noticed by a small but short and clear stream, not only is food abundant and of a peculiarly rich nature, but the fish are also less numerous, and the area of water is greater than in any of the other lakes. In it, moreover, the trout present the appearance and other qualities which have led scientists to describe Loch Leven trout as fish descended from land-locked migratory sea trout, which by a long-continued compulsory "non utendum" of their migratory instinct, have merely retained the external features of their sea trout origin—in shape, activity, and a greeny-yellow silveriness of normal colouring best seen in death, and a latent tendency to migrate downwards whenever, as is alleged, the opportunity arises, or, as I maintain, when necessity calls the instinct into active being.

The trout in this last lake never migrate under ordinary circumstances. Even under abnormal conditions, when continuous heavy rains have made all the lakes practically one, they rarely do so. If they did, when the waters had subsided it would be a not infrequent occurrence to take one of these fish, instantly distinguishable by their exquisitely brilliant colouring in life and most characteristic shading in death, their size, shape, and general contour from the different "varieties" of trout in other lakes. On the contrary, though the fish of the other lakes occasionally find their way into the spreading waters of this most ideal home for lusty fish, with its stretches of fair sand and shredded weed, its pure clean water, its patches of reeds and weeds, its shell-encrusted stones and ideal spawning grounds, yet the compliment is rarely returned, for these home-keeping trout would only display "homely wit" if they took to wandering or migrating to less choice pasturing grounds.

One moral of the lesson taught by these Hebridean lakes is clear. It shows conclusively that the tendency to migrate is not an absolute but a relative tendency, conditioned by the necessity for its exercise and proportioned in its intensity by the degree of that necessity. When the tendency becomes a habit through the gratification of the particular appetite which calls it into play, then the fish becomes truly migratory, and not merely a non-migratory fish with a latent migratory tendency. It is also obvious that a fish will continue longest in the element, or, in other words, the adopted environment which best suits the gratification of that appetite deserving for the time being to be designated the overmastering sensual impulse.

It may possibly appear that I have already dwelt at too great length upon that variety of lake. the Hebridean, and have elevated it to a position amongst British lakes out of keeping with its merits. I would suggest to the critical reader who holds this opinion to tax his patience by re-reading the very simple but most satisfying lesson in fish habits and characteristics which the dilation on the five Hebridean lakes should have taught him. Nay more. I would even suggest to all students of fish, particularly of the salmonidæ that a month or two spent amongst the waters of the Outer Islands might result in a greater acquisition of knowledge than many laborious years spent in studying waters less adapted by nature for the reading of him who runs. Hebridean lakes do not, it is true, exhaust the world of waters, but they form a chapter in the book of nature which no student should miss reading. No passages are wholly dull, though some are naturally more interesting than others.

Resuming, however, the general subject, here is another simple but pregnant example of the lessons of lakeland. You are fishing, as a man may, with a light heart where the larger air sweeps in free draughts across the moor, and suddenly you notice that you are casting over bright sand of virgin purity and that the water is so shallow and clear that any fish that are around you should be perfectly visible. You throw your flies without hope, but as a matter of habit over the apparently tenantless portion of water in front of you. There is a flash from nowhere and you hook, play and land a trout. Examine the fish and you will find that his back is a light tawny yellow, his belly and sides almost white. You leave that spot and fish over sand of a darker hue patched with greenish weed. You raise, hook and kill another fish and on examining him you discover that his back is a deep olive hue, while his sides have a yellow tinge, fading to white. Presently you cast over shallow water above a bed of green grass. You see no fish, but eventually you kill one. His back is almost green, his sides a deep yellow, the green of the grass, the yellow of its kindred weeds, the firmer roots that are the foundations of the green home which is his lurking place. A light breaks in upon you and the Great Mother stands revealed. You have probed the secret of her maternal care for the least of

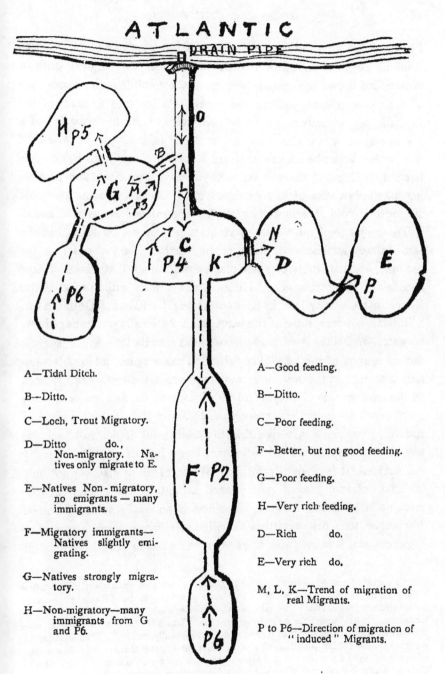

A—Tidal Ditch.

B—Ditto.

C—Loch, Trout Migratory.

D—Ditto do.,
Non-migratory. Natives only migrate to E.

E—Natives Non-migratory,
no emigrants — many
immigrants.

F—Migratory immigrants—
Natives slightly emigrating.

G—Natives strongly migratory.

H—Non-migratory—many
immigrants from G
and P6.

A—Good feeding.

B—Ditto.

C—Poor feeding.

F—Better, but not good feeding.

G—Poor feeding.

H—Very rich feeding.

D—Rich do.

E—Very rich do.

M, L, K—Trend of migration of
real Migrants.

P to P6—Direction of migration of
"induced" Migrants.

ENVIRONMENT AND MIGRATION.

her cold-blooded children. What though the pessimistic analyst, who robs all beautiful thoughts of their charm, with the surgical knife of mis-applied reason, whispers in your ear that the children are unconscious of their parents care, you can rise superior to the cold accuracy of the formalist by remembering that the pantheism of the fluttering fall of a a single sparrow is a Christian philosophy of faith simply because God and nature cannot be thought of apart. Nature not only feeds but clothes her children, and in these three casts you have learnt that her protecting mantle is a coat of many colours, swift to change to the hue best suiting the child that lurks beneath his apportioned share of raiment.

To the lakes of the Southern Hebrides, it cannot be said, that the same interest attaches as to those of the North. The lochs of Jura, for example, are deplorably common-place, even though that island of deer and fabled mountains of gold does boast a loch with, perhaps, the longest name of any lake in Scotland, Loch Joch-Darach-Ghlinn-Astir.

In Islay, however, some of the lakes are exceptionally interesting sheets of water, and three * of them have some peculiarities which suggest further lessons of the lake. They are cited as examples, not as object lessons that exhaust the didactic aspect of the world of meres. Loch Guirm, on the western side of Islay, is a lake without, so far as I am aware, any great depth of water throughout its mile and a half by half a mile of surface. Now in a lake like this the thoughtful angler will look for some lesson deeper than the water lying below its surface. One of many will suffice. It is obviously an ideal lake in which to discover not only the effect of environment upon general habitat, but of special environment upon particular habitat. The first is an easily solved problem. The angler soon discovers that he kills more fish in some places than in others, and it is easy also to see that those places afford the greatest

---

* I exclude from the interesting lakes of Islay the tarn said to contain the so-called tailless trout, which a recent writer on the fauna and flora of the Hebrides erroneously placed in Loch Finlaggan. The lake in which these trout were said to occur is now tenantless. It lies cradled far up in the wilds of Ben Bhainn. It is a curious lake and the bottom is simply heaped with jagged rocks " confessedly hurled." The native theory was that the fish rubbed their tails off against the rough edges of these rocks. As a matter of fact, Islay trout are subject to a disease of the tail ray which causes it to dry up and drop off, and it is a common thing to catch a trout with a quarter, half,or three-quarters of his tail gone. Tail ray abnomalities are not uncommon, and my friend, Dr. Stewart, "Nether Lochaber," records the case of a mackerel-tailed trout in lone Loch Lydoch, on the Moor of Ranroch.

degree of shelter conjoined with the maximum of food—a golden mean
of monopoly at which trout and indeed all fish aim.

To prove, however, that the fittest demonstrate not only the rule of
survival but that they are the lords of particular and very choice castles
and keeps, strong lurking places set in a land of easy plenty, is not quite
such a simple matter.   You must either raise and closely note without
hooking some specially large fish at an exact spot easily identified, say,
beside a certain stone that rises above or is clearly visible below the
water, or you must land some such fish, mark and return him unharmed
to freedom.   If a day or two after you can raise and kill him at the same
spot you will have proved that even in lochs fish have homes that are their
abodes of choice and not of chance, which they hold against all comers
so long as they have the power.   If they are big, powerful Rob Roys
of the lake you may rest assured that the spot is a specially choice one.
From this analogy, you can run through the whole field of nature and
see a new, certainly a truer, meaning in the doctrine of evolution.

Two other Islay lakes have a different, but equally pregnant lesson to
teach amongst the many lessons all lakes, as all nature, can teach.   The
lesson I choose is one of exceptional interest to the stocker, and the
lochs which teach it are Ballygrant and Lossit.   The first of these is a
typical small Argyleshire lake of the best and most beautiful kind, a
wood-crowned water abounding in food and in trout of the Loch Leven
variety, as well as in native trout of most excellent quality.   Of late
years the loch has been somewhat over-crowded, and the fish have
deteriorated in size in spite of the rich feeding.   Lossit is an ordinary
rough and ready small lake, half tarn, half loch, which nevertheless
has some good feeding ground and is usually rich in surface flies, best of
all food for trout.   It is connected with Ballygrant by a small stream
of easy descent, while out of Ballygrant flows the river Sorn, which at its
place of exit is fenced with barrier-wire impassable to fish.   Twenty
years ago in Lossit you could have killed any average day in the week
some dozens of small confiding trout running six, seven, and eight to
1lb.   In Ballygrant you would rarely have got a fish under one pound,
and many would have reached two, some three, and a few even four
pounds or more.   At present your fish will average about 10 ounces,
with an occasional large one.   In Lossit, on the other hand, instead of
killing any number of little fish, you will kill and would have killed for

the past twelve years on a good day a large number of fish running from six ounces up to and over one pound. Twenty years ago 100 fish would have weighed from 14lb. to 15lb; twelve years ago an actual basket of 103 fish I killed one afternoon weighed 38½lb., and I presume a similar number would, if killed during the present season (1899), weigh even more. There is here not only a very excellent example of the side-charms of angling, but of the lessons which the lake and perhaps the lake alone is able to teach. It is obvious that there arose in Ballygrant a condition of affairs analogous to that in an over-populated country. The struggle for existence became too fierce. The fittest were faring best and the loch was threatened with an oligarchy of avoirdupois—a despotism of the few that were heavy and strong. Certain emigrants of necessity, affording another fine example of the origin and limitation of the migratory habit, essayed the burn and won their way to Loch Lossit. These few established themselves there amongst the pigmy savages, intermarried with some, and ate others up, until, being joined by others from the lake below at intervals, the character of the fishy people inhabiting Lossit and of the " country " itself* was changed and the lake became a sort of United States to the Great Britain of Ballygrant. There is, therefore, in a study of these two lakes to be found not only an object lesson in fish life, but also a sort of rude justification, based upon what is essentially a natural law, for the usurpation of the places of weak peoples by strong races, and a very excellent example of the kind of might that really is right, the might that gives as much as it takes and only asserts its right by recognising a corresponding duty.

Even at the risk of tediousness I will venture upon further illustrating the lessons of the lake from yet some other points of view, premising that in dealing with the more practical aspect of loch fishing I shall possibly have occasion to " moralise " in a similar strain. The aspects of the lake by which I would further illustrate its didactic character may be put in this way.

A certain worthy who was an authority on " finds " used to lay down the law to the fox-hunters of his district in the pregnant words " Them

* It is a necessary conclusion from the observation of fish life that a strong " people " can extract more out of the same environment than a weak, though the position may not be permanently maintained and decay grow by what it feeds upon. There are many forms of food which the feeble people or the decaying race cannot annex or assimilate.— Vide chapter on " Habits of Loch Trout."

places that seem the most likeliest are often less liklier than them places that seems the least likeliest." Mutatis mutandis this phrase of classic purity of diction appears to me to be eminently applicable to angling days. Days that are full of promise in the morning too often close in disappointment, and days that promise nothing are often the richest in fulfilment. A cursory glance over my angling ledger, reveals many such days, sandwiched between days on which the sun shone on the waters of promise. Possibly this contrariness on the part of nature, and the most fickle and most meteorologically responsive of her many children, may account for the fact that my best days on certain lakes should, according to the dicta of the angling Cockers, have been my worst.

Nature in all her aspects, and certainly in her didactic character, is ever an ideal economist. She wastes neither lessons nor moods. It is possible, therefore, that, if you placed me by a Highland loch side, when the wind was coming in cold gusts from the south-east, a leaden sky stretched its cold dome from horizon to horizon, and the mist-laden hills loomed a ghostly grey with blurred outlines through the driving rain, I should be right if I laid down the absolute rule that on such a day there would be no rise of fish in a stiff water, and that only an occasional " mad one " would reward your obstinate perversion of the Shakespearian dictum, " Home-keeping youths have ever homely wits." If, however, I found after experiment that the fish were rising and feeding with a persistency I had never seen them equal in the water in question, I should at once look for nature's lesson hid in the midst of her unwasted mood with its retroactive influence on the humour of the apparently unconscionable trout, who seemed to have thrown axiomatic truth to the south-east wind.

Nor would the reason be far to seek. Analogy is the best interpreter of natural mysteries, for analogy of all methods combines the synthetical with the analytical. I would remember that I had seen grouse sit close on wet stormy days, when the weather seemed to have been broken on the meteorological wheel beyond the surgical skill of its clerical dispenser and from the dust of old oblivion I would rake the experience that such days of " grousish " perverseness have invariably been followed by spells of fine weather. From this analogy, aided by similar experiences drawn from the angling past, I would surmise, and surmise correctly, that the depression was only temporary, and that the trout knew it, and were already hailing in fancy a smiling morn on the morrow.

This is one of the charms of sport. The student of it who can rise above the mere killing of fish and bird and beast catches something of the wisdom of nature, the lessons of very little things that tell great stories. We are more self-sufficient than wise and more simple than natural, else we would employ men to study animals and prophesy the weather "from the birds" instead of those instruments which are for the most part still the masters of their own truths.

I have, however, already said sufficient to prove that the raising and killing of fish does not exhaust the joys of the loch. Lakeland has charms other than those which appeal to the sense of the beautiful in form. It is replete with the beauty of the fitness of things—of the slavish ministry of all nature's parts to the perfect whole, the kaleidoscopic balance that flits and changes, but never fails to produce a perfect picture of symmetrical design.

Those great yellow argosies of summer—the fat May flies, that flop up and go quivering down the wind in aimless fluttering to the casual eye, are nature's provisional insurance against the rainy day when the shrimps floating past in their dead hundreds may fail to be fruitful and multiply. The gulls that swoop and dip after them on all hands insure that they shall not be wasted when the troutish cupboard is full. Away in the amber shallows you will see countless little black and wriggling objects, like semi-colons, now clinging to the rocks as if for safety, now making little sinuous voyages of no great purpose from one fastness to another amongst the hard but kindly stones. These tadpoles have their place in the economy of the loch. They are the solids that flank the daintier dishes—the last resource of noble troutish bodies when other things fail. They dwell in the shallow sanctuaries for there alone is safety assured.

Search the lake through and through, study it with the eye, not merely of the angler, who desires to bring down its fish to the grave with blood, but with that of the student of the great lessons of little things, and you will find that in the lake as in the whole cosmic order co-operation which exhausts the ideal of economic demand and supply is the ruling principle of the universe. This is the last, but not the least, if indeed it is not the consummation, of the sermons in brooks—sermons of which the lake is but the larger expression, deeper may be, but not a whit less clear.

CHAPTER III.

The Darwinian dictum that the most intelligent of monkeys are divided by a greater gulf from the least intelligent of men than divides the highest from the lowest races of mankind appears, as a necessary conclusion from the observations of the practical evolutionist, to convey the suggestion of a somewhat similar dictum in the case of the salmonidæ. The analogy, is, of course, in many aspects far from being perfect, for the simple reason that there are no monkeys or what would correspond to monkeys in the family of the salmonidæ, though as between trout in all their varied gradations from the civilised trout of our best waters to the puny trout of our poorest waters and fish in general, the comparison is not wholly unjustifiable. It may be presumed that the monkey would resent as an injustice the placing of the blind eel-shaped fish of the caves of Adelsberg with their lizard-like fins in the same position relatively to the trout as the monkey occupies to man. Yet such a comparison is not wholly unjustifiable on psychological, if not on physiological grounds. In any case if evolution can presume, on the plan of the geologist and contrary to the reasoned belief of Lord Kelvin on more or less intelligible grounds, an eternity for evolution to work out the mysterious ends of the Creator, which we see clearly in the tree and dimly in the bud, the ichythologist, whether scientific or merely practical, may be permitted to borrow an odd million or two of the twenty-five allotted by the learned Glasgow professor for the emerging of the world from primeval chaos to present order.

That we must become the debtors of time to explain the differences that exist between the members of the same family of fishes—differences that do not appeal so strongly to the man of science as to the practical student of fish—is aboundantly clear, when yet one stands on the very threshold, and the fish world is still absolutely a region of virgin

mystery. Even after one has wandered for years amongst
its thousand charms for the speculative mind, it remains still a region
with whose external features alone the observer, to whom the tracking of
the old mazes with fresh feet is a labour of love, becomes intimately acquainted. Nature seals certain chapters in her great book, and has
fenced round the world of fish as commoners of water with an elemental
barrier that has sentinelled from time immemorial, and may sentinel
until chaos is come again the mysteries of subaqueous existence.

It is possibly to this intuitive appreciation of the limitations of our
power, not less true as yet of air as of water, that we owe not only the
fabled monsters of the deep from sea serpent to kelpie, but also
the origin of Daedalus and his thousand and one imitators. Possibly, too, it was the same spirit which induced the builders to start
work on Shinar's plain and create the first boom that history or its hand
maiden tradition has recorded, antedating even the apocryphal giants
war with the gods of Olympus.

These reflections are apparently somewhat of a divergence from loch
trout. As a matter of fact they are suggested by a very complete chain
of ideas associated with loch trout, whose very differences, united as
they are by a bond of family likeness of a general as well as a special
kind, necessitate, if they are to be accounted for at all, the hypothesis
of a common ancestor. From this common ancestor loch trout have, it
is true, widely diverged if one is content to regard the matter super-
ficially; a very little consideration, however, soon shows that the degree
of the divergence is more apparent than real

A priori reasoning in problems of this scientific and historical character is a most dangerous and misleading guide. Yet few who have
considered this question can have failed to ask themselves whether, if
we could even conceive of that imaginary golden age of angling, when
fishing was not a pastime, that calls forth, if pursued in its true spirit,
the best qualities of the heart and the highest energies of head and hand,
and awakens from its necessary associations and surroundings the noblest
and loftiest thoughts of which human nature in its best moments is capable, but was merely a portion of the daily or occasional quest for food
in which the hunting man in the ancient sense was ever engaged, would
we find the same or nearly the same differences in trout as now exist?
How far we should have to roll back the years, it is not altogether idle

speculation to ask, as we shall presently see, so far as the solution of the
practical problem at issue is concerned. Imagine for a moment,
however, that period when the rivers of Britain poured their dark
waters through the wild glens and primeval forests, and the
lakes expanded their lone bosoms to the sky, when the
light of each returning dawn was shed in vain, for no man arose with
hope renewed to reap the spoil of their teeming waters; when the full
pride of day poured its glories on swirling pool and laughing lake and rising fish that knew not, and had never known, the dangers of dancing fur
and feather cunningly interblended in varied contrast of colour and form
across the surface of their home; when the soft and fading splendours
of the dying day crimsoned and empurpled the hills, and steeped in a
myriad of varied hues that phantasy of massed clouds which attend the
sun in his going down, and no man came to angle at that most pleasant
and often most profitable period of the whole day. At that period, and,
as scientists reckon time, it was as yesterday, presupposing the conditions
of existence were otherwise the same as those of to-day, if man and his
works were removed and the evil they have done were undone, it is safe
to presume that the order of things, so far as the salmonidæ is concerned, would be as they are.

To go back to remote periods as the zoologist, and still more as the
geologist, regard remoteness, would be to explore a world of very different conditions of existence. if that is to say we are to presuppose a common ancestor of the salmonidæ. Such a supposition if evolution means
anything, is a necessity of thought, but at the same time to assume a
physical postulate which we must formulate but cannot trace is only to
acknowledge, so far as fish in general and any species of fish in particular are concerned, that scientific history is only exact when it is analytical
and is largely speculative and wholly inferential when it become synthetical. If zoologists cannot discover the missing links in the great
chain of evoluted life, then surely ichthyologists can afford to stand
and wait, content with the knowledge that if they cannot trace the salmonidæ through all the chances and changes of years back to a common
ancestor they have at least been able to assure themselves of the link
between the existing varieties of the family and to attribute the differences to their proper origin and cause.

Turning from the temptation to speculate in wider fields, and confining my remarks so far as possible to loch trout, as we know them, it is undoubtedly difficult to believe prima facie that the great differ-ences between the trout of lochs are entirely due to corres-ponding differences of environment operating through thousands ot years or through periods of sufficient, if of indeterminate duration, to produce the results which we see.

Who, for example, comparing an excellent specimen of the fish of Loch Coil-a-Bharra, in Argyleshire, Lower Bornish, in South Uist, and Loch Sarclett, in Caithnessshire, three lakes whose trout are unsurpassed in beauty of shape and richness of colouring by those of any lake in Scot-land, with the black and yellow dwarfed fish from some of the peaty tarns of Jura, Harris, or one of the few South Uist lochs carrying such fish, would not find it difficult to believe that the obvious difference, not merely in size, but in stateliness of being was entirely due to years, probable centuries, perhaps aeons of difference in environment? The difficulty of grasp-ing what evolution as a practical process means is as great as the en-deavour to realise infinity in time whether looking forwards or back-wards. Yet it is equally a necessity of thought. We fail, it is true, to see far up the long slope of time down which the countless years have rolled, and by processes that are bewildering have produced the infinite variety of fish life with its subtle connecting links from the lowest form of it seen in water animals that are a mere congeries of nerveless ganglia to the most shapely and dashing of fish with their fixed habits of ap-parently reasoned purpose. If we take not merely an order that has branched into a genus, and that again into a species of fish with its varieties, as modified by the special conditions of environment, the mind in endeavouring to grasp the infinite number of moving incidents by flood that have produced the subsequent different development, is lost in a maze of physical causes, real and supposed, that is as perplex-ing as the labyrinth of the higher problems of metaphysics, the origin of rights and responsibilities belonging to the moral and not the material order. Yet we know that from time immemorial those laws have ever been at work, and have operated mighty changes before men discovered them or gave them formal recognition. It has been finely said that natural law, in the widest sense as embracing all the laws of the physical and moral order was extant " long before Moses was born,

before Aaron rang his golden bells, before there was a phrophet or a
judge in Israel." Presupposing, therefore, what is practically an infinite
period for their operation, it is easy in theory to grasp as a whole, though
impossible to do so in detail, how the infinite variety in fish life arose.
Ichythyologists by their researches of a scientific, and in many cases of
an anatomical, kind have not left us altogether in the dark as to the connecting links between the higher and the lower forms of fish life, using
that phrase to embrace all animals that live in water without being under
the necessity of coming to the surface for air.

As an example of this connecting link which may help to simplify the
problem, in one of its aspects, of the differences observed in loch trout,
lampreys, and lamperns may be cited. These interesting water-animals
belong to the order cyclostomata, the genus petromyzontidæ and have
been sub-divided into four species, the last of which has two variations,
or to speak by the card, is known by two different names, one derived
from its habitat, the mud, the other from its lack of visionary power.
Some of these species of lamprey affect the sea and one of them, the
true sea lamprey, is known as the lampern, and will attack even such fast
swimming fish as the mackerel and sea-trout. In proof of this interesting
fact I may here interpolate that I once secured in a Hebridean loch a
sea-trout of 1lb. with a large hole clean through it; the surface of the
wound was rough and the formation of the pinkish cicatrix, perfectly
healed, suggested the pulpy condition to which the circular motion of the
adhering teeth of the lamprey would reduce it. The other two species of
lamprey are migratory, while the third is found only in rivers, in which
all the four species spawn. Finally it may be mentioned that the mud
lamprey for the first three or four years of its existence has the habits of
a worm, a fact which emphasises the position that the borer and that
very minute "fish" the lancelot seem to be decayed members of the
lamprey family, or elevated members of the worm race; in any case they
seem to be the connecting link between the annelids and the petromyson-
tidæ. A casual observer would class the latter order with the eels or
anguillidae, and, indeed, in some places, Scotland, for example, they are
called lamprey eels. As a matter of fact, they belong to a class of their
own, and differ in many essentials from eels and from all other fresh
water fish, the majority of which, including eels, come under the order
physostomi, fish, that is to say, having a duct from the air bladder to

the throat which permits the fish to adapt themselves to the varying pressure of the water. In some aspects, and this is the reason why 1 have selected them as "missing links," the lampreys are not true fish at all, but seem to rank mid-way between a true fish and the annelid or worm family, while in the shape of their mouths, owing to the absence ot true jaws, they approach the tadpole; moreover, the vertebrae, though completely arched, are not separated, as in the case of undoubted fish. Their brain, however, both in formation and nerve branches, is the same as in other fish. The most strongly marked characteristic is the mouth. This organ, armed with strong suckers, enables them to adhere to stones and other substances with the tenacity of a parasite. There are no scales, and a glance at a specimen reveals the total absence of any lateral line. The bronchial gills (invariably seven in number in adults, the eight of the embryo and undevolped petrmyzon being lost in development) are another marked and leading peculiarity. All the different species, unlike the eel, always, as already stated, spawn in rivers, the sea variety ascending them for the purpose. We have here an obviously instructive lesson which, if it does not teach us how the differences between fish arise, at least succeeds in showing that those differences if enormous are not wholly destructive of the traces of a common ancestor. The lampreys are connected with fish, in the popular and in some sort the scientific sense, and possess certain characteristics common to all fish, yet are differentiated from all other fish by characteristics peculiar to themselves. The history of the evolution is a sealed book, but in theory at least, analysis gives to the mind a general idea of the synthetical process that has operated these wonderful ramifications in fish life of which the classifications of the ichthyologist are the chronicles.

CHAPTER IV

Loch Trout and Evolution. The Effects of Particular Environments.

If the problem of accounting for the infinite variety of fish life as a whole is, as I have endeavoured to show, not altogether inexplicable, and the root idea underlying its solution be kept in view, it becomes abundantly clear that the differences between the trout of various lochs are capable of a very simple explanation.

In the first place those differences are differences of degree and not of kind, and we have in consequence a much more limited field of investigation to cover. When we remember the many variations in form fish life has assumed, while still preserving, as in the case of the lamprey, certain common characteristics, and note that as between the trout of this loch and of that we have not the abstruse problem of connecting links to solve, it becomes still more obvious that with the exception of certain analogies, which are first principles in the theory of evolution, we have the question of environment, and of environment alone, to consider. Environment is to fish-life as important as the " standard of comfort " is to our social life, and once a " standard " is set up by environment any departure from it creates precisely the same discontent and unrest in a community of fish as it does in a community of human beings. Happily therefore so far as loch trout are concerned, environment, using the word in its widest sense, is a factor in evolution which we can study in operation without presupposing any such eternity as the geologist, and in some respects the zoologist, is under the necessity of assuming. We will not, it is true, be able by observing its effects to trace the rise of new species, but we can undoubtedly notice its effect, as a powerful cause, upon different communities of the same species. I have already in a previous chapter cited a singular instance of how a more powerful and in every way a fitter race of loch trout were forced through the conditions of their environment to invade the territory of a more feeble race—springing, of course, from a common ancestor—whose feebleness was the result of the long-continued operation of precisely the same causes as compelled the invasion to wit, overpopulation, an excess of fish over food, and the overmastering in the struggle for it—in the fight for the condition of existence, of the strong by the weak. I showed that within at least eight years, this invasion by a stronger and larger race, conjoined with the partial extirpation by and partial fusion of, the weak with the strong, the small with the larger, had resulted in the production of a race of trout, occupying a middle position between the fish of the upper and those of the lower lake. The invaders being a more powerful and virile race and descended from "fitter" ancestors have naturally been able to make more of the conditions of the same home than did the puny race, whose decadence once established grew by what it fed upon. Possibly the new race may in turn decay. Possibly their virility may enable them by cannibalistic predation to maintain the balance of nature. In any case they at present afford a most perfect illustration of that law of evolution, the survival of the fittest, and illustrate with a clearness that he who runs may read, one at least of the causes that produce the differences which we see in loch trout.

The illustration which this example affords of the effect of environment and the struggle for existence upon the trout of a particlar loch, is very far from exhausting this aspect of the subject, though it not only exemplies the progressive power of environment, but also the retrogression which environment can bring about.

As an example of the retrograde effect of environment, premising that its operation as a deteriorating or ameliorating influence is the same on all members of the salmonidæ and therefore that the analogy is absolutely logical, nothing can be more pregnant of the truth I am endeavouring to elucidate, than the effect of captivity upon the migratory salmonidæ, particularly upon the truest migrant of the three great recognised migrants of the genus, the salmo salar.

It is now, I presume, an accepted fact that up to its assumption of the smolts livery of splendid silver the salmon is a fresh water fish. That marvellous change occurs when the salmon is in a state of nature, or in other words is a free denizen of river or lake, in a few cases during the April or May following its birth, in most cases during the second April or May, and in some instances

during the third recurrence of these months. In all cases when
the sea thus casts its silvery shadow before, the change is co-incident
with the first dawning, so far as we are aware, of the restless desire for
the wider range, the richer tables of the deep, for what, in a word, may
be the natural home of the fish as a worker in the field of nature. It is
not necessary for my purpose to follow the fish to the sea, and I content
myself with pointing out that once he feels the salt water the salmon's
habits change. From being a contented pigmy he speedily has the ambitions of a giant and battening on the choicest pastures of the kindly
deep with an appetite in strange contrast to his not wholly voluntary
abstemiousness when he returns to the river, he realises with incredible
rapidity his wildest hopes of changing the condition of a puny dweller in
the stream to that of a leviathan. Interesting as is the rapid growth of
the salmon when he can enjoy the rights of freedom, he becomes, perhaps, doubly interesting and illustrative of the effect of environment
upon fish, quantitatively and qualitatively considered, when he is made
prisoner and is deprived of his rights as a commoner of water. The
effect of this deprivation is more pronounced in what I may term artificial captivity, when, that is to say, the salmon is imprisoned in a confined area equivalent to a cell and is not merely, so to speak, exiled
or transported. The effect of the deprivation will, in other words, vary
in degree with the amount of liberty allowed him, and will naturally be
more pronounced if the fish is confined in a small pond corresponding
to a prison cell or is allowed the freedom of a largish sheet of water or
a river, corresponding according to their dimensions and the jus spatiandi
they afford, either to the condition of an exile on a small island, or to a
prisoner on a great continent fenced by the inviolable sea. When in
confinement such as a mill pond connected with their native river by a
race, the behaviour of smolts shows what an overmastering
impulse is the desire for the sea. I have seen them leap
clean out of the pond on to the banks and even when they
do not thus commit unconscious suicide in their despair, their restlessness is pitiful. The environment which the sea alone can give is absolutely necessary for their intuitive ambition and deprived of what they
appear to feel is a right, their development is almost as phenomenally
slow under the unnatural conditions of existence forced upon them, as it
is phenomenally rapid when allowed to gratify their instincts. Possibly

in a large sheet of water abounding in food they may occasionally grow with the normal rapidity of non-migratory salmonidæ, but in no case and under no circumstances, that are not natural, do they ever show that tendency to rapid growth displayed by them in the sea. When imprisoned within narrower confines, their growth, even when food is plentifully supplied, is still more markedly arrested. Indeed the unnatural environment of the fish pond will occasionally produce effects upon fish, which clearly show the desperate struggle between the hereditary instinct that is the result of environment and the new characteristics that are wholly the result of altered and, from the traditional stand-point, unnatural environment. I have observed at least one case in which a four year old land-locked salmon, though a bright fish of about ½lb. in weight actually retained the parr marks, which stood out against its white, rather than silvery sides, with far more clearness than they did even during its true infancy.

It is clear, therefore, on this analogy that if a change of environment can reduce the salmon from the condition of a quick-growing and comparatively large fish to that of a very slow-growing and comparatively small fish, environment, rather than an apparent difference in race, the difference being due to environment, must by itself be sufficient to account for the varying size and varying quality of the trout in our lochs.

Another and peculiar example of the retrogressive effect of environment came under my observation in the Hebrides, and as it was the means of establishing the fact that trout and fish generally are subject to tuberculosis—a discovery which, so far as I am aware, has not been followed up—the circumstances of the case may be detailed here. In 1890, while fishing in a South Uist loch, I killed on the same day a couple of trout weighing about 1¼lb. each. These fish were long and lank. They were not, however, merely thin. They were emaciated, and had the sickly, unnatural look of animals suffering from a wasting disease.* Over and above their emaciated consumptive appearance, they

*All or nearly all the symptoms here described are very frequently observed in trout when they reach old age and are about to swim into the waters of everlasting shade, that glide with noiseless ripple through the happy hunting grounds, or as the unpoetic small boy put it, are about to fall into "the everlasting sleep of Haddies." I note the circumstance, as it is just possible, that the trout of the second lake mentioned were old fish that had ceased to be fruitful. It is certain that the sanitary condition of their home had been altered for the worse by the lowering of its level. I desire, however, to avoid confusion of causes as well as of effects. Nevertheless, if the signs of old age and

D

presented another and unusual feature. They bulged out at the belly, and both fish looked, in consequence, as if they had a paunch, or had swallowed a stone or an india-rubber ball. This paunch, in contrast to their leanness and lankiness, gave them a most ungainly—almost a ludicrous appearance. My gillie, one of the quaintest Highlanders who ever made a bad day into a good one by letting his Celtic fancy have free play in broken English, at once christened the fish " big heads," and declared that a few of the lochs abounded in such fish—a statement which I subsequently verified.*

Curiously enough, three or four similar fish, rather larger in size, were brought in the same evening by another angler, who had been fishing a loch that had practically lain fallow for a number of years. As the house was full of doctors, and the matter was worth sifting, the young-est of them, who was a very skilled anatomist, speedily laid one of the trout on an extemporised dissecting board and revealed, as I had ex-pected, the presence of large ovarian cysts, which may be described, though not defined, as bags appearing to contain yellow glutinous mat-ter of a morbid nature. It then occurred to me to suggest, pursuing the first train of thought which the fish had conveyed to my non-scientific mind, that the fish were suffering from a form of consumption, or, in other words, from tuberculosis. With the idea of demonstrating the truth or fallacy of this suggestion, the fish were carefully preserved for analytical investigation, which established beyond doubt that they contained the bacilli of consumption, and were, in a word, tuberculosed or consumptive fish.

Now in both these lochs the conditions producing the disease ap-peared to be precisely those insanitary conditions, which, mutatis mutandis, authorities declare to be the cause of tuberculosis in cows. One of the lochs carried a large head of fair conditioned trout up to ¾ lb.; anything above that weight appeared not only to be underfed but " cribbed and confined," for the lake was undoubtedly too small for the number of fish in it. The environment was, in other words, tending to-

the signs of consumption in trout are the same, then the extremely instructive inference may be drawn that most trout die of consumption. It is, however, possible that the signs of old age may be mistaken for those of consumption. A trout register of births. and deaths should easily avoid such confusion. We do not know the age to which a trout lives in a state of nature.

  * Such fish are in Austria called Quixotes or adventurers, and in Sweden "big-heads."

wards the deterioration of the fish in quality with their increase in number, and the big fish were dying out. In a few years I have no doubt that the trout of the loch will be found to have altered their character. The process of decay had certainly set in.

In the other loch there appeared to be only large fish, and the whole of them were in shocking condition and, in fact, diseased. The retrogression was due not only to the loch having reached its carrying capacity through not being fished, but also to the fact that drainage had shrunk its area, and rendered it a less fit home for trout of a large size than it, prior to "modern improvements," had been. In both cases the environment was the direct cause of the deterioration, partial in the one case, complete in the other, but in both proportionate to the change for the worse in the conditions of existence.*

Before passing to another example of the effect of environment, I would point out that the case of these South Uist fish disposes of the claim of certain French experimenters that they were the first in 1897 to discover tuberculosis in fish. The method of their discovery was as follows: Into a pond in France tuberculous matter from the lungs and digestive organs of a patient was thrown. The fish—carp—were afterwards noted to die, and the germs or bacilli of consumption were found in plenty in their bodies. Moreover when these bacilli of the fishes were given to other fishes, they proved fatal in the same way. Presuming that the common carp is meant (for there are a good many varieties of carp and of fish that are half-carp half-bream in appearance, which on the Continent might be called carp) it is rather curious that I should have had two carp through my hands which were certainly suffering from ovarian cysts, if not from tuberculosis, and presented precisely the same appearance, in a modified form, as the South Uist trout.

I had been asked by Lord Loudon to come up and witness the netting of a large bream pond at Willesley Hall in Leicestershire, and to give my opinion as to the advisability of stocking the pond with trout. I described the netting of this lake in the " Field " a week or two after it occurred, and mentioned the circumstance that the two carp referred to

---

* While these pages were in the press (in June) I found that many of the trout of a certain loch, thick-set fish of 1½lb. to 2½lb. were long, thin and attenuated owing to the dearth of fly, May fly and ordinary, as well as the demise of nearly all the shrimps. The long continued cold weather of a phenomenally late season was the cause of the change in environment and in the condition of the trout.

were suffering from ovarian cysts, though, unfortunately, through other matters occupying my attention, I did not take away either of the fish, and so failed to carry the investigation further. If these two carp on being submitted to analysis and miscrospic examination, had been proved to be suffering from tuberculosis, as well as from ovarian cysts, the circustances would have been both interesting and instructive. That they were so suffering I have little doubt, but presumption is not proof.

These tuberculosed trout not only proved that environment is the great factor in producing size, beauty and health, particularly the nast named, in trout, but they also led me, after some observation of their habits, to draw a somewhat speculative inference. In drawing this inference I may have mistaken a cause for an effect, or vice versa. In any case the conclusion which I drew was the rather startling one that fish suffering from tuberculosis develop a sort of blindness.* My difficulty is that I am uncertain whether the tuberculosis causes the blindness or the blindness acts as a predisposing cause towards tuberculosis. In the human patient we know that visual power is often strongly dependent upon bodily health, in the absence of which the patient may either see nothing or things which do not exist to be seen—a paradox which is self-explaining when one remembers that all our sensations are dependent upon the perfect working of a most intricate and complex system of what one may term nerve-signalling.

What I observed was that when these trout fish rose to the fly they took a long time to locate it, and seemed almost to grope for it like a blind man. Their play, allowance being made for their invalid condition, was not merely lethargic, it was purposeless and lacked method. Near the landing net they were unstartled by quick movements of it, and, in a word, betrayed all the symptoms of fish whose sight was defective.

Now, here it may be very properly asked how could, or why should, trout affected by partial blindness take the artificial fly, a lure which can only owe its attractiveness to sight? The answer to the question is simple, yet it might form the text of a hundred angling sermons. Such trout as those with which I am dealing only rise when there is a great rise or " move " on, and when, therefore, rivalry for flies is sufficiently keen to rouse them out of their lethargy. They follow the crowd, so to speak, and because something is stirring bestir themselves. Moreover,

---

*This is another occasional but sufficiently characteristic symptom of old age.

there is an element of chance in their taking the fly, for partially blind fish are very apt to go bobbing about the surface in an aimless kind of way. When behaving thus if your flies light at their noses they take them in their listless, uncertain fashion.

It would appear, therefore, that, if the fish of a lake rise in a very list-less manner, it is just possible thin in this, apart from their condition which can only be seen after they are hooked, there is prima facie ground for the presumption that something ails their environment.

There may be more blind fish than we are aware of. But it is not probable that there are, for the struggle for existence must with them soon end in death. My own experience it that blind fish are not easily come by for purposes of observation. Many years before I caught these Uist trout I had secured some strange lizard-looking, olive-green so-called fish in the mysterious river that passes through the great stalactite grotto at Adelsberg, in Hungary, but these threw no light on the habits of blind fish. Luckily, in 1893, I was fortunate enough to come across a blind trout in a pond, and to be in a position to remove and place him for purposes of observation in a shallow stream. He was a long and lank fish of most sorrowful countenance, and lay like a log wherever he was placed. Often, if one sent a stronger rush of water over him than usual, he would be washed away with it until, to use a nautical phrase, he was brought up " all standing " against some friendly stone or some-thing that gave him a holding ground against the force of the current. He was totally blind, yet he found his food by smell and touch, and was fed, like the other fish in his pond. He pined away to a shadow, how-ever, and finally died after presenting all the appearances of a consump-tive fish, and showing all the movements characterising the fish proved to be consumptive and presumed to be partially blind.

I may say in general with regard to consumption in loch trout that I have observed a great increase in its apparent occurrence of late years. The first suspicious case I remember noting was in Loch Skene some 19 years ago. Since then and up to 1890 I observed isolated examples of it in lakes as far sundered geographically as in character. Since 1890 I have naturally been on the outlook for examples of trout either really or apparenttly thus affected. I regret to say, as I have already pointed out, that I have observed an increase, and that, too, even in lochs where the conditions appear not to favour the development of the disease, at least in epidemic form. Possibly the increased number of cases I have observed may, as the statisticians say, be due merely to a better system of personal notification. If so the increase may be occasional and perhaps much more apparent than real. Possibly drainage may be affecting our lochs as adversely as I believe it has done our salmon rivers. In any view, it is to be hoped that there is no real danger of the fell disease which man is preparing to combat with the weapons of simple sanitation, curative and preventive, but which at present claims a yearly sacrifice from our midst of 70,000 human lives and 40,000 of the cattle on our hills, invading with deadly purpose our choicest lakes and decimating their lusty fish.

Tidal lochs afford another and most excellent example of the effect of environment upon fish. As a rule, to which there are, of course, exceptions (Loch Stennis, in Orkney, and the so-called loch at Strome Dearg, in South Uist, the former to a most marked degree, may be instanced), the common trout found in most tidal lochs or lochs invaded by the tide are small and poor, so long, that is to say, as they remain loch trout pure and simple and do not better their environment. That the tendency of fish to better their environment is one of their strongest impulses goes without saying, and when I come to deal with the future of our lochs, I shall naturally have something to say on the point. In the meantime I venture to lay down the rule, (also subject to exceptions which the tidal loch illustrates), that all trout, who have any necessity to do so, occasionally visit the sea, if, that is to say, they are able to make the trip. This is a statement which must, as I have already indicated, be taken as a mere generalisation. Trout in the upper reaches of a river like the Wharfe in Yorkshire or the Derwent in Derbyshire will never visit the sea if only because there are barriers in the way which no trout can surmount. Nor will they do so if the predisposing cause, lack of food, be absent. If, however, the trout in certain reaches of these streams were deprived of their natural food they would speedily migrate in search of reaches where food might be more abundant., and if the sea were near or easy of access they would most certainly travel as far as the estuary.

The point I desire to emphasise is this : If the life conditions of trout are such that the waters they frequent can be invaded by immigrant food from the sea, then it stands to reason that such fish, if their food supply otherwise is meagre or insufficient, will follow the food back to the sea. Fish far removed from the sea show a similar restless tendency, and the allurement in all cases is food. Many anglers of the older school, who were much less fastidious in their methods than we are to-day, have set it on record that they have drawn fish from long distances up to their fishing point by the use of salmon roe. Its power to attract they have variously attributed to smell or the operation of shredded portions of it as ground bait. The former explanation is a fanciful one, and on the analogy of the effect of ground bait the floating particles are probably the cause of the trout being drawn up towards the original source of the food.

It is, at any rate, clear (and I have in a previous chapter quoted a singular New Zealand case in which non-migratory trout, so-called, became migratory through visits to the sea rendered compulsory by the lack of and the search for food) that if fish in tidal waters have their appetites stirred by food coming in with the tide and are capable of responding to the suggestion, they will go back with the food and with the tide, in precisely the same way as herring and other tide-feeding and tide-ranging fish do. Now the curious part of the matter is, that the vast majority of the trout in the tidal lochs of the usual type are not in the least degree influenced either by the food borne in by the tide or by the incursion of the tide itself. They seem content to keep up a frail and feverish being in the loch, and their environment being barren and miserable, they are, as a result of it, extremely poor and small specimens of fish, mere fingerlings when they might be giants. A few wiser or more fortunate members of the community do make a trial trip to the sea and speedily attain to a large size, which they no doubt maintain when they return temporarily to the loch by preying on their fellows and by developing the migratory habit. I find by reference to my fishing ledger, that I killed with the fly within a short period more than one of these fish in a certain tidal loch. One weighed 5¾ lb. and the other 3¾ lb. Both were superb fish in form, colouring and strength, yet the average ordinary trout of the loch was about one ounce in weight, and in colour was a hideous black, in form an emaciated pigmy, and in strength could not match a rather weak minnow. Here obviously a change of environmen at once wrought a corresponding change in the fish and I feel assured that had the position been reversed and large trout been turned

into the loch and the small fish removed, the big fish would either
have developed the migratory habit or would speedily have died out
leaving behind them an inferior progeny, and they again the "dwindled
sons of little sons of little men" until finally the old order was established
and the loch once more was reduced to its former position as a lake only
holding and only fit to hold small and poor fish so long as they were
non-migratory. The example of the tidal loch is, perhaps, the most
convincing I have yet given to prove that the differences in the quality
and size of our loch trout is entirely due to environment and has practically but little to do with "breed,"* a fine breed of trout being, on
the last analysis, the result of environment.

Many further examples could be quoted in support of this contention.
I could cite cases of lochs with water exceptionally well suited for trout
but poor homes otherwise, which hold very beautiful, but small fish of
excellent quality, such as Loch Tanna, in Arran, and Loch Stullivaule,
in South Uist; I could adduce many example of very large fish in lochs
abounding in small as proofs that the Titans having by chance overcome
the difficulties of environment have by this fortuitous victory become
superior to environment by creating an environment of habit, the habit
of cannibalism and the power to obtain and devour other animal food
beyond the reach of their small brethren; and lastly I could adduce
examples of fine fish placed in an unsuitable home that because their
environment was not imported with them have either died out or been
succeeded by a gradually dwindling and decaying race. Enough has already been said, however, to show that the differences in size and quality
observed in the trout of our lochs, striking as they are, are the result
not of racial or inherent superiority, but of environment. The finest
races of men are not the growth of, but must perish in the desert, and so
is it with fish. The pigmies of Central Africa are not more truly an example of men who have dwindled because nature conquered and dwarfed
them by her own magnificence and prodigality than are the trout of certain lochs the product of that niggardliness with which she has furnished
their home. Nature knows. if man does not, that the fish should not be
there. She vindicates her own laws by pointing to their condition and
it is for us to read and learn the lesson that she has written so plainly
on many waters.

---

* The only advantage a good breed possesses is noted on page 20. It should be
noted that the higher the race, the higher is the standard of comfort.

CHAPTER V.

FISHING AS THE HAND-MAIDEN OF SCIENCE.

It must often have struck even the casual student that our scientific ichthyologists are better classifiers from the anatomical than they are from the practical standpoint, that they more often chronicle the experience of others than their own and more often quote the observations of previous writers than set forth the results of their own observations.* Nor is the circumstance matter for surprise. The range of the ichtyhologist is not specialised but general, and he must make himself not only master of the structural peculiarities of the fish that swim, as it were, past his door, but also of their kindred in, if need be, the virgin waters of almost untrodden solitudes. If it were possible for the man of science to know fish in the haunts of nature as well and as fully as studious hours in the laboratory have enabled him to know their structural differences, then ichthyology would rise nearer to the level of an exact science than it is to be feared it has done. At the same time all science is complementary and the experience of no practical observer of fish and their habits, however limited his knowledge of scientific terms, whether anatomical or otherwise, can be ignored with advantage by the scientist, whose eye and ear he is. The fishing-rod may, in this aspect, be called the key of many mysteries, because the angler who can rise above the mere slaying of fish is necessarily a keen, because an interested observer, of the multiform varieties of fish life. And even if, as sometimes happens, his whole soul be bent on slaughter, this fact in itself necessitates some study of the habits of his quarry. He may fail to see the beauties of the subject he studies but he cannot wholly miss its practical

---

*The following is a good example of the way in which the scientist pure and simple writes of the trout from the practical point of view :—"They live on insects, molluscs, spawn, worms, and small fishes, and rush *perpetually after gnats*, which skim over the surface of the water. When their weight is about two pounds, they are as greedy as pike." Comment on this would ruin its sublimity, yet it is an extract from a standard work of most admirable range and great scientific accuracy. The observations on habits are obviouly borrowed and are not the result of personal experience.

lessons. In either case the utilitarian value of angling to science must be immense, and would become greater, if any unity of purpose pervaded the angling world on this important point. Let me here cite, perhaps, the most common example of the aid angling has been to science. I refer to the entomological angler, whom one may in all honesty of purpose term, the blue stocking of the angling world or to give him a more imposing and a more original title the Neo-Imitationist.

In his proper sphere, the Neo-Imitationist is an entomologist who is a specialist, and devotes his attention to the study of those insects which are either water-born or spend their brief hour of life flitting above or floating on the surface of our rivers, I do not, advisedly, add " and lakes." Scarcely a week passes without the " Field," the " Fishing Gazette," or " The Angler " chronicling some example of his work, pregnant with knowledge of the little ephemerids that claim their share in the great heritage of life, those " small things " loved and sung by the poet, whose short share in time might pass unchronicled into oblivion, and their habits remain unknown were it not for the enthusiasm that hurries the entomological angler to probe the mysteries of their little life.

Beyond this point, however, praise will not carry me, because I draw a line of demarcation between practical angling and entomology, that is a kindred study, and taboo the latter when the entomologist angles only as a man of science and indulges in too fine distinctions. I trust I may be forgiven for pointing out that we are in danger of becoming too entomological; by placing a value upon the intelligence and discriminating acumen of the trout, for which there is no reason, we may find that we have dropped the substance of angling for a very vain shadow. If trout have the power of noticing that a leg is missing from a fly, that a colour is accentuated, and that there are three strands instead of five in a tail, as the purists would have us believe, then why do these educated entomological trout take an " Alexandra " or any other fancy fly at all? They should be able to murmur " lusus naturæ," wink the one eye, shut the other, and go and have a feed on what any trout, even the most common, must know is the gammarus pulex. This is possibly a reductio ad absurdum; but what I desire to emphasise is that the moment angling becomes a serious pursuit of purely scientific aim, it may cease pro tanto to possess the interest which is the esse as well as the posse of observation. Memory and indeed reason can be easily deceived into observing facts presented through the medium of what is a real or imaginary pleasure, which both might fretfully overlook, if the pleasure ceasing to be a labour of love, becomes an apparent, as it is a real, labour of duty.

Far be it from me to maintain that the delightful art of taking fish by imitating nature, known as " dry fly " fishing is not the acme of scientific sport, much more of sport in its imitative aspect, but what I complain of is that it has bred a race of prejudiced, exclusive and pedantic entomologists, amongst whom may be found not a few examples of the angling hypocrite and the angling Pharisee. These I should be inclined to class with those who make a desperate splutter about the vital necessity to their health of a cold tub in the morning when the weather is at its very " iciest," but which no one sees them take.

The entomologist angler of the best type, if he is a bit of a pendant, is an extremely interesting person who has caught the true secret of angling, not as the art merely of catching fish, but of studying the life of many waters. His side issues are intensely instructive and interesting, but when he applies the rigid exclusivism of his scientific discoveries to practical sport he becomes, as I have already pointed out, a sort of reductio ad absurdum.

Still when I have blown this blast against his exclusivism, the entomological angler is, perhaps, king amongst us all, especially in the direct aid which he gives to science. The entomologist, for example, will willingly consult him. and has not Professor Miall said of him, " The names employed by anglers should be noted, as much information respecting the habits of aquatic insects can be extracted from anglers by those who speak their language "? I do not know what the learned professor meant by " speak their language," unless he alluded to the popular nomenclature of flies and so forth, but of this I am assured, our friend the Neo-Imitationist is a useful person to the scientist. His great fault is that he attributes a knowledge not only equal to his own, but far greater than his own to the trout which he endeavours to catch.

I cannot leave him, confirmed malignant as he is in the eyes of the loch fisher, who claims for his sport recognition amongst the branches of scientific angling, without quoting an example of his methods. " The only legs," says one of the school," that would strike the observer, whether he were man or fish, are the posterior pair which larixæ use to propel themselves through the water." A fly lacking these legs is, there-condemned as a useless imitation which no entomological trout will take!* It will be observed that the information is of scientific value and interest, while its practical application to angling, with the wet fly at least, is utterly absurd, or argues a nicety of distinction no hungry trout (and these are the only fish of general angling interest) is ever likely to show.

The imitative or rational school of anglers thus conjoin an extremely interesting study of entomology with angling, which is most commend-able and praiseworthy, and read and expound not the least interesting chapter in that great book of nature studied by all true sportsman that love fin, fur, and feather.

As a further example of the complementary position angling occupies towards science and as a preamble to the point to which I am leading, namely, certain observations in particular lochs, not only of the differ-ences in their trout, but also of the special causes of those differences, I may here cite the possiblv well known anatomical distinctions between well-fed and ill-fed fish. The ichthologist has certain trout submitted for his inspection. He dissects them and discovers that the degree of their plumpness or condition varies, under certain exceptions, with the number of the pyloric caecal appendages. When he notes in a still large large number of examples that the relation between the number of cœcal appendages and condition is more or less proportionately constant he draws an inductive inference and formulates a law. He is, however, not wholly enlightened as to the cause though he sees the effect. It is here that the utility of the angler to science comes in. He should be easily able to satisfy the ichthyologist as to the character of the home from which the fish have come and should thus enable the scientist to lay down the principle that the number of the coecal appendages is de-dependent upon food, is a sign of the abundance or scarcity of food and is valuable as a guide to specific character only so far—and I have already indicated that it is considerable—species depends upon environ-ment and the conditions of existence.

*As another, and perhaps a fairer, example of the assistance the entomological angler affords science, it may be stated that Mr. Halford was the first to discover that the colouring of the larvae of certain ephemerids varied and was not constant.

The obviously complementary character of the discovery that the better fed a trout is, the greater become the number of appendages referred to is a very clear example of the use of science to angling and angling to science. From the practical standpoint of the stocker it furnishes a rough and ready means of obtaining a diagnosis of a reliable character that has nowhere been more clearly proved than in the case of the British trout imported into the waters of New Zealand. Its value is enhanced by the fact that it becomes specific and is not merely a chance symptom in isolated cases. In other words any marked decrease in the number of these appendages even when trout retain external health and condition may be taken as a danger signal that the race is in peril of decaying, and as a sanitary warning that something ails their home.

Though the subject is a tempting one yet its range is so wide that I will content myself with but two or three further exa np.es of the co-relation of science and angling, or with practical fishing generally, of which angling is a specialised department.

Scientists would, for example, have had considerable difficulty in establishing the habits of the salmon in the sea, had not those working on our coasts with stake-nets been able to vouch from their personal observation for the undoubted fact that salmon are, of all fish, the most gregarious and widest-ranging when in the sea. At such a suitable station as the East side of the long peninsula of Kintyre I observed a very striking example of this truth. Up to a certain period of the season not a single fish was taken in the nets at another station higher up the east side of the peninsula and in the Sound of Kilbrannan. The first morning any fish were taken at the North station the haul was not only a record one, but consisted of many varieties of salmon, including Irish fish. Exactly a week afterwards the first fish of the season were taken at the more southerly station. This, too, was a record haul and consisted of the same varied assortment of salmon as the first haul at the other station. The distance between the two stations being ascertainable, the character of the shore and its feeding being known, and the identity of the two lots of salmon as part of the same shoal being established, it was here possible for practical fishing to aid science in establishing the gregariousness, nomadism, and rate of travelling of salmon in the sea under ascertained circumstances.

I have already, though I shall have to recur to them as dealing with
practical loch fishing, given two illustrations of the value of lake-trout as
weather prophets and as illustrators of the law of "albinism," and will,
therefore, further exemplify the mutual assistance which science gives
to angling and angling to science by a fact concerning the sea-trout,
which is of the first importance.   In angling for sea-trout in lochs which
so far resemble the sea on a rock-bound coast that there is a considerable depth of water not far from the shore, feeding and hence
taking sea-trout are invariably taken right on the beach amongst the
breaking waves when there is a breeze and with their noses apparently
on the rocks when it is calm.   It is a curious fact that the darker the
the water of the loch is, the more pronounced does this habit become.
The circumstance is singular because it is a regular night habit of the
sea-trout in the sea, as the "splash netter" is aware, to lie right on
sandy beaches and as close up to rocky shores as it can get.   It is true
that so far as the latter are concerned the same habit marks it when
feeding by day.   As, however, the sea-trout is not much of a shore
feeder by day and prefers to range the freer water of the estuary when
the sun is at his prime, the circumstance in no way robs the fact of its
significance.   Reverting to the effect of the darker or lighter colour of
the water of a loch upon this shore-resting habit of feeding sea-trout,
though it is possible that the height of the loch (fullness itself, be it
observed, being as often as not a cause of deep colouring) may have
some influence on the location of the fish, yet a comparison between the
habits of the sea-trout in two connected and in every respect, save colouring, identical lochs, led me to draw the above inference.   In the
one loch, which as it so happened was nearest the sea and subject to
invasions of the salt water at every tide, the sea-trout, though to be
taken close in by the shores, were to be had in greater plenty in the
central and other portions of the loch.   This feature of the loch was admittedly more pronounced when the loch was low and when, therefore,
its water in part hill, in part sea-fed, was in its clearest condition than
when full and discoloured through the burn which fell into it coming
down in peat-stained flood.   The water of the other loch, fed as it was
by a greater number of burns whose channels were steeper and whose
flow was therefore more constant, was invariably darker, while its hue
was not robbed of its peaty inkiness by the invasions of the green and

rushing tide to which the other lake was subject.   In this second lake
the vast majority of the taking fish lay close by the shore, so much so
that on the first occasion on which I fished it, remembering only the
lessons of the first lake of which this one was the putative mother, I
killed but very few fish, until, setting my reasoning powers to work, I
conjectured the very truth which I am now endeavouring to illustrate.
The thought was a happy one, for I killed in something over an hour
and a half some 36 sea-trout off the first bit of shore I tried, taking the
fish as fast as I could raise, hook, and land them right amongst the
yeast and spume of the breaking waves.

Read with other ascertained facts of a similar kind, science has here
a very useful lesson which practical fishing has been able to teach and
whose accuracy practical angling appears to corroborate. It establishes
very clearly certain habits of the sea-trout which differentiate it from
the salmon when, as I have said, the facts stated are added to other ascertained facts. I may mention finally in this connection that when
dealing with the habits of sea-trout and salmon in lochs I shall further
explain the principle involved by pointing out and illustrating by examples the curious fact that while in the sea the salmon has no habitat
or locus, in a loch, unlike the sea-trout, he is apt to establish himself in
a fixed hole or home—a fact which shows that the fish reverse their
habits of the sea when in lochs, though it must be observed that in the
case of the sea-trout there is nothing inconsistent with his confirmed
nomadic habits within a certain range in the fact that he should decline
to remain a fixture in or about a certain spot in a loch.

A very remarkable instance of the light which fishing, again using the
word in its widest sense, has thrown upon the idiosyncrasies of the
salmon in the matter of colour and the special share angling has had, in
preventing a popular belief from becoming a scientific prejudice, is afforded on the one hand by the practice of " burning the water," and on
the other by the fact that salmon are particularly partial to a boiled
prawn and are by no means indifferent to a bright red fly.

The former practice is largely based on the love of the salmon for
bright objects, the glare of a torch seeming to have the same attractiveness for a salmon as the beacon of a light-house has for birds.

As to the latter, it was held by many fishermen that salmon had a
similar antipathy to anything red as they had love for something

white—a popular belief that might have passed into a scientific prejudice had not anglers with the red prawn and with flies, either altogether
red or with red as their most outstanding colour, demonstrated that
there was not the slightest ground for this alleged characteristic.

A curious example of how angling may aid science, is
afforded by the fact that the presence of lake-balls in
certain of the lochs of South Uist was discovered by anglers.
These lake-balls do not, I believe, occur elsewhere in the
United Kingdom, and though classified by botanists amongst the algae,
their life history is still a mystery. I took some specimens of these balls
to the British Museum (South Kensington) in 1891, and as there was
not a single specimen of this most curious of all water-plants within
its walls, the value of the discovery of them by anglers may be imagined.
The balls, I may mention, vary in size as a rule from a walnut to an
orange, but I have found them as large as a cocoanut, and in a few
cases even as a boy's football. The Botanical Section gave them
special accommodation in tanks in a large room and endeavoured without, I believe, much success to solve their whole mystery of which their
mode of reproduction and growth, together with the fructification of the
green moss interspersed with bell-shaped stems that covers them at
certain seasons, were the most interesting features. This example of
how angling aids science is, of course, in a different category to the
cases I have been considering and which I now resume.

There are, however, cases in which angling experience does not supplement science, cases in which, as a matter of fact the dictum of the
scientist is directly opposed to the experience of anglers. Two of the
most pronounced examples of this difference of opinion are the feeding
of salmon in fresh water and the continued classification of bull-trout
and sea-trout as the same fish. When dealing with the question of
salmon and sea-trout in lochs, I will have to recur to both these questions and in the meantime will content myself with stating a case
analogous to the first, namely the feeding habits of barbel in winter. I
do so to illustrate not only the methods by which angling and science
aid one another, but to show that an observer noting that the habits
of two fish are identical, can draw by analogy an inference which experience may or may not verify, but which remains a logical deduction
until disproved.

AN UNNATURAL POSITION: SNAP SHOT OF LEAPING SALMON.

In considering the question whether the salmon does or does not feed in fresh water I came to the practical conclusion that so far as the angler was concerned, it was really a matter of no moment whether or not the salmon feeds in fresh water, so long as he takes with a varying avidity the angler's lures, fly, prawn, worm, phantom minnow, eel's tail, gudgeon, or whatsoever lure he thinks or finds best. Even the most practical angler, the angler for whom angling consists in trying to kill fish, must necessarily study the feeding habits of the object of his quest, and it is, therefore, impossible for him to avoid making those habits more or less of a study if he is to realise even his low-placed ideal of the art of angling.

Some years ago this reflection was suggested to me by the fact, and it is at this point the object lesson begins, that I raised a hornet's nest about my ears for daring to reason as to the possible feeding habits of the barbel in winter, from the fact that lampreys and barbel seek the self-same deeps when the air grows chill. I suggested that it was just possible that the barbel might feed on lampreys, and urged some dweller on the Thames or Trent to try by experiment the truth or fallacy of the generally accredited belief that the barbel does not feed in winter. My conclusion was drawn, not from any special knowledge of the barbel, but from a love of studying fish in general, and an appreciation of the exquisitely balanced and ideally economic laws of nature. One blameless enthusiast in particular made my fad, as he was pleased to term it, a very personal matter, and had the temerity, after roundly proclaiming my ignorance of barbel and barbel-fishing, to offer me in the " Sportsman " a ten-guinea silver cup if I could catch a single barbel in winter with lamprey or any other lure. The challenge of this omniscient dweller by the Trent, whose knowledge of fish and fishing was entirely derived from experience by that stream, I naturally ignored, though as another equally opinionative enthusiast had previously offered me a guinea for every salmon I rose with the fly in the Trent, it was clear that I had thrown away a piscatorial Klondyke.

Nemesis, however, came to my aid, and abundant proof was soon forthcoming that even in the Trent barbel had fallen to the lamprey in winter, while it was proved beyond dispute that in the Thames the barbel will take the lamprey with great avidity, and that fish had fallen to that lure on too many occasions in the past to necessitate the chronicling of separate cases or going into the matter more fully.

E

The instance cited when analysed is most instructive, for my reasoning was based on the fact that the barbel and the lamprey frequented the
same kind of water in winter and on the general principle that
if nature compels a fish or an animal to adopt a certain habit and frequent a certain habitat she will provide means of sustenance either in
animal or in vegetable form to the degree that is necessary to the fish
or animal. If she does not provide it, then the fish or animal (a fish is,
of course, an animal) will decline to be bound by the chains of that
habit or the prison cell of that habitat, and will seek new quarters and
acquire new habits. It is to this very cause, the absence, that is to say,
of suitable food and its varying quality and quantity, that so far as sea-
fishing station are concerned, is due the recurrence of good and bad
seasons. It would be the height of illogical folly to suppose that the
great rule of the life of the sea is not equally applicable to the more
confined areas of river and lake.

I have already referred to this principle and shall have occasion to
frequently refer to it again, not only in the chapter entitled "The
Philosophy of the Fly," but also in that dealing with the somewhat
speculative habits of salmon in the matter of food, and hence of locus, in
fresh water lochs, so far as these habits are of importance to the angler.

As a last example of the aid science gives to angling and vice versa,
though certain aspects of the subject have only been suggested not exhausted, I would cite an example of science correcting what at one time
appeared to be a conjecture that anglers were only too ready to snap up
because, as the "Fishing Gazette" pointed out, it appeared to
offer a most glorious excuse for a bad day and "missed fish."
I had observed that on bright, breezy days loch trout
were very apt to miss the fly through failing to locate it. They seemed
to rise and attempt to seize the fly not at the exact spot where it was,
but where, as I thought after considering the matter, refraction made
it appear to be. It was obviously a very pretty notion, and appeared so
eminently original that I consulted Lord Kelvin on the point. The
great scientist at once demolished my castle in the air. He declared
that the moment the fly touched the water refraction ceased. There
was, however, in this dictum not a complete, but only a partial demoli-
tion of my theory. So long, that is to say, as the fly was in the air and
had not lighted on the water a portion of the ray coming from it, which

and not the fly is what the fish really sees, to put a scientific fact in semi-scientific language, would be reflected, while the ray—all as aforesaid—would be refracted and so deceive the fish as to the exact spot at which the fly was going to alight. In this half-hearted fashion I consoled myself over the fragments of my actinic hobby.

Lord Kelvin's dictum is obviously one of considerable moment to the purists. Dry flies and all flies that imitate natural flies are dressed in the medium of air, and are therefore seen by the dresser through that medium, whereas they are seen by the trout through the medium of water. As, however, it appears that even the most optimistic of ento-mological anglers does not pretend that human skill has yet succeeded in imitating natural flies to perfection even in a state of rest much less in that condition of life or liveliness which, or its absence ex hypothesi, the trout must be able to note, the position is, perhaps, not so very important. It certainly suggests, however, a fine sample of the irony of dilemma, when one accepts the contradictory hypotheses of the school, which maintains, on the one hand, that imitations of unnamed and unclassified aquatic animals should be made and used under certain circumstances, while laying down the rule that a trout will not take maimed real, or imperfect imitations of, flies in a "state of motion" though they will take the undamaged fly and suck in the approximately perfect imitation " in a state of rest."

Apart from the physics of the question and the effect of the media through which the fly is seen before alighting, as it frequently is, and of the medium through which alone on lighting it can be seen, the intricate problem just suggested may never be solved, until experi-ments in virgin waters analogous to dry fly waters as we know them have established beyond dispute the degree of education to which a trout, whether by sensational or reasoned memory, can attain. So far at least as lochs approximate virgin waters, and so far as loch trout may be presumed from the nature of their home to be less sensationally educated, or in other words, less frequently alarmed by apparitions than are the trout of certain rivers, it is certain that they take with greater avid-ity a wet fly that imitates a swimming aquatic animal—classified or un-classified—than they will any of the imitations of real flies, whether floating or wet. It is also certain that at times they will take no kind of fly—using the word to cover all combinations of steel, fur and feather—at all and appear to be just as cautious of imitations in certain lights as are the most "highly educated" trout of chalk streams. So much is this so, that even sea-trout will act like their brown brothers. The problem whether the caution is a mood of matter (or in other words is due to appetite), or is a mood of mind, I do not here pause to discuss. In its proper place in a later chapter dealing with the "Philosophy of the Fly," this and kindred questions are treated at considerable length. In the meantime, therefore, I postpone all consideration of the question, both in the case of loch trout and the "Dons" of the clear rivers of the South.

CHAPTER VI.

THE LESSONS OF SOME LAKES

Angling is such a speculative subject and embraces within its sphere so many problems and side issues that it is almost impossible to avoid certain digressions from the main subject under discussion and the introduction of what lawyers call irrelevant matter or irrelevant issues. Yet as I regard and interpret angling these speculative digressions, these wanderings into the happy hunting grounds of the unknown are always justifiable and sometimes profitable. It may happen that they throw some new light on old problems, just as little excursions up side paths off the beaten track often reveal hidden beauties whose claim to recognition the more celebrated and obvious charms of "show places" may have overshadowed. It is possible, however, that when the range of a subject and its kindred subjects covers a wide field, one may be merely lost in the maze without solving any of the mysteries of the labyrinth. It is, perhaps, impossible to wholly dismember angling and treat the infinite variety of parts that make up the pastime as a whole as separate and distinct branches that have nothing in common save a parent stem. The co-relation of all branches of angling is, however, such an obvious fact that it is doubtful whether the minnow fisher, the bait catcher, or the gentleman with a jar seen on the banks of a midland canal on Saturday afternoons do not, mutatis mutandis and to a degree that varies with circumstances, put precisely the same sort of skill in practice, set the same sort of ideas working, reason in the same way from different premises, as does the far and fine "dry fly" angler of guileful method worthy of the Red Indian.

The field of "Lochs and Loch fishing" is, therefore, by parity of reasoning not bounded, qua subject, by the thousands of lakes, large and small, good and indifferent, holding great fish and fingerlings that lie within the territories washed by the four seas of Great Britain. On the contrary the fact that Grassi discovered amidst the swirling tides

of the Straits of Messina that eels spawn not in the river, but in the
deep sea may be quite relevant evidence if one desires to illustrate the
analogical method of deducing inferences from facts, or even as an
absolute fact if it has to be proved that habits are merely conditional
opportunities realized through the heredity of long continued pre-disposing circumstances. While this is true of general principles, it is
obviously impossible to exhaust the features of lakeland by particular
examples that would be guides to lakeland, even as it falls within the
observation of a single angler. For my own part I have fished within
the last fifteen years in upwards of 200 lakes that are not mere nameless
tarns unsung in the prose, that is ever poetry of angling literature as
written from week to week, but lakes of some repute. In these lakes I
angled in six seasons alone on 279 * days. It is obvious, therefore, that
out of this great chain of lakes and this necessarily wide field of
experiences, one must eliminate many lakes, and in the matter of experiences condescend only upon generalities that are universal, read and
interpreted though " specialities " that may be exceptions to the rules.
With a view to limiting my remarks on lochs as homes for trout, and as
waters giving them their characteristics as lake fish I may, therefore,
confine myself to a selected few types.

An ideal angling loch from all and every point of view does not perhaps exist, because ideals vary from person to person, and the degree of
sport a loch yields may not be judged by the same standard by all
anglers, namely, the difficulties that have to be overcome to obtain it.
Some men, for example, would prefer to angle always in a loch like Roag
in South Uist, Loch Stack in Sutherlandshire, and Loch Voshmid in
Harris, all sea-trout lakes in which the fish are not only so numerous,
but as a rule so accommodating that some measure of sport is assured
before the rod is put up. On the same principle some sportsmen prefer
the certain shots of a big cover " shoot " to laborious hours spent in cir-
cumventing a wild goose, or a solitary day on rough ground on which
one has not only to find and kill, but also to carry one's spoil. It is
not, however, merely from the point of view of the sport which it yields
that a loch is to be judged, because it is an obvious truism that the

---

* The greatest number of days on which I have angled in lochs in any one season
was 65 in 1886. I was then in the happy position of a happy Captain Clutterbuck rather
than a Captain Do-little.

more nearly a loch approaches the ideal of a trout-home, the less likely, under certain exceptions, is it to yield sport with too great and too accommodating complaisance to the rod—or to speak by the card, to the fly. It is perhaps a bold assertion to make, but I know very few, if any districts, holding within a comparatively limited area, more thoroughly difficult and " stiff " lochs than the Crinan district of Argyleshire. While, however, certain lochs obtain an undeserved reputation for " stiffness," simply because they are rarely fished " with the head," to use a cricketing phrase, yet on the other hand it is equally certain that there are many lakes in which the trout do not, for reasons that are not wholly speculative, rise at all well to the artificial fly. It sometimes happens that such lakes do not readily admit of the use of methods differing much from the traditional, but it frequently happens that after a day of vain casting with the fly, a minnow spun from the shore close by the weeds will produce a fish every cast and prove that the apparently tenantless lake is really teeming with fish.

There is just such a lake as the one described in the Crinan district, and it is far from being an ideal sheet of water. Curiously enough it lies in close proximity to a lake that as nearly approximates the ideal as any loch in Scotland, with which I have an intimate and not merely a passing and casual acquaintance. The lake in question is called Choil-a-Bharra, a name that by some intricate philogical process has been corrupted into Culiper. It is a lake of singular beauty for the lover of nature, but possesses even greater charms for the student of fish. It lies cradled among hills, whose rocky and wood-clad sides rise steep from its margin, while throughout its whole length, save at either end, the branches weep and wave over its shore waters. Sunken rocks and deep abiding places are everywhere to be found in its waters of swift descent in many places from shallow to comparative deep, but there are no portions so deep that fish may not be seen to rise to the fly, or to use an expressive coloquialism, " to themselves." When surveyed as the angler surveys a lake, it is found to be an epitome of the world of lakeland. It has a few bays in which the depth of water being uniform and the bed stony, fish are always to be found, while here and there up its picturesquely wooded and rocky shores occur stretches of shallow, and a central bed of " below-water " reeds seems to run up its

whole length with ramifications to north and south—the whole affording
admirable shelter and food for fish. At its westerly end tall reeds grow
in beds and the bottom is more sandy and weed-strewn. Up its length
of shore on either side it is practically unapproachable from the land,
the cliffs rising sheer, and the trees growing with dense and rank luxuri-
ance right to the edge. In the matter of food, the lake is unique. Its
surface larder, if one may use the phrase, is stocked with a lavishness
I have never seen equalled on any lake. Under the fretted sunshine of
the branches thousands upon thousands of flies dance the mad dance
of sun-kissed life, while for quite three weeks in an average year the
May-fly appears with an abundance that is almost incredible. On its
waves thousands of flies are constantly being washed shorewards, while
almost every yard of surface bears a dead water-shrimp. In the shallows amongst the crevices of the rocks thousands of tadpoles make
their homes, basking in the generous warmth of the sun and seeking
sanctuary from the great lithe enemies of spotted sides of gleaming
yellow that move with such incredible swiftness to their undoing. Food
in this lake is not only equally distributed, but it is actually too abundant, and much of it is wasted, for though it is impossible to question
the general claim of nature to be described as an ideal economist, it occasionally happens that in the world of waters her distribution of
the good things of fish-life is not always equal. Where migration is
possible nature affords a means of adjusting the balance ; where it is
not possible—and many lakes are in this position—the lake either holds
poor fish or, in terms of the law of the survival of the fittest, fish of
quality varying with the excellence of the " pasture " they are able
to occupy. The strongest will naturally hold the best feeding grounds,
and the difference in quality thus literally grows by what it feeds upon.
In Coil-a-Bharra the accuracy of this theory is fully borne out. The
food is so equally distributed that there are practically no choice spots,
and as a consequence the fish are not only of a large but also of
a uniform size, so that if you killed or could secure some hundreds of
them, there would be scarcely a fish under $1\frac{1}{2}$lb. and very few over
$2\frac{1}{2}$lb.*

Reasoning from the analogy of other lakes where the distribution of
food is more unequal, one would naturally look for an occasional heavy

---

* I revert to these environments and their effects upon angling in a future chapter.

fish and would be almost certain to exclaim after securing a dozen in a day weighing about 20lb. " There must be some very heavy trout in the loch." That there are no fish in it over 3lb. and very few under 1½lb. may, however, be inferred from two facts. I have never heard of a monster being even raised, much less hooked, and though hundreds upon hundreds of fish may be observed during the spawning period, no trout exceeding in size those actually falling to the rod has ever been seen. The conclusion, therefore, to be drawn from this interesting lake is that where food is uniform and abundant—and perhaps also when it is of a particular type—the trout produced by this kind of environment while uniformly large and excellent do not, so long as they are numerous attain an exceptional size. Another and possibly a corrollary conclusion is that they do not develop cannibalistic tendencies —a fact which properly analysed is both an effect and a cause. The fish are under no necessity to prey on their fellows when food is abundant. This may be the cause of their not attaining a great size. On the other hand the effect of the abundant supply of good food is to produce a quick growing race of trout, soon placed beyond any danger of attack from their fellows—an immunity which the physical features of the loch, abounding as it does in hiding holes and places of r.egative strength help to enhance. There is a last aspect in which the limitation of size may be regarded. The fish are prisoners and there is for them no change of scene, of water and of food.

I may here interpolate a few remarks on certain points that may be controversial and have been raised by my observations on the trout of this loch. In the first place I do not suppose that it will be disputed that an abundant, indeed a superfluous, supply of food equally distributed will fail to produce a quick-growing race. All stockers admit that fry * and very small trout will not forage for food, and justify the narrow confines of their fish ponds on the ground that the fish cannot miss the food. In a lake like Coil-a-Bharra it is " brought under their noses " in a similar manner.

In the second place I presume that it is an equally accepted axiomatic truth that though all trout are cannibals, the trait, when it becomes pronounced, is the result of circumstances special to the environment or to the fish and will vary in degree with the necessity for its exercise. As

* Rainbow fry may possibly be an exception to this rule.

a result of this general theory I presume that I am not wholly wrong in concluding that when other food is abundant, even the omnivorous trout will display a dainty and discreet, if not a pampered appetite, and will prefer delicacies to gross fare. The Rainbow trout, we know, is rarely a cannibal save from necessity, and yet the Rainbow is, we are also aware, a fish of most healthy appetite which, qua gourmand if not gourmet, can give other trout a few worms, flies, etc., "and a beating."

As to the effect of places of shelter upon the fish life of a lake, it must be abundantly manifest that when small trout can find sanctuaries which render them immune from the predatory attacks of their larger brothers, the fact will not only discourage cannibalism, but will also in a loch where the sanctuaries are well provisioned, result in the water being thickly populated with fish of very level size and uniform quality. There are such sanctuaries in all lochs, but it is in lochs where the food supply is uniform that their presence is most beneficial. In Loch Leven, for example, the fry frequent shallows and are, I presume, not only safe, but also decently fed, for the fish in the loch are of fairly level excellence. On the other hand, there is a loch in Orkney in one portion of which alone one kills good fish, and in the rest fingerlings. The juveniles have no real sanctuaries, much less is their daily bread assured. As a consequence the fish of the loch continue, as a rule, small and poor in all save a certain reach, only the fittest of the general body survive to become denizens of this choice bit of "pasture," and the race is slow-growing and dwarfed—a mixture of many pigmies keeping up a frail and feverish being in the regions outside the aquatic "margin of cultivation," and of lusty giants, comparatively considered, battening on the choice reach referred to, and not only driving off invaders but making also occasional predatory invasions when cannibalistically inclined.

To illustrate by an example from another field the effect of sanctuaries upon fish life, it may be noted that at a meeting of the West Cumberland Fishery Board a member told a story of a duel, which he appears from the report of the meeting to have witnessed, between a large salmon and a large eel in one of the lakes of the county. At the end of the duel, the salmon was left dead "on the field" with a big hole in its side. It was added that large numbers of salmon had been killed by eels of late years in the lakes referred to. This story and the addendum to it can hardly be accepted as they stand. The facts as stated are opposed to my experience. I have frequently observed large numbers of big congers inside the " house " of stake nets in the sea, but I can only recall one instance of a conger securing a salmon—as a matter of fact it was a 3lb. grilse—as its prey. The conger in question was a comparatively small specimen, not more than 8lb. to 10lb. in weight, and it succeeded in swallowing the grilse whole tail first, the only damage the latter suffered being a slight " pulping " just above the wrist similar to the " pulping " an otter will make on the shoulder of a salmon. Even when imprisoned in a stake-net, where the movements of a salmon are slow and somewhat stupid, the conger is no match for the king of fish in agility, and though I have seen over 100 salmon imprisoned with as many congers and have frequently observed the chase of the former by the latter, I can only recall the instance already cited of a successful capture. Another difficulty remains. No fresh water eel—even a specimen of the apocryphal monsters said in the local legends of South Uist to haunt a certain loch and to attack those who venture into its waters—is, as a rule, large enough to tackle a salmon, while even if large enough, the salmon, given space, is far too agile for the eel. Even a small trout is rarely taken save by an ambushed eel. Indeed observation enables me to state that eels never attempt to take trout save by the guile of an ambuscado.*

It is obvious, therefore, that sanctuaries play a not unimportant part in the life of lakeland.

I will now take another type of lake, one whose physical features are different, and in which, though the trout are, as a rule, of the same equal quality they do not display either the same uniformity or the same limitation of size as in Culiper.

Of the type of lake referred to it would, no doubt, be possible to name several, so far as mere variation in the size and quality of the fish frequenting them is concerned. As, however, I am dealing wtih the conditions of existence as affecting the size and quality of fish in the same lake with a view to discussing in another chapter the future of our lakes as fish homes, it is obvious that I must choose the most instructive lakes—lakes, that is to say, containing not only the most, but also the most useful, lessons.

* Vide the chapter on " Habits and Habitats of Loch Trout."

It is for this reason that I choose three lakes which, though they have
certain common characteristics, yet differ in essentials, namely Lower
Bornish and Loch Bee in South Uist, and Loch Stennis in Orkney.

Taking these in the order named I have already pointed out some
of the leading features of Lower Bornish. It differs from Loch Coil-a-
Bharra in the following essential characteristics.

It is not, in the first place. cut off from connection with the sea or
with other lakes. On the contrary the road to the sea is of the simplest
and easiest nature. A ditch, or small burn, runs from Bornish across
the narrow neck of land between it and Upper Kildonan, which is only
a stone-throw distant. Into this ditch the Bornish trout frequently
go to feed, and in it as well as in similar drains falling into the loch they
also spawn. From Upper Kildonan to the sea as stated in a previous
chapter, the passage is short and of the simplest kind. The importance
of this facility for migration is obvious, for though the trout do not,
so far as I am aware, avail themselves largely of their opportunities, yet
that they do so occasionally and return refreshed bearing external
evidence of their marine dip I have more than once had occasion to note
in specimens taken, not only in the loch itself, but also in each of the
two connecting and larger lakes as well as in the ditch that is the common road to the sea.* This " open door " has, however, far more important effects upon the conditions of existence in the loch. The animal food
of the loch is undoubtedly affected by its presence, but I will only
condescend upon the most important aspect of the influence thus exercised upon the environment. The sea-trout of the lower lake though
spawning for the most part either in another lake or in a more pretentious burn than the little effluent from Bornish to Upper Kildonan
occasionally penetrate into Upper Kildonan and spawn in the said small
effluent. In the fry and non-migratory stage these young sea-trout
haunt this effluent and the lake above, and being less to the manner
born than fish destined to be permanent denizens of its waters, they
fall a ready prey to the big brothers and sisters of those congenital
denizens. As a consequence of this and the fact that Bornish is frequented by large numbers of stickle-backs on which all Hebridean

---

* This opportunity to migrate is, perhaps, of greatest importance by reason of the
fact that the fish do not feel themselves to be confined—a consideration of moment in
the case of trout of supposed descent from migratory trout.

trout feed, the fish of the lake, from this difference in the conditions of existence, vary far more in size than do the fish of Coil-a-Bharra, though they appear to be equally numerous. Nor does there appear to be any limitation imposed on their growth, though I have been unable to even hear of, much less see, a specimen over 4lb. in weight. In a loch of similar environment in another part of the island, fish of that weight are, however, common, though curiously enough they are never taken with the rod. As illustrating the effect of this difference in environment upon uniformity in size, I quote the weights of some fish, comprising two small baskets of the same number of fish taken from these lochs : Coil-a-Bharra, 6 trout, 10½lb., 2½lb., and five other fish an ounce or so above 1½lb. each; Bornish, 6 trout, 10¼lb., 2½lb., 2¼lb. 1¾lb., 1½lb., 1¼lb., and 1lb. The weights in both cases are approximate.

In this connection it must also be observed that Bornish, being a lake lying in a plain and possessing a bed of sand and gravel, does not afford the same natural shelters or abound in those sanctuaries with which Loich Coil-a-Bharra is so richly endowed, a circumstance which, other things being equal predisposes towards a greater degree of cannibalism, and hence tends to inequality of growth.

Nor is the surface food of Bornish in the form of flies to be compared in plenty with that of Coil-a-Bharra. There is, for example, no rise of the May Fly, while other flies found on the surface of Coil-a-Bharra in thousands, such as the red ant, are conspicuous by their absence. On the other hand the corixæ or water bettles exist in immense numbers, as do water snails and small shell fish. The fish are, in consequence, more predatory and the competition being keener they also display greater variation in size than, as already noted, do the fish of the other lake. That this difference in character is due to such differences in environment as I have noted, goes, of course, without saying.

Loch Bee is simply a second Bornish with this difference, that it is connected with the sea at both ends, though upon this clear connection man has imposed an artificial barrier in the form of tidal gates. It is much shallower and has a more sandy bottom than Bornish—the latter a legacy of its sea-birth. Fish here can and do migrate, though not to the extent that one would expect, while to a limited, but still a marked, degree they enjoy the bountiful table of the true migrants and grow with a proportionate measure of their marvellous rapidity when

in the sea. Occasionally they become true tidal trout and then attain
a large size, assuming with increased weight a silvery sheen over the
yellow of their sides thickly coated with large black spots—a colouring,
I first observed in the trout of salt-water rivers in the Hebrides, at the
same time as another observer was noting it in similar waters in Canada. I·
have mentioned Loch Bee simply as a stepping stone to the environment
of Loch Stennis, between which loch and Bornish it is the connecting
link in the chain of environment from Loch Coil-a-Bharra to the Orcadian water. It will be observed that as the environment in one aspect.
improves, it also in another aspect approaches more closely, what must.
have been if not the real, at least, the possible environment of the common ancestor from which all the species of salmonidæ are sprung. My
principal, though not my only object, being to illustrate by natural.
environments, the effect of environment upon both the bodies and the
minds of trout, or in other words upon their varying size and habits,.
their specific differences and characteristics, I could hardly have chosen
a more happy example than Stennis, the home of the so-called Salmo
Orcadensis, closely allied to the black-finned trout when anatomically
considered in terms of the principles ruling or misruling the classification of the salmonidæ..

Loch Stennis is in many respects unique amongst British lakes be
cause here we find the common trout in what is really as much a salt-
water habitat as a fresh. We find it afforded also as many opportunities of quickly growing big and lusty as is the smolt or grilse when
they migrate to the sea. As a consequence of its environment Stennis.
is frequented by fish of all sizes, which without presenting any specific
external, anatomical or structural differences, so far as I have observed
or am aware, vary in weight from a few ounces up to 30lb., or to speak
by the card to 29lb., that being the largest Stennis trout on record..
That this fine fish represented the maximum growth of trout in Stennis
I do not suppose, but that it was far above the average to which even
the best of its trout attain may be assumed, but not with confidence.
It was a beautiful fish, and as instructive as beautiful, if only because
it did not present any of those " deformities " of age and great size—
from the symmetrical and aesthetic point of view—so frequently observed in abnormally large trout from other waters. In a word the
Stennis trout resembled, metaphorically speaking, a perfect female sal-

mon of the same weight, coloured like a trout and naturally fed on a. marine diet, or to drop the suggestion of metaphor which I have recognised in the above comparison, it was as perfect a trout as a three-quarter pounder taken from a good loch or river, after feeding on fresh water food. Now the conditions of existence in Stennis differ but little from the conditions of existence which the salmon finds in the best-furnished estuaries that approach in size the dignity of what in. Scotland are termed Firths, long lochs, that is to say, of salt water in which some of our larger rivers urge against the ocean their " rival seas. of roaring war." Every form of marine fish food and every variety of sea fish are found in these Firths and, with some exceptions, the same may be said of Loch Stennis, so that while you are angling for trout with. the fly, a lobster fisher may be lifting his creels, another fisherman may be taking herring, and a third may be catching cod, saithe, laithe and. flounders. Nay more. Fresh water forms of food from flies downwards* also abound in it, so that, like certain other waters of a different and more confined type, Stennis is a sort of " No Fish's Water," the debatable land of the great world of waters, that stands and divides the empire of sea fish from the kingdom of fresh water fish. A minute study of its environment I do not undertake. I simply desire to point out. that it completes the ascending scale in environments from the true fresh water environment of Loch Coil-a-Bharra to the most marked example of the mixed environment—more salt than fresh, which it affords.

In its didactic aspect the Stennis environment is of but little utilitarian value because practically incapable of imitation unless one were. bent on creating an artificial lake or founding a fish hatchery, with Stennis. as a model, by the sea. Indirectly, however, Stennis is in itself an object lesson in environment since it proves conclusively—as certain. Continental lakes also prove, that, given anything like the same conditions of existence, the trout can attain almost as great a size as the salmon, and that, too, with a rapidity which if not equal to that of the salmon, is certainly unknown in confined waters or in waters affording only a limited dietary—a rule that will, of course, so far as rapidity of growth is concerned be subject to exceptions. I base this conclusion as to rapidity of growth, rivalling, if not equalling, after a certain.

* No flies are hatched out in Stennis but many are blown on to its surface.

period of existence that of the salmon, on the apparent lack of any
signs of old age in the large trout of Stennis and particularly in the
largest recorded specimen to whose beautiful symmetry of form I have
already referred.   That this rapid growth and attainment of a large
size in a suitable environment, capable of creating what men of science
have with a charming inconsistency called new species in some cases and
not in others, is not confined to the operation of what I may term the
blessings of a quasi-marine home, is proved by the growth of British
trout in the waters of New Zealand, where statistics seem to show that
the rate of increase, varying in this country from one-third of a pound
as the minimum to half a pound per annum in adult specimens, actually
doubles, quadruples, or becomes even six times as rapid in the rich
and generous waters of the Britain of the South.   The cause of this
rapid growth in both the Stennis and the New Zealand cases is the
same.   It is simply the difference in food and in the general conditions
of existence.   These great facts may be best left to " tell their own
story greatly."

Loch Stennis finally is a loch in which we might look for specific
abnormalities or developments in contour such as occur in sea fish and
give them a far greater variety of appearance than fresh water fish
present.   So far as I am aware, however, Stennis trout do not differ in
this respect from other trout, and are no more affected in the direction
indicated by their quasi-marine home than are salmon—a fact which,
when one compares the " many-formed " and variously shaped sea fish
with the " uniformed " fresh water fish—lampreys, eels, sturgeons, and
flounders being all migratory fish—seems to assign to the common
ancestor of the salmonidæ a fresh water origin.   Like all well-fed fish
Stennis trout are remarkably fickle and the larger specimens, so far as
I am aware, never, or very rarely, rise to the fly—a peculiarity shared by
the so-called salmo ferox of other lakes, though the latter do not carry
their objection to fly food to anything like the degree of aversion to it
shown by the big trout of Stennis.

As this fickleness is a trait of all trout in most brackish waters that
are well supplied with food, I may here serve a double purpose by a
description of two somewhat similar and yet different environments in
South Uist, those of the famous Howmore River and Loch Roag, and
of the no less famous Strome Dearg—one of the few salt-water rivers

in this country. To these, as their description involves a slight digression, I shall give a separate chapter by way of break in the continuity, so that the reader, if he pleases, can skip it or read it as a study interesting in itself, but possibly rendered dull by my handling of it.

CHAPTER VII.

The Salmonidæ in Brackish Waters.

Hamlet speaks of "the fruitful river in the eye," and the phrase always suggests to my mind's eye a river, if it can be so called, whose anomalies, not only as a fish holding. but as a fish yielding water, have often afforded me food for conjecture and speculation. It could only exist under its own peculiar circumstances of land configuration. The Obbe and the tidal pools of the South Lacisdale in Harris, some of the Ythan in Aberdeenshire, and of the Kyle of Sutherlandshire, the Wester in Caithness-shire, and a few of the voes of Shetland, and the bays and creeks of Orkney and other the like places, may have some resemblance to it; but in its outstanding features, and in many so to speak, personal. idosyncrasies the Howmore is unique. Rising away up in the hills beneath the shadow of Ben Mohr and another mountain with an Icelandic name, it is for miles merely a dry mountain torrent bed, rocky and. stony, with only a trickle of water in ordinary weather from basin to basin in its steep descent from mountain and moor to the green of a. level plain; when in flood, however, it comes down with the impetuous "Wha' dare meddle wi' me" fierceness so characteristic of all mountain torrents. As soon as it enters the plain it subsides, when in flood, into a smooth-sliding stream; and when low, or even in its normal state, is broken up into currentless and almost isolated pools. After a mile of this canal-like, reed-fringed water (save for its colour it might be a canal in the Midlands, but the peat saves its Celtic character), it expands into a small shallow loch of about two-thirds of a mile in length by 500 yards across, of surpassing excellence for sea-trout, sandy bottomed, rocky-sided, and absolutely free from weeds and reeds. From. this loch again there runs up another ditch, with lochlets here and there. in its course to another and larger loch, into which, again, a fair-sized burn flows, and so to other lochs. At the extreme right-hand corner of the lower loch, looking seawards, the so-called river emerges once

SOURCE OF A SALT WATER RIVER.

ON A SALT WATER RIVER

more. When the tide is out (the pools are only fishable then), the superfluous waters of the loch pour seawards beneath two bridges with no
great force or depth of water in normal weather, while, immediately
below, the river expands into a fine pool, with green banks, sandy bottom, and dark water, with ramifications here and there, of no use for
fishing, which is confined entirely to the main stream. The river then
twists and twines in such a way as to make five pools, which though at
no place of much depth are shallower at some places than at others;
then comes a long stretch of sand and shallow water, three small pools,*
a shallow over sand, and finally a very large pool indeed—the Atlantic !

When the tide glides up these sands the brown river vanishes, the
water becomes deep green and swirling, the pools disappear, all is
uniform, and the water pours into the loch with great force. To see a
high tide bring up hundreds of large sea-trout sporting and splashing,
and the new life which it puts into the old denizens is a sight worth
some travel; but it is not of invariable occurrence. Formerly there
was a sort of gate between the loch and the river to keep the fish in the
tidal pools, but as it was not specially efficacious, it was removed.

This curious water is manifestly ideal for sea-trout, though it has a
strange effect on their moods. In the tidal pools the fish either take with
an alarming avidity, and you get a rise or two rises every cast, or you
might as well emulate Simple Simon and angle in a pail so far as success is concerned. Incredible as it may appear, I once killed 28lb of
sea-trout in twenty minutes in one of the pools (beaching all the fish),
and never got another rise the rest of the day. Eight fish were beached
with the first four casts. The very first cast I ever made in the river I
rose a large bull trout, with my second cast I rose, hooked, and lost
an eriox of perhaps 12lb. Not another bull trout did I afterwards rise.
These curious circumstances shows how extremely fickle fish can be in
brackish water.

There are more fish in the river than in the loch; there is, in fact,
no comparison between the numbers in each, their respective areas considered, yet as long as they are in the river, so long are they fickle. Once
in the loch, their fickleness vanishes, and though on some days they

---

* There is a tributary ditch, leading to another chain of lochs, near the mouth of the
Howmore. The influence of this on the angling of the river is noticed in a later chapter
when dealing with a special aspect of topographical environment and its effects upon the
habits of sea-trout in lakes.

take better than others, yet an angler would either need to be very unskilful, or hit on a very bad day, if he did not do some execution. My
average of all days, long and short, good and bad, over four seasons
on the loch, was twenty-seven sea-trout, 37¾lb. per occasion,* in the
tidal pools it was only fourteen sea-trout 14lb. 1oz., a strong disparity
both in number and in size; yet a draft of the net in the pools, with
reverence be it said, would fully have deserved the title of miraculous.
Restlessness and high feeding, combined with the regularly recurring
invasions of the salt tide, are no doubt the reasons of this fickleness,
yet the tide always invaded the loch strongly, and there was no period
(especially in spring) during which the fish took better than just before
the tide came into and when it was leaving the loch. The constant
food supply in the river and its comparative absence in the loch account
for the different behaviour of the fish, while it is extremely probable
that the invasion of the salt water into the loch, by its enlivening effect
and its suggestiveness of food makes the fish rise freely.

In all brackish water sea trout are apt to come short; this was a
marked feature of these pools. One also loses a large proportion of fish
after hooking, for their mouths are invariably very tender. Though in
swift running brackish water, or in wide expanses of it, the minnow,
sand eel—et hoc genus omne of lure—are very deadly, no fish was
killed save with the fly. If one tried bait (worm) one caught nothing
but eels and flounders, or perhaps a few small yellow trout, of a particularly pretty colour, fine flavour, and shape, peculiar to the river. The
prawn was offered in vain. Small flies alone persuaded the fish to
their doom, a daintiness in the salmonidæ under certain circumstances
to which I recur in a later chapter.

There are two other kinds of fish in this river, namely, the estuary,
slob or tidal trout and a remarkably beautiful hybrid—apparently either
between the said tidal trout and the sea trout, or between the latter
and the common trout. An occasional large common trout has been
killed in the loch above up to 4½lb., but slob trout are rarely taken
in the river, where they are said to attain the weight of 10lb. and
over. The extremely heavy loch trout occasionally killed in Lochs Baa
and Assapool in Mull, are probably of this family, and though in these
lochs they have been reported up to 15lb., the other islands have not

---

* I only once devoted a full day to the loch and killed 52 sea trout—104½lb.

produced a specimen over 6lb. They occur occasionally in the lochs under tidal influence, but, as a rule, are killed either in the sea itself, or in those peculiar " stromes." or salt water rivers, which one occasionally meets with round the Hebridean coast.

The other fish is presumably a hybrid. It reaches occasionally the weight of 1lb., but is rarely over, and generally under, ½lb. This fish does not appear to spawn, but is numerous. What goes on at the bottom it is impossible to say, but when the sea-trout, etc., are off the feed, these fish take greedily, and vice versa. The fact that these hybrids are strongly gregarious in their habits may to some extent account for this, and immense shoals of them, comparatively speaking, will suddenly invade a shallow, clear pool in some disorder, as if driven thither by powerful enemies. These hybrids, without being specially pink in the flesh, are the most delicately flavoured fish of the salmon kind which I have ever eaten. To complete the peculiarities of the whole place, and the eccentricities of the inhabitants, there is no month throughout the whole angling year during which the pools do not contain fresh fish, though some months are, of course, superior to others.*

Now here we have a type of environment which has undoubtedly some of the effects noticed in Stennis, but which, as it is for the most part in the tenancy of migratory salmonidæ, does not, of course, produce the same large specimens of non-migratory trout. Moreover the area of rich feeding is practically limited to the river, and the loch above could not, it is certain, in spite of the invasions of the tide, carry anything like the same number of non-migratory trout as it can accommodate of migratory trout to whom good feeding in a loch is not, as we know, so essential. Finally it will be observed as an effect of environment that in the tidal pools where " bottom " food is not only plentiful but greedily devoured, the fish are as a rule indifferent to the angler's lures, whereas in the lake, where similar food is scarce and surface food is fairly plentiful, they are as keen risers as one could desire.

" There is a river in the ocean " are the opening words of a standard work on physical geography, but it is not to rivers of this class that the salt-water river called Strome Dearg, in South Uist, belong. The Strome —a name-survival of the old Norse days—is about 2½ miles from Loch-

---

* A similar charteristic distinguishes some of the other lochs in the Uists and a few in Harris and Loch Dhu, near Inveray, the two last in a less mark d degree.

boisdale Hotel, and may be fished by residence there.   Its general configuration and character mav be thus described.   From a most admirable
loch for yellow trout, Loch Hallan, there runs down a ditch some 15ft.
to 20ft. in breadth, with an average depth of 3ft. and a clear sandy bottom.   This ditch is practically currentless, and would be invaded
strongly by the tide at each recurrence were it not for a strong wooden
tidal gate, which bars further progress.   The consequence of this, bar-
ring of the ways is that the tide expands over a natural basin or hollow,
and so forms a salt-water loch, about 300 yards long by, say, 100 yards
across, gradually narrowing down at the point of entrance and exit ot
the tide.   The basin in which the river has its source would naturally
receive the superfluous waters of the ditch when the loch above is too
full, but in the normal state there is no current, and this fact, combined
with the barrier, enables the tide to pour up and down a narrow rock-
bound channel as it ebbs and flows, filling the large basin with
its inward rush and emptying it with its outward flow, pouring in mad
tumult back to the parent sea.   These salt-water rivers are thus peculiar;
they flow, as it were, both up and down their channels.   As a consequence of the configuration of the land, which slopes towards the sea,
while the inward rush by reason of the resistance to its oncoming
is generally the more tumultuous, its outward flow is invariably the more
rapid.   The loch never entirely disappears, even in the lowest of low
tides; it is absolutely salt save after very heavy rain.   After leaving the
loch for some 50 yards the water moves swiftly along past high rocks
on one side, and a shingly shore on the other.   It is here from 6ft. to
10ft. deep, according to the state and the nature of the tide.   At the end
of this smooth portion, rough water has been created by a unique and
most curious tidal dyke or bridge, according as one regards it as intended for a barrier or as a means for crossing the stream.   The intention of its builders was that it should serve the dual purpose of checking
the tide and transporting people across it, and to some extent it fulfils
its double mission.   It is a concrete structure some 20 ft. high above
the water, and solid save for two holes (with movable tidal gates), which,
however, the strong rush of water now upwards and now downwards
(but more especially the latter) has much enlarged and rendered of
irregular shape.

The barrier bridge to which I have already referred is a solid concrete structure raised many feet above the roaring tides below, and as it is only some three feet wide, ends at both banks in a rock up which one has to scramble, or down which one has to slide and hit the bridge, it is a trying place for one not used to it. To cross it is, moreover, a matter of peril, for it has neither rail nor parapet to assist the wayfarer over its ridge-like summit.

Farewell, a long farewell to him of the unaccustomed step who, dazed by the altitude at which he stands and the ceaseless din of the water below, loses first his head and then his feet and falls headlong into the swirling tide. If he escape injury from abutting rock or buttress of the bridge, he would need to be a strong swimmer to win his way safe to the rocky sides of the stream, which, like a second Orinoco,

> " Against broad Ocean urges far
> A rival sea of roaring war."

It is just below where the tides pours fiercely and strongly through the arches of this bridge, and in the smooth running water above and the broken run below that the very cream of the fishing is obtained. From the dizzy height of the bridge enormous sea-trout can nearly any day be seen lying with their heads turned towards the descending tide apparently waiting for coming food, though no one has ever seen them feeding. To fly and minnow, sand eel, or any form of lure, they are, as a rule, quite indifferent, and when the rare event has occurred of one taking either fly or minnow, the battle has been short and fierce, the whole drama consisting simply of the rise at the fly or seizure of the minnow, followed by a wild rush through one of the holes with jagged edges, a breakage, and an angler on the bank excited over the possibilities of the place and lamenting its sad realities. Some little distance above the bridge it is, of course, possible to land a good fish, but even there, owing to the abundance of long trailing weed and tangle, and the excessive strength, activity, and tender mouths of the fish (these three features being specially pronounced by reason of the water being salt), it is a matter of extreme difficulty, though not of impossible accomplishment. The ordinary sea-trout in the loch and river weighs about ¾lb. Even these small fish give ideal sport; they are never in the water, so to speak. I have seen one of 1lb. jump seventeen times in succession with incredible rapidity. The rush of a big fish, anything from 5lb. up to 8lb. or 9lb., in the rough water below the bridge, is one of the very finest things in angling. It is true that, so far as is known, no fish over 6lb. has ever been landed on the fly, but at the same time some magnificent sport, so long as it lasted, has been obtained from these giants. No doubt the man who will be the first to successfully combat one of these monsters has yet to come. Below the bridge the river runs for a few hundred yards between high, rocky banks, finally losing itself in Loch Boisdale. From about thirty to forty yards below the bridge, however, it is very difficult to fish. The rod for this sort of place should be about 14ft. in length, and the reel should carry a good supply of line, say seventy or eighty yards. The gut should be strong, and carefully washed in rain water after use, as salt-water oc-casionally rots gut. Though one fly should be used, having regard merely to the advantage thereby gained when playing a trout, yet as two flies raise more fish, and, as the angler must make up his mind beforehand to get more sport than fish (the ambiguity will be readily understood), the advantage is more apparent than real. Small flies are commonly used flies, that is, of the size employed in South Uist lochs. Ordinary sea-trout patterns kill best. Double hooks are preferable to single, as they hold better. The fish usually rise low and require no striking. When playing them, they should be kept " high " and landed as speedily as possible, and at the first opportunity.

Besides sea-trout this salt-water river is frequented by a species of yellow trout with extremely large spots, a feature observed in similar waters in the Far West. These fish, it may be stated, have been caught as heavy as 5½lbs., and generally belong to the slob or tidal variety. A marked characteristic of the fish is that it grows dark, almost black, after it has been some time out of the water.

These salt-water rivers are certainly interesting and novel. Though big baskets are not often made in their weed-haunted and tumultuous waters, yet they almost invariably afford sport if not amongst the sea-trout, then amongst the brown; if not from the brown trout, then, may-hap, from the grey mullet; and if the mullet be not present, or " dour," then certainly from the lythe; but there the line must be drawn, for though there is a local legend that a flounder was once taken on the fly, the possibilities of the place are sufficiently satisfying without exacting further demand on our credulity.

I have, it will be observed, in treating of the salmonidæ in brackish

HALF TIDE ON A SALT WATER RIVER.

SALT WATER SEA-TROUT LOCH: HALF TIDE.

water as exemplified by the fish of the two environments resembling Stennis sufficiently closely in certain respects to be, mutatis mutandis, analogous, allowed myself much more latitude than I did in my remarks on that famous, interesting and peculiar sheet of water. I was tempted to do so by reason of the fact, already stated in the case of the Howmore, that the environment is so good in both these waters, that, as in Stennis, it makes the fish most fastidious. Further as the Strome is frequented by yellow trout originally from Loch Hallan and other lochs the peculiarities of its environment have practically succeeded in producing a new species—or at least a variety of the trout of the loch referred to. This new species or variety attains a recorded size of at least 6lbs., or three times the size which the trout, from which it is a specific environment-born off-shoot, is known to attain. I cannot conceive of any object lesson in the influence of environment that would be more instructive, nor of any illustration, borrowed from my own experience that could better demonstrate the important position environment occupies as the chief producer of size and quality in fish.

CHAPTER VIII.

MORE LAKES AND FURTHER LESSONS.

Leaving such great, dignified and aristocratic waters as Stennis, the Howmore, and the Strome, let us stand for a little by the shores of a lakeland gem set like a jewel rich and rare to flash back the sunlight on the grim hills amidst which it lies embosomed far up in the solitudes some 1,500 feet above the sea.* Its clear, shallow and limpid water flashes green against its granite bed as its waves roll shoreward and it looks, and in a measure is, a cold and hard dwelling-place for the trout that call it home. Yet in some aspects it is an oasis set in the sterile rocky desert of the grim peaks of Arran. It is true that its people are but pigmies, but it is also true that they are beautiful pigmies, their dwarfed condition being due to a too generous response to the great command "Be fruitful and multiply." If, however, a race of very small anglers happened upon their lake and angled with rod and gear so proportionately small and fine as to make these fish 2lbs. or more, they would declare that they had lighted on a trouting paradise. The flesh of the trout is distinctly pinkish in hue in spite of their small size, and they are, as I have said, unsurpassed in beauty of contour and richness of colouring. They are, however, incredibly numerous, and though the loch lacks but little to make its environment capable of carrying a large head of good fish yet it is obviously capable of improvement, and has equally obviously produced this dwarfed race while preserving their beauty and sustaining its own character for being equal to the requirements of much better fish if they came in companies and not in battalions. This lake, small and unpretentious as it is, is in this aspect as full of instructive matter as are its larger brethren of greater name and fame. It suggests apart from the general problem of environment, the enormous importance of proportion as a question of environment. By proportion, I understand, the head of fish a lake, pond, or stream

* One of the most elevated lochs in Scotland is curiously named Loch Brandy. It is 2,070 feet above sea level.

should carry relatively not only to its area, but what is more important, the quantity of food it holds. It is this lack of proportion between head of population and the food-producing powers of a country that in human communities is the cause of emigration or of colonisation. Whenever, that is to say, the number of people requiring food—leaving labour and other problems out of account—exceeds the food-producing capacity of an isolated country, ipso facto you have, a priori, emigration or colonisation, or, as an alternative, a race that is physically dwarfed into what the poet called "dwindled sons of little men." Human beings can, as a rule, avoid this final catastrophe, but in Africa, as we are aware, they have not always done so and pigmy races occur. Trout, however, are not always their own masters. They cannot always migrate and are often the slavish ministers of circumstances which preclude migration. When, therefore, under such circumstances this lack of proportion between their number and the food supply becomes pronounced, they at once begin to grow smaller and smaller in size and poorer and poorer in quality, adapting their persons by a beautiful example of specialised evolution to the requirements and possibilities of the conditions of their existence.

This is precisely what has happened in Loch Tanna, the loch to which I have been referring. It is a bright, brisk, cheerful loch which seems to have given such a measure of the same characteristics to its fish that boon nature, taking pity on their decaying condition, has sent just enough food in the form of flies, beetles and so forth to save the "character" of the race.

A student of environment would suggest the adoption of means to restore the proper proportion, or, in other words, the balance of nature. It is not improbable that some would recommend decimation. Personally I urge the claims of a study of environment and of environment-cultivation and thus avoid the slaughter grim and great for which it may be shown there is no necessity. Amelioration of environment seems a plan more in keeping with our boasted modern knowledge than the cutting of the Gordian knot of this and other lakes—by the sword. However, I do not desire at this stage to anticipate the succeeding chapters, and will content myself with merely indicating the remedy.

As the antithesis of Loch Tanna, a few lochs could be instanced in which the trout, without any change in environment in the strict sense, have nevertheless suffered such a change in the conditions of their existence that from being numerous and small, they have become scarce and comparatively large, thus indicating that when the proper "propoṟtion" of food to population is restored "by the sword" the fish respond to the change. A typical example of this change is afforded by Loch Fraochie in Perthshire. Some forty years ago Fraochie was a lake in which it was possible to kill trout by the dozen. Indeed, a near relation, who used to fish it with the late "Rorie" Anderson, of Dunkeld, and a minister, whose name I have forgotten if I ever knew it, informed me that he and the two other "rods" took some 120 dozens of very small trout in one week. Pike shortly afterwards were introduced or found their way into the loch, and my earliest recollections of the lake, dating as they do from about 1870, carry me back to a stiff and cheerless water which, on the first occasion I floated in a boat on its surface, did not yield either a single fish or a single rise, but produced interminable stories of its past glories from both the near relation already referred to and the boatman. Being a small boy I became a confirmed laudator temporis acti so far as Fraochie was concerned, and voted angling on it but little removed, in these days of decay and pike, from the inglorious condition of a fraud. Now I believe the angling is better, but the fish are still comparatively few in number and of a much larger size than in the old days that ante-dated the pike. Here, then, we have an excellent example of the effect of the law of proportion, though, as I have said, decimation is not the means by which the law should be recognized.

Before passing to consider the future of our lakes, I shall briefly notice some other indirect causes operating on the environments of to-day—one of too common, the others of as yet infrequent occurrence. so far as lakes are concerned.

Most authorities are agreed that there is a large and wasteful destruction of winged insects and their larvæ, which has been brought about by draining swamps, hill sides, and moors, all of whose surplus water of old found its way on the surface into our lakes and, of course,. rivers. Now, as most of the drains are underground such insects as. they sweep down are staid by the earth, and few or none of them reach the lakes. That this is of some importance goes without saying, and as. there is no diet so good for trout as flies it must adversely affect the fish. The growing of abundance of trees and bushes by the banks is.

the most natural solution of the difficulty, which is one aspect is part
of the problem of proper proportion.

The prevalence of poaching in England, Ireland and Scotland and
the absence of a close season in the last-named country, are powerful
deterrents to the improvement of our lakes and active agents in the
destruction of their fish. Whether the somewhat arbitrary rule by
which the close time for trout in Ireland is the same, with power to
alter but not to shorten its duration, as for salmon is, or is not, a wise
regulation, I do not pause to discuss, but will content myself with
pointing out that long or short, arbitrarily or judiciously fixed, the
blessings of a close time cannot be over-estimated. From the absence
of such a close time and the peculiar character of the Scottish law as to
the right to take trout, the lakes and rivers of the country suffer to an
incalculable degree. The personal, rather than the topographical,
"environment" of the poacher could easily be remedied, if our legislators
could only be brought to see the immense moral and political influence
angling is able to exercise over the community. The fishing rod is the
best policeman, as Nottingham and Sheffield know, and Solomon were
he now alive would alter his famous dictum "Spare the rod and spoil
the child" to "Spare the rod and spoil the people." In Scotland the
absence of a close season conjoined with the fact that the right to take
trout is a pertinent of the land has nowhere borne more baleful
fruit than in the Orcadian lochs, which now hold very few trout compared with the immense numbers that used to jostle one another in the
race of life in their bountiful waters. An Orcadian innkeeper lately
wrote me a letter in which he stated that poaching was a thing of the
past. As a matter of fact "poaching" is only less rife, because there
are fewer trout to "poach," if one can apply the term to men who as
owners of a square foot of territory on a loch side have, in Scots Law, the
right to fish all over its waters. A few years ago one could take baskets
of from 35lb. to 40lb. on Loch Harray. Its deterioration began with
the institution of poaching by set lines and nets, and has been steadily
maintained. In one season a single Orcadian sent 1000lb. of trout to
Billingsgate, and there are some hundreds of nets—the number is by
some placed at 1000—on this lake alone! So far is poaching from
being at an end in Orkney, that enquiries made at Billingsgate while
these pages were in the press, elicited the information that thousands of

trout still come from the islands to the great London fish market. The fish have sadly deteriorated in size and are now rarely larger than a hand's length. Finally, the depopulated Harray is no longer able to supply the London market, and the demand is met by laying all the lochs on the various islands of the Orcadian group under contribution. The destructive trade in trout if it has reached its climax in Orkney is, assuredly not confined to that region. It exists all over Scotland to the detriment alike of lakes and rivers. That this state of affairs should be endured for a single day is a social and political crime and a standing reflection upon the narrowness of the horizon of legislative life as it appears bounded to those who make our laws. A two clause act, or one a clause longer than the Eels Act of 1886, would remedy the evil. All over the United Kingdom a legal size limit of sale is sadly needed, similar to that which sends annually thousands of helpless lobsters from the market and over the quay end to be devoured in their defenceless condition by the waiting crabs. Lobsters appear in the financial returns of our sea fisheries, but trout do not. Hinc illae lachrymae. It is, therefore, the irony of fate that the lobsters rejected by law should nominally be saved because returned to the sea, but really perish because so restored when " snicked " and unable to defend themselves. This, however, is legislation on a par with the lack of it, which denies a legal size limit of sale to trout and procrastinates the granting of a close season to Scottish trout, and the making of the sale of trout absolutely illegal in Scotland, as it is in England and Wales, during certain periods of the year. Until this close season is established and the other necessary steps are taken to protect Scottish trout, we strive in vain to realize the ideal of Burns and apply it to loch trout :—

> "Shame fa' the fun, wi sword and gun
> To slap mankind like lumber !
> I sing his name and nobler fame
> Who multiplies their number."

Finally, there is the question of pollution. A few but not many of our lakes suffer directly from this ; all must in a measure when the drains already referred to carry down not food but injurious mineral matter. The kind of pollution to which I refer is, however, that from which Loch Lomond suffers.* I mean the pollution after it has left

---

* That our ancestors fully appreciated the effects of that other form of topographical environment—the dam—curse of the Don and other rivers, may be gathered from the

the lake of the effluent that connects it with the sea. Happily the case of Loch Lomond is as yet exceptional, but how long it will continue to be so I do not care to contemplate when I remember Kelvin, Clyde, and Cart, the inky Irwell and hundreds of other English rivers, of which many of the streams of Yorkshire, once fair and pellucid, but now black, greasy, evil-smelling, and foul, are not the least saddening examples.

So far as the stream is concerned that sweeps from under the shadow of the Ben with all the clearness and much of the grace that the lordly Tay bursts from the confines of its parent lake, I have no hesitation in saying that if " Turkey Red " ceased to be an object of commercial desire and the Leven were restored to its pristine sanitary glory, Loch Lomond would be the finest sea-trout and salmon loch in the United Kingdom. There is, it is true, the Clyde to consider— that polluted river which bears the black burden of the dark sea-born city's foulest product. Still, even that difficulty, great as it is, salmon and sea trout would overcome. Possibly unless the Clyde poured as clear a tide as it did in the days of when " Richard Franck, Philanthropus," wrote his " Northern Memoirs " as a rival book to Walton's " Compleat Angler," the glories of the Leven and the Loch Lomond* of the seventeenth century might not be completely restored. In any view, so far as lakes are concerned, we have happily only for the most part to deal with the prevention rather than the cure of pollution as a means of bettering environment. Prevention, as a rule, is much easier than cure, and this is truer of the sanitation of lakes and rivers than perhaps of anything else in the cosmic order. I leave the subject with reluctance, but must pass to the more or less practical application of certain of the lessons which the waters I have mentioned should have been able to teach, unless I have wholly failed, as I feel to some extent I have failed, to state these lessons clearly.

following extract :—'' It is said that the raising of the dam head at Partick Mills, upon the Kelvin, is the sole cause why the fish come not up in rodding time to the Glagert."— P. Camps: Statis., xcc., xv. ; 321.

* These glories are referred to in a later chapter. When the Glasgow sewage works which now deal with about one-fifth of the sewage of the city are completed, there is not merely a possibility, but a reasonable probability, of the Clyde being sufficiently purified for salmon to ascend. In any case the Clyde must affect the Leven and Loch Lomond less adversely than it does at present.

CHAPTER IX.

The Future of our Lakes.

" There were giants in those days " is the natural thought of the man with memories, whose tendency, indeed certain fate, is to become a laudator temporis acti unless he keeps his admiration of the glories of the past within due bounds by taking an optimistic view of the possibilites of the future and ignoring some of the sternly sad realities of the present.

Those whose patience has enabled them to read the all too hastily-penned generalizations and ancient and modern instances, not always relevant and but ill-arranged and worse digested in the previous chapters, will now be in possession of the views I hold with regard to environment and its effect upon fish. I have endeavoured to show that species is nothing and that environment is everything, and is in fact the cause of specific differences.

The importance of this position is very obvious when one comes to discuss the future of our lakes, since it is clear that the theory of environment as stated makes the question of what fish our lakes, as they are, can carry of even less importance than the problem of what fish they can be made to carry, when, by the exercise of a wise and reasoned study of the conditions of lake existence, the " standard of comfort " is appreciably raised.

In the old days, before the march of events and the force of circumstances called the fish-farmer into existence and the demand for fish to re-stock naturally barren, unsuitably populated, or decimated waters had not arisen, anglers were content to let nature work out her own ends and did not seek either to improve upon her or to come to her aid by artificial means. Anglers have, however, so increased in number of late years that, the water area remaining constant, it is no longer possible to rely solely upon nature for repeopling waters that have been decimated or overfished.

The causes of this increase in anglers are not far to seek. The means of communication have been so improved in every way that people are now encouraged to go a-fishing who formerly would have stayed at home. Angling grows by what it feeds upon. If a tourist pure and simple be carried, through the agency of modern conveniency in travelling into an angling region which in the older days he would not have visited, and finds himself in an angling hotel, with its fish-flavoured atmosphere and its constant buzz of enthusiastic angling gossip, if not too far gone in cynicism for recovery, he will reason from effect to cause and, in many cases, will turn angler, in the belief that there must be something specially enjoyable, something peculiarly attractive, in a pursuit which seems to stir up such enthusiasm and to afford food for such endless speculative discussion to its votaries.

True, there is your out-and-out ignoramus—your cynic of the "malignant" type—who, never having even essayed to wean himself from his abstemious folly, accepts as satisfying the time-worn definition of the great lexicographer; but this class is nowadays in a hopeless minority.

Many anglers have become so by force of example, and there is no doubt that angling fever is strongly infectious. This unpremeditated meeting of non-anglers with anglers when in angling and "angling-talking" vein is certainly one of the principal causes of the great increase in the number of anglers, especially of those coming from large towns and non-angling centres.

With another generation the thronging of the ways will be even greater, for an angling father is likely to have angling sons, on the very same principle that one rarely finds in thorough angling centres—such, say, as Tweedside—a native who is not more or less enthusiastic over the sport. It is the same, of course, to some extent, with regard to every sport; but there is this difference between angling and most other sports—one must be an active participator, not merely a spectator. There are thousands of ardent supporters of cricket and football who never handle a bat or kick a ball; but angling's categorical imperative is, "Thou shalt fish thyself or know not my true joys."

Fashion has no doubt, at least in the case of wealthier anglers, a good deal to do with their becoming anglers. When fashion is the cause of a man turning angler it has had this effect: it has made angling waters more valuable, therefore more to be desired, and hence

G

has increased the number of exclusive waters, and thronged more closely what one might term the open and non-exclusive watery ways.

Whether the angling Press—papers entirely devoted to angling in all its branches, and those which give it a more or less prominent place in their pages—has been born of the increase in anglers or has caused, to some extent, the increase is a question admitting of a double answer. The increase in anglers primarily, no doubt, gave birth to the angling Press, and the angling Press again multiplied the number of anglers.

At first sight, this thronging of the ways would seem to mean ruin to angling through the depletion of the steams and lochs ; but, on the contrary, it may confidently be asserted that it may ultimately have no such effect. The selfish angler, who hates to see a brother of the craft fishing his favourite stream and so on, is a being with whom most of us have no sympathy, and whose interests need not be regarded. The very size of the army of anglers has called attention to the importance of fish preservation and culture. Pollution has been guarded against ; wholesale and unreasonable destruction legislatively forbidden ; illegal methods of capture have been defined ; boards of conservators guard the interests of the fish ; while scientific fish culture provides the assurance that the supply, even if naturally exhausted, may be artificially renewed. The thronging of the ways with anglers is thus not a subject for fear or for doleful plaint, but one for congratulation, for there is no department of sport which has such an influence for good amongst the masses, none which engenders so much benefit socially, physically, and morally, amongst all classes of the community.

While all this is very true, yet it is at the same time only too clear that many of our lakes have by the severe and continuous castigation by rod and line to which they have been subjected fallen away from their high estate, while the efforts that have been made to remedy the evil by the introduction of artificially reared fish have not always been directed on proper principles. It is indeed almost a platitude in these days to urge that to put good fish in an unsuitable home is not to secure any improvement in the fishing, but to tempt further deterioration through the operation of a law of nature taking vengeance on its outrage. Though the law of environment is, however, thus recognised in theory, it is to be feared that either wilfully or by way of experiment, it is frequently ignored in practice. It is for this reason that I venture to urge not the re-stocking of our lochs, but an enquiry into the conditions of existence they offer, and the means of improving these conditions. That the production of first class environments by artificial means is always possible, I do not assert, but that there are few environments which cannot be improved goes without saying. The relatively greater importance of improving environments to merely breeding strong trout for whom a naturally suitable environment must be found, or who must be placed in angling water irrespective of its suitability to their requirements, may be illustrated by an imaginary but conceivable case. If we take a certain water that is an admittedly bad environment and by comparing its possibilities with the actualities of a water that is a good environment, formulate a specific plan of improvement which when carried into effect produces such an amelioration in the natural conditions of existence in the water which places it, quoad environment, almost on the same level as the water which we took as the standard to be attained, what is the obvious result? Not only can we, if we please, introduce trout of almost the same quality as the standard water will carry into the amiliorated water, but we may even leave the improved environment to work out the salvation of its original denizens.

It is true that if we adopt the latter plan, we shall have to exercise patience and cultivate the contentment of abstention until the change in size and quality has been slowly but surely accomplished, but this fact does not alter the general accuracy of the principle involved either in its theoretical or in its practical aspect. The axiomatic truth remains the same, whether we artificially stock or leave the natural law of environment to operate its own vindication, the only difference being that in the former case we secure the desired end certainly with greater rapidity, possibly with greater certainty, seeing that we have anticipated the specific change that nature would have brought about, and do not have to wait for the law of evolution to afford one of the most speedily accomplished examples of its operation.

That our fish farmers are fully alive to the importance of the truth just enunciated goes without saying, but that they always give it the recognition it merits in practice is, I am afraid, a proposition that cannot be urged with the same degree of confidence. Our fish farmers are, after all, men of business, and may urge the very same excuse for their neglect of this aspect of fish culture—the culture of fish homes—as do

our theatrical managers for submitting a certain class of plays, which
they admit are poor stuff, with pernicious tendencies, but for which there
is a popular demand. As a matter of business, therefore, the theatrical
manager does not sacrifice his banking account at the shrine of art, and
for this surrender to expediency calms his conscience by the reflection
that he is merely the involuntary and compelled source of supply that
meets a demand. The fish farmer argues in very much the same fashion
and though he protests against the unfairness to his "goods" of placing
them in circumstances that do not tend to show off their good qualities,
yet in the main his efforts are directed to the production of these good
qualities and to the breeding of good fish that will sell and meet
the demand. Within his own ponds, however, be it observed, he
recognises how much more important environment is than "quality,"
which is not inherent but acquired, and a result of environment
dependent for its endurance upon the continuation of the conditions
producing it. He supplements nature by artificial means—an aspect
of the question which requires separate treatment—and while thus
emphasing the importance of environment, makes but little more than
a half-hearted protest against its almost total neglect by his customers,
as something possibly as capable of artificial production as the
finest breed of trout that ever cut with their golden oars the silver
stream or the dancing waters of the lake. My position is this, that what
is recognised as possible, and indeed as necessary, in the fish pond, is
equally possible and by parity of reasoning equally necessary in the
lake. If we can, by a study of good environments—of good conditions
of existence in certain lakes—formulate a theory of "lake farming" that
when practically applied, will improve the standard of environment in
our lakes, then not only will we improve the fish already inhabiting
them, but we will have solved a problem that is a corollary to the
problem of how to produce fish of good quality, and one which,
within the limits of "the fisheries" has already been solved.

I am, of course, aware that all our fish farmers have devoted considerable attention to the study of aquatic plants suitable for the
production of water-insects and flies on which fish feed, but so far as I
am aware, none of them have placed the general question of the cultivation of environment in natural waters before every other question,
or have conjoined the study of that aspect of fish-farming within their

own ponds, with the study of what I may term "comparative environmentology."

If, for example, a complete survey of the conditions of a natural lake affording an ideal environment resulted in either the reproduction of that lake, with all its physical features on a small scale for experimental purposes, such as the cultivation of its many forms of living food, ard of the vegetarian growths that in turn foster that living food, or, failing such reproduction, in a theory of lake-farming, then I am assured, that the future of our lakes would be even more hopeful than it is.

That we possess the means of ensuring the future of our lochs goes without saying, and the problem in the aspect in which, up to this point I have regarded it really resolves itself into the question of how these means are to be applied. My contention is that we shall have to study the creation of good environments, and that until we do so, we can only partially avail ourselves of the means which science has placed at our command. The botanist and the entomologist must come to the aid of the fish-breeder pure and simple, while he cannot dispense with the services of the lake architect who studys the best and not the worst of nature's models. Happily in the case of lochs we have not the sanitary difficulty to face and overcome. As yet our lochs, like the sea, are practically unpolluted, and though there are a few lakes, notably Loch Lomond, which suffer as homes for the migratary salmonidæ through their pure effluent waters being polluted and poisoned in their course to the parent ocean, yet all or nearly all the lake-homes of trout that have to be ameliorated possess the first essential to fish life and good environment, the blessing of pure water appreciated by none more fully than by those living in a beautiful county of once fair but now fœtid streams on whose pellucid waters commercialism has put the imprimatur of its black and inky curse.

CHAPTER X.

FISH FARMERS AND NATURE.

"Great Nature spoke,—observant man obey'd."—Pope.

Head-lines, as the sub-editor understands the art and science of using them, are designed either to attract the eye by indicating the nature of the copy or matter which follows them, in which case they are apposite, or they are designed to excite the curiosity, in which case they may be the opposite of apposite. A similar rule applies to titles whether of books or of chapters, and I therefore make no apology for the above heading, other than is contained in the context, which deals with the effect of early environment on hand-reared fish, especially when descended from hand-reared fish whose little and easy life has been bounded by the narrow horizon of the fish pond.

Before proceeding to discuss the problem—which might be otherwise entitled "Memory in Hand-Reared Fish"—some preliminary observations are necessary. Certain fish-farmers, as business men and otherwise, have taken exception to my views, as expressed in the angling press, and have maintained both in the columns of the papers referred to and also in private correspondence, that trout when once beyond the fry stage (they except, as already indicated, rainbow trout fry from the helplessness of other trout fry) take anything and eat anything when hungry irrespective of environment, and irrespective of the conditions under which their early days have been passed, or the ancestors from which they are sprung. This, it will be observed, is a mere petitio principii. It ignores the finding of food, the earning of bread and butter, so to speak, by the wag of the troutish tail and the questing of the troutish eye. All men we know can eat, when hungry, if food be placed before them, but men reared in the lap of luxury, and unused to earning their daily bread, find it much harder to adapt themselves to conditions necessitating such toil, than do those used to it from their youth upwards. I waive the question of "standard of comfort" in the quality and quantity of food, though it is a concession that, strictly speaking, no Materialist, in the best and proper sense of the phrase, can be called upon to make.

I point out further to avoid initial misconstruction that the most helpless of animals are those which receive most attention, the most dependent, those in whom the quality of dependence is cultivated by materialistic agencies, and that what is true of the individual is true of the race to which he belongs. A baby, when it survives being born, is the most helpless and dependent of all young animals, though sprung from the king of animals, and after birth would as often as not die did medical skill not forcibly beat it into life. The physiological or material causes of this are so clear that they need not be stated, and there are numerous analogies. The pampered, useless pet dog is one example; an over-fed pointer is another. Once the latter is fed he loses his sense of smell and becomes, pro tanto, less of a gifted hunter, whose power as a food-searcher is impliably dependent on the sense of smell. I do not desire to labour the point, but merely to indicate that certain faculties may, a non utendo, become rudimentary attributes, just as certain muscles may become, and have in man become rudimentary organs by the same long prescription. Further I should point out that my theory of fish life as I have already, I trust, made sufficiently clear, is that of the Sensationilist or Materialist. Sensationalism and Materialism may, it is true, present some subtle doctrinal differences, but as the discussion of these differences is a question of moral philosophy and not of physiological moment, there is no necessity to debate the problem of freedom of will and responsibility as applied to our friends the trout. Whether therefore, Sensationalism or Materialism is a satisfying theory of the cosmic order as a whole it is certain that in the narrow world of fish life—in its mental as well as its physical aspect—Materialism is a whole truth. Fish are governed by two great impulses of purely sensational origin which rule their being—the impulse to reproduce their species, and the impulse to feed and claim the right to continue to be as a postulate of their being. The gratification of these appetites, the one an occasional but regularly recurring impulse, the other a constant motive, are the autocratic dictators of their habits, conditioned only in their law-giving and will-imposing categorical imperative, by the circumstances of their environment as favouring or hindering, rendering

easy or difficult the due satisfaction of the great ends of the lives
of fish as sensational entities.

It is to those differences in environment and in the degree of reproductive facilities, that to a large extent must be attributed the specific
differences, the varying manifestation of the migratory tendency and
other habitual characteristics shown by the different members of the
great family of the salmonidæ.   Finally I would point out, by way of
introduction, that fish are said to have no brain cortex—the place where
" memory holds her seat."   Nevertheless we hear so much in these
days of " educated " trout that if the Act of 1870 does not apply to our
fario, through the saving grace of the dry fly and the entomological
angler, Sensationalism, as already indicated, must know its very highest
development in the trout, whose really wonderful memory for things
that are good must be attributed to the association of sensations, if not
of ideas, conjoined with an optimism that enables him to see something
good to eat in all things.   Of course the purist will say that our friends
the trout—most interesting because most humanly companionable of all
British fish—in a state of educated nature have reversed the ordinary
sociological rule, and have proceeded from contract to status.   At one
time, in other words, they took any kind of lure wholesale, by contract
so to speak, now, as a rule of their social order, they stand,
examine, and doubt, until they reject under normal conditions every
fly that is not an exact imitation of nature or behaves in a way that is
not according to " Cocker."   A leg beyond the number boon nature
has provided, or one that gives an extra kick or kicks with a muscular
action foreign to the mechanical anatomy of the real Simon Pure in flies,
is said to be at once rejected as a lusus naturæ that contains a hook.
The ghost of Colonel Hawker would find, says the purist, if he rode on
horseback from the Shades and essayed to wile a Test trout with one of
his flies, that Cocytus held no more shadowy fish than those which his
antiquated feathered fancies would lure to their doom.   Whether this
cunning of the fish is due to reasoning or merely to some form of
neurosis that has attacked the trout, as the other form of neurosis has
the men and women of the age, it might be inquiring too curiously to
ask.   The fact remains, and seems to prove that fish in a state of nature
can develop a sort of neurotic or sensational* memory which is only less

* This theory is developed in the chapter dealing with the "Philosophy of the Fly."

remarkable than the singular power tame fish in captivity or hand-reared fish in ponds develop of recognising persons and of associating for very long periods after their release to freedom and the conditions of a wild environment the presence of a human being with something good to eat.

Personally I do not wholly accept the educated trout theory. The most "educated" of trout, I am aware, lose all or nearly all their so-called cunning when the May fly is "up and down" (which should be the technical phase to express its birth, brief course and death), simply because appetite overcomes every other sensation from the visual shadow that carries with it, as it falls on the water, the terrors of the unknown,* to the substance of that shadow which catches the sharp troutish eye at other and less exclusively sensual seasons than the May fly festival, and drives the trout away, whether he be a denizen of the limpid water of a chalk stream or a roamer in the shallows by the untrodden shores of some lonely lake in the West.

I will here cite two most curious examples of this effect of appetite upon what one may term the sensational timidity of trout. I was fishing a very sporting loch in Argyleshire and observed a fish feeding, as is their wont, over a range of some ten yards of shore. In the dead calm I made several long and light casts in the endeavour to bring my flies under his notice. This I could not succeed in doing. As I was finally withdrawing my flies to rest him, he suddenly charged out after them, every fin in his body and his body itself quivering with unsuppressed eagerness. He was a big fish and I saw him as clearly as if he had been in a stream. He came straight for the boat and reminded me of a certain adventure with a torpedo I survived in foreign seas. But that is another story. Involuntarily I raised my hand to turn him. Whether it was my hand or whether it was a sudden memory of the substance he was leaving for the shadow, the fact remains that he turned and swam back as quickly as he came until lost in the fretted sunshine under the boughs. I cast in his line of march and he at once took my fly and was duly landed. The whole operation which I have described occurred in a second. He was a 2½ lb. fish that should have been 4 lbs. The other case occurred on the Hebrides. I was taking a boat from one loch to another up a short and shallow ditch and the

* Sea-trout show at times precisely the same distrust in a fly.

task was a matter of some difficulty. When it was nearly accomplished
I disturbed a trout of about 2 lbs. that had evidently been feeding in the
ditch and he ran out over some shallow sandy water that stretched for
some distance on either side of the point of exit of the ditch. As the
trout went slowly out I seized my rod and made a long cast over him.
To my astonishment he took the fly and was duly landed He was a
fish of 2¼ lbs. That it was hunger made both of these fish indifferent
to the terrors of my presence I do not doubt, precisely on the
principle that grouse on stooks and even wild geese in April among potatoes
(certainly Hebridean wild geese) throw their natural wariness and
suspicion to the winds. Otherwise the cases are instructive examples of
the effect of feeding habits upon fish and afford another remarkable
example of the sensational aspect of fish life, which in dealing with the
effect of artificial feeding on fish cannot be wholly ignored and is
certainly of some didactic value.

I have found it necessary to make these preliminary observations to
prevent misunderstanding as to my theory, while the problem initially
raised as to the effect of the habits of the fish pond upon the habits of
artificially-reared trout set free in a lake or river, lead me to ask the
following questions : Do hand-reared fish retain for any length of time
the memories of their comfortable sojourn in the fishery ponds, when
they sweep through the spreading waters of a lake or dash through the
thousand runs of some brimming river ? Does the fierce and sharp
thunder plump lashing the surface of their new habitat awaken by
association memories of their first home and the spluttering fall of
chopped liver and longings for the vanished hand that fed them ? Or
does the hissing of the hail-kissed water no more affect the troutish
brain than it would stir the emotions of some animal low placed on the
scale and boasting a system of nerves and ganglia as its only claim
to intelligence ?

We hear continually of so many hundreds or thousands of artificially
hatched and reared trout being put into our waters yet, so far as I am
aware the question has never been raised as to what effect, if any, the
fact that fish have for the first period of their lives been hand-fed, has
upon their subsequent habits, or to put the matter colloquially on what
we term their " tameness ?" Authorities are dumb on the matter. At
the same time, it is clear that, if two-year-old trout (and some hatchery-

reared fish of that age may by many be esteemed takable) retain the greedy and confiding habits of the pond in which they have been reared, a single day of angling slaughter might easily decimate a stock of 1,000 fish.

The answer to these questions may, perhaps, be found by a consideration of the subject of this chapter "Fish Farmers and Nature," which as a title covering and implying an important problem in pisculture so far as the future of our lakes, and also of our waters in general, is concerned, will now be better understood.

It is a curious fact, but is for the writer a matter of observation, that hand-reared fish turned out to enjoy the freedom of commoners of water in some broad spreading mere that dwarfs to insignificance the confined area of their old and original home, will yet crowd into some narrow bay and gather in their tens and hundreds at the approach of a man to its shores, especially if by chance he can happen on some of their number and excite them to rise as decoys to their brethren. Nay more. Even after long years of sojourn in spreading waters the fifth or sixth generation sprung from hand-reared trout—particularly from trout whose wild ancestors were of a migratory tendency or showed to an uncommon degree the traits of the great common ancestor of all the salmonidæ—will travel in shoals, as brethern and kindred may, ready to rise obsequious to the fly if only the leader or "king" fish shoves up his shoulder to show how trout may be done. Stranger still, though this applies only to hand-reared fish not long released to enjoy the laws of liberty, a hail shower flashing amongst the swirl of the waves or tearing the calm surface with its countless spluttering boils will often excite such fish to a ready activity, as if they associated with its fall, not, indeed manna from heaven, but the old sound of the chopped meat scattered broadcast on their former home.

As to the first of these tendencies if I am to draw any inference from a recent experience in a thirty-acre reservoir stocked with exactly 500 fontinales, the inference would necessarily be that even in such a large reservoir relatively to the number of fish in it, a skilled angler fishing diligently and with intent to kill could in the course of a couple of days practically depopulate any water of moderate size of its artificially-imported and artificially-reared inhabitants. He might, it is true, fail to locate the fish, but once he had found their favourite haunt I have no hesitation in predicting that the imported would soon become the departed, for they would practically be at the exterminator's will, and decidedly "within his danger." Nor would other circumstances, not of a fortuitous but of a reasoned nature, fail to assist the wilful agent in such a slaughter grim and great as this massacre of the innocents would assuredly prove. I do not state it as a speculative inference from this isolated experience in the reservoir, but as a deduction from the whole range of my observation during an experience which has been both wide and keen, that artificially-reared trout of every kind imported into strange sheets of water invariably display such strongly gregarious habits that it would be a matter for surprise if the capture of one such fish were not at once followed by the capture of others, the number actually taken depending upon the direction of the shoal, the ability of the angler to judge this direction, and the continuation of the, fish in a taking mood. Gregariousness is, of course, a characteristic of less moment, but its value as indicating the retention of the fish pond "habits" is obviously of considerable importance when the question of dependence and all the consequences of its presence and absence are considered. I am also aware that it is sometimes a specific characteristic, but as specific characteristics are the result of environment, the fact so far from being inimical to my theory actually strengthens it as the necessary theory of the Sensationalist.

If then this gregariousness, which I have repeated proved in loch fishing, be a characteristic of imported artificially-reared trout, even after a few years' sojourn in such large sheets of water, as many of the Highland lochs are, how much stronger must the tendency be in small reservoirs and lakes amongst fish fresh from the nursery? This leads me, naturally, to point the moral so far as stockers, and particularly stockers of public and "corporation" waters, are concerned. It is obvious, to take the latter case, that if a corporation goes to the expense of introducing say 2,000 two-year-old trout into a reservoir, and places no restrictions either of time or size upon their capture, the ungrateful angling lieges may in a week depopulate the reservoir and levy upon the ratepayers a charge of 3d. for every fish! Most corporations recognise this possible extermination of the ratepayers' fish, and place a size limit on their capture. They do not, however, prohibit all angling for a period of sufficient duration to accustom the fish to their new life with all the responsibilities of freedom which it brings, much less to attain that size which may prove their best protection against the angler's wiles. When a size limit alone is fixed and angling is allowed, some fish are always taken and many fish are injured. Anglers, when a time limit is imposed, are apt to grumble, but when the prohibition is regarded in a philosophical spirit, and anglers remember that if the fish were not there they could not angle, forbearance for one year is cheerfully agreed to and is rewarded the next.

To resume the general argument, it is obvious that the retention of the old memories of their "tame" days is a bad trait in fish from a stocker's point of view, and I doubt if it has ever been satisfactorily proved whether trout that have been hand-reared develop the same wariness as wild fish, and give, therefore, the same sport—the more difficult it is to persuade a fish to rise the greater is the sport, being an angling paradox that is self-explaining—as fish born in natural surroundings that have fought the battle of life, learned its lessons of prudence and wisdom, and possess as well those hereditary, as distinct from acquired, faculties of suspicious caution which descent from a long and noble train of savage ancestors can alone confer.

We have here a suggestion of two qualities—the qualities of independence and self-support which together give that strength to fish and all animals summed up in the famous adjective the "fittest."

The absence of habitual independence and of reliance for food on their own exertions which distinguishes hand-reared fish, may be complementary to their tameness, but it is the cause rather than the effect of that tameness, and being habitual is, therefore, of far greater moment to the stocker than is the personal trait of merely sensational familiarity that has bred contempt of danger, and trust in all men as like Nathaniel without guile. At the same time the line of demarcation is faint, and the distinction is so subtle, that it may be safer to ignore it and simply to accept even hand-reared trout as fish with natural powers—instincts if you will—somewhat diminished in strength by non-use.

That these powers—the ability chiefly to "do" for themselves—must be diminished to a greater or less extent is clear when we consider the usual environment of a hand-reared fish as well as his descent. Taking the latter first, the fish may be sprung from wild fish who have sojourned for so many years in the narrow confines of their pond that not the fish

of Lethe itself could be more oblivious of the free and unfettered dash
through stream and lake, of the old days when food had to be sought
even by wide-ranging to the kindly sea, by midnight prowling on the
dangerous shallows and by many a moonlit foray or sunlit raid of
incredibly daring conception, and still more dauntless and dashing
execution.

Hand-reared fish, again, may be sprung from parents that have never
known any home but the fish pond, whose egg stage and alevin
existence were passed amid the roar and tumult of the rushing water
of the hatching house, whose earliest hours of conscious being saw
them forming an integral portion of that kaleidoscopic life of perfect
sanitation and well-guarded immunity from the perils of troutish babyhood, whether of temperature, of flood, of storm, or of things great,
greedy and hostile that love to prey on things small and helpless in the
ever-raging battle of chance and change, whereby nature preserves the
balance of the powers that make and never mar her rule ; whose yearling
world was bounded by the narrow horizon of the straight-banked pond,
and whose dependence, until their second year, was fostered from
alevin to mischievous youngsters of lusty growth, by the hand that never
omitted to feed them, and was watched over by the eye of a providence
in tweeds and tall boots, who never failed them in the hour of danger,
of sickness, or need of every degree and kind.

Fish sprung from such parents, and themselves reared in a similar
environment of easy peace and plenty, of familiarity with man as a
bountiful food-producing machine, guide, philosopher, doctor and friend,
all rolled into one great benevolence of masterful but kindly purpose,
who have never had to seek board or lodgings in the cold streets of the
brimming river, who have never seen a pike or the shimmering sheen
of an otter passing like a shadow of black purpose through their pools,
to whom the hand of the "guddling" youngster would be a sign
manual of kindly faith, the long-legged heron—sentinel poacher of the
reed-girt pool—a playfellow of clumsy movement, until the treacherous
lance of his beak shot like muscular and feathered lightning to awaken
doubt, merging into the darkness of death, to whom a fly had never
borne a sting, nor a worm held a steel back bone,—such fish are but
poorly equipped either for fighting the battle of life or for giving that
sport of which wariness against wile is a condition precedent.

Yet these are the kind of fish with which we are stocking our rivers and lakes in the hope that they will thrive and multiply, and give as much sport as the congenital natives that have fallen victims to the march of events.

Fish farmers may maintain, and indeed have done so, that these arguments are based on partial assumptions, but they do not wholly deny the accuracy of the premises and, naturally, cannot do so, so far as very young trout, but little removed from fry, are concerned. As to yearlings and two-year-olds, they declare that fish of these ages—I cannot say fish of these "sizes," since all "lots" are not level and age is, in trout, a most deceptive guide to size, yearlings varying from one inch to six inches in length—eat when they are hungry and can get food. I presume that the contention is that given a suitable environment they cannot fail to find food, and that one of the two great impulses of their life will drive them to seek it. I do not doubt it. I question, however, their ability to find it, and I fear that it will be as a hungry, voracious, gregarious, quarrelsome crowd that they will give a new form to the miracle of the fishes without the loaves. I observe, too, that even fish farmers are not quite so confident in practice as they are in theory of the truth of their contention that one year of dependence has a more deteriorating effect upon a trout's ability to "do" for itself than have two years of the same pampered life* on fish sprung from aristocratic ancestors that have lived lives of such luxury and easy plenty as never to weigh less than 6lb.

Feeding yearlings for a month or two after being turned out into a pond has been recommended, but a pond is not a lake, as fishes coming from a small home even with natural food at their elbows, so to speak, will speedily discover. Morover, it is not easy to see, unless a suitable environment be presumed, why fish not merely descended, but actually the sons and daughters of great lusty well-fed, well-cared for fish are likely to thrive in environments usually inferior to those which gave their fathers and mothers the right to feel as bloated and as proud as any fish may feel with a clear conscience who have been fed on an "unearned increment" of peace and plenty.

* The contention here is that two-years-olds, because they are two-year-olds, and therefore are more experienced, are better fish than year-olds. The questing habit is more fully developed because the fish have been hand-fed for a year longer than the year-olds !

I am here endeavouring, it should be explained, to put certain
theoretical suggestions before fish farmers, and my object is, if possible,
to ascertain how great or how little is their practical value. In the
preceding chapter I urged the cultivation of the study of environments
in lakes as of the first importance. The problem I am now discussing
is complementary to, and, in fact, a corollary of the other problem. It
is really the problem of "set back" in its relation to environments—
new and old. No one would rejoice more heartily than myself, were it
satisfactorily proved that the so-called "set back" of imported fish
suddenly placed in a new environment merely entailed a conquering of
its conditions by familiarity with them, and the active exercise of latent
habits, powers, and instincts, which a few short "generations," departing
by force of circumstances from atavic characteristics "in being" and
capable of recrudescence have rendered only dormant and not dead.
The term "dead" is, I am aware, a highly improper one, and I do not
defend its application, save in so far as the stocker may find that though
theoretically a faculty is a possession for ever, practically its temporary
aberration may mean its death in use.

This last position is of great moment, and, as a rule of animal
existence, is, I venture to think, in accordance with the best thought
on the subject.

That artificial feeding and an assured supply of food which has not to
be sought for engender dependence, and must necessarily be destructive of the power to gratify the impulse to feed, which at the same time,
it leaves in unimpaired, if not enhanced, strength, is a proposition that
can scarcely be disputed, when the strongest of all materialistic
arguments,—the "standard of comfort"—is not only recognised as a
natural law of cosmic existence but is also realized "in time and
circumstance" as jurists understand the phrase. I have already indicated that the cultivation of good environments and the general
bettering of the conditions of existence in lakes on approved models of
lakes with good environments, is of more importance than the production of fine breeds of trout or specimen yearlings that are of no value
without suitable environments, and are certainly in unsuitable environments of less value than indifferent fish. Though the improvement of
environments may thus solve the problem under discussion, yet even
under the best of new conditions, the effect of the dependence begot of

old conditions cannot be ignored. It is in consideration of this fact that in the succeeding chapter, read of course in relation to this chapter and the one preceding it, I propose to offer a theoretical answer to the whole question so far as it has not been already answered.

CHAPTER XI.

The Theoretical Solution of the Problem

Certain fish farmers have been pleased to term much of what is contained in the two preceding chapters, mere theorising, because it is clear that if not dismissed as inaccurate "theorising" by sound arguments, it may, by the use of that vague and flippant word, be temporarily "scotched."

I have, however, shown that it is a law of nature that specific and individual differences are the result of environment, and hence that not only is environment more important than "species," as produced by artificial environment, but also that the effect of artificial environment must necessarily be, ex lege, to produce species bearing specific characteristics due to that environment.* If evolution means anything, this conclusion is inevitable unless to suit the purposes of our fish-farmers, fish are to be exempt from the operation of natural laws because they have been artificially reared—an arbitrary assumption that destroys the declaratory character of all natural laws. The object of all fish-farming is to perfect nature in the sense only that is implied by the giving of what would be perfectly natural conditions by artificial means. Unfortunately fish farmers have gone beyond nature, and by ceasing to imitate her best moods merely, have produced unnatural fish, on which the self-avenging laws of nature take revenge for their outrage whenever once more the fish come within the jurisdiction of the Great Mother and pass out of the protection of their human owners.

Many of our fish farmers are ready enough to lay down the great natural law of environment and to give it a limited recognition within their fisheries in order that they may, like other merchants, be in a position to offer to the public fish which can be truthfully described as not wholly fed on artificial food, fish, that is, accustomed to feed on the natural food that is purposely cultivated in the ponds. So far as

*Another and important effect is to produce specific necessities which only a particular and special kind of environment can satisfy.

natural food within the limited area of a fish pond can teach a fish independence, the power to do, the will to dare in the battle of life fought on the wider field of nature, fish-farmers by the very recognition of its importance place themselves in a position of approbate and reprobate with regard to the principles I have been enunciating. They give a limited recognition to the great natural law of environment and then they describe as "theorising" the application of the law in its entirety to hand-reared fish bred in conditions of existence wholly different to those natural conditions under which the law will enforce its recognition.

Do our fish-farmers recognise the great truth, as true of the moral as of the physical order that natural law, as embracing all positive law or laws, is absolutely inviolable? Do they recognise that logic was used and abused in the Garden of Eden, before Aristotle was born or Wheatley gave it formal life, that houses fell by the law of gravity before Newton watched another pippin drop that rivals the apple of Eve in fame? Do they not know that arbitrariness gives to all human law and all human justice its essential weakness, and that all human law that is just or approximately just is declaratory of great principles that are eternal and merely vary in realisation with the circumstances under which they receive that concrete realisation which we call positive law? Do they not recognise that the laws ruling fish life are older than the fish farm, and hence that the fish farmer cannot arbitrarily ignore them without suffering these very consequences of their violation, which are as inevitable as that two and two make four?

The theory of fish-farming has not, indeed, run counter to the great principle to which I have been referring. Applied to trout the law of environment is the great natural law that must be clothed with a declaratory character and realised in circumstances, if fish farmers would produce races or species of fish equal to the races or species of fish produced by the unfettered operation of that law in the realm of nature.

The nearer fish-farmers approximate the conditions of existence on their farms to the best natural conditions found to produce a race of strong healthy fish, the more closely will they approach the declaratory realisation of the great law of environment. The mere crossing and re-crossing of species to produce better breeds of fish within the farm as a solution of the difficulty is but a petitio principii. It ignores the law of environment and assumes that the best traits of species will be repeated in progeny, and is, therefore, not declaratory. The traits of environment remain, as we know they remain in sheep and stock generally. That they should remain is a consequence that is inevitable, unless we ignore principles that are laws of nature, wisely left by the Creator to slowly evolve chaos out of order and species out of protoplasmic life. This is a truism accepted equally by the jurist and the geologist, the physiologist and the metaphysician, the physicist and the physician, and yet the fish farmer would rise superior to it and would maintain that those students of fish who are not in the trade, merely " theorise " when they urge its full recognition as the first principle of scientific fish-farming. So assured do I feel that the fish-farms of the future will be great natural nurseries on a scale hitherto unattempted, and certainly unrealised on any fish-farm, that I venture to assert that in a few decades fish-breeders will be able to produce, by a study of environments, fish of specific characteristics suitable for all environments that are capable of amelioration. A movement in this direction has already set in. How it must eventually culminate I have already indicated.

Environment is the cause of all specific difference, the source of good qualities and bad, of racial excellencies and racial defects. The proper study, therefore, of fish-breeding mankind is environment, and not how to produce good fish by selecting sires and dams and placing their progeny in an environment of assured excellence, that is within the arbitrary control of their owners.

The practical problem, in other words, which fish farmers have to solve is to construct homes that afford their fish, after a certain period in their existence, perfectly natural conditions of life framed on the most educative models fashioned by nature. The conditions arrived at must necessitate hunting for natural food and must be calculated to cultivate in the fish independence and the power of being self-supporting. Living under such conditions not only will the trout which breeders supply be sprung from practically wild fish, but will themselves be wild fish that have lived a life as nearly approximating that of freedom and nature—of commoners of water—as it is possible to secure without sacrificing protection or running those risks to which capital sunk in absolutely free fish living under absolutely natural conditions would be always exposed.

If the truths which I have been enunciating were mere idle speculative theorising, I should delete the qualification which the last sentence introduces, for, strictly speaking, I have insisted upon absolutely natural conditions which would include certain perils of juvenile troutish existence highly educative to the young fish.* At the same time as the endeavour of the fish farmer is to realise a civilised ideal of communal life in the fish life of his farm, it is possible for him to reconcile the reign of law with the reign of liberty. The apparent anarchy of nature is in reality a cosmic order resulting in what we properly term the preservation of her balance. Within the fish pond the circumstances under which the law of nature is recognised vary, and therefore the imposition of order is merely the recognition of the same law in terms of the difference between the circumstances, which may, when specialised to the case in point, be termed the conditions of existence.

Finally the study of environment in nature and its application to the conditions of existence in the fish farm, does not exhaust the problem of the future of our lakes and rivers. It only solves one half of it. "Environment-farming" must be made complementary to fish-farming, for it is as certain that environments can be improved, as it is that the existing bad environments in many of our lakes and rivers have produced the inferior races inhabiting them. If environment can produce specific differences, it is clear that the study of and consequent improvement in environments can, without stocking at all, result in the production of superior races. In lakes, however, in which trout are already too numerous, the process of amelioration in the fish would be a comparatively slow one, in spite of the example of Loch Lossit. On the other hand, in such a lake as Loch Fraochie, the introduction of fish would have to proceed pari passu with the betterment of the environment in all its aspects, the disturbing causes hindering the amelioration not being quite the same in all respects. In any case it is obvious that until fish-farmers and their customers give to environment in both its aspects the recognition it deserves, the future of our lakes in the fullest sense cannot be assured. Compared with the task of restoring our rivers to their pristine excellence, the problem of securing the future excellence of our lakes is comparatively simple. The area of pure water is prac-

* Let a two-year-old fish get into the yearling pond and the lesson he could teach is not suffered by the fish-farmer to be taught.

tically unlimited, and the question of pollution scarcely arises, though examples of its disastrous effects have occurred and been duly quoted.

It is when one considers what is involved in the solution of the prob-lem of ameliorating environment, that its importance becomes of almost appalling significance.

The fallow lakes of this country that have run to seed and are either weed-covered and almost unfishable, or have, through lack of cultivation of their natural capabilities, become the home of "feeble peoples" like the conies of Scripture, are so numerous, their neglected condition so obvious to the eye even of the chance wayfarer who visits their not always desolate shores, that one wonders why the "cultivation of environment" within their waters has been so long postponed. In the case of some districts this neglect may be traced to the abundance of other waters to which boon nature has been kinder than has man yet found himself under the necessity of being to their sister lakes. But the thronging of the angling ways is the shadow of the coming Nemesis. Lakes that used to yield full creels are being slowly but surely robbed of their denizens, and even if these are re-peopled there is still the thronging of the ways with an ever growing crowd crying aloud for more water in which to relieve the cacoethes "anglendi."

In South Uist alone there is one acre of water to every ten of land; in Benbecula the proportion is one to seven; yet on both islands the hundreds of acres of water, whose environment could be cultivated are allowed to lie fallow and to become the prey of natural decay. In Islay, Jura, Harris, and all the Northern and Southern Hebrides a similar state of affairs prevails. In Sutherlandshire, Caithness-shire, Argyle-shire, and in fact all over the mainland it is the same. What we do for our land we decline to do for our waters. That good crops cannot at once follow "breaking-in" we recognise so far as land and the extension of the margin of its cultivation are concerned, but we decline to extend the recognition of the principle involved to fish-farming in the widest sense of the phrase. Without first cultivating the environments of these fallow waters, to stock the majority of them would be a waste of money; to cultivate and improve their environments would, in many cases, render subsequent stocking unnecessary. In any case the breeding of good fish for stocking purposes is of secondary and supplementary im-portance in some cases, and can only be of complementary utility in all.

How true this is has often been borne in upon me, when on visiting a fish farm I have spent an hour or two in the nursery amidst the roar of waters and have noted the eggs of the great Bavarian trout, of crosses between the sea-trout and the fario, of Loch Levens, and of the common trout all hatching out, or in the alevin or fry stage, and have from thence followed these fish of varied parentage and descent to their environment in the fish pond, which, for one and all is to be practically identical. When I have pictured these fish being turned out into environments that may or may not suit their racial and acquired characteristics without any previous acquaintance with their new environment or with a "wild environment" of any kind, the theoretical and practical difficulties of proper stocking have assumed enormous proportions. When I have further considered the many species of trout of scientific and popular classification that occur in European waters, or even in the lakes and rivers of England, Scotland, and Ireland—each and all of which are the growth of environment, and if not separate species then assuredly geographical or topographical varieties of species —surely I am justly entitled to ask whether all these varieties or species born and reared in the same environment will adapt themselves to any environment; much more will they all find environments suitable, not merely to their common and acquired habits, but to their separate and racial characteristics? When I find that smolts born in the hatchery and reared in the ponds are turned out in the estuary of a river in the belief that such a river will see these, its adopted children, return as grilse, and when I read this example and other examples of sublime faith in chance, in the light of the general theory of environment, it is no matter for wonder that I am forced to regard the cultivation of environment as the only sure means of securing permanently the future well-being of our lakes.*

On the commercial and moral aspect of the problem I will scarcely touch. I will content myself with pointing out that there is a good deal of capital sunk in angling hotels the owners and lessees of which cannot afford to neglect the broad issues involved in the problem of

---

*The Utopian scheme, recently mooted, which proposes to convert the Thames into a river frequented by the migratory salmonidæ will not abide discussion. A study of the topographical environment of the Thames is sufficient to convince any student of fish acquainted with the Trent, and the causes of its decline as a salmon river, that the Thames scheme is premature and must result in costly failure.

the future of our lakes, as I have stated these issues and suggested their solution.

As to the moral aspect of the problem angling is one of the few sports that must do a nation good, and cannot possibly do it any harm. Its proper pursuit ensures hygienic conditions that are excellent alike for mind and body as the medical faculty both by precept and example are constantly urging. In its political aspect, in the widest sense, it is obvious that the problem of how to obtain wild, strong, natural, healthy, and sport-giving fish is only a part of that wider problem of innocent substitutes for injurious pleasures whose solution will help to solve the great problem of the age—the satisfaction of that discontent by material agencies to which the raising of the standard of comfort has given birth. The tendency of the best legislation of the age is to reconcile the reign of law with the reign of liberty, and there is no doubt that the providing of angling, as a compensation for the curtailment of individual license in other directions will eventually be recognised as a means of saving grace which will not only improve the moral well-being of the people, but will also, by the necessity it entails of securing the purity of our rivers and preserving that of our lakes improve their material well-being and aid a sanitary reform of incalculable benefit.

CHAPTER XII.

British Lakes and Foreign Fish: Rainbow and Fontinalis.

British pisciculturists in their search for good species and with that enterprise, which distinguishes them and which competition fosters, have not confined themselves to the denizens of British waters. Amongst foreign fish on which they have cast the eyes of speculative love are the rainbow trout and the fontinalis. It seems necessary, therefore, that I should devote some of my space to both these fish and their possible future place in the economy of the lake. Of the two, the rainbow trout is, I need hardly say, by the far the more interesting fish, and the question of its introduction into British waters is such an obviously important one that I make no apology for summarising the discussion to which its attempted naturalisation has given rise. Though originally a river fish the suitability of the rainbow for lakes, I may premise, is not, under reservations, disputed, but it is impossible at the same time, to discuss its future in our lakes without having regard to its alleged imperfections. It is for this reason that I state the practical issues at stake from the general standpoint before dealing with the fish as a future denizen of our lakes.

The opponents of the rainbow trout have a two-fold objection to urge against its introduction into British waters. They allege (1) that the fish is a cannibal of lusty appetite, whose primest condition is contemporaneous with the spawning time of our common trout; and (2) that the fish is of such strongly marked migratory habits that it disappears from all streams in which it is placed if any road of escape is left open to it, whether to the sea or to the more confined waters of lakes to which the streams are tributary. It is, of course, obvious that these pleas are what lawyers term alternative, and are not, therefore, necessarily contradictory. At the same time, it may be pointed out that if the fish do not take up their permanent abode in streams from which they can escape to the sea or elsewhere, their introduction into such streams is a perfectly safe experiment, for the injury they can do to the native trout must be as evanescent and passing as their cohabitation with them is temporary, being, in fact, measured by its duration.

Presuming, however, that the case against the rainbow depends upon these alternative pleas, it is clear that the question of its introduction into British waters—lakes, ponds, and rivers, as distinguished from rivers merely—must be conjoined into two issues. In streams, for example, with a sea or large lake connection, already frequented by the common trout, either in such numbers or of such a size as to warrant their being described as trout streams, it is obvious that either of the objections would, if substantiated by satisfactory evidence, be fatal to the rainbow's claims to recognition as a desirable fish in British waters of this class. If a cannibal in a worse degree than that stigma attaches to all or nearly all of the Salmonidæ, and to most fresh water fish, the only justification that could be urged in favour of the rainbow would be his superior intrinsic merits as a sport-giving fish. Into the discussion of that wide problem it is not necessary to enter in a mere statement of the propositions which embrace the practical issues to be decided. Such a side issue can only arise as a dernier ressort if the main issue had been decided against the rainbow. By parity of reasoning, if the main issue were decided in his favour the side issue referred to would not arise at all. In the second place, it is obvious that if the fish can be proved to be of so restless and migratory a nature that they never take up their permanent home in waters from which they can escape, or in other words, if our waters do not afford a suitable environment, then the first issue will not arise, and the advisability of their introduction as a problem in practical pisciculture solves itself on grounds that are at once economic and utilitarian.

In streams, again, that cannot be called trout streams in the strict sense of that phrase, the decision for or against the rainbow will depend to a very large extent upon the degree to which these streams are frequented by the young of the migratory salmonidæ, presuming always that one of the main issues is the existence or non-existence of what may be termed a super-cannibalistic tendency in the fish. The destruction which the rainbow may cause to the spawn of the migratory salmonidæ in such streams will be a question of less moment than in the case of trout streams, though still a problem of considerable gravity, for the spawning times of the rainbow and of the migratory salmonidæ are divided by a minimum period of five weeks—a fact which cannot be overlooked when the possible depredator is a fish of such admittedly keen appetite as the salmo irideus. The second of the two main objections, namely, that the rainbow will not stay in streams from which he can escape, may, however, in the case of streams of this class, be fairly stated as the principal issue to be decided. It is only necessary, therefore, to repeat that if his nomadic instincts in our waters are established beyond doubt, his introduction into such streams would be a mere waste of money, unless he were artificially confined. This is a particular and not a general issue, the answer to which would depend upon the sporting value and quality of the stream as a salmon, sea-trout, or mixed river. It does not, therefore, fall within the scope of the broader issue, and is, in fact, a side issue of relative intrinsic importance.

The adaptability and suitability of the rainbow to lakes and ponds is, as I have already pointed out, scarcely disputed, even though the fish in its original home is essentially a river fish. At the same time, as natural lakes—these, as a rule, being the only waters of this class in which the public are interested—are of different characteristics, it may serve a useful purpose to state the practical issues at stake. Mutatis mutandis, they scarcely differ, either in degree or kind from those to be decided in the case of rivers.

Lakes may be divided into several classes, the advisability of introducing the rainbow into each of which will depend upon the answer given to the two main issues already stated in the case of streams. In a few exceptional instances, neither issue will arise, at least in their direct aspect. Presupposing, therefore, the same main issues, lakes may be divided as follows:—

(1) Trout lakes with no effluent.

(2) Trout lakes with an effluent.

(3) Mixed lakes frequented by either (a) salmon, sea-trout, and brown trout, or (b) sea-trout and brown trout, or (c) " sea-trout and salmon," or (d) "sea-trout," or (e) "salmon "—all of which must necessarily have an effluent.

(4) Lakes holding few or no trout, and having no effluent.

There are, of course, other kinds of lakes, those, for example, holding coarse fish, but to take such lakes into consideration would be irrelevant to the issues.

To discuss the practical problem to be decided in the case of each of these varieties of lake seriatim would involve, it is clear, a repetition of much that has been already stated in the case of streams. It is obvious, for example, in the case of trout lakes with no effluent, that the question of migration does not arise, and that the only issue to be decided is the cannibalistic and spawn-destroying tendency of the rainbow. If the common trout and the rainbow can be proved to be mutually destructive or the latter can be proved to be inimical to the interests of the trout, then we are once more confronted with the side issue of their relative merits and advantages. To follow, therefore, the application of the two main issues to each and all of those different kinds of lakes would be merely to reiterate with a greater or less degree of appositeness the points already indicated as falling to be decided in the case of streams of different characters.

There is, however, an aspect of the question, not yet stated, which can scarcely be overlooked, but which nevertheless is of minor importance. The rainbow appears to be able to conquer the common trout, and like a strong invader it can either reduce the common trout to a state of subjection or drive it forth from its old haunts to seek new quarters. In a later chapter I describe a duel, which I had the good fortune to witness in a stream, between a female rainbow and a female brown trout—a combat in which the former held the upper hand—but in the meantime I will content myself with quoting a single example of the apparent superiority of the rainbow over the common trout, when the possession of water is put to the dread arbitrament of the sword.* The example of the rainbow's might of right is afforded by an interesting experiment recently made by Sir Peter Walker on his Osmaston estate, Derbyshire. Two years ago he placed 5,000 yearling rainbows in a trout stream just above a couple of small lakes. Now these yearlings appear to have entirely displaced the native trout and to be in the position of beati possidentes, not only of the two lakes, but of the whole of the stream below. In the course of two years they have attained an average weight of ¾lb., and as already indicated seem as they grew in size and strength, to have gradually overpowered and finally to have driven away the native brown trout.*

* I could have here quoted a recent Tasmanian case, but prefer the Derbyshire instance as more relevant to the issues to be decided in British waters. The Lancashire, Argyllshire, and Perthshire cases, subsequently quoted, more than counterbalance the Derbyshire case.

This may or may not be considered strong evidence against the rainbow. The facts of the case are singular. An army of 5,000 rainbows is a host of dread power, and I have no doubt that 5,000 Loch Leven trout, if the conditions had suited them equally well—and to judge from the rapid growth of the rainbows the conclusion is irresistible that the conditions would have suited them—would have effected precisely the same clearance, if the law of the survival of the fittest has any meaning. The only inference, therefore, that can be drawn from such cases is that they are typical examples of the operation of the law referred to. In view, moreover, of the instructive Islay case on which I have already laid such emphasis, the case quoted, is simply an example, mutatis mutandis, of a strong people and a finer race displacing a weaker people and an inferior race. Finally, and on the last analysis, the question resolves itself, from an angling point of view, into one of comparative utility. If the rainbow be the conquering fish, he is, ipso facto, the better fish from the absolute standpoint. Relatively, when sentiment intrudes and the stream ripples to the tune of " Auld Lang Syne," he may be the inferior fish, but the only moan we can make or are justified in making is based on the patriotic sentiment of old association—the mournful music of the laudator temporis acti, summed up in the famous triad, " old wine, old books and old friends." Ignoring, therefore, this special aspect of the question as really included within the two main issues, I content myself with stating these main issues, which are :—

1. Is the rainbow trout of such cannibalistic and spawn-destroying habits that, his prime being contemporaneous with the spawning time of the trout and almost contemporaneous with the presence of the maximum quantity of trout fry in various stages of growth in our streams, his introduction would prove the means either of (a) practically exterminating our trout, or (b) seriously diminishing their numbers?

2. Does the rainbow trout develop such strongly marked migratory habits in the unsuitable environment of British waters that unless confined by artificial barriers it will descend to the sea or elsewhere never to appear again, and, if so, is its failure to return voluntary or involuntary?

In the absence of sufficient data from the experience of stockers, it is clear that these issues can only be decided by experiments carried on in waters where very peculiar conditions exist, if, that is to say, the experiments are to be undertaken without serious risk to streams of existing sporting value and sport-yielding excellence.   In other words, some water adapted by Nature to sustain a good head of lusty and fair-sized trout must be found, which is practically without trout or a large head of fish of any kind, whether migratory or non-migratory salmonidæ, or coarse fish.   A stream absolutely fulfilling these conditions, and having the further qualifications for an experiment of this kind, of being situated near an established fishery and having a clear and unobstructed connection with the sea, does not, perhaps, exist in the United Kingdom.   If such a stream did exist and were divided into two portions, the upper of which could by an insuperable artificial barrier be entirely cut off from the sea in such a way as to bar the descent of all fish placed in it, while the lower portion remained an open door to "old ocean," an ideal water for the experiment in both its branches would be furnished.   If an equal number of ordinary and rainbow trout were placed in the upper and lower portions referred to, the contest, if any arose, between the confined fish in the upper water would settle the first issue, while both issues—particularly the second— would be helped towards solution by the result of the co-habitation of the two species in the lower portion with the open road to the sea.

I have stated the problem and formally suggested an experimental solution simply because both the problem and the suggested solution are equally interesting.

In the meantime I need not pursue the subject further, but will merely state my own impressions of the rainbow and a few facts concerning the fish that appear to be of moment in the matter of his future status amongst the denizens of our lakes.

If the rainbow were all his traducers have painted him there would be considerable danger in introducing the fish into our lakes, and it would be as mistaken chivalry as that which may have lost Flodden, to grant salmo irideus a fair field and no favour.   We can at least keep an open mind on the subject and await results in certain waters which will prove whether the rainbow is a fish to be trusted in British waters in general.

Since, however, he is not all his traducers have painted him, I may say from my own observation of him in tanks, ponds, and streams that the salmo irrideus is a masterful fish, and a keen fighter.   He is also blessed with an abnormally keen appetite, but he is not a cannibal,* and is a fish of a somewhat frank and trustful nature. Possibly this simplicity may be due to his belly being an imperious cupboard-ringer; but in any case the fact remains that the rainbow is a gentleman, a fish of aristocratic appearance, of Bayard's mood, who loves fighting and puts faith in man, scorns to prey upon his fellows, and is more of a gourmand and less of an epicure than the common trout, omnivorous though the indigenous dweller in our streams may be.

In the fish ponds the big rainbows win many hearts. No sooner does the visitor take up his stand than the great handsome fish congregate at his feet. When a handful of food is thrown in, they make the water boil, cutting it with their silver oars dashed with red, and displaying an activity that might make even a sea-trout green with envy. They are truly magnificent fish, these four and five pounders, and come of a race for whom a great future may be safely prophesied if only British waters prove kind. They are lithe and eel-like in their quick and graceful movements as pisciculturists know, and the average fish-farmer would rather rob one hundred ordinary fish of their spawn than help to exude the ova from a single rainbow; they will never submit with gravid passivity to the restraining hands, but wriggle and fight to their own danger during this important operation. Finally, as the rainbow is in season when the trout is out, is a better and truer riser than the grayling, suits either lakes or rivers, grows to a greater size, and is a better fighter and a hardier fish in every way, one may safely venture to say that in time, if all goes well, he may drive the fickle, flirting thymallus out of popular favour.

I hear good accounts of the rainbow in streams from time to time. If these came only from fish-farmers, I might view them with the eye of a gentle sceptic, and might doubt the accuracy of the information without questioning the veracity of those submitting it to me. They come, however, from quite independent as well as from naturally prejudiced

---

*An extremely interesting experiment lately fell within my observation. A certain number of yearling trout were placed in a pond containing large brown and Loch Leven trout. They were eaten up to a yearling promptly and voraciously. Of a similar number of yearlings placed amongst large rainbows not a single one was touched I have frequently seen small trout consorting with perfect confidence and trust with large rainbows. The rainbow is a masterful and imperious, not a cruel and cannibalistic, fish. Force him to cannibalism and his healthy appetite does the rest. It is, however, his poverty and not his will which consents.

scurces, and are therefore evidence of a most unimpeachable character. They prove, it is true, nothing definite, and will not admit of being generalised into a conclusion for or against, and simply amount to this: that in certain streams into which a good head of rainbow trout were introduced the fish have remained and thriven, and not migrated or disappeared. What is perhaps more important, I hear that in one stream in particular, a Lancashire water famous for its trout, the rainbows have not only thriven (the evidence does not warrant adding, and multiplied), but have in no way injured or even interfered with the original and imported common trout in the stream. The trout is not a "short-generationed" animal like the rat or the dog or the felis domesticus, and you must therefore give a fish plenty of time before he can establish himself and obey the scriptural dictum: "Be fruitful and multiply." It may, therefore, be quite a decade before the rainbow bears fruit, though it may not be quite so long before we shall be in a position to forecast the nature of the harvest.

His future in our lakes as distinct from our streams seems now, however, to be practically assured, and the good news slowly accumulating as to his naturalisation in our lochs must be for all anglers very welcome tidings.* I addressed a number of enquiries on this subject to Highland landlords, and in all cases in which they have had the courtesy to reply the answer has been favourable. Mr. MacFadyen, of Cuilfail Hotel, whose good example as a "stocker" many lessees of Highland inns are now following, tells me that in his lochs the rainbow is flourishing and is growing fast, though curiously enough he did not condescend upon any particulars as to its increase in numbers. In suitable lakes, (which are, I may say, lakes in which they can be confined until acclimatised), Mr. MacFadyen tells me that the fontinalis is quite at home and grows as fast as the rainbow. From Perthshire I have equally favourable replies in the case of the rainbow, and indeterminate answers in the case of the fontinalis. Most of the Perthshire lakes have effluents, and this facts may easily account for the disappearance of the fontinalis. This evidence not only shows that the rainbow is capable of being

---

* No prudent lake owner would dream, in the light of our present knowledge, of introducing rainbows into a loch holding fine large trout, unless he desired to ensure winter sport from quick-growing and free-rising trout and were willing to risk his summer sport. I say "risk" advisedly, for though the rainbow is at home in lakes, it is not yet proved that he is a fit consort for our loch trout.

acclimatised in our waters, but also that all that is necessary to his acclimatisation is a suitable environment.* It is just possible, indeed it is highly probable, that his restlessness—real or assumed—in our streams may be largely due to the fact that the winter life of those streams does not afford the rainbow a suitable environment, and hence awakens, on grounds already formulated, the migratory instinct. The fish is undoubtedly a fish of mixed and even of indeterminate descent, and as some of his ancestors at least were assuredly migratory, that trait, long latent by compulsion and " scotched " by environment, is naturally liable to recrudescence when environment calls it into being and opportunity for its display is not lacking. In some, at least, of our lakes, the rainbow has, however, found a congenial home and has certainly thriven if he has not multiplied, for on the last point statistics, as already pointed out, are not forthcoming. It would appear, however, that just as the best rainbows for stocking purposes are those sprung from the ova of British-reared fish, so the tendency of the fish is towards assimilating its period of spawning with that of the fario of our streams. This, however, is as yet only a tendency, though it is a perfectly natural evolution from the somewhat altered conditions of existence, from those to which its ancestors were accustomed, which the rainbow in our waters has to endure. It is, of course, from some points of view not wholly desirable that the times of spawning of the rainbow and the fario should approach too closely, even though the approximation caused one of the alleged objections to the former—that which urges its vices as a spawn-eater—to vanish. The question is one of compensation. As a fish who is in his prime season when the trout is at his worst, the rainbow is, apart from the comparative value of trout and rainbows as sport-giving fish, most to be desired as an addition to what are called our game fish ; on the other hand if his spawning season were the same as that of the trout, would we gain more by the security against his destruction of trout-spawn which this assimilation of spawning time might imply than we would certainly lose by the sacrifice of a

---

* Loch Katrine, to quote a "lake" example, affords precisely the sort of environment that is assuredly suitable for the rainbow. The trout of this romantic and beautiful loch though numerous are, as a rule, of singularly poor quality. If the proposal to further raise the water level, contemplated by the Glasgow Corporation, be carried out, the suitability of Loch Katrine as a "rainbow" home will be enhanced, while it will probably have an injurious effect upon the sport which it yields amongst the common trout to the fly fisher.

I

winter sport-giving fish which it would necessarily entail? As it is
highly probable that the temperature of our lakes will in time alter the
spawning season of the rainbow, this question of compensation cannot
be overlooked. We must, however, await until the passage of time
answers this and other questions of a similar kind.

Whatever be the doubtful demerits of the rainbow, on his absolute
merits as a bold, brave Bayard of the lake, a sport-giving fish that yields
only with his last breath, an aristocrat at once in shape, in colouring
and stateliness of being, a gentleman in all his instincts, no one, not
even his most bitter and prejudiced foe can cast the shadow of slander.
Possessed of that superabundant activity that is the chief charm of the
sea-trout, he has none of that fish's wayward fickleness, and when he
rises in a blaze of living and swirling red, his intention to take the fly
is never in doubt. When hooked, he gives play that the sea-trout cannot surpass, while he never acknowledges defeat until on the very
threshold of death itself. When one adds that he attains a great size,
is a rapid grower, a fish of a hardy constitution, and even in the fry
stage shows independence and the questing instinct, the merits of the
rainbow make him a fish to be desired. That he may adapt himself
to British waters and refute the timorous calumnies of his traducers is
the earnest wish of all those who admire great and good fish, and to
whom the sounding swish of a taut line is as the song of the bow of
Odysseus when battle was in the air.

The salmo fontinalis, as most anglers are aware, is called by courtesy
the American brook trout, but it is really not a trout at all. It is a true
char with the habits of a lake or pond trout. That appears to be a
satisfying definition of the fish so far as its habits and sport-giving
qualities to the fly-fisher are concerned. The char, as we know him in
English and Scottish lakes, is by no means a free riser to the fly. Indeed, when he does take the fly with any degree of avidity he is either
rather out of condition or he takes it when the angler indulges in a
mongrel kind of fly-fishing—the trailed or sunken style which necessitates the use of a couple of dozen of close strung flies weighted with a
few shot, for all the world as if a Clyde angler had suddenly gone mad
and attached sinkers to the horse hair on which are mounted the dozen
flies of his reelless line, tapering from the rod point to the tail fly of
his long drawn out troutish peril. For a time it was feared that the

salmo fontinalis would not develop the "rising" faculty but would display the characteristics of his English brother and remain rather a useful and ornamental fish from the gastronomic standpoint than a sport-
giving denizen of our lakes.* As a matter of fact the fontinalis has proved
himself to be in lakes a fish of quite "another kidney." He rises as
boldly and as truly as a tarn trout on a fine June evening, and when he
comes he means business, just as the tarn trout does. Still he is a charr,
not a trout, though after all there is nothing in a name.

In appearance he is, on the whole, a very pretty fish, though his rather
ugly head, with its long, pikey look, and square level under-jaw, as
often as not overlapping the upper, and giving him the "smug" appearance of an attenuated tench or surly carp "reconcentradoed" to a
shadow, rather prejudices his claim to the added glory of being also
described as handsome. An Irishman might say, "Cut off his head and
is he not an illigant beauty?" but I prefer not to indulge in such a
Gordian-knot style of piscine aestheticism; and will content myself with
calling the fontinalis a fish with a beautiful body and an ugly head,
like the veiled prophet of Moore's poem. When he rises he either
gleams a bright silvery white dashed with green, or flashes back the
sunlight in wave rings of pale whirling red, the difference of the hue
of his rise depending upon the light and to some extent upon the colouring of the fish, which varies with the bottom, though not in the same
marked degree as does the colouring of our native trout. For the rest
he is a pretty fish of light green and grey, flecked with rich red spots,
while over him all is that suggestiveness of burnished dull metal, to use
a contradiction in terms, which is the badge of all his tribe. He attains
a large weight (many pounds) speedily, and is essentially, in this country
at least, a fish only suited for lakes, reservoirs, and ponds, for in British
rivers he has hitherto proved and is likely to continue to prove a failure.

The friends of the fontinalis do not, I think, desire to place the fish
on the same pedestal as the common trout or the rainbow, but it may
safely be said of this foreign char that he is a game, sporting, and free-
rising fish† well worthy of cultivation, and of the attention of the angler

* I have killed over 100 fontinalis with the fly in a day in an English lake.

† When the fontinalis grows thus large, he ceases like all big fish of the non-migratory
"salmon kind" to rise. His strong jaws and big head argue descent from a race that
has indulged in predatory habits. The recrudescence of this hereditary trait will be
conditioned by his environment.

in suitable waters, to wit, lakes and ponds that are not so well adapted for ordinary trout. Further than that, as a prudent man, not ashamed to confess the present imperfect state of my knowledge, I do not venture to go in praise of the fontinalis.

We can, in the meantime, afford to ignore the other varieties of foreign sporting fish that may yet find a home in British waters and a warm place in the hearts of British sportsmen. If I am to judge, as already stated, from certain letters I have received, while these pages were in the press, from Highland landlords who have stocked some of their lakes with rainbow and fontinalis, the results are eminently satisfactory in so far as no complaint as to the lack of adaptability shown by the first of the two species has been made, and the complaints in the case of the fontinalis are due to defects in the homes provided, and not in the fish themselves. It may, therefore, be assumed that the fontinalis, that pretty, gamesome fish, whose main artistic defect is his somewhat ugly head, redeemed by his colouring of red-spotted, green-grey, lacking something of the variety of the parti-coloured trout, and the lordly rainbow, that fish of exquisite hues, of graceful form, dashing courage and superabundant activity, are destined to delight the hearts of anglers in certain Highland lakes and other waters of a similar nature, whether the former ever becomes a permanent denizen of our streams or the latter endures each dire inclemency to become the successor in sporting office of the " fickle flirting grayling," when October leaves are sere and the grip of winter is over all the land.

CHAPTER XIII.

FURTHER LESSONS OF LAKE-LAND : SOME SALMON AND SEA-TROUT PROBLEMS.

"Nature abhors a vacuum," facetiously interpreted is a phrase that does not apply to sea-trout and salmon in lakes in which, by a wise provision of nature environment, so far as it means food, does not appear to be a matter of moment to the migratory salmonidæ, though in certain of its other aspects, namely, the topographical and the sanitary, environment is of as much importance to salmon, sea-trout and bull-trout as it is to the most confirmed non-migratory trout acting in whole-souled defiance of the Shakespearian dictum "Home keeping youths have ever homely wits." I have used the phrase "by a wise provision of nature" advisedly, for it is to be supposed that we must now accept the dictum as true which our scientists have laid down, that if salmon, and ex hypothesi sea-trout, do feed in fresh water, nature has provided certain anatomical changes in their digestive organs, which practically render the mastication and swallowing of food a mere useless formality, a jaw exercise on Father William's plan that argues a dog-in-the-manger stomach. Now though the problem of salmon and fresh water feeding is a very ancient, it is also a very interesting, problem. This, therefore, must be my excuse for here dwelling very shortly upon it and stating one or two theories on the subject which, so far as I am aware, have never before been formulated. In the first place I presume that it is not disputed that salmon do feed in fresh water. If, however, proof were needed, a remarkable rise of salmon I once observed in an Islay river and chronicled in the "Field" at the time of its occurrence would, as that paper remarked in noting it, be sufficient in itself to disprove the statement that salmon never do feed in fresh water. I quote the following extract from the article referred to :—

"I had been lucky enough to obtain leave for one day on a fairly good West Highland river of the smaller class, but, as the stream had been for weeks running clear and low, and crystal waters are more beautiful to the eye than calculated to satisfy the cacoethes, my title to fish seemed doomed to be as empty of advantage as the river of water. Two days, however, before "my day," down came the rain, and my spirits rose as the drops fell. One can get too much of even a good thing, and so it seemed likely to prove, for the river, when the morning of the auspicious day dawned, was in such a dirty and flooded condition, that angling with any hope of success seemed as vain a task as that of the builders on the plain of Shinar. Sadly I sat me down to dream of the death of kings of the salmon race; but ten o'clock saw my patience exhausted, and myself close by a long, still pool, in which I knew, from personal observation, that before the spate came, there were, at least, fifty-four salmon. The pool in question was about 100 yards long, and, in any ordinary flood, was too "dead" for fishing unless a strong breeze ruffled its surface. To-day the current was pacing its lazy way through it with many oily swirls, and there was a fair ripple; so, despite its discoloured condition, I determined to give it a trial. Suddenly I noticed salmon rising in all directions, like trout, and my spirit of heaviness vanished. The fish were apparently rising and feeding on the small flies swirling on the surface. My 12ft. rod up, I dropped my flies (a teal and red, and turkey and yellow) over a fish which was rising close by the bank at my feet; he came at once, but missed. However, the next cast I was fast, and after a merry bout of five minutes I landed a nice little fish of 6½lb. In his mouth was a ball of small flies. I was certainly excited, and whilst playing him wished I had as many arms as Briareus to wield fifty rods—the two hands for the pipes and one for the sword for which the Highland piper yearned would never have satisfied me—for fish were rising everywhere."

After chronicling the raising, hooking and landing of fish after fish and the escape of others, I then described how the "rise of salmon" came to an end. "I had been at the pool for only an hour, and a phenomenal day seemed in store for me, but just as my last victory was secured, the sun burst through the clouds and a rich gladness filled the air. The long trailing shadows through the woods; that indescribable sweetness of nature during the first hours of sunshine after rain; the green glories of the meadows; the autumn tints of russet that clothed the feet, and purple that crowned the summits of the distant hills, were for once wasted in vain on me, for the rise of salmon was over for the day, and in the bright beams of the " all-seeing cycle of the sun," which, like a second Prometheus, I invoked to take pity on my woes, my efforts were only rewarded by a few sea and yellow trout of no great size, though that hour in the morning was worth many hours of profitless toil by unyielding pool and stream, and made me in my dreams struggle the livelong night with salmon so great and mighty that not even the wildest waking fancy could conceive their immensity."

This testimony, it will be observed, is quite unique. It raises no question of mere playfulness on the part of the salmon, no doubt as to taking the fly for a whim and so forth. The fish were feeding precisely as trout feed. Nay, more. During the rise I killed them with trout flies as fast as I could raise, hook and land them, the rise lasting for an hour and being terminated as stated by the sun bursting through a cloudy sky, routing the dense battalions that had obscured him and pouring his victorious rays on land and water.

Without further supplementing this remarkable example, which many modern instances of similar, if not identical, occurrence prove to be no exception to any rule, I may, in stating my theory of salmon and fresh water feeding, enunciate as a preliminary the broad principle that the salmon is, as a rule, not only under no pressing necessity to feed, but also is scarcely tempted to feed when in fresh water, particularly when in rivers, for the niggard table spread on the bed of streams or carried down as a running feast on their currents, must after the thrice glorious feasts, the incomparably rich banquets of the teeming and kindly deep appear to salmo salar as prison fare on a deal board. One cannot wonder, to put the same idea in another way, at him scorning the crumbs that fall from the table of a river Lazarus, when he has been an honoured guest and eaten of the fat, and drunk of the strong salt wash at the table of a marine Dives, companion at cup and board to Neptune himself.

Presuming that those digestive changes which really amount to a closing of the orifice of the stomach, though strictly speaking, this is not quite what happens, we have here, read in the light of the "rise" just cited, a marvellous example of the economy of nature. To fully explain, however, what follows I would very briefly recur to a circumstance I have detailed at more length when dealing with "Fishing as the Handmaiden of Science." In that chapter I referred to the feeding of barbel in winter and explained how I came to the conclusion that though the commonly accepted belief that the barbel did not feed in winter was in the main correct, yet that from the fact of the barbel and the lamprey frequenting the same kind of water at the same period of the year, the inference was permissible that barbel feed on lampreys.

This surmise, I pointed out was verified by experiments. I have mentioned the circumstance again because the analogy is extremely instructive in the matter of the problem of salmon feeding in fresh water. It suggests that the salmon though not feeding regularly, may like the barbel not decline food placed in tempting or even tantalising juxtaposition to his nose, especially if the temperature of the water be calculated to make him " hungry." I have naturally read most carefully the report of the experts on the changes which occurred in the digestive organs indirectly, and in the alimentary canal directly, of certain salmon examined by them, and after comparing it with my own experience of the feeding habits of the fish, I have come to the conclusion that the facts do not prove that salmon do not feed in fresh water, but that nature has provided in her own inimitable way for the temporary disuse of organs which the circumstances of the situation do not render imperatively necessary for the salmon's safe survival during its sojourn in fresh water. I base my conclusion first of all on the general principle that nature is an ideal economist and never confers upon an organ what lawyers term a jus nudum, which may be physiologically interpreted as a function whose exercise would be a waste of energy. Salmon in fresh water have, as already pointed out, little to feed upon, compared with the boundless wealth of food borne for their delectation and fattening by the teeming sea. Therefore, says Nature, I will suspend the digestive organs and preserve them in the beauty of their perfect strength against that time in the sea when assimilation failing, a severe tax may be put upon their digestive and excretive powers.

Again, I argued, assimilation of food being the first law of sanitary digestion, the suggestion is irresistible that at no time in its life does that prince of assimilative digesters, the salmon, exercise the excretive function with the frequency and marked quantativeness of the gross-feeding but by no means so rapidly assimilative trout. I recall, in

proof of this, that in few or none of the many salmon I have taken out of nets—not after meshing but after calmly swimming round the "house" of a stake net, has excrement been present, and I surmise, therefore, that it is to conserve the digestive and assimilative powers of the fish rather than to prevent it feeding in fresh water that nature suspends partially or wholly the function of the most imperious of all organs.

Falling back from this conclusion (and it is by no means based on a priori reasoning, though I have used the word surmise) on the facts of experience as well as of observation, what do I find? Precisely such instances of actual feeding as that to which I have already referred. More, important, perhaps, than such cases and the commonplaces that salmon are taken with worm and prawn, known foods, both stationary and moving, is the analogy of trout and eels, fish that can endure, and are forced to endure, long periods of starvation.

It is, in fact, no usual thing for an eel to be long confined in an eel trap, when eels are scarce, awaiting without food a sufficient number of his fellows to make the lot worth sending to market. It is, moreover, not merely usual, but absolutely necessary to confine and starve trout for from ten days to three weeks, according to the weather and their condition, before dispatching them on a journey in fish cans. That animals can exist for long periods without food is also a commonplace of knowledge, and that they can store the energy that means life, as the camel, in a limited kind of way, stores water against the desert march is another matter of common knowledge.*

Nature, as I have said, is an ideal economist, and knowing that the salmon must necessarily for the purpose of propagating his species enter rivers where food is scarce, she has contrived means as part of her constructive economy whereby the fish can withstand the period of deprivation without losing that exciting cause towards assimilation called appetite, or if the phase be preferred, that sensational mnemonic impulse of habit which makes him occasionally feed, and what is more important rise with keen obsequiousness to the fly. The conclusion, therefore, is that the salmon, if he does not feed from necessity in fresh water, can claim no virtue by reason of his abstention, for his appetite and its display are merely conditions of environment arrested in their

*.Strictly speaking the camel is not the travelling reservoir he is supposed to be.

action by the retroactive force of a temporarily suspended function, and the subtle mutual reaction of a mental impulse upon its material gratification. Nature alone understands the physiological mystery of this strange suspension of a function while the animal retains the instinct to gratify it, but surely nothing could better illustrate her beautiful balance than the conservation of an instinct by use to preserve a function from abuse against the day when that instinct must know its fullest activity, and the corporeal garrison must, after Dalgetty's plan, be provisioned against the state of siege and starvation of the river? Instead, therefore, of expressing surprise at the order of things, we should throw up our hands in wondering amazement at the simple wisdom of nature's masterly plan, based as it is on the conservation of energy principle, and an economic ideal such as man can only imitate, and can scarcely hope at present to initiate in solving certain social and sanitary problems that vex the public mind of to-day.

As a corollary to this theory of salmon and fresh water feeding—and the theory appears to me to reconcile the two schools of thought on the subject—I would point out that the salmon in lakes far more closely resembles the salmon in the sea, both as to food and space environment, and possibly temperature,* than does the salmon of the river. This resemblance of the lake-salmon to the sea-salmon will, of course, cease, pro tanto, when the lake is a small lake and one of inferior quality in the matter of food. The consequence of such a diminution in the space-quantity and the food-quality of a lake environment is a remarkable prima facie vindication of the accuracy of the general contention. It reduces the salmon in the matter of feeding habits to the same level as when in the river, for it is a truism of angling experience that, exceptis excipiendis, salmon in the small and poverty-stricken peaty tarns of the Western Islands rise with greater avidity to the fly than they do in any of the larger lakes of the mainland. Moreover they take, though not with the same avidity and in a far more limited number of lakes, the worm and are not, as a rule, partial to the prawn—which, by the way, I regard as a deadly bait through the suggestion of sensational memory—or the minnow.

On the larger lakes of the mainland and indeed in most lakes on the

---

* It is a known fact that salmon feed or at least "take" better in certain temperatures of water than in others.

mainland, it is the exception and not the rule, to find salmon rising with any degree of avidity to the fly, and in certain lakes there is not a recorded case of their having done so. Properly interpreted this theory contains what is, at the very least, a feasible explanation of a mystery which has long agitated the minds of anglers. From time immemorial the problem why salmon in Loch Tay and other lakes will take only the " phantom " or other spun lure and will not take the fly, has vexed the ingenuity of ingenious and accurate students of such questions. This " sea-suggestiveness " contains, as I have said, at the least, a possible solution. In the particular case of Loch Tay it works itself out with most plausible persuasiveness. Loch Tay is large and deep. Like many lakes of its class it affords feeding infinitely superior and more easily come by than do most Scottish salmon rivers. The salmon do not take the fly, but they do not disdain a very large phantom when brought under their notice—a phantom reminiscent of the dashing sprat, in fancy suggestive of the still more glorious herring, a fish which the salmon loves with such an intense stomachic passion that I have known him in the sea gobble up a piece of it on a flounder line and fall an ignominious victim. These same fish on their passage up the Tay would take the fly; when they leave the Tay and enter the River Dochart the habit is resumed, and when they enter Loch Dochart it is still in evidence, only Loch Dochart being a small sheet of water with not over rich feeding, the salmon take the same small flies that tempt them to their doom in Hebridean tarns.* Nor, in this connection, is it possible to ignore the strongly corroborative proof afforded by the pronounced partiality for the fly displayed by the salmon of Loch More, in Caithness-shire—a lake which may be called a very over-grown pool of the Thurso river and one which used to afford, and will yet again afford better sport amongst salmon to the fly than any loch on the mainland of Scotland. A few years ago when the Thurso was a better river than it is at present, and yielded a dozen salmon in a day to a single rod, Loch More during April, and certainly during May, was frequently equally prolific of sport. Indeed, so keen were the salmon frequenting Loch More for the fly, that the ordinary number of flies

---

* I state the problem in this aspect as it is usually stated. Up to their entry into Loch Tay, and as long as they are in Loch Tay, the salmon are Loch Tay fish.—Vide supra the chapter on " The Habits of the Salmonidæ in Lochs."

mounted for loch fishing, namely three, were occasionally used, and a case
is on record of two salmon being hooked at one cast and finally landed.
Now Loch More is a small, shallow loch nowhere more than nine feet
deep when in its best fishing condition, and is, therefore, in every way
the exact counterpart of all the small Hebridean lakes which afford
the best sport amongst salmon to the fly. No evidence could be more
emphatic, especially when read in the light of the fact that other larger
and deeper lakes in the same district frequented by salmon, such as
Loch Naver, yield sport only to " spun " lures.

That there is something more than mere plausible theorising in the
suggested inference from these facts goes, I venture to think, without
saying, but that the theory advanced exhausts the whole truth I do not
pretend. It, at least, illustrates one way, and that a most important
way in which enviroment affects the salmon.*Whether it applies to sea-
trout is another matter. In fact it may be said that it does not apply
to   sea-trout, as will appear from the conclusions I will shortly   draw
from certain sea-trout problems I am about to state, and to attempt to
answer.

It has always struck me as a somewhat singular, but not wholly inexplicable circumstance that while a very great deal of attention has been
given to and much ingenuity and labour have been expended upon
salmon problems, but little energy of a similar kind has been devoted
to inquiring into the haunts, habits, life-history and utility in the world
of fish economics of the sea-trout. The reason of this neglect, possibly
more apparent than real, is two-fold. It has been assumed that in the
solving of the mysteries of the salmon is contained the solution of the
mysteries of the sea-trout, while it has been taken for granted that if the interest of the salmon are regarded, then ipso facto,
those of the sea-trout are rendered secure. Neither premise is wholly
wrong. On the other hand neither is quite right; they are both half-
truths. In their habits and life history the salmon and sea-trout
have much in common, and up to a certain point and within the river or
lake itself to which both migrate " from the sea," the interests of the
two fish in the matter of environment, in the widest sense of the phrase,

---

* I have purposely refrained from enlarging upon how the temperature of such lochs,
possibly approaching more closely the average temperature of the sea than does that
of most rivers, may affect the salmon frequenting them. Our knowledge on the point is
too indeterminate.

are practically identical.   Their habits, however, diverge with the
estuary while their environment, keeping in view the retroactive influence
of life conditions on habits and of habits as qualifying through heredity
the relative and not the absolute conditions of existence
necessary, postulates certain requirements for the sea-trout with which
the salmon can afford to dispense.   It is by no means a mere wild conjecture, whether we regard the trout or the salmon as the first or last
link in the short evolution of specific divergences in the salmonidæ, to
assume that the salmon, sea-trout, bull trout, estuary trout, and common trout form a chain with the links in the order named, each species
being evolved in terms of the theory of environment from conditions
special to a series of ancestors and continued for a sufficient period of
years to produce its species with its specific habits and specific characteristics whether of a structural or other kind.

I was some years ago forced to observe a very patent fact, namely,
that in some districts the salmon and the sea-trout are set in a strange
antagonism while a peculiarity of this apparent matching of mighty
opposites was that the " baser nature," as represented by the bull trout,
was permitted to pass between the fell incensed points with apparent
immunity.

The general conclusion at which I was forced to arrive may be thus
put in axiomatic form.   Wherever the salmon is found in numbers and
of a large size, the sea-trout is not numerous, or if numerous is not of
a large size ; the converse axiom is still more striking and is in the
main much nearer the truth ; wherever the sea-trout is large and numerous, the salmon is either not numerous, of if numerous, is of a small
size.

There are, of course, many exceptions to both rules, but it is the lessons of localities approaching the possible life conditions of the primeval
order which are on this point by far the most instructive and not the exceptions of which one could quote so many.   Let me cite only two.   In
the river Laxford and in Loch Stack, both salmon and sea-trout attain
to a large size ; but the sea-trout rarely reach the high standard attained
by the fish in those purely sea-trout localities which teach the lesson referred to.   In the Tweed, again, monster sea-trout are from time to time
killed ; but in the Tweed, that is prcisely what one would expect.

It is to the Outer Hebrides, those strange islands whose land is ever at war with water, into whose shores the deep has bitten far and left many gaping wounds washed by the salt tides, and into whose many basins the fresh water from a thousand springs has poured, until they are a strange medley of fresh water lake, salt sea and pools that are tributary to both—it is to these islands of estuaries, tidal lakes and salt water rivers that we must turn, if we would discover what appears to be the truth.

Now what are the conditions we find prevailing in these islands? In Harris, large sea-trout and small salmon exist side by side, notably in South Lacisdale, Lochs Scurst, and Voshmid; of the last two there is a tendency for salmon to prefer the one, and sea-trout the other. Thus, though Loch Voshmid is a good salmon loch, it is much better for enormous sea trout, which run heavier than the salmon, while Loch Scurst, again, is more affected by the salmon, and the sea-trout suffer thereby. South Loch Lacisdale is, however, equally good (though only a tarn of very small dimensions) for both kinds of fish, the sea-trout reaching, comparatively speaking, fabulous weights. In the Lews, again, sea-trout run very small, salmon having a most pronounced ascendancy while it is an exception for the sea-trout ever to approach the salmon in weight, low though the average weight of the latter fish may be. The results of the fishing in the Grimersta river for some seasons clearly show this to be the case. North Uist again ranks midway between South Uist and Harris so far as the commingling of salmon with sea-trout is concerned.

Salmon do ascend into various lochs in North Uist, but they are not nearly so numerous, nor do they run so heavy as the sea-trout, which seem to gain the mastery, or to have the field left to their undisputed possession, as we approach South Uist. That island shares the unique distinction with the Orkney and Shetland group of containing the only waters in this country of any angling importance entirely given over to the sea-trout; for though an occasional salmon may be killed in the lochs of these places, it is such an exceptional circumstance that it may be entirely overlooked. It has always appeared to be a singular and important fact that it is in South Uist, and in Orkney and Shetland, that the sea trout attains its largest size in this country—that is to say, it is in those islands that the greatest number of large sea-trout are found, and certainly by far the greatest number fall to rod and line. Some curiosity on the point led me to investigate statistics so far as obtainable, and the result was as follows: In six seasons' fishing, the capture of sea-trout, by the comparatively few anglers out, in the somewhat limited sea-trout water attached to the Lochboisdale Hotel was 4,195. Of these 4,195 trout, no fewer than 259 were 3lbs. or over in weight, the average size of fish over that weight being 4½lbs. (nearly); their aggregate weight was 1,161¾lbs., while the largest trout weighed 10lbs. These fish, with one or two exceptions, were killed with the fly. The total number of alleged salmon captured during that period was only sixteen, averaging about 7lbs.; and I have very good grounds for thinking that these so-called salmon were in reality only bull trout, which had been "up" for a very long period. In a later season, during which 1,036 sea-trout were killed, the number of fish over 4lbs. was increased relatively to the statistics just quoted. A comparison of these figures with those of the Waterville river and lake in Ireland in a certain season during which they yielded respectively 3,257 sea-trout and 3,810 sea-trout and 736 salmon and 126 salmon, is instructive.

The largest sea-trout killed in the Waterville lake and river in that season was 4½lbs., while it may be pointed out that if the number of salmon killed in the lake, namely 126, seems small, it is because most of the salmon running up the Waterville river are killed at the weir, 736 falling up to July 15, and 3,810 sea-trout, so that both lake and river are "salmon and sea-trout" waters, and not sea-trout or salmon waters exclusively. In South Uist one fish in about sixteen killed reaches 4½lbs.; in Waterville lake and river one in 7,067 reaches 4½lbs. This seems to me to point to the conclusion that the one fish suffers, in size at least, if not in number, from the presence of the other. Why South Uist and Orkney and Shetland should be the exclusive possession of the sea-trout is a question more easily put than answered; but there can, as I hope to show, be no doubt that some very natural explanation exists. Mere volume of water has nothing apparently to do with it. If a 10lbs. or 12lbs. sea-trout, or even a 7lbs. or 8lbs. fish, can find ample scope in every way, the smaller class of salmon should certainly be able to do so also. The analogy of the co-existence of the two fish (the retention of comparative size supremacy by the sea-trout being understood) in certain of the Harris lochs darkens, rather than elucidates, the mystery. Further round the coast

of South Uist, salmon of the largest class regularly travel, and have
been from time to time captured; but so far as I know they never ascend
into the lochs.

There is here, therefore, a problem which, if incapable of a solution
that will satisfy all students of fish, is not wholly insoluble if one is
content to accept a theory, that is sufficiently reasoned to be something
rather more than merely plausible.

We have from the Lews to South Uist as will be seen from the
facts stated a gradual mastery of the salmon as we travel north, and of
the sea-trout as we travel south, so that on the interesting battle field
lying between the Butt of Lews and the Sound of Barra we have, if
not an actual conflict, then the results of specific distribution that have
followed specific war and for aught we know a specific pact.   Possibly,
however, environment has acted as a sort of arbitrator and solved by
its more peaceful and less sharp, but none the less decisive methods, the
mastery of those territories that might have been the cause of ceaseless
war or the prize of its victorious waging.   The latter alternative is certain the more instructive and to optimists who love the peaceful assertion of cosmic order, it is also by far the more acceptable.*   In its physical aspects the Lews—and this applies also to Harris, is much less
of a divergence from the normal or an approach towards the presumed
primordial than are the more southerly islands, North Uist, Benbecula
and South Uist.   It seems possible, therefore, to find a more or less
satisfactory solution of the problem in the differences in topographical
environment.   In Harris, for example, there are practically no tidal lochs
save the Obbe, a sea pool which can only by courtesy be termed a true

* It is interesting to note that so far as South Lacisdale, Harris, is concerned a recent
experiment, initiated by Lord Dunmore, seems to verify in the most complete and
satisfactory manner the theory here advanced as the result of my personal study
of Hebridian waters as formed by nature.   Near the mouth of the tidal waters of the
Lacisdale an artificial lake has been constructed in such a way that the old sea wall of
rocks is one of its confining boundaries, while the loch is, strictly speaking, only fully
tidal at the very highest tide.   Up to this point—and the loch is about a year old and is
called after the Earl of Dunmore's heir, Viscount Fincastle, V.C., who so distinguished
himself on the Frontier—the sea-trout seem to have made the loch their own, to haunt it at
all seasons of the year, and to have compelled the salmon to continue to seek the small tarn
and deeper pools above, as they have done ever sinc ethe lake and the burn that connects
it with the sea have had an angling history.   The case is most instructive and intensely
interesting for a topographical environment similar to those common in South Uist has
been artificially created with a result similar to that produced by the natural topographical
conditions prevailing in the more southerly island—the home of the sea-trout.

A SOUTH UIST SEA-TROUT " RUN."

[This semi-artificial ditch is tidal.]

tidal loch. On the other hand most of the roads connecting the lochs with the sea, if amazingly small and narrow paths for the crowds of ascending fish that throng them, are, nevertheless, in all cases, and most markedly so in some instances, examples of the true burn or river type of connecting effluent.* A picture of one of the Harris burns is here figured. It represents the short link which connects three lochs, known as the "Ladies Lochs" near Amdhuinnsuidh Castle, with the sea. Lady Farquhar figures in the picture, and the juvenile lady angler with the rod is essaying her 'prentice hand with the fly on the hundreds of salmon that must be running the flooded burn, if one is to draw any inference from the immense shoals of fish showing in the sea just below, but not, of course, visible in the picture. Now though all the Harris burns are not of this size, yet all are, with one or two exceptions, of this nature, and are larger streams than, and of a totally different character to the tidal ditches or tidal pools connecting the Uist sea-trout lochs with the sea. It is obvious, therefore, that the topographical character of South Uist differs from the topographical character of Harris to a degree sufficient in itself to account for the sea-trout preferring to make the lochs of the former an exclusive, the latter a joint, possession with the salmon. By way of contrast and of emphasising this truth two pictures of a South Uist tidal ditch are also figured.†

Moreover there are no common trout lakes of any note either in the Lews or in Harris—a fact, which in considering a problem of this nature, cannot be overlooked. Small trout are not " enemies of environment " to salmon, but allies of a humble but useful kind, when the right of might is considered in relation to the utilitarian aspect of environment. Moreover there are few or no tidal trout in Harris and the Lews, if only because the physical conditions are not such as induce the evolution of that variety of the common trout. The principal point, however, to be remembered is that salmon and sea-trout ascend rivers both in Harris and in the Lews and are not tide-carried, at least to the same degree as are the migratory trout of North and South Uist.

* A similar remark applies to the Inner in Jura. The first time I visited that connecting link between the sea and Loch Knockbreac—a fair salmon lake—I stood on its banks and asked " were the river was "? It was hidden by high heather and one might easily have stept across it at places.

† The tidal pools and estuary of Loch-na-Bharp in South Uist might perhaps have better illustrated the estuary habits of the sea-trout, though they would not have shown so clearly the differences in topographical environment.

K

To the lochs and connecting estuaries of North Uist, South Uist and Benbecula, on the other hand, the road is as free to the sea-trout in most cases from the sea to the loch, as it is from the loch to the sea to the loch trout. Nay more. For this very reason there is a constant sug-gestion of the sea borne in upon the loch trout by each rising tide while each ebbing flow from the loch carries to the sea-trout an invitation writ in the fair round hand of nature to visit the loch above. In North Uist this exchange of suggestive force is less pronounced than in Benbecula and South Uist, and we have seen that the mastery of the sea-trout pro-portionately corresponds to the degree of the difference. The inference appears to me to be irresistible. The sea-trout is essentially an estuary fish—and this fact alone in the case of polluted estuaries differentiates his interests from those of the ocean-ranging salmon—coming and go-ing with its tides, sweeping up with a great and frolicsome joy when the green and swirling water brings back to parched weed and thirsty whelk, greeting its advent with a hissing kiss of love, the generous moisture that is their life, now pushing on through the gateways of the loch, now halting at its portals to turn with the turning tide but where he can— and in the chosen land of saltwater rivers and lakes that are vassal to old ocean the power is a possession for ever—ever maintaining his char-acter as an estuary fish. Nor does he lack stout allies, the allies of a common birthplace and ancestry in holding this chosen home of his race against his greater kindred by descent, the lordly salmon. The estuary trout, fewer in number than his own silver clad warriors vie with him as brethren-in-arms, but rivals in renown. Both increase in size and number by the ideal conditions of existence that have made them the fish they are, until the salmon, conquered as much by nature and the great law of environment as by force of arms, have abandoned the field on grounds that are expedient in relation to their own interests and cos-mic in relation to the physical order.

In the matter of the evolution of the species of salmonidæ, the facts that have led to this explanation of the triumph of the sea-trout in South Uist are equally instructive. In the first place the salmon of all the Outer Hebrides are small fish—a circumstance which may either be at-tributed to a poverty in diet or what is the same thing, ex hypothesi, a more limited ocean range than the larger varieties of salmon cover. In either case assuming that the conditions of life in Hebridean waters

THE END OF A TIDAL DITCH, SOUTH UIST, AT LOW WATER.

[At high tide, their running "period," the sea-trout ascend through a drain
pipe.—Vide Environment and Migration, p. 13—16.]

approach in their mixed character the primeval order, the relatively small size of the salmon, and the large size of the sea-trout indicate an extremely interesting assimilation in this direction as much the result of environment as is the structural differences which remain constant. When we add the connecting links, the bull trout and the estuary trout, both of which approximate to this level quality of size we get a chain of connected species, which read in the light of the conditions and whole circumstances of their existence, cannot for instructive pregnancy be excelled in the whole range of piscine being. My reasoning may be based on speculative premises, but they are speculations that have been borne in upon me by the Hebridean breezes. Often, as I have passed from lake to sea and from sea to salt-water river overcome by the mysteries of weird land and water, thoughts have come on the green tides, ideas have cleared the tangle and floated up from the limpid depths that seemed whole truths when fresh from the hand of nature, if idle speculations in the colder and more artificial air of the city where dwell the critics who do not feel the inspiration which the mysteries of fish life give to the student and to him alone who studies them in their very home and most ancient and secret places.

PART II.

PRACTICAL LOCH FISHING.

CHAPTER XIV.

The Evolution of Loch Fishing : A History of Negatives.

Herodotus with that charmingly simple faith in human credulity, which always distinguishes the true historian, describes in a certain part of his marvellous work a primitive, but none the less perfect, kind of fly-fishing practised in the remote period with which he is dealing by certain of the dwellers in that land of marvels—Africa. On translating, whether by the aid of a crib or otherwise, this portion of the works of the father of history, the average schoolboy who knows anything about rods, other than the kind advertised by Solomon, permits himself the luxury of a chuckle, and if a rude boy puts his tongue in his cheek, raises the digital finger of his right hand to his nose and by an exercise of his comparative faculties, that does him more credit than the facial and manual exercises first mentioned, dubs Herodotus the father, not merely of history, but of the fish story. Though this mention of fly-fishing by Herodotus may thus make the unskilful laugh, it has the effect of making the judicious think. The result of such contemplation usually is that Herodotus is hailed as a sort of Darwin of historical evolution, or in other words, as a very keen observer who has noted many things that might have escaped the eye of one less richly endowed with what we now-a-days term the journalistic insight and intuition. Herodotus may not have seen all he says he saw, but seeing something resembling what he described, he grasped intuitively what the Scottish pundits would have termed, its "infinite potentiality" and evolved from his inner consciousness with the aid of a prophetic eye playing on a few isolated facts the theory and practice of fly-fishing as time was destined to perfect it.*

This dipping into the future a good deal further than the average

---

* Other and equally ancient authorities could be quoted to the same effect—dubious save by implication.

human eye can see is no doubt a characteristic of all writers capable of grasping the infinite posse that is in every esse, and on the same principle it is highly probable that when Watt kept his eye on the lifting lid of the kettle, he saw not a little iron vessel in sore travail, wrestling with the giant force that was within it, but thousands of tall chimneys belching the black wealth of smoke, trains annihilating distance in every land, steamers ploughing every sea, and this great giant made the slavish minister of man's will. The ancient legend of the genie confined in pots only, I suppose, tells the same lesson when one comes to comprehend its true inwardness.

There is, however, a reverse side to the picture of great men contemplating the future with the eye that can read the potentialities of the apparently little facts of the present. Great men, and little men who are their feeble imitators, are equally apt to read the past in the light of the knowledge of the present, and hence to produce such a priori history which, if interesting reading is obviously to a very large extent a fine example of the greatest of all assumptions or in other words, of the speculative inference. We admit and accept as true history that which is the result of comparative method of inquiry. If, for example, comparative philology shows by an analysis of the root ideas of certain words that a people, whose story is otherwise lost in the mists of a hoary antiquity, were a pastoral people, we accept that evidence, in the absence of more direct proof, as sufficiently convincing to make the inference possible, and perhaps probable. If some enterprising antiquary—and one word of a dead language is, we know, sufficient to cause a " rise " of antiquaries, discovers a milk pail amongst the regions which the alleged pastoral people are said to have inhabited, then we sup the lacteal fluid from it with " Aiken Drum's lang ladle," and the comparative method of enquiry sets all the purely a priori gentlemen by the ears and registers a very great triumph indeed. Still when all is said that can be said, there is just as much vulgar incredulity in this world as vulgar credulity, and the number of people who stand, doubt and examine would, if marshalled in battalions, probably form as large, if not a larger army, than would those persons of simple faith who accept the marvellous with all the avidity with which tarn trout take the fly, simply because it is the marvellous and appeals to that deep-seated love of the sensa-

tional and the unusual which is one of the mysterious weaknesses of
human nature, largely taken advantage of by the American press.
Nevertheless, to hark back to Herodotus, the fact that he mentions fly
fishing at all is a great fact, which not only speaks aloud for the antiquity
of the practice if not the art of fly fishing, but also largely justifies those
a priori writers to whom I have already referred.   Of these writers the
chief is Scott.   The fact is interesting because in the endeavour—and
I admit that my researches have been both hastily conducted and mostly
on the surface of the wonderful land of literature—to trace the history
of loch fishing in books, the earliest recorded reference which I found
occurs in the "Fair Maid of Perth."   Now Scott we know was not an
angler ; the fact is writ large in those few passages in his works in which
he refers to angling.   For example he makes Darsie Latimer use a plum-
met to sound the depths of a stream—a thing no Scottish
angler ever does—and enables the trusty henchman of Vich
Ian Vohr to take a sea-trout in a Perthshire lake—a triumph
no angler would accord even to such "a pretty man."   These and many
other angling solecisms in his works might, it is true, be pardoned in
any other writer than one who lived in that chosen home of the angler,
the region where the silver Tweed ever makes gladsome music in the
ear, who wandered in the romantic valley of the Yarrow and stood by
the shores of lone St. Mary's lake with his great contemporaries that
were anglers, who saw the chain of lochs that grace the Trossachs as we
have never seen them, who could remember to record in the finest war
poem in our language that the leaping trout of Loch Achray "lay still,"
before the pealing of the banner cry of hell, and who stood upon the
shores of Loch Coruisk, when the proud Queen of Wilderness could still
remember the rude homage of Cormac Doil, and yet failed to chronicle
in lofty rhyme the fish that peopled its virgin waters.   But if Scott were
not an angler, he was assuredly a great antiquary, steeped to his very
fingers in the legend that is history, the history that is romance of
those deserts his magic wand has made blossom like the rose.   We may
rest assured, therefore, that if Scott made Simon Glover angle in Loch
Tay and fish that lake from a boat, he did so because he had some solid
ground for believing that in the days of the good King Robert, lake
fishing was actually a sport—primitive no doubt, but still a sport—as
well as one of the many means whereby the hunter of the day in the wid-

est sense of the term, supplied by the family or tribal larder.*
By parity of reasoning, if he fails to enter into details and
to chronicle the lures used or describe the flies, it is probably because
he would have felt precisely the same lack of confidence, had he been
compelled to describe the lures employed by and the general modus
operandi of the loch fisher of his own day, or even of the Tweedside
angler with whom he must constantly have been rubbing shoulders.

It is instructive at this point to note, if the comparison of very small
with very great things be permissible, that writers, who are at least
sufficiently devoted to angling to know something of its mysteries, would
certainly not have failed to chronicle the angling methods of Simon
Glover in Loch Tay in the fourteenth century—an age when the sword
was ostensibly mightier than the pen, and the spear was more often
grasped than the rod, whose history is written in blood and whose
monuments are forgotten graves. So to chronicle the methods employed and the lures used might, it is true, have involved the writers in
a priori and speculative angling history. On the other hand it is not
improbable that angling intuition, which I take it is in this connection
the re-building of the past by the light of the present, might have enabled
a writer blessed with a little imagination—that best of handkerchiefs in
a game of blind man's buff with the facts of history—to fashion a nar-
rative of such plausible probability that, in the lack of proof to the contrary, it would secure a ready acceptance by the credulous half, or
whatever be the proportion, of the world. For example, a few years
ago I attempted in a small story called " The Angler Hermit " to fill in
some of the blanks left by Scott in the picture of Simon Glover fishing
in the virgin waters of Loch Tay. The story, I may mention, is supposed to be told by a Scottish angling clergyman of the older school
who " prefaces it with " a long and learned preamble on the antiquity
of everything (manifestly based on the text " There is no new thing
under the Sun "), in which the reverend gentleman as a divine has
striven sore with the very old Adam within him as an antiquary, and
mixed heathen superstition with Christian precept and fairy lore with
the Gospel according to St. John in such a manner that only his utter

---

* Scott says that the recreation of the Highlanders of that day were fishing and
hunting while their trade was war. He does not condescend upon details in the case of
the first mentioned though he describes "hunting matches."

incomprehensibility can have saved him from an interview with the Assembly.

The story is introduced under the following circumstances. I was fishing with a certain parson on a very stormy spring day in a Perthshire loch. Finally we are driven before the wind to seek shelter in a spot which is thus described. " It was indeed a calmly tranquil spot in which we found ourselves, a sort of cradled bay with an extremely narrow entrance. Overhead and outside roared the storm; we could hear the sough of the wind through the firs above and see them bending to the blast and tossing their arms wildly before the gale; could mark the flying clouds and the drifting snow and spray that flew overhead in blinding masses; but underneath a hanging cliff all was as calm and still, if not quite so warm, as if a July sun had been pouring its rays on a glassy lake with the mountains shadowed on its calm surface. A gentle shingle and a pier rudely fashioned made landing easy, and we made our way by a somewhat precipitous and twisting path up the cliff-side towards where a rivulet leaped sheer some feet in a crystal cascade from the summit of an abutting rock. Arrived there, we entered a roomy cavern with an inner and an outer cave, the latter much overgrown with trailing brushwood. Its floor was composed of rock and sand, and from it there welled a spring of pure cold water bubbling up through the bed. Its superfluous waters found their way to the adjacent burn by a course which seemed almost artificial, and no doubt to some extent was. Here and there on the walls crosses were carved, ancient memorials, intermingled with names that were evidently the work of visitors of a more modern and less religious kind. A rude stone bench fashioned from the wall ran up one side, and somehow, I know not why, one could not help feeling that it had once been inhabited, and had a story."

At this point the following dialogue occurs and as it repeats in somewhat different words and possibly puts in another light my previous remarks on the probable antiquity of fly fishing and loch fishing, I need offer no further apology for quoting it.

" This is the Angler Hermit's cave," said my friend; " the dwelling of the first angler I have ever heard of; he lived and flourished nearly 500 years ago."

" Perfectly possible," said I; " Scott is my authority, besides, a kind of fly-fishing as old as the Pyramids is mentioned by Herodotus."

" Herr Dotus, is't," said Donald, who was, or pretended to be, somewhat deaf ; " anither bit German body I'll be thinkin'. If he kens nae mair aboot fishin' than Herr Bratvurst wha' was here last year I'll no be thinkin' much o' his opeenion onyway. A wee bit feckless body was the Herr wi' blue glasses and an owergrown heid ; he was aye howking and slashing in the wames o' the fish—and few eneuch they were—and wasting time running after butterflies and a' manner o' fleas—Effie Merrals, or some sic name he ca'ad them by—talking a kind of jargon that was neither English, nor Latin, nor his ain outlandish gibberish—a kind o' far awa' cousin of the kindly Scots tongue spoiled by ower muckle foreign air. Herr Dotus, I wouldna' fash ma thoomb for all the crood . of such bodies. Oor Jock could ding them a'."

" Herodotus," I said, " not Herr Dotus, nor any other ' Herr.' "

" Oh, Herodotus—why did ye not sae sae—the chiel wi' his Greek blethers. Oor Jock kens him fine. He's college learnt, and reads bits frae him whiles o' an evening, and a muckle lot o' trash it is. Jock says he was the faither o' history ; the worse for him then, says I, for he maun be the faither o' lees. Faither o' history, indeed ; maybe he is, but if so he doesna' ken his ain bairn."

" What do you say to Scott, then? He makes people angle just at this very period."

" Whatna Scott?" said Donald, who evidently had not heard my previous mention of the great writer's name, " Tam Scott, the lang pedlar wi' the langer tongue, or Willie wha' teaches the bairns at the Brig doon bye. The yin is a fine bletherer about silks and satins and pirns o' worsted an' buttons and sic like trash that are guid eneuch for the foolish womankind, but I never heard that he kenned muckle aboot the thread of history, and as for the ither, he minds aye the book ; he can drive the A.B.C. into a bairn wi' the tawse, and tho' he's aye in the past, it's little he kens aboot it or onything else."

" Sir Walter Scott," I said.

" Oh, Wattie, is't," said Donald with the grand air of a man who would have called the great Napoleon Nap over the first, and Nappy over the fifth tumbler ; " ah, he was a man. If he said it, enough said ; it maun be so."

" Well, well," said my companion, interrupting, " to-night you shall read all about it in a manuscript of an old minister of the Parish, who died when last century was young, and long before Waterloo was lost and won."

After certain other matters have been explained not revalent to the question in hand, the supposititious manuscript referred to proceeds to fill in as follows the blanks in the picture suggested by Scott's creating of an angler out of Simon Glover.

"About his origin and the relationship of the lad to him, the Hermit's lips were ever sealed, and there was not a man dared ask him, in part by reason of the stern glance of his steel-grey eye, that bespoke him a man of courage and action, however peaceful his present life, and one prompt to resent such idle curiosity, by the whole physical force of his giant frame and sinewy limbs, and in part by reason of the awe, amounting almost to superstitous dread, in which he was held. So far he might have been forgotten, as many such hermits were, men who had turned from war to lead an ascetic life for reasons known to themselves, had it not been for one outstanding peculiarity. He was devoted to the chase, but more particularly to the catching of fish, great and small, which he had so elevated into an art as to win for himself the title in those days of the Holy Fisher, now changed through the course of time into the legendary name of "The Angler Hermit." According to the gossip current in my youth his skill in angling fell but little short of that of our most accomplished modern professors of the gentle art though his mechanical contrivances for the capture of fish, particularly rods and flies, were necessarily lacking in that exquisite finish, that admirable equipose of lightness and strength which distinguish the masterpieces of our day, when the art of rod-making has apparently achieved its goal and is incapable of further development.* 'His rod was made, as I have heard, of two pieces, sometimes of stout yew, of which wood were the bows, sometimes of the hardy ash, the pieces being joined together by wire or stout thongs of leather

It was both polished and stained, according to the story current in my youth, while the rings were of a construction peculiarly cunning, lying out stiff from the rod by means of a bridge-shaped wire, and not complete circles like those of the present day, that hang pendant sheer from the rod itself, and are apt at times, I admit, to wear the line and prevent its true and rapid passage through them when the line is heavy

*A wise prophet the parson !

and swollen with moisture and a great fish is fighting for his liberty
in a flooded stream. I have also by much inquiry discovered that, according to the legend, his top ring lacked also the chaste and rounded
symmetry of that which adorns my rods, and was fashioned after the
style of a pulley, and depended somewhat below the line of the rod
when held in a horizontal position. As to his reel or pirn, this was,.
I believe, of great size, though the legend is obscure on the point, and
constructed of wood, and must have been somewhat cumbersome and
ill to guide, especially in wet weather, or when by the chances of angling it had become immersed in the water and swollen from the contact.
The lines which he employed were framed of silk, brought with him
from Spain, the secret of whose manufacture must have died with him,.
for it is unknown to modern times. The most curious of all his angling
furniture was, however, his lures and the substitute for gut which he
employed to fasten them to his line. On this point the legend is most
emphatic.

Soon finding that the salmon frequenting the lake would not take
any of the flies (about which I have been able to gather nothing), and
could not be persuaded to look at any lure such as worms or a dead bait
of young trout or the like, he devised a most ingenious lure fashioned
after the shape of a young trout, and painted and coloured in such
exquisite style (this art, I take it, he must have acquired in his youth in
some monastery at the same time as he mastered reading and writing) as
to deceive anyone, and certainly the salmon and trout frequenting the
spreading waters of the loch. This lure he trailed behind his light
curragh, and many a lordly salmon and great trout fell by its allurement
to his prowess. In these old days, as all or most men know, artificers in
steel had great skill in the fashioning of all manner of things made
therefrom, fine hauberks of rings and the like, and in
this craft the Hermit was skilled, for he fashioned steel wire of such
exceeding fineness and small links, made with great cunning that it
vied with the web of the spider at once in firmness and in strength
for the web of the spider is for its girth the stoutest thing that is spun
or made.

The pastime of angling he followed with such devotion as seems to
me only justified by its apostolic origin, for certainly I should lose somewhat in the eyes of my flock of my humble reputation for sanctity were

I to devote so much time and energy to a pusuit which many of my more
seriously-minded parishioners would regard as unbeseeming in one
devoted to the service of God, though I believe that more may be learnt
of Him and His ways by the riverside and amongst the mountains and
the lakes than ever our words accomplish even in such few inspired
moments of lofty thought as the sinful nature and frailty of humanity
permit us to enjoy. No doubt, however, in those days his prowess in
and devotion to the chase added to rather than detracted from the
reverence in which he was held. Apart from angling, to which more
legitimate branch of sport he was most addicted, the venerable Hermit
had many other cunning means for the capture of fish. The use of
the spear, water burning, and of the net were of course understood of
the people, but one ingenious method which he introduced I must mention, of driving fish until they congregated in one pool, and fell easy
and terrified victims to the spear and net. He caused them to secure
two or three dead otters, and these being properly guided by thongs
were made to appear at the neck of pools and in the verisimilitude of
the live animals to hunt the dubs, so that the fish, in terror of their
foes, left them and were crowded into one pool fenced with nets where
they fell easy victims.* This sport, being better understood and more
in keeping with their instincts, was much loved by the people and won
him great credit, which was not diminished when, having captured
several young otters, he trained them very cunningly to hunt the pools
in lieu of their dead relatives just as a pack of terriers will hunt the
cairns and rocks for the fox in spring time."

Further than is set forth above I did not venture into the dangerous
regions of the a priori, if the latter portion of what I have just quoted
can be fairly termed a priori matter at all, seeing that it is certain that
people took fish from lakes from the very earliest times, and that in
this aspect lake fishing is as old as the lakes themselves. If, therefore,
a professed angler and a dabbler in the literary pleasure of angling
writing, did not dare to complete the picture of the Angler Hermit,
who is only, qua angler, Simon Glover turned hermit with a few qualities
tacked on, it is scarcely fair to condemn Scott for failing to condescend
on details, which, if they had been as accurate, as those he usually is

* Lord London once informed me that he had either seen or heard of, I forget which
this method of poaching being actually put in practice in Scotland.

able to command of the habits and customs of the forgotten peoples whom he has made to live again in the manner in which they lived, would have been intensely interesting and particularly valuable to anyone endeavouring to trace the rise of loch fishing—particularly with the fly. As it is, I am forced to confess that the history of loch fishing has never been, and probably never will be, written without indulging in speculations, which, however interesting, are not facts and are largely a priori inferences. However the fact that fly fishing is as old as Herodotus and was practised long before his day on the Nile, and that Scott gives the weight of his authority to Simon Glover angling in Loch Tay in the fourteenth century, together warrant the assumption that loch fishing, after a sort, is as old as lochs.*

By the time of Queen Mary, that is to say by the sixteenth century—for we may afford to ignore all the a priori fly-fishing monks of the monastery ponds—we begin to reach a period in which fly-fishing in lakes, as well as in rivers, seems to have been a recognised sport. Yet it is no easy matter to find any authoritative utterance as to the methods employed by our angling ancestors to wile the loch trout to his doom. Jamieson will wax, as is his wont, extremely learned, if not indeed pedantic, on the derivation of the word loch and its cognate terms lough in Erse, laug in Icelandic and so on and after pointing out that it is of the same root as the Latin lacus, will finally ask you to believe that it is derived from lavo " I wash." He will quote Barbour

" Between a louchsid and a brae."

and " the loch of cair " mentioned in the " Palice of Honour," but on loch fishing he is dumb. It is true that his silence may be discreet, for when he does mention angling, it is to explain that it is derived from the Teutonic anghelen meaning to sting and hence to angle or fish. The connection between this learned reference and fly-fishing is not clear, until one is informed that the kind of stinging implied by anghelen is that of bees and hence by implication of all flies. " Rodding-time " looks but it is not a more hopeful reference for on searching deeper one discovers that it is only spawning time and, therefore, an

---

* It is a remarkable fact that fly-fishing is now practised on the Nile, and loch fishing is a possible sport in the Holy Land.

obvious corruption of redding-time, the very season when all save the
black fishers of old and the triangle-wielders of to-day

> " Hang in idle trophy near
>   The basket, fishing rod and spear."

—a trilogy that has the sanction of Scott for its classic lack of sporting appropriateness.

Nor is Boswell more fruitful of light of the proper kind on the mysterious darkness in which the history of loch-fishing is enshrouded.   He
speaks of " lochs, as they call them, or arms of the sea which flow upon
all the coasts of Skye " and dismisses them otherwise with the same ease
as Johnson emptied his " crowning dish of tea."   One and all appear
to have a most serious objection to dilating on a subject in whose
exposition they are not calculated to shine and even Jamieson declines
to hold further debate on the subject of the lister, than to dismiss it
as a spear for killing fish and what is more instructive as a word without
a root.   I find, it is true, a reference in P. Arroquhar: Dumbarton
Statistics , Act III., 434, to Loch Long in which it is stated of this
arm of the sea " the fish that frequent Loch Long are cod, haddock seath,
lythe, whiting, flounders, mackerel, trout and herrings."   As the only
trout recorded by Colonel Thornton as coming from Loch Long turned
out on inspection to be whiting, it is obvious that this very ancient reference is not worth following up.*

The search for facts as to the mode of fishing employed on our British
lakes is, indeed, a vain task and the lack of interest shown by some of
our leading sporting antiquaries is truly lamentable.   Strutt, for example,
absolutely refuses to join issue with the subject of angling and thus
summarily dismisses it: " But with regard to the latter (fishing) I have
not met with any particulars sufficiently deviating from the present
methods [these after the manner of his tribe he takes for granted and
does not describe] of taking fish to claim a place in this work."† Pride of
of place is accordingly denied them and one is forced to turn elsewhere

---

* Colonel Thornton tells an amusing story with regard to these whitings.   His landlady, when the Colonel came in hungry after a day on Loch Lomond, held a lengthy
debate as to the respective merits of the trout of Loch Lomond and Loch Long with the
object of deciding whether a dish of trout from the former or one from the latter should
figure on the supper table.   Finally, by way of clinching the argument, she produced the
Loch Long trout.   They proved to be whitings !   This explains the reference.

† P. 38, Sports and Pastimes, Hone's edition, 1845.

L

for even such small rays of light as here and there illumine the darkness in which the history of loch fishing appears to be impenetrably enshrouded, unless one boldly adopts the a priori method and lights the lamp of speculation.

I have said that in the time of Queen Mary, or in other words in the sixteenth century, loch-angling appears to have been a recognised sport, followed, however, if one is to judge from the single reference to it in literature dealing with the period, only by " the wise and noble." Scott is once more my authority, and as his references are of some personal interest as well as germane to the subject, I will quote them verbatim. They occur in the " Abbot " and the anglers are Roland Graeme and George Douglas. Scott makes Roland Graeme, when in a temper, say " I will speak with George Douglas when we go a-fishing," which is a concession for him to make inasmuch as it shows that fishing was then, as now, the cure for all ills, and Scott, as will presently appear, was no great friend of the pastime.

The picture of loch fishing in the sixteenth century does not, however, continue for long to present such a pleasing exterior. It is recorded of George Douglas that he " in his usual mood of silence sat in the stern of the little skiff which they used on such occasions, trimming his tackle and from time to time indicating by signs to Graeme, who pulled the oars, which way he should go." Now though the sorting of tackle has been known to lead to loss of temper, yet it is in the main a genial, as it is a congenial pastime, and most of us had we had Roland Graeme, the page of one of the most beautiful, most interesting and cleverest women of all time and fresh from her presence, as our gillie on Loch Leven would have assumed our most pleasant smile and thought ourselves the very button on fortune's fishing cap. These immortals of fiction never are and never have been opportunists, and the chance, like all the leviathans, is lost and Scott treats the angling as of secondary importance. We shall presently see how Queen Mary with her womanly tact and insight better appreciates the possibilities of the situation, which seems forced on Scott simply because the scene of his story is laid on an island on Loch Leven—a lake not to be thought of apart from trout.

Let us, however, resume our seats in the boat beside Graeme and Douglas. On doing so we will hear the latter utter words pregnant with meaning. He says: "But row towards Saint Serf's island—there is a breeze from the West and we shall have sport, keeping to windward of the isle where the ripple is strongest. We will speak more of what you have mentioned when we have had an hour's sport." "Their fishing was successful though never," says Scott, "did two anglers pursue that silent and unsocial pleasure with less of verbal intercourse."

There is perhaps no reference in literature more pregnant than this of internal proof of the personal predelictions of a great writer. Scott betrays what his own feelings are towards the pastime of angling with a clearness that is all the more convincing because it may have been unconscious. Possibly it might not have carried the same weight had he not specialised it to the proprieties of the drama he is unfolding and made it personal to the characters of his actors. "That silent and unsocial pleasure" is as Scott would himself have said, as pregnant as the "expressive nod of Lord Burleigh's head." One may well exclaim on reading these lines O Tempora! O Mores! O Noctes Ambrosianae! Scott missed one lesson learned by the contemporary suggested by the last phrase to the full, ahd it is sad to think, when one regards the possibilities which lay in angling had Scott learned to love it, the literary treasures his magic would have won from mere and stream, that there may have been, indeed was, a missing link in the chain of sweet affinity that bound the poet of nature to the land of the mountain and of the flood, who called it not vain that fountains taught

> "Their rushing wave
> To murmur dirges o'er his grave."

Nor would this conclusion be influenced by a story of Sir Walter told by the Hon. Mrs. George Edgecumbe and recalled by the death of that lady in Florence while these pages were in the Press. Mrs. Edgecumbe was a daughter of Sir John Shelley, and one of the Sussex Shelleys of whom the great poet must ever remain the chief. She knew Sir Walter well, and early in the twenties visited Abbotsford with her father. Scott, as it happened, was at that time "busily idle" writing "The Talisman," and one morning after breakfast retired to add a chapter or two to that wonderful work. While he was writing—and no doubt, more suo, was scattering the sheets of his copy all over the floor of his library—Sir John Shelley returned "radiant from the Tweed, whence he had landed a magnificent salmon." At once, according to Mrs. Edgecumbe, Sir

Walter rose, "the Talisman" quite forgotten in what seemed the far
more important task of weighing the salmon for which purpose the
whole party descended to the kitchen. Arrived there, Sir Walter ad-
justed the scales and noted the weight with a dignified solemnity which
Mrs. Edgecumbe never forgot. And no wonder. Scott weighing a salmon fresh from the silver stream of his beloved Tweed was a sight at
once for gods and men. If, however, the story is intended to imply—
and there is no escaping from the conclusion so plainly suggested—that
the salmon, as a fish taken with rod and line appealed to Scott as an
angler with more irresistible force than the building of "The Talisman,"
it is a conclusion quite opposed to the internal evidence of his works,
to his known predelictions and to certain recorded facts as to his angling
knowledge. The story merely confirms what we all know that Scott
was a courteous gentleman and an admirable host who threw aside the
work in which he was immersed because he saw with that intuition of
the "perfect gentleman" that to appear interested in the salmon would
be to please his guest and add a fresh glow to the joy of the triumphant
angler. Sir Walter was Pleydell and I feel assured that he viewed the
salmon, as that hero of High Jinks would have viewed it, not only,
that is to say, as a fish in situ giving him an opportunity of displaying
his innate courtesy and kindness of heart but also as, in prospectu, a
very worthy inmate of the "kettle." Scott, as the apostle in romance
of diners and drinkers, always dwells with a wealth of detail on the cook-
ing and eating of fish which is in strange contrast to his curt, fragment-
ary and often wholly erroneous descriptions of the methods employed for
their capture other than by illegal or non-sporting means.

We may, therefore, not only set the general evidence of his works
against the implication of this story, but may reduce it to a merely
interesting tour de force, by recalling the fact that we owe the Waverley
novels, according to Scott's own story, to his one day going to a drawer
and while searching amongst the lumber of papers, there consigned to
the dust of old oblivion for some tackle for a friend, discovering the
discarded manuscript of Waverley. An angler would only have looked
in such a drawer for tackle for a foe, presuming any angler, much
more the genial Wizard, could have an enemy. In any case no angler
would have been under the necessity of searching in such a place for
tackle, nor would anyone acquainted with the first principles of practical

angling have ventured to offer gut that had lain in such a receptacle to any brother of the guild even as a dernier ressort. We may take it, therefore, that Scott's general attitude towards angling was if not to the " North side of friendly," then certainly one of uninterested indifference, while his knowledge of it, in the absence of all interest in it, was merely superficial.

Yet beneath the surface we may find the reason for this lack of love of a sport that is essentially the sport of a lover of nature as Scott must have known, unless Walton spoke to him in vain as the representative angling son of the Great Mother who most of all men has mingled fishing jargon with the sweet words of the most natural of all philosophers, the wise man who takes the lessons of little things from the things them-selves. This manifest lack of love of angling may always have existed in Scott, but I venture to think that his prejudice became a rooted dislike after he had edited the edition of Franck's " Northern Memoirs " published in 1821. Now Franck was a practical angler who could afford, qua angler, to call Walton a " muddler," but otherwise he is an intolerable bore and his " wise saws " and philosophising make him as inferior to Walton as a writer—a philosopher of nature—as Walton was inferior to him as an angler. Had Scott edited an edition of Wal-ton, and never been forced to conn with laborious care the pages of Franck, who is only interesting to the practical angler and lacks the root of the matter which might have wooed Scott from indifference to interest and from interest to love, we might have ranked him amongst the immortals that have made angling the stepping stone to higher things. Yet ever between Walton and Scott, stood the bogey Franck in all his terrors. If Walton could not woo him to love the rod, no one could, Walton who more than any man that ever breathed the larger air realised the Falstaffian ideal of babbling of green fields, who was one of the very few that have truly read the books in the running brooks and has left as a last and best legacy to anglers the inspiration to rise above the mere killing of fish to feel the very breath of nature in every breeze that shakes the humblest flower in the meadow, the les-sons that open in all their sweetness and light with each returning dawn, that fall with the golden rain of noon, that in myriad form lie cradled in the massed fantasy of evening cloudland, that rise with the rising moon until even such a stern land as a rock-strewn island of the West

becomes silver-studded in the soft blue radiance of a summer night.
Viewed under the inspiration of the first angler that read the great book
of many chapters the lily is wiser than Solomon, its array still more
splendid than the purple and fine linen of the king.

It is a vain dream now to think of what Scott might have done for
angling had he fallen under the spell of Walton and not the practical
disillusioning influence of Franck. My present task would assuredly
have been easier, for Scott would with his wizard power have found
those very facts in the history of my subject, which I have to seek in his
pages and would have given us a perfect, instead of that imperfect, picture of loch fishing in the sixteenth century of which I now take up the
thread. It will be observed that Scott makes Douglas speak favourably
of the island drift on Loch Leven and from this we may infer that it
was not without repute in his day. He shows, however, that he did
not know much from personal experience of Loch Leven when he makes
Douglas speak of the West wind as favourable, though it must be observed that Loch Leven trout have had not a few changes of mood in
their time and that as a generalisation the favourable character of a
West wind is absolutely justified.

Nor does Scott refuse us some further insight into the fishing knowledge or angling beliefs, as I fain would persuade myself, of the 16th
century. He thus proceeds " With the peculiar tact and delicacy which
no woman possessed in greater perfection she (Queen Mary) began to
soothe by degrees the vexed spirit of her magnanimous attendant. The
excellence of the fish which he had taken in his expedition, the high
flavour and beautiful red colour of the trout, which have long given
distinction to the lake, led her first to express her thanks to her attendant for so agreeable an adjunct to her table especially upon a jour
de jeune; and this brought on enquiries into the place where the fish
had been taken, their size, their peculiarities, the times when they were
in season and a comparison between the Loch Leven trouts and those
which are found in the lakes and rivers of the South of Scotland. The
ill-humour of Roland Graeme was never of an obstinate character. It
rolled away like mist before the sun, and he was busily engaged in a keen
and animated dissertation about Loch Leven trout, and sea-trout, and
river trout and bull trout and char, which never rise to a fly and par,
which some suppose infant salmon and herlings, which frequent the Nith

and vendisses which are only found in the Castle-Loch of Lochmaben."

But here be it observed the raison de'etre of this concession to angling intrudes again and Queen Mary grows sad because as the lakes and rivers of her kingdom were enumerated " imagination cheated her," and she ceased to think of fish, but of her share in the misfortunes of " the hapless Stuart race." No doubt if we knew the truth Scott got his information from some member of that jovial crew of good fellows who never left a " tappit hen " behind them when the Vendisse Club dined under the shadow of " the royal towers of Lochmaben." In any case the dissertation such as it is throws no more light on the methods, gear and flies of the loch fisher in the time of Queen Mary than do any of the previous generalisations. Interesting as Scott is—and still more interesting, alas, as he might have been, he was merely at the best, as he says, in the preface to Franck's " Northern Memoirs," quoting John Richards, " No fisher, but a well-wisher of the game." Still we may assume that he had a better authority even than the work referred to for suggesting to the mind the existence of the art of loch fishing not only in the days of Queen Mary, but also in those of her ancestor Robert II. He leaves us, it is true, to fill in the picture for ourselves, because he lacked all personal interest in the antiquarian research which he was better qualified to carry through to a successful issue than are the majority of the dwindled sons of the little men of to-day—of which majority parva pars sum. In thus leaving us to our own devices and presenting us with one authoritative fact—the fact that loch fishing was practised hundreds of years before the Loch Leven Angling Association was registered as a company, or before a Loch Tay landlord hailed the Sassenach as an itinerant gold mine—as a basis for an a priori filling in of the picture by the inferences of evolution—he has given the fancy free play and the imagination a most excellent jus spatiandi. We may go back to our ancient ally Herodotus, that down the long array of years where the shadows frown from the twilight forest of the rods of the centuries, holds up to our view in the dim light the first fly that stained with parti-coloured hues the white radiance of the faith of fish in man as like Nathaniel without guile and we may evolve from the simple study of this progenitor of the " Jock Scott," this common ancestor of " Red and Teal " and " Zulu," and every species of fly that swims and floats, holds the mirror up to nature or breaks the entomolo-

gical angler's heart, the history of the thirty centuries which
angling man has from father to son failed to hand down. We may infer
that loch fishing as now practised always was practised, mutatis mutandis, for there is no new thing under the sun, but only a constant changing and developing of the old order.. From the primitive willow rod
and bait, we would pass to the primitive rod and the natural fly ; from
the primitive rod and the natural fly, to the primitive rod and the
artificial fly, if indeed the primitive rod and the artificial fly were not
contemporaneous. We will, however, find but little in general and relatively less in special literature to aid us in arriving at the true facts
of the evolution. If we take up Franck's " Northern Memoirs," we will
find not only that there is no direct reference to loch-fishing as a separate art,* but further that for the most part, he assumes that his readers
know all about the antiquity of fly-fishing in general as an art and desire
only such practical details as he can impart of how it is pursued in
Scotland which he describes as "a legible fair draught of the beautiful
creation dressed up with polished rocks, pleasant savannas, flourishing
dales, deep and torpid lakes, with shady woods immerged with rivers and
gliding rivulets, while every fountain overflows a valley and every ford
superabounds with fish." No doubt had Walton undertaken the Northern tour instead of Franck we might have had "from the good old man
who had so true an eye for nature, so simple a taste for her most innocent pleasures and, withal so sound a judgment, both concerning men
and things," a better picture of the Scotland of the days of Cromwell
as her natural beauties and the lessons of her lakes and rivers caught in
the one case, his eye and, in the other, filled his Arcadian imagination,
but it is highly probable that we should have had the same historical
silence, the same taking for granted of the commonplaces of knowledge
which, traditional in those days, are now almost a sealed book.

Even Colonel Thornton comparatively recent as was his " Sporting
Tour" is not half so explicit as is Franck. He does not even condescend to tell us as does the rival of Walton to " remember always to

---

* Sir Herbert Maxwell, M.P., to whose kindness I was indebted for the use of an
excellent copy of Franck's rare book, told me that it contained no reference to loch
fishing. Strictly speaking this is both accurate and inaccurate, and my observations, as
above, represent the facts. Franck's experience of Scottish lakes, Loch Lomond
excepted, was unlucky, and for this he had to thank a certain witch.—Vide the chapter
on " Pike Fishing," supra.

carry your dubbing-bag about you; wherein there ought to be silks of all sorts, threads, thrums, moccado-ends, and cruels of all sizes and variety of colours; diversified and stained wool, with dog's and bear's hair; besides twisted fine threads of gold and silver: with feathers from the capon, partridge, peacock, pheasant, mallard, smith, teal, snite, parrot, heronshaw, paraketta, bittern, hobby, phlimingo, or Indian-flush; but the mockaw, without exception, gives flames of life to the hackle. . . . Should any man, under the pretence of an artist, remain destitute of these prenoted qualifications, proclaim him a blockhead; let him angle for oisters."

The "angle for oisters" is good, and were it not ironical from my personal standpoint, I, for that very "word," could forgive Franck all he has omitted to state and all he might have learned but, as it is, it is not easy to forget that he stood beneath a tree of knowledge that did not bear forbidden fruit and failed like so many of his compeers to taste its apples and leave behind him a legacy that would now be precious to the curious student of pastimes. Finally, as I have already said, Colonel Thornton's "Sporting Tour" though abounding in descriptions of loch-fishing, makes no reference to its antiquity, and if the truth be told not only throws no light on the history of methods, but also leaves his own methods dubious when of a character which, according to our standard, could enable us with a clear conscience to call them sportsmanlike. The Colonel used largely what we call trimmers, and he dubs fox-hounds presumably as a salve to his sporting conscience. Once he speaks of "my favourite black fly," but he does not describe it, while he almost invariably refers to the "rises" he secures while trolling. He had marvellous sport in Loch Lomond—even though in his day the Leven was already beginning to be polluted—and in other lakes and clearly indicates that the sight of a rod in the Highlands last century, when yet Inversnaid held a garrison, was a familiar and well-understood sight. Yet if a bit of a poacher—from our point of view— Colonel Thornton is not a Captain Grosse and his evidence only proves a negative; it shows that the art of loch fishing was not new. There we may leave it for within the past fifteen years, still more within the past thirty the science and art of loch fishing has altered beyond recognition. Like all other departments of angling, it has advanced with the rapidity of the times. With improvements in gear have come corresponding advance in methods, until loch fishing is now both a science and an art. How this evolution and revolution have been accomplished may be judged by the succeeding pages.

The ancient worthies whom I have consulted have, it is clear, failed to throw much light on what is admittedly a difficult subject to elucidate. They have for the most part contented themselves with making us feel that we have been born either before or after the golden age of angling, judged merely from the tables of the slain. Possibly there were such fish in Loch Lomond in the days of Colonel Thornton, as perch that weighed " 7lbs. 3ozs. or thereabouts,"* possibly baskets of 58 trout with a best fish of six and a half pounds, could be killed in its spreading waters and possibly there was some necessity for printing the word " fly " in italics when it is stated that it was used ; possibly five salmon from 4r to 9lbs. could easily be killed in the Leven both in the days of Franck and of Thornton ; possibly also it was necessary to explain to English readers of the latter period that whisky was " a spirituous liquor, extracted from oats." For these days of vanished abundance and of touching innocence I make no moan, but I do permit myself the luxury of raising a wail of regret to shiver to the tingling stars that the Antiquary did not find a fish hatchery of Roman construction on the Monkbarns boundary instead of a putative castrum of doubtful value and that Edie Ochiltree did not unearth the rod of a Roman instead of that long ladle which once called Aiken Drum lord and master. I might then have achieved something more definite as to the evolution of loch fishing than a mere history of negatives.

* P. 43, Thornton's Sporting Tour. The Colonel gives this big fish a variety of weights which only correspond in all being between 7lb. and 8lb.

CHAPTER XV.

THE LOCH FISHER'S OUTFIT.

The "American Breeder and Sportsman" in reprinting a series of articles which I contributed on the subject of loch fishing to an English sporting weekly, gave as its reason for doing so the great increase in the number of anglers who prefer the quiet and peaceful, and in some aspects, the luxurious catching of trout from a boat to the rough-and-tumble work by the riverside. It at the same time paid me the possibly undeserved compliment of calling my remarks authoritative, and as applicable to American lakes as to those Scottish lochs to which they were primarily intended to refer. In those articles I found myself naturally compelled to refer to the loch fisher's outfit, and as my remarks on the subject appeared, in common with the rest of the articles, to have a cosmopolitan interest, and a measure, at least, of cosmopolitan value, I need scarcely make any further apology for a chapter dealing with matters that are assuredly somewhat dry and with questions that may well resolve themselves into problems in taste usually solved in terms of the individual angler's idiosyncrasies.

At the same time every little counts in angling, and it is just as important that the loch angler should secure, if possible, the best type of boat suitable for his purpose, as it is that he should use the flies most suitable for the water he is fishing.

It may here be stated, that for reasons which a subsequent chapter will reveal, two anglers should never fish from the same boat save under the most exceptional circumstances, and hence there is no necessity that a boat for loch fishing should be large, provided it is seaworthy, of sufficient beam and depth to be stable, and is otherwise sufficiently roomy to give greater freedom of movement than the limitation to "coughing and sneezing" implies.

Presuming that the loch fisher from a boat fishes alone the proper length of boat is one of some twelve feet. It should be sufficiently

light to be easily rowed, turned, and generally manœuvred and transported from loch to loch, and yet, at the same time, as already stated,
of sufficient beam to be steady, and of sufficient strength to resist
not only the buffets of the deep, but what is more important, the
frequent and generally unexpected impact with sunken rocks and
gravel banks.

Rowlocks will, in all cases, be found much better than tholepins, for
the oars can be turned in towards the boat, and allowed to rest with
much less risk of their slipping overboard. The oars should be
made fast when practicable, and a rest aft into which they can fit is
desirable, if not absolutely necessary. A locker aft will be found
extremely useful, while the boat should have both painter and anchor
if the angler must drift on stormy days—a proceeding which, however,
I hope to show to be not only unnecessary but even unadvisable.
There are three other important matters which should in no case be
overlooked, a spare oar, an iron-shod staff of considerable length—a
boathook will do—to clear away weeds should a fish get into them, and
the angler not know how to get him out, and, above all, a broad board
to run from gunwale to gunwale, on which the angler can comfortably
sit, and from which he can comfortably cast. To fish standing up
cramps the angler and is theoretically wrong, for he sees too much of
the fish. Moreover, on a clear day, in clear water, with the sun at the
angler's back, loch trout, though they do not mind a boat, are apt to
come short when the shadow of a man is thrown across the fly.

Were certain advantages, of which quickness of movement and ease
of propulsion either ahead or astern are the chief, the only features of
a good loch boat that had to be considered, I should have no hesitation
in recommending a "double-prowed bark" as the ideal vessel, but mere
" fore-and-aftness " is not everything. Room, and hence a measure of
comfort, are as important factors in successful fishing, as is the standard
of comfort in social content. Hence a roomy square-sterned boat
is undoubtedly the best, provided it fulfils those other requirements
which I have indicated. Collapsible boats have, of course, their
advantages, but I speak from personal experience when I say that it is
perfectly possible to secure for loch fishing a light boat that can be
transported to any loch in Scotland, either deserving or necessitating
the use of a boat. I am at the same time reminded by the mention of

collapsible boats of one of the strangest blendings of assured comedy and possible tragedy that ever occurred on a Highland loch. Many years ago my venerable angling friend, the Rev. F. Simpson, of Foston —a typical Yorkshire sportsman who could at 86 ride as straight to hounds as any man in the Broadacres—had one of those very collapsible boats which he used both on the Islay and Jura lochs. He was in the habit of regulating its rate of drifting—on the good old plan—by throwing out a stone attached to a rope made fast to one of the thwarts. An Islay and "very Hielan" keeper borrowed the boat one day and duly prepared his sea anchor. Instead, however, of fastening the rope to the thwart, he made it fast to his foot. As he subsequently upset the boat in the middle of the loch my reference to a comedy that might have ended and nearly did end in a tragedy will readily be understood. As most of us have more sense than to commit *de facto* suicide after the manner of this sapient Highland keeper, collapsible boats, if not wholly desirable, nevertheless have their occasional uses.

Though we may land many trout in a river—and even in a loch when angling from the shore—without a landing net, it seems scarcely necessary to point out that in boat fishing a net is an indispensable adjunct. It is true that I have heard of a certain Colonsay keeper who had the knack of lifting trout of a pound and a pound and a half into the boat by a careful, but unconscious study of the laws of kinetics and resultant forces, but as I never met this wonderful Celt and only heard of his method "second hand," the landing net so far as the loch fisher from a boat is concerned, may still be suffered to hold an honoured place in the catalogue of fishing requisites. It is a much more important adjunct than one might, on a cursory consideration of its status suppose. There are landing nets and landing nets. Some nets are only fit to catch minnows, and many are only adapted for the pursuit of the butterfly. Cheap nets are, moreover, an abomination, though there are some nets which unite utility with little cost. On the whole, however, if the angler be wise he will avoid the false economy of purchasing cheap goods as carefully as he must avoid using too small a net in loch fishing. In the first place every loch holds the possibility of a monster fish, and may not only be a very Triton amongst the minnows, but may also be lost by being asked to finish his days by slipping into a net several sizes too small for his dignified, venerable, and portly person. That there are such giants even in lochs holding, as a rule, only small trout, experience is ever showing, and, amongst many examples which could be quoted, the one which occurs to me most readily was the capture of a trout of nearly 9lb in weight in a loch where his brothers ran as a rule about 2oz and were, no doubt, made painfully aware of the fact when Goliath was out on a cannibalistic cruise.

In the second place a big net is just as serviceable for little fish as, for large, and, moreover, can be used for all purposes from salmon fishing down to tarn fishing. Since one really good landing net can thus be utilized for many purposes, it is obviously the part of the economic man to provide himself with an all round article of this description. In the third place cheap nets do not endure long; most of them are apt to shrink; many of them are not made of strong material but are easily torn, while the rings with which they are adorned are usually of poor metal and so contrived as to their joints that the careless hand of a gillie or the well-meaning hand of a servant —her ignorance wins her this saving grace of distinction—can break them in two. Finally most cheap landing nets do not fold themselves away in such a small space as do the dearer and in every way better quality of nets. A landing net for loch fishing should be deep and made of non-shrinkable material; it should be at least of what is called grilse-size and their is no objection to it being salmon size, while it should be fitted to a very long handle, as long a handle as is used by some roach fishers. The handle cannot be too strong, but it should not at the same time be too heavy, for reasons which I shall state when dealing with the landing of fish, but which may here be summarised into the dogma "the angler must land all his own fish, big and little." I should perhaps hesitate to recommend any particular type of net, made by those very ingenious gentlemen, the fishing tackle manu-facturers, who have not only responded with marvellous technical skill to the advance in scientific angling, marking the past decade, but have also as practical anglers turned their own experiences on the river to such profitable account that they have been largely responsible for the very advance to which I have referred. Palmam qui meruit ferat and if I did not think that the landing net, called by Messrs. Hardy Bros., of Alnwick, the "Collapsing," was the best net for loch-fishing on the market I should hesitate to say so. The curious part of the matter is that this net is not intended specially for loch-fishing, but I have found it so admirably adapted for that purpose, possessing, as it does, all the qualities that make for greatness in a net, that I have no hesitation in awarding it pride of place amongst the various landing nets at present obtainable. One of its leading features, apart from the qualities already enumerated, is the leather thong which unites its two extremities and holds the net in position. Fish I find slip over this into the net with great ease, while the possibility, always present in nets with metal rims, of broken barbs is practically avoided not only by the small surface presented by the thong, but also by the sides being made of wood. For many years I used a net which I had specially made that was simply, so far as its ring was concerned, a mere barrel ring fitted with a net. It had sharp edges, and as such nets are still on the market and are excellent in every respect save in so far as they cut and fray the gut, their use is not advisable. I have dwelt at length upon the landing net, because it is one of those adjuncts apt to be dismissed as of very secondary importance, whereas, on the contrary, it is to the loch-fisher a part of his equipment of such paramount importance that it often makes all the difference between a good day and a bad day. This difference as I interpret it, does not consist in the number of fish slain, absolutely considered, but in the number of fish killed relatively to the opportunities offered and the difficulties overcome.

If fish are lost that should have been killed, simply because the angler uses an unsuitable net, then he has a bad day if he slays hecatombs of fish; if, on the other hand, he kills only a few fish, and "has to fish" for them and does not lose them through, inter alia, using an indifferent landing net, then he has a good day, though he has only half a dozen fish to show as the spoil of his labourious but ever instructive and pleasurable hours on the lake.

With waders, baskets and other impedimenta of that nature, the writer on loch fishing has no concern. To speak of them would be wholly irrelevant, for the boat once you are in it, is, so to speak, a fortress and not an army on the march. It is, of course, true that in the case of the loch fisher who angles from the shore, basket, waders, &c., are of the same importance as they are to the river fisher, but that very fact excludes their discussion as subjects not special to the lake.

I pass, therefore, to the great and vexed question of the proper rod to use in loch fishing for trout, as distinct from the rod to use for salmon and sea-trout in boat angling. In treating of the rod, I can, of course, only condescend upon generalisations and lay down certain rules which experience has suggested ; between the limitations these rules suggest the angler can, of course, please himself, for it is axiomatic that use is everything in a rod, and that the dictates of what appears to be the custom are on the last analysis, really the declaratory laws of individual strength, whether that strength is expended in casting, striking, playing, or landing, and exemplifies mere muscular endurance of wrist and back, a lack of scientific delicacy of touch in handling, or, an intuitive appreciation or otherwise of the proper application of the vis major both in time and circumstance. One might, on this subject, wax extremely learned if not obscure, by pointing out that the choice of a rod necessitates as great a regard being had to the psychological as to the physical differences in anglers, since it is obvious that the impatient angler who lacks self-restraint and is ever keen to be " into a fish " in the angling sense and not after the fashion of Jonah, must have a different kind of rod, and indeed different gear generally, to the self-contained angler whose deliberate actions are all based on the principle that the consummation of angling art is to extract the last " foot ounce " of strength out of the gear at his disposal. It is equally clear that the strong man, if he be also the skilful man, can use a heavier weapon with greater ease than the man of weak wrist and frame that cannot endure laborious hours. To discuss these problems would obviously be not to generalise but to particularize, and hence I avoid the debatable aspect of the rod question, by laying down the rule that no angler, whatever his strength or weakness, physical or mental or both, is or can be justified in using any but a light single-handed rod of a maximum length of 12 and a minimum length of 9 ft. 6 in. for loch fishing for trout with the fly. It is, of course, but natural that loch fishers, following the march of angling as a progressive science daily imposing higher standards of sportsmanship on its votaries, by rendering the use of gear proportionate to the size of the quarry, and of lures that by reason of their imitative character are necessarily instructive

lessons in the life of river and lake, part of the unwritten constitution of
its code of honour between man and trout, should some years ago have
abandoned the use of those ponderous weapons which most of our
angling fathers used, and which, by their power, rendered the playing
of a pound fish no sport at all, and by their sullen irresponsive stiffness
compelled the use of tackle fit to drag Leviathan himself from the
deep. Yet there is nothing more remarkable in the history of angling
than the rapidity with which this reform was accomplished, unless
indeed it be the stubborn conservatism of purpose with which certain
of the older school of anglers continued to use those mighty two-handed
weapons between which and the graceful single-handed rods of to-day
there is the same difference, whether in strength, bulk for bulk, or in
skill in use, as there is between the two-handed sword of Wallace and
the keenest scimitar that ever called Damascus its birth place or the finest
single rapier that ever flashed back the lightning of personal war in the
hands of a master of fence.

Even my young recollection extending over an "intelligent" period
of more than 30 years has not to strain itself unduly to remember the
"other" days, and remember them too with reverence, for the old dogs,
if they refused, more suo, to learn new tricks, were wonderfully skilful
manipulators of the ponderous weapons with which use and wont, conjoined with the bliss of ignorance, had made them familiar. Probably the
loch-trout of these days were fish of simpler faith, with less keen sensational powers of discrimination; possibly they were actuated by a
sense of chivalry and suited their latter end to the circumstances
of the hour. In any case there is no doubt that they were killed,
and killed too in a style which, according to the lights of that ruder
angling age, was considered in keeping with the standard of sportsmanship.

As Poquelin's doctor changed the position of the heart, so we have
changed the standard, and it is part of the code of angling honour to
use weapons and gear directly proportionate in size and strength to the
quarry to be captured. By this reform we have gained far more than
we have lost, for we have made sport assured by acknowledging the sense
of proportion just indicated. Nay more. We have turned a toil into
a pleasure, for it is possible with the rods of to-day, not only to kill fish
that our fathers would have looked at in helpless despair, the while they

M

whistled for a breeze with the fervour of the sailor who prayed to Saint
Antonio, but also to take such a joy in the mere act of casting, in
watching the graceful sweep of the lissome rod, the gossamer curve from
the wrist-delivered under cast with which the flies and gut ascending
high fall as gently as the snowflake on the river, that the mere killing of
fish becomes an accessory and not a necessity.   It is true that the old
angling Adam, that best heritage of the flood, does sometimes cry aloud
for blood, but as a rule, thanks to our modern appliances and the
scientific longings that gave them birth—that acquired appreciation of the
wisdom of adapting ourselves to the conditions and not waiting for the
conditions to alter until they suit our purpose and render its accomplishment an easy task—it never happens in practical loch fishing that the
circumstances are such as to render the taking of fish an impossible feat.
The methods whereby all conditions can be made the slavish ministers
of our will, do not fall within the scope of the present subject, for the art
of casting with a rod in a loch is obviously a different thing from the
choice of a rod to use.   At the same time, the value in use, to quote an
economic phrase, of a rod will naturally wholly depend upon its all
round excellence—its power that is to say not only to throw a line far
and fine, but to get one out in a strong wind, when working up against
the wind.   It is obvious also that a thoroughly good loch-rod must
have considerable holding power and in a word must possess most of the
all-round qualifications that go to make up a good rod no matter what
sort of fly-fishing may be indulged in.

So far as length is concerned for general loch trouting I have but
little hesitation, taking all the circumstances into consideration, and the
possibilities of giants, in fixing eleven feet, as the best length of rod for
loch fishing for trout.   At present I use a Hardy " Hotspur " which is
the best rod at the price I know.   At the same time all our better-
known rod-makers, such as Foster, of Ashbourne, whose steel-ribbed
rods make, I gather from the experience of friends, admirable loch-rods,
uniting power with delicacy, Burrow of Preston, Cummins of Auckland,
and amongst Scottish builders, Robertson, of Glasgow, turn out rods
for loch fishing that leave but little, if anything, to be desired.*   Rods

*Amongst other Scottish rod-makers the name of R. Anderson & Sons of Edinburgh
deserves honourable mention.   The Messrs. Anderson and Mr. Robertson are experienced
loch fishers and know exactly the sort of weapon required.   It may here be explained that
a twelve foot rod possessing the necessary qualifications—lightness and strength—is the

are a lottery and though cheap rods are as a rule to be avoided, yet occasionally one picks up a weapon cheap that proves in use to be as good and faithful a servant as the highest priced rods. I had such a rod in use for many years. It was an American built cane and though I killed with it among other fish upwards of 80 trout between 2¼lbs. and 10lbs., it was as good a rod when the last fish was landed as it was when it received its baptism of fire on a big day when 85½lbs. of sea-trout yielded themselves victims of its prowess.* The rod may, there-fore, under the generalisation already indicated be left to the discretion of the angler, though I would offer this advice to all those who lack confidence in their own discretion or are bewildered by the plethora of choice. In the first place, your rod must not exceed your powers of endurance, since continuous casting is the first essential in successful loch fishing. In the second place go to a good maker, trust him and do not grudge the initial expense, for a good rod should last a good angler all his days, even until the "night cometh" when no man may angle but when all hope still to pursue that pastime of the immortals.

Finally there remains the reel and those important adjuncts casts and flies. The last of these three subjects and to a certain extent the second I am dealing with separately, but the first may be summarily dismissed. Precisely the same individul pecularities in the angler, the degree that is to say with which he uses vis major, must be recognized as are recognized in the choice of a rod, under the proviso always that rod and reel must balance and be otherwise proportioned the one to the other. The two essentials therefore in reels for loch fishing are the balance and the check. As to the latter, sudden and unexpected rises are of frequent occurrence in certain kinds of loch fishing, and in many cases they lead to quick and forcible striking, which again often results in a breakage or a break away. Now, though I shall revert to this

best all-round rod, since it is unnecessary then to use a different rod for brown and sea-trout and the risk of loss of skill, which the change for a time inevitably entails, is thereby avoided. I have never used the "Hotspur" (11 feet) for big fish in weedy water, but in 12 days killed with it, inter alia, 93 trout from 1½ to 2¾lb., securing every fish risen on six of the days in water in which reeds and weeds both occur.

* I never had occasion to use the second top of this rod, which owed some of its power to the fact that I had one of Robertson's (Glasgow) patent steel rod-tips added to it—a most excellent contrivance ; it adds to the casting and holding power of a rod to a marvellous degree. The rod in question killed in my hands 456 sea-trout, weighing 628¼lb. ; 789 brown trout, weighing 454¼lb. ; and was, as stated, as good a weapon after landing these fish as when I made my first cast with it.

matter, yet it may be pointed out that the proper way to strike, if one must strike at all, varies with the angler. If he is self-controlled, deliberate and cool, he should not strike from the reel, but should keep the line fixed with his forefinger and strike from the point of pressure. A "hard-striker," on the other hand, should strike from the reel, which should therefore, in his case, be a reel of easy-running action—such an one, in fact, as is used in "dapping" in lochs with the natural fly. A stiff winch should always be avoided, while the ideal and scientifically correct reel is a happy medium between the two.

Forty yards of line is quite enough for loch fishing from a boat, whether for brown or sea-trout, however large the fish. The reason for this I will state when speaking of playing the fish and enlarging upon my method of doing so.

I do not presume to offer any advice on the subject of lines, but will content myself with saying that while lines for loch fishing may vary in "size" with the strength of the wind and the height of the wave, yet the angler should always have at his command a line suited for the finest class of fly fishing and adapted for use during those periods of dead calm and bright sunshine, when loch-fishing yields its highest joys and becomes, in the truest sense, a branch of scientific fly fishing.

It is obvious from certain *obiter dicta* as well as from the whole tenour of all that has been already said, that I regard the observance of proportion between quarry and gear as not only the criterion by which the sportsmanlike angler is to be judged, but also the standard by which his skill is to be estimated, his pleasure is to be measured,* and his success apportioned. There are, however, in loch fishing certain circumstances, to wit, the conditions of wind and wave, and the strength or weakness of the light, which must be regarded as modifying to some extent the application of this general rule. A fair fishing ripple is precisely the same to the average loch fisher as a properly coloured water is to the average wet-fly fisher in a river, while a whole gale and in some instances a dirty loch—the two conditions are in some lochs invariably, and in others occasionally, conjoined—may be taken to correspond to the conditions prevailing in a river in full, but

---

*I have amongst my happiest memories, a fight on a ten foot greenheart, made by Robertson of Glasgow, which endured for about 15 minutes and led me over a mile of storm-tossed water. The fish was a 6½lb. sea-trout.

not unfishable flood. It is the custom of some anglers, having regard to these varied conditions, to lay down the rule that the strength or stoutness of the gut should vary with the amount of wind and wave and the discoloured state of loch. Exceptis excipiendis I accept the rule, which is one, I find by reference, that I have myself laid down in different articles dealing with this very subject. The exceptions referred to are important. The first and, perhaps, the chief, is that the moment the observation of this rule panders to the fear of the fish certain anglers show, and whenever and as soon as it sacrifices the principle of proportion, on which I have already laid so much stress, it should be thrown down the very wind that gave it plausible birth, and on the other hand, when the strength of the wind renders the playing and landing of fish more difficult or necessitates harder, wilder, or more frequent striking, to the degree that it does or appears to do so, and to that degree only is an angler justified in increasing the strength of his tackle. By observing this rule within a rule he preserves that principle of proportion on which, under easy angling conditions, the claim of loch fishing to be a branch of scientific fly-fishing rests.* There are, it is true,'circumstances under which one is justified in throwing morality to the winds, and in adopting a thorough-going utilitarianism. We may desire to kill a great bag of fish, or we may desire to kill a few fish quickly, say during a short rise on a difficult day, or on the last day of one of those all too short angling holidays which are the oases in the desert of work-a-day life that is not wholly eye-wearying. On the same principle we could, however, use an "otter" or a net, or even condescend to the lowest of angling Infernos and troll with the minnow. I consequently hold that it is best to adhere strictly to the rule of proportion without any right or left hand deflections from the straight path, and to fish with tackle varying in fineness with the size of the fish, and with his natural allies that lurk beneath and above the water such as tall reeds, sunken roots and kindred foes of the angler and friends of the fish. These, of course, have their uses. They add to the difficulties, and, from the sporting point of view, increase the charms of any lake. A similar exception might also be made in the case of lakes holding large fish. The finer the tackle one uses the better is the

---

* Personally, I use an × fine Hercules cast, and this quality of gut is the proper quality both on moral and expedient grounds.

chance of success, while it is obviously a greater triumph and is assuredly a greater pleasure to give the fish the advantage and make up by skill, what one has sacrificed in strength. I deal with the question of flies in seperate chapters, but as part of the angler's outfit I may recommend the "Stuart" tackle box—figured at the end of this chapter—made by Mr. W. Robertson of Glasgow. It holds sufficient tackle for a month's fishing, and is, in every way, a most convenient receptacle. If made of a horse-shoe shape, its excellence would, however, be considerably increased, as its only present defects are its rather sharp edges and slightly inconvenient shape otherwise.

It will also be observed that I have omitted all mention of that important functionary the gillie or boatmen. I have done so of set purpose. Many gillies, if questioned as to the most important item in the loch fisher's outfit, would answer in stentorian tones of emphatic assurance "the gillie." Nor would they blow their loud-voiced trumpet without just cause. The gillie is a factor of such immense importance that I devote a seperate chapter to a description of the general merits he should possess, to detailing some of his peculiarities by personal reminiscences of individual gillies, and to demonstrating generally his power as the autocrat of the lake, to make or mar sport for those who, North of the Tweed at least, never are the boatman's patrons.

THE "STUART" TACKLE BOX.

CHAPTER XVI.

The Virtues and Vices of Gilliedom.

A weird land, that is usually wind-vexed, given over to the hush and silence of a deep calm; overhead a blue sky with only a faint line of saffron clouds, where the eye bids farewell to the ocean, and sea and sky are one; at our feet the loch, its smooth surface reflecting the grey hills, patched with heather, that rise all round its rocky shores, innocent of ripple from side to side for even the leaping trout to-day lies still; on every hand rock and the gleaming waters of a thousand tarns; over all the hushed silence of heat-worn nature, broken only by the occasional hoarse croak of a raven far up amongst the cliffs of a scathed ben, at once the monarch and senior of them all. The lowing of the calves, pent in the fold out in the field by the machar land, no longer comes in plaintive petition on our ears, for their mothers are resting up the loch side among the boulders; to sight and smell they are alike lost, and the calfish mind is oppressed and the long drawn "luig" is silent on the hillside. Even the insatiable lambs, with their constant crying after wandering dams—that libellous bleating which so unjustly reflects on the maternal instincts of sheep—is to-day stilled; while the honk of the geese on the seaboard, which in its crude harshness so aptly suggests at once their vigilance and veteran toughness, startles not the ear. Silence and quiet rest on all things, save for the hoarse challenge of the raven, and the thunder of old ocean on a western beach.

. . . .

In all its length the lake lay wind-vexed, its waters tempest tossed into mighty waves for so small a sea, in which the somewhat frail and unseaworthy craft in which we had braved the perils of the deep seemed in dire danger of being engulfed, while across it there tore in mad fury a winter gale, with clouds of flying spindrift here traversing it with the hissing rage of hail, there twisting and twirling in spiral form like an aerial maelstrom under the fierce squalls of cyclonic strength that ever and anon burst with threefold force from the glens. Overhead the

grey storm-clouds drove in angry chase with rifts between their torn and
ragged edges through which a greeny-blue sky looked coldly down;
the great hills white to their far summits, save where a rock showed
swart or a mountain torrent wound its snake-like length down their sides,
now stood out in dazzling brilliancy as the clouds lifted, and their
peaks cleared, now loomed ghostly white through the veil of flying
snow, and anon vanished in the greyness of some fiercer and darker storm
cloud that wrapped them round; to its far shore, which showed a line
of twisted black, where the snow lay not, stretched the lake, a dull cold
grey with patches here and there of colder blue, everywhere flecked
with white, marking where the waves roared towards the rocky shores.

.   .   .   .

When you have looked on these varied pictures and realised the
angling conditions they imply you will at once admit without parley the
importance of the gillie, not only as a stout ally who must pull at the
straining oar when the wind "doth speak aloud," but as the friend that
must share with you the companionship of nature, your comrade at
once in the stricken fields of elemental war and the piping times of
peace when nature sleeps and her noisy forces rest with her.

In the former character a gillie of steady sobriety, that yet does not
scorn the "cheerers" when the blood of John Barleycorn is shed at its
proper season wisely and well, a man of stout frame inured to each dire
inclemency, a William of Deloraine of the lake to whom July's pride
and December's snow are alike, he is as necessary to your sport as rod
and tackle and the lake itself.   Scotland rears many such men, who can
row from morning to evening, who in all their actions in a boat display
that steady skill, that enduring physicalism which only a healthy life
and a diet of oatmeal can give.   On the other hand the hills of the
North look down on cocks of a very different feather, that are only good
boatmen in the tap-room, when inspiring bold John Barleycorn has made
them in their own fancy what they might be in reality, but men on the
lake to whom angling spells whisky, a foolish generation and as feeble
as fain.   Happily the days of these drouthy "die-hards" appear to be
numbered, though not a few still exist, the scorn of the fate which they
have so often tempted.   In such a gale on a loch as I have described
they are worse than useless and positive Jonahs—not a source of strength
and security, but of weakness and danger.

Nor on the social side of the question which the other picture presents do they shine with any greater splendour.   Their ideas, angling and otherwise, are narrowed to the compass of a single thought and with them custom has become such a second nature, that, enshrouded as they are in an impenetrable conservatism rendered the more tenacious of its effete notions by the mist of whisky through which all reforms and all ameliorations in methods are viewed, they regard all departures from the time-honoured lazy, traditional, non-reflective methods of loch fishing as invasions of their rights justifying surly service, as burdens not to be endured without special reward, golden and liquid, and as in themselves a ridiculous waste of time and energy which might be much more profitably employed.

Contrast these creations of the pint-pot and a lazy life, these longshoremen of our inland seas, with the alert and keen Celt in his primitive simplicity—at once a child, a gentleman and a student of nature with a mind as healthy as his body, poetic as the child of nature must be, simple yet profound in all his thoughts of the Great Mother, simple because he has none of the acquired knowledge that is dangerous, profound because he has drunk deep of the purest spring with the thirst of a commoner of the larger air, a gentleman, because in him respect for others and self-respect strike the golden mean,—these are the qualities that make for greatness in a gillie, not merely as a companion when angling is a serious business, but when the rod is laid aside and fishing gives way to musing on the death of kings.   Gillies of this ideal type are by no means uncommon.   When found they should be bound to the finder by ties of personal regard and a community of interest, not merely in the pursuit of fish, but in the world of wondrous mystery and mighty thoughts that lies within the compass of the smallest lake.

Such gillies, and my old friend and companion Neil Campbell, of South Uist, is typical of the class, are not merely good servants in the angling sense; they are men worth knowing and worth studying, who unite in themselves a readiness to learn, a keenness that is catching, with the power, by the very charm and quaintness of their thoughts and language, of turning a good day into a bad, and of keeping "the heart aboon" when it is sorely tempted to let the pessimism of unrewarded effort hold it in bondage and the stubborn sulkiness of unrequited zeal take the place of patient hope.   And if they have this social quality

which Dugald Dalgetty thought a good trait in a horse, they have also
that sense of discipline and of training which enables them, on the one
hand, to obey orders with unquestioning implicit fidelity, and on the
other to act in an emergency, when no order is issued, with that clearness of judgment and cool self-control which drilled experience of the
hurly-burly of fishing battle confers. Many gillies that are men of
sober life and robust frames still lack the brain of ice that can think
or act in an emergency for itself and seem devoid of the intuitive knack
—which may be cultivated—of always doing the right thing at the right
moment. They lose their heads in crises and though obedient and
willing in all save the supreme moments, yet fail when the desperate
issue between the mighty opposites hangs in the balance. A momentary
loss of head, of confusion of ideas in a desperate pass, when the fate of
a battle between man and fish hangs in the balance and a stroke of the
right oar instead of the left may mean the yielding to the fish a position
of strategic importance that can or may never be re-won, is obviously a
fatal defect in a gillie which is probably natural and can only be driven
out by the mind-strengthening force of education.

When I come to deal with the actual fishing of a loch, with the raising, hooking, playing and landing of fish, for the gillie though he should
not use the net, nevertheless plays an important part in the final death-
scene, what I have said on the qualities of good and the characteristics
of bad gillies will have a deeper significance than it appears to possess
when read only by itself.

I cannot, however, leave such an important factor in successful loch
fishing without expressing in more concise and possibly in clearer
language the imperative necessity of securing the services of a man
possessing as many of the good qualities enumerated as your varying
field of choice permits of. A gillie that is willing to work and to do
as he is told and does not assume the position of mentor, critic and
dictator is obviously on practical grounds the sort of gillie who will
enable you not only to put your best mechanical skill in practice, but
also to exercise that intelligence in all you do which is the essence of
good tactics in angling war and one of its chief joys as the contemplative
recreation of the man of action with a keen and alertly opportune eye.

A gillie who is sober and reliable, of stout physical frame and as
skilful as he is strong, is obviously the kind of man one should search

ffor with a keen eye, and when found bind to oneself with the bonds
of mutual interest.

Finally in selecting a gillie you must study the man as well as the
machine, the mind as well as the body. A surly or stupid, or lazy, or
drunken gillie will, if you once choose him be as surely your enforced
companion in what will prove durance vile even on good and a very
iinferno on bad days, as will the cheerful, intelligent, willing and steady
gillie be your comrade alike when you are under the feet of fortune or
the very button on her cap. Such men are the unpaid jesters as well
as the paid feudal retainers of the over-lord of the lake. Their quaint
conceits, the play of their untutored fancy, their optimism, the inspiration of their experience, their stories of mighty deeds done, of great battles fought in the water off the very rocks beside which your flies are
ffalling, some legend of a great fish that ranged the shore under those
very boughs, by these and other charms they ensure success by the
renewing of the hope that sustains effort.

Their obedience to orders, their power to think and act for themselves, only when silence gives consent, and even to cover a blunder
render them allies of the very first importance and certainly warrant,
when united with the other attributes detailed, the assumption by the
gillie of that pride of place which the only intelligent and self-willed
portion of the angler's auxiliaries, that can make or mar his success, is
entitled to occupy. Example is ever better than precept, facts than
theories, just as wisdom is never taught by the penalties paid for impersonal folly. I, therefore, quote some instances of the practical effects
following the attendance of good and bad gillies.

My first sample of the degenerate boatman was a native of and
dweller in the sporting county of Perth. He was a fine type of his class,
and was, I may say, engaged in a Dutch market, for he happened to be
the only available man in the district on the day on which I enjoyed the
privilege of his advice and manual services. He was in appearance a
sort of Andrew Fairservice, and he had all that worthy's superiority of
manner and none of his mother wit. He had to be primed with two
stiff cheerers before he would consent "to gang," and he had also to
be provisioned otherwise "with a bottle." He objected to walking to
the loch and dropped broad hints about "most gentlemen driving."
Finally in great ill-temper he set forth, and we reached the lake. He

had, however, taken sundry nips en route and by the time we were
afloat his ancient brain was out on a loch of its own—floating about in
whisky. He kept up a constant chatter of drivelling nonsense, and
passed through all the stages from familiarity to respectful love, and
from obsequiousness which did not fit him to an assertion of independence that became him even worse. As a result fishing was at a discount,
and when finally he tumbled overboard with a splash* that awakened
the sleeping echoes, I had very serious doubts as to my proper duty
under the circumstances. Fate had clearly indicated her will; it was
but retributive justice that the trout should pick his bones; on the
other hand, death in a Highland lake was too noble an end for this
product of civilisation. I, therefore, took my revenge by saving him
from the fate of a Celtic Clarence. He went ashore after drinking the
rest of his bottle a wetter but not a wiser man, and rolled home down
the road like a whisky and water cart. Comment on such a case is
superfluous.

My second example was also a native of the same county. He was not
quite such a venerable physical ruin as the first, but he was an even
more seasoned toper in a special sense. He drank all the whisky he
could come by in summer because it was hot, in winter because it was
cold; in spring because it was alternately hot and cold, and in autumn
because the corn was ripe and bread and brandy were alliterative cousins.
My experience of him began and ended in the winter solstice of the bottle, and extended over two days. His voice first broke in on my ear
from the taproom where he was waxing eloquent under the influence of
his second "morning" and proclaiming himself a sort of Highland
cousins of Grace Darling and Isaac Walton rolled into one. As the
courage inspired by these morning cups evaporated in the course of
our drive to the loch, his eye never left the luncheon basket, and his
fears rose as his spirits—natural and acquired—fell.

Finally when we emerged from the shelter of a friendly wood at the
foot of the loch and wild stormy grey clouds came rushing up on the
wind, a thick snow shower obliterated the hills, and reached us with

---

* The manner of happening was this. Our worthy had, with a bland smile, suffered
the boat to drift too close to a wall built sheer from the loch side and rising above deep
water. He rose to shove off, but, unfortunately, placed the oar in a crevice of the *other*
wall. The rest was, more or less, silence.

blinding force, he boldly declared that it was " unco' cold " and dived into the basket.   He annexed his bottle and by the time the storm had
cleared was sufficiently restored to draw my attention to the glorious
sight the loch presented.   The great hills on either shore were white
to their far summits, save where here and there some steep rock, on
which the snow could not lie, showed swart against the white; above
storm clouds were scudding before the wind, while away in the distance
another shower was gathering to the attack.   At our feet lay the lake,
its calmer portions a dull greyish black against the white, with a fringe
of dark shore on the lee side, its stormier portions a mass of foaming
waters, with waves crested as white as the snow that lay around, and
the spindrift whirling across it with a demoniacal glee, as if the spirit
of the storm were in the hissing spray.   While, however, I was drinking
in the majestic, this untutored child of nature was busy imbibing
" Mountain dew " with the result that when we did get afloat, we were
speedily reduced to the condition of a mere runner before the gale,
the while our Highland Bacchanalian sang snatches of song.   In the
end I had to put him ashore with a ten mile walk home before him
that may have made him slightly sober.

My share in the day's work was a stern row back to the
starting point and my spoil was nil.   He turned up next day smiling and
was engaged of malice afore-thought, for it is not constructive murder
in the legal sense to suffer a drunken boatman to cease to exist—on
Sir John Ramorny's plan—by the temptation he affords fate.   It was a
bleak day that had dawned grey and cold and damp.   The rude wind
still howled and tore with mad fury over hill and dale, but it no longer
carried snow on its rushing wings, but something infinitely worse—sleet.
It seemed the height of winter-end madness to venture forth on such a
day, but I was inured to " each dire inclemency," and revenge is sweet.
The horse, as we drove up to the lake, seemed to regard me as the
Rev. Bide-the-Bent did Capt. Craigengelt, as past praying for, and
ploughed along without any head shaking, but with that swinging motion
which horses adopt when facing a storm.   The loch we found more
stormy than ever; the prospect was even more cheerless than the day
before; there was no longer the grand vista of water and the hills tower-
ing in white majesty; the landscape was blurred and indistinct; there
was nothing but mist, grey clouds, cheerless water, and the sleet-laden

air. But my friend had a cure for pessimism. He had "gotten a job,"
and with it credit and a bottle of the biggest belly possible. He was
suffered to "gang his ain gait," and as he was more interested in
whisky than in loch water, when he was sufficiently "glorious" he was
again deposited some miles from hame which he did not reach until the
next morning. He was effectively cured for some little time and if he
ever again passed from the condition of ebriolus or half seas over to that
of ebrius or as drunk as the Baltic, it was not because I failed to make
him a homeless inebriate, in a sense not intended by the Act.

My next experience of this class of boatmen was, I regret to say, on
Loch Leven. I arrived by the loch side on a glorious August evening
—one of those nights which are inspirations, when the splendours of
the dying day defy description. There was that hush over nature which
shows a response of all her parts to the mood of the whole. The lake
itself was glassy calm, but I secured a boat and began fishing. It was
only, however, when I suggested to my boatmen the possibility of
catching fish by casting over the "odd" trout that were rising here and
there that I discovered their glorified condition. They had, it would
appear, consumed their allowance, and if they had not supplemented
it, it must have been a liberal one. They maintained—possibly under
the spur of a thirst which only the loch could in the meantime quench—
that to fish under such circumstances was absurd, and clenched their
arguments with so many surly and uncomplimentary criticisms—but
thinly veiled—that fishing was almost hopeless. I did kill four or five
trout, but might have killed many more had the knights of the oar not
had their thoughts fixed on the tap-room. I refrain from further comment, though I drew down on myself glances of scorn by sternly order-
ing one of the men to put down my rod—a favourite one—which he
had taken up for a cast as if he and not I were the angler and owner.
I record this instance with regret, but it is an undoubted fact that on
too many Scottish lochs the joy of angling is marred by experiences
such as I have described.

Of a different type, but still a bad type is the autocratic, dictatory
boatman, given to laying down the law, simply because most of his
customers—one dare not use the word patron North of the Tweed—
are content to place themselves in his hands and not only accept, but
seek his advice as to flies, tackle and methods generally. Now the

whole duty of a good boatman is only to offer advice when it is asked, to keep his tongue under control, to obey orders implicitly without questioning or reasoning why, and to develop the bump of locality, and know every nook and cranny, all the lies and holds of fish and the banks and shallows that are not obvious to the eye of even the most experienced of anglers unacquainted with the particular loch on which he follows his interesting and instructive occupation. Now the boatman in my mind's eye, was a very excellent man off the loch at all times, an admirable gillie for a tyro when on it, and most accomplished when he chose to do exactly what he was told to do. He was, however, so accustomed to having his own way and so used to the role of a dominie of the mere, that, on the one hand, he would rarely condescend to do anything save in the way he was used to do it—that is in the easiest way for himself, and, on the other, invariably shouted "There he is," when you rose a fish and gave such irritating directions when playing one, as to render cool and deliberate striking or abstention from it impossible, and proper mastery a hopeless task.*

Such gillies are not irreclaimable. Once gain their respect by a show of skill and they will develop new traits and become, at least when out with you, faithful servants who respect your methods as rational, even if revolutionary, and yield a ready obedience to all your orders. It is, however, a pleasure to turn from the contemplation of such gloomy pictures of the night-side of gilliedom to its brighter aspects as seen through the haec olims of happy memory—of days spent with Highlanders that still preserve the best traits of a race of natural gentlemen and have been tutored in the school of modern practical angling. Such graduates had angling minds that were tabulae rasae when they took their first lessons in the art and being simple " biddable bodies " free from prejudice and totally lacking the wrong sort of self-importance, make as good gillies as they make soldiers. I cite only one case of their prowess. I had been fishing without reward and putting all the wiles at my command in practice and was casting without hope, but still cheerfully, for my companion at the oars, had been answering questions in that quaint way peculiar to the Celtic thinker speaking English in Gaelic idioms, when suddenly by the reeds, and within half a foot of their shelter a giant fish loomed slowly up through the water,.

* The fault of this class of gillie is that they treat all the world as pupils.

and quietly took my fly. Trained to preserve silence even if a kelpie rose
and was hooked, my gillie's prattle ceased. He sat with the silent,
alert look of a disciplined soldier waiting for the word of command before acting. It was a "tight" place but two words were sufficient.
Keeping a steady strain on the fish who hung as big sea-trout will hang
before making his first charge, the boat was round and in the reeds in
a second. The strain was towards the reeds and the fish went out,
clearing their outlying sentinels and no more. What followed was
simple; it was the emergency that showed the man and only three or
four four short, sharp words of command had been uttered. I was
the general and he the army and our intercourse was dropped for the
discipline of angling war with the enemy in touch. Under such circumstances a self-willed, undisciplined, prejudiced, conservative, didactic, disobedient gillie would probably in the first place have startled
me into missing the fish by an impatient strike, or failing that would
have hesitated to act or have disobeyed orders, with the result that
I should have bidden a long farewell in the reeds to greatness, as per-
sonified in that fish.

I need quote no more modern instances; the principle is the same in
all and the result of the application of that principle does not vary.
I cannot, however, leave the Highland gillie without giving some instances of his excellent social qualities as a companion framed to
keep the angling heart from being bowed down. I do so with the
apology to Erse, Cymric, and North of England boatmen contained in
the explanation that if I knew them as well as I know their Gaelic
brethren, no doubt I should chronicle such of their sayings as can
compare with the inimitable quaintness of language with which the
Highland gillie clothes what are the merest commonplaces when robbed
of their "philological kilt."

Before chronicling a few of these quaint sayings I would point out that
the popular belief that humour cannot cross the Tweed in a northerly
direction would be more fully justified by the facts of the case if it
were added that humour cannot cross the Tweed without the border
river absorbing its moisture and leaving it dry. The Scots as a race are
more caustic of tongue than they are of thought, and their wit as something more often thought than expressed—well or ill—does not necessarily indicate their feelings. At the same time its leading charact-

eristic is eminently national in its ironical, and at times, satirical depth, the mere superficiality which distinguishes cockney chaff being as unknown as the blunt down-rightness of Lancashire and Yorkshire is obnoxious to the Scot. Highland humour, however, is a thing apart from Scottish humour, and divides itself into several classes. Highlanders have, in other words, a "cosmopolitan" wit and a native wit, the latter being essentially racial, and for that reason fanciful, since the Celt of all the races that have made the British people of to-day is imaginative and poetic and hence artistic in the best and fullest sense of the phrase. Apart from this peculiar genius which is independent of expression and belongs to the domain of thought before it finds utterance, there are two kinds of Highland humour—as distinguished from wit—or of "funny things" said in the Highlands. One is dependent for its humour on the fact that the idea is conceived in terms of Gaelic idioms and expressed in English; the other is purely adventitious and depends for its laughter-provoking power on the speaker's plentiful lack of knowledge of the English language. Such a form of humour as the last is no doubt displayed by every one struggling to express his thoughts in a language with which he is imperfectly acquainted, but in the Highlander it is more quaint, more characteristic, often more pregnant, and sometimes more dignified—the word is used advisedly—than in any other race with whom I am acquainted.

Some samples of the last kind of humour that have fallen within my observation may best illustrate its efficacy as a factor in the gaiety of nations, particularly those that angle and whose spirits must be kept to the casting point.

Faring across one of the loch-studded islands of the West with a young gillie, since prematurely gathered to his fathers, and now sleeping peacefully with the surge and thunder of ocean on a western beach as his requiem, I pointed to a certain loch, and asked if there was any burn coming out of it. "Na, na," replied the gillie, "there's no burn; there's only a smaal river." This is exquisite when you come to analyse it, and contains a most tempting philological problem on which the ingenious can exercise their leading faculty.

This use of the word "smaal" (Anglice small) suggests yet another peculiar use of the same, which is equally rich and rare. At a certain hotel two gillies were seated side by side at breakfast. They did justice

N

to the good things provided in a style that Dugald Dalgetty or Dandie-Dinmont would have admired. Herrings formed the staple article of their breakfast, and on one of them showing not so much signs of being satisfied as of bashfulness at the extent of his meal, the other thus encouraged him to greater deeds of " herring-do." " Have another herring, Donal, you've only had nine and wan of them waas a smaal one." That " smaal one " is a leviathan when it gets its due.

Still another " smaal " story is worth repeating. Fishing one day with the Neil Campbell I have already mentioned, Neil, who was always keen on what he called " doing funs " in the intervals of bad angling days began to enlarge upon his domestic and financial affairs. " I was buying a sheeps," he said, " from Mr. MacLean the other day, and he waas a very kind man and waas only asking four shillings for it."

" Four shillings!" said I, " why, Neil, what kind of a sheep can you get for four shillings?"

" Well, well," said Neil, it waas not a very big sheeps whatever chust " (and here he cudgelled his brains), " chust as big as a smaal young dog."*

I leave to the anti-vegetarian fancy this problem in the mensuration of puppy mutton.

The same gillie could rise to higher things and yet use the " smaal " idea. Fishing with him one day in a loch from which another loch with two anglers and their gillie in the boat were visible, Neil surprised me by saying with most pithy scorn, " Three mens in a boat and one smaal trout." The explanation of his acquaintance with Jerome's book was simple. The anglers in question had read long extracts from it to him in idle moments, and as the humour was to him incomprehensible, and their baskets small, Neil had conceived a fine Highland scorn not merely of the anglers, but of poor Jerome, who had done nothing to deserve this setting of the heather on fire.

When on the subject of size, it may be mentioned that your Highlander is a bit of a natural philosopher in the ordinary as distinguished

---

* This reply illustrates the truth of Solomon's dictum that "there is no new thing under the sun." Herodius (Book III., cap. cii.) expresses a similar idea. He says—" In the vicinity of this district (Pactycea) there are vast deserts of sand, on which a species of ants is produced *not so large as a dog*, but bigger than a fox." Pliny, it may be mentioned also speaks of these ants, which he says *are of the colour of cats* and as large as the wolves of Egypt. The triple coincidence is curious.

from the applied sense of the phrase. Driving home one day my driver and my gillie began to theorise on the stocks and stones plentifully scattered about. Out of compliment to me—though a Highlander by descent—their remarks were couched in English.

"I'll be thinking," said the driver as we passed a pile of rocks great and small, "that stones will be growing just like other things."

"That's just because they'll not be all being the same size, Kenneth," said the sapient Neil.

"Not at aal," said Kenneth, "it's chust because some will be stoppin' growin' and others will be keepin' on."

"Well," said Neil, "if it was stopping growin' only just look at Ben Koinnich. If I was growing like that I would be chust as big as a mile high, and the Ben's aalways been there." This cogent argument for the presumptive eternity of geology may be presented to Lord Kelvin as a proof that all natural philosophers do not differ from the hammer-wielders.

It will be observed that the humour—if it fully deserves that description—of the foregoing is not wholly unconscious. Perhaps that of the following story is equally dubious. A certain well-known surgeon was thus addressed by a gillie, known as "Red Donald."

"I'll be hearing that you'll be a grate dochtor."

"Well, Donald," replied the amused but gratified chirurgeon, "I make enough at my profession to keep myself."

After a pause Donald continued insinuatingly, "Now I'm sure, dochtor, it will be two chemists shops you'll be having."

"I'm afraid not, I'm afraid not," said the surgeon, hurriedly and a little hurt.

"Dod man you'll get them yet," was the consoling remark of the unabashed Donald who was either unconscionably innocent or equally unconscionably and consciously ironical.

That the gillie can be consciously caustic is illustrated by the following: I once unintentionally touched the racial pride of my gillie by asking innocently why it was that when I had distributed certain small gifts amongst the old women of the parochine, they had invariably used some strange English out of their very slender stock in which the words "goot woman" were the only intelligible phrase. He replied with an excess of politeness, "Waas you wearing your kilt at the time?"

The irony, sarcasm, or satire of this is better understood when one considers that I had implied by innuendo that the venerable ladies were confirmed beggars and had picked up their only English phrase by a series of mildly predatory and usually successful forays on the wives of Lowland farmers in the district, whose presence was more or less resented as a reflection upon the indigenous agriculturists. Its irony is further emphasised by the fact that for some reason or other Highlanders rather despise Highlanders-born, who by the chance of circumstance have either forgotten or can speak but little of their native Gaelic—a predicament in which I happened to stand.

Of a wholly different class of humour are the following stories, which are entirely dependent for that quality upon the adventitious fact that the heroes of them did not know Sassenach.

A certain keeper of one of the Southern Hebrides astonished and wholly disgusted a Southern angler by informing him that "his guts were rotten," but changed his frown of disapproval into a smile "confoundedly loud" by looking up at the sky and declaring that he expected "a shower of milestones." He meant hail stones, and if they had fallen in the Brobdignagian form indicated they would, no doubt, have come in handy as tombstones in a country that combines rockiness with thrift.

It would puzzle a student of idioms to know why a gillie should use a phrase like "What'll I can do now." But there is no doubt about the strength of its despairing inquisitiveness to express the last argument of a keen gillie on a bad day. Equally pregnant was the phrase of a gillie who was travelling "cabin" with a steerage ticket. When requested "to go forr'ad," he said, "I'll go, but I'll no be put." That sums his race up. Of powerful, almost poetical descriptive phrases, the gillie who said of the rise of a salmon, "Mon, he chust came up like a naked man," would be hard to beat, though the following story illustrates this power more amusingly. In describing the playing of a big fish when out with a friend to whom I had "lent" him the previous day, a certain famous gillie used the following original and graphic phrases, "Och man, he first rushed away—oh as far as yon" (pointing to a distant loch) then he came back growlin' like ———— and turnin' the stones over with his nose." The phrases are so magnificently expressive that the man who even thinks of a dog fish in their presence should suffer the fate of Morris and be thrown into a Highland loch with a stone at his heels.

The blank in the foregoing which stands for what the reporter called a " cursory remark " reminds me of a wholly incomprehensible practice of mixing things sacred and most profane in which the gillies of a certain Roman Catholic island of the West indulge in moments of supreme excitement. I was never more surprised in my life than when, during the mighty burst of a great fish far out into a stormy loch in the gathering dusk—a fish that ran straight away from the shore for 100 yards in a piping gale and appeared to be a demon trout—my gillie dancing about on the shore behind me kept shouting " Holy ——" using the most sacred of names and " Holy ——" using the most lewd of expressions in alternate breaths following up both ejaculations with the strangest medley of Gaelic and English, curses and prayers, it has ever been my lot to hear. " Wit " of that kind can be thought and expressed.

Highlanders are not given to making puns and I can recall only one instance, and that a doubtful one, of an apparent pun.

Neil Campbell, already noted, had been out with two anglers who had indulged in a big lunch and a " solemn tankard " as that phrase is understood in gilliedom. " They waas mens," said Neil, " very found for (fond of) their meat and drink, but they waas puttin' too much Angus Stuart in their whuskey. I waas havin' a tartan head every day whatiffer."

Mention of " whatiffer " recalls something that the same gillie said which might have emanated from a much " smarter " source than the gillie is supposed to be. As it also proves that the gillie is, like the Dugal Cratur, not such a fool as " his English " would sometimes make him appear to be, and as many think him who do not know him I will give the story. He had been twitted by a party with whom he was out on the use of the phrase " whatiffer." The party made it appear that he did not use the expression. They further said that it was de rigeur in a gillie and part of his duty to use the phrase to amuse his " patrons," (a Thames phrase, which would not suit the haughty Highlander), adding that the Sutherlandshire gillies never failed to come up to expectations in this respect and to provide " sport " of this kind. Now Neil did habitually and naturally use the phrase and he saw at once that the Sassenach was chaffing the Gael. He said nothing but thought a great deal and avoided the expression, until it slipped out, whereupon he promptly added to the "It was a good fush whatiffer," the saving clause, "as the Sutherlandshire gillies say." It was an undoubted Highland victory. The Sassenachs were fairly beaten at their own game and Culloden became Prestonpans.

These stories from real life may be fitly concluded with an alleged Highlander's prayer for whose authenticity the writer cannot vouch, but which aptly illustrates the Gaelic line of thought. The prayer is said to have run as follows:—"Oh, Lord, send us rivers of whuskey and worlds of snuff and a breat and a cheese as big as a Ben Lomond, and bless the MacIntoshes, the MacPhersons and the Caumills and make them all lords and dukes and to mine ain 'sel be'the glory, Amen." This explains why the angler never kills any fish and why the gillie tells his next customer after he has left you, "I killed a fine fish off that point last week."

Before, however finally dismissing the Highland character I may point out that a great deal has been written since the publication of Stevenson's "Kidnapped," Munro's "John Splendid," and Cobban's "The Angel of the Covenant," on the subject of Scott's conception of it in its various manifestations in high and low life. Possibly the critics who have praised the latter-day painters have in their desire to do them justice done an injustice to the Old Master—the Great Wizard who inspired them. Scott's Highlanders of the "Dugald Cratur" type have been condemned as exaggerations and as mere casual sketches thrown into the canvass with that sublime indifferences which characterises genius when dealing with subjects not calling for its highest efforts or with characters dwarfed by more engrossing figures in the great whole. Yet after all even the "Dugald Cratur" is true to life and is the gillie of to-day as I have attempted to pourtray him and as the English sportsman knows him when he penetrates into the few lone places of the North which the railway has not tinged with its character-destroying cosmopolitanism and reduced to the dull level of the ever-growing plain of life. Your Highlander is a blend of natural courtesy that shades of into the pride of all mountaineers—the pride than can be led not driven, the independence born of living in regions of natural sanctuary, of hospitality that is the product of the indigenous inhospitality of rude rock and barren hill-side, of prompt ire, the hereditary trait of a race who have suffered wrong, the breath of whose nostrils was battle, whose hand was ever on the sword to win back the spoil from the spoiler or take revenge for wrong in a wrath nursed to warmth in the upland solitudes. Yet withal a simple man, steeped in the philosophy of stocks and stones, the poetry that is amongst the lonely hills, the rythm that is in the temptest's breath, the solemn dirge of ocean on a Western beach, the superstition that is nature-born in a land of lone moors and sedgy tarns, given over to the past—a land repeopled by a thousand legends only with the dead and the mysteries of life—the unknowns that are terrible in animal and spiritual existence. Those who know the gillie as he is, know him to be all this—a "Dugald Cratur" in English, a philosopher, poet and man in Gaelic. "The Dugald Cratur" must be judged rather by his deeds than by his words. By that standard he is not a literary creation of a casual kind, but the progenitor of the Highlander of his own class. "John Splendid" and "Allan Breck" are non-existent types. Our interest in them is not a living but an historical interest, when they are viewed in their broadest aspect, and it is very doubtful whether Vich Ian Vohr and the dapper little robber of the Perthshire cave are not truer in some aspects to time and circumstances than are the more recent creations. The critic cannot forget that Rob Roy was scarcely cold in his grave when Scott was born; that he knew men who knew Rob Roy; that the Highlands he described were de facto the Highlands of his day, and that Loch Coruisk, to quote only one example, was the Loch Coruisk of Cormac Doil when Scott invaded its solitudes and drew inspiration from the chief seat of the proud Queen of Wilderness. Scott's style is for the most part so simple and direct that readers in an age in which a certain literary mysticism is supposed to give depth* are rather apt to dismiss some of his less carefully drawn characters as superficial. There could be no more profound error in criticism. It is a safe presumption that Burns will outlive Browning in the great heritage of transmitted thought that is the common poss-ession of all ages, of all men and of all climes, yet Burns, judged by the standard of style, is the most direct and simple of all poets—great phrase-

---

*Scott never committed the fatal error of mistaking Edinburgh schoolboy "English" for the Scotch of the time of Rob Roy. Nor did he confound the confusion of tongues by mistaking a mere oddness of expression for philological and archæological accuracy in dialectical dialogue. If he had done so, "Ivanhoe" would be unintelligible.

maker though he be—whose verse appears on the surface, at least, to appeal only to the feelings, while Browning, ignoring the lessons of the last analysis, seems to appeal to the intellect only, and to those emotions which are metaphysical and are supposed to be at war with " the baser nature," the very aspect of our nature which in the hands of Burns proves that " love is heaven and heaven is love."   So is it with many of the characters of Scott; they are so simple that they appear too natural, and are occasionally, therefore dismissed as unworthy of his genius by reason of an inequality of delineation that exists only in the critic and not in the character.   To me his Highlanders are the Highlanders of to-day, the Highlanders I love and to whom my heart will ever warm, until, to quote the phrase of the great Argyle, " it is cold in death."

CHAPTER XVII.

THE PHILOSOPHY OF THE FLY.

A fly contains the essence of a thousand philosophies. To cover all that it suggests, simple compound as it is of fur and feather, of tinsel and steel, would be to range over the whole field of philosophy, to exhaust physiology, essay the sublime heights of pyschology, run through the whole gamut of human feelings, and preach a thousand sermons that are in running water or hidden in the mysterious bosom of the lake. To the angler a fly epitomises by suggestion every problem that has ever vexed human ingenuity with reference to fish, their modes of life and, if we may dare say so, their habits of thought, since in these later days, there are said to swim in our rivers, and possibly in our lakes, fish that are called educated trout.

It seems strange, but is nevertheless true, that such a matter-of-fact, prosaic congeries of fur, feather, tinsel and steel should in a measure be able to revive the old difference between the Idealistic and Sensational schools. Yet if one considers for a moment what reasoned memory in a fish means, it becomes clear that if a trout is to be credited with the power to discriminate by means of the images of memory, or in other words, by association of ideas between certain flies that are and certain flies that are not imitations of nature, and between certain flies, whether imitations or otherwise of nature, that behave naturally and others that behave unnaturally, the problem of the proper fly and the proper manner of working it, becomes at once a sort of semi-psychological, semi-physiological question of an extremely intricate and interesting kind.

If man, a conscious being, sensible, to use an ignoble word, of his own thoughts and a student who can study himself through himself, is unable to separate his physical appetites from his mental powers, and is not only bewildered as to the origin of sensations proper and thoughts proper, but is even incapable of a dogmatic cataloguing by differentation of each, how can we hope to lay down with any degree of scientific exactness the dividing line between a presupposed mind and an ascertained matter in such a non-responsive, subtle, mysterious, uncompanionable animal as a fish?

No authority, indeed, who recognizes the limitations even of speculative thought, would dare to dogmatise, so far as man is concerned, on the point where knowledge due to sensation ends and that due to man's power of abstract conception and non-sensational acquisitiveness begins. The reader is dependent on his eye, the hearer on his ear, the thinker on knowledge acquired through both these sensational media which bring the raw material to that factory the brain, itself a physical mystery, whether it registers the lowly sensation of a mean appetite gratified, or thinks, in what are vaguely termed moments of inspiration, through all its convolutions of grey matter the thoughts of God Himself. Genius we know is itself not a thing apart from the material home in which it dwells, but is the result of the proper and regular application of brain muscularity to the problems of life, whose solution it translates into the language of art or of literature, or, in fine, into that tongue which commands the senates of the world and of all time. The physical aspect of intelligence or, in other words, the physical conditions which determine brain power cannot be overlooked, whether one discusses its manifestation in a Socrates or a Shakespeare, or in a mammal of the tertiary period, or in a hand-reared or wild trout of to-day turned forth to enjoy or born in the freedom that is the joint heritage of all commoners of water.

If, therefore, we are to judge of intelligence by the size and structure of its physical source, the brain, it is, I am afraid, a sternly sad duty to write that animal the fish down an ass, strictly and literally, and irrespective of the Dogberry vein. This of course is the fish's misfortune, and not his fault, though the Neo-*Imitationists* and ultra-Scientists of the angling world would fain have us believe that "reading and writing" in the troutish sense "are the gift of nature." Nor need one pity the Purist as he lies impaled on the horns of the dilemma to which this attitude necessarily gives birth. The Purist lays down a rule "No trout in certain streams is or should be killed save with the dry fly." The principle, on which the rule permitting the use of the dry fly only rests, is an assumption that the casting of a dry fly is the most difficult

:and, therefore, the most " sportsmanlike " method which the angler can
:adopt. Admitting the accuracy of this assumption, the inevitable
-conclusion is that it is easier and pro tanto less " sportsmanlike " to kill
trout by other methods—wet fly, minnow, worm—than with the dry fly.
If, therefore, educated trout can be more easily killed by methods, ex-
hypothesi, coarser, and requiring less skill, on which horn of the dilemma
will the pharisaical type of Purist choose to rest? Will he admit that
his exclusive rule is a mere arbitrary enactment based on an ascetic
.abtsemiousness savouring in its worst aspect of sophistry, pedantry and
hypocrisy, and when most favourably interpreted, capable of being
·construed into a categorical imperative not justifiable even from the
absolute standpoint and wholly unjustifiable considered relatively to
the feeding habits of the omnivorous trout ? Or will he admit that the
.advantages of education are exaggerated because the education itself is
.an assumption not warranted by the facts of trout-life? If he will
.accept the theory which I am developing he may escape both horns.
If he is prepared to admit that the special topographical environment of
·clear water and the mood of the fish—the result of a specialised or
:temporary condition of environment—creates, in the one case, a
:sensational fear of, and in the other, a sensational aversion to, all flies
which he can present for acceptance, then he sacrifices nothing of that
:skill which the all-round angler is willing to admit that he displays in
placing and floating a fly over a fish in a natural, masterly, and
convincing manner. I will shew in a later chapter that not only do the
loch trout of certain lakes holding large fish " smut," " bulge," " tail,"
and reject flies after "inspection," but also that sea trout, who cannot
be educated, display as much cautious cunning, as much diffidence of
approach, as much apparently reasoned initial doubt and final rejection
of a fly after examination, as the most educated fish that ever gave the
·dry fly man some ground for regarding the Test and other streams of a
:similar character as watery universities.
　　Now it is extremely hard on those writers who are always using that
ill-advised phrase " educated trout " thus to have to deprive them of the
merit of having turned out pupils who do them so much credit ; but
there is no escaping from the physiological truth that,. though water on
the brain is a common enough thing in land animals, much brain in
animals that live in water is absolutely unknown. To speak of the

cunning of a sea serpent would, in fact, be to argue oneself a fit and
proper person to act as historiographer to the Horse Marines, or to fill
the situation of war correspondent to an American paper.   Fish are not
intelligent animals, though they have pronounced habits of sensational
growth founded on their appetites and on what excites those appetites.

I must not, however, be misunderstood when I appear to thus
undervalue the intelligence of fish.   To declare that they are without
reasoning power "after a sort" would be to reduce the fish of the chalk
stream to the level of the fish of a Highland burn, to attribute to the
greedy little fish of some upland tarn, whose shores are rarely trodden
by the foot of man, above whose waters no rod ever flashed back the
sunlight, the same cautious fastidiousness shown by the great trout of
some difficult lake, as the phrase "difficult" is used by the President
of the Transvaal Republic.

That there is some difference must be admitted.   It is, in fact,
impossible to read the many books and articles published on the art of
dry fly-fishing without the conviction being borne in upon one that all
dry flymen believe that the introduction of the dry fly has acted upon
the trout of England as a sort of compulsory education act.   Purists
do not hesitate to give a list of the streams in which the trout are said
to like "their fly cocked" just as if they were speaking of a human
epicure who would only eat trout, if he were wise, after it had been
"green kippered."

The effect of modern methods upon the trout and, indeed, as "Red
Spinner" has suggested, but whether in irony or deadly earnest I am
unable to say, upon the "flies" of to-day has certainly been some such
reductio ad absurdum as I have indicated.   The probability is that the
trout of certain streams have from time immemorial not been specially
easy to take,* and so far as the philosophy of the fly admits of statement
I will here venture to propound what appears to be the truth.

I am not prepared to deny that Master Trout has advanced with the
times in certain waters, but I am quite ready to maintain that the
angler is for him merely an ignotum pro terrible, and that the trout of
much-fished fine waters no more associates the angler's fly with a
known and reasoned danger than does the trout of a stream across
whose virgin waters no rod has ever glanced.   Such a sweeping assertion

* Colonel Hawker only chronicles his successful days on the Test.

is not, of course, intended to be literally interpreted. It merely assumes a position which marks the opposite extreme to the attitude taken up by the "educated trout" school of anglers. Both views, like most extreme opinions, state a half-truth. It is, however, easy to see that the whole question of association of ideas in fish is a difficult problem, since it involves another problem, whose main difficulty is one of definition, the difference, to wit, between what we are pleased to term instinct and what we arbitrarily call reason. I presume that man, even in his highest individual developments in the highest developed races, is a mixture of animal impulses or instincts and rational restraints upon their indulgence, whose equipoise is virtue, the source of all wisdom, of all prudence, of all forethought, which bids him avoid this or that folly on moral as well as material grounds, and which induces him to advise his fellow-creatures, in any particular matter, "to the contrary" or otherwise. This, after all, is the sort of moral utilitarianism which sums philosophy up when it does not dash its hoary old head against those barrier-problems on which finite thought has hurled itself in vain ever since time bridged one of the unfathomable abysses of eternity.

Such a consideration must give us pause, for it necessitates the question : Is it possible to conceive of a fish, whatever be his vexed opportunities of associating things with the ideas they convey, rising above the animal impulse to take what is good under the influence of a reasoned conclusion that the thing taken is bad for him on ascertained and formulated grounds of material damage if he gives way to the natural impulse and animal instinct ?

The school who believe that super-educated trout exist will, however, almost go the length of giving in adherence to such a doctrine as this question answered in the affirmative would imply. They will maintain that no really "educated trout," say the fish of such a stream as the Test, will ever again take the fly as they did in the days of Colonel Hawker, a worthy who seemed able to catch them by the dozen, and even throw a fly from horseback with success. In this they will speak · accurately. When, however, they assert that the reason why the trout in the Test are shy is because they know a wet fly imitation from the real article, and are rationally afraid of a thing they understand and can define and associate with danger, I confess a desire to smile and a yearning to ask why such trout take the deceptive dry fly at all,

admittedly imperfect imitation as it is, if they are so superlatively acute·
and suspicious?

In reality the assertion covers as I have said a half truth, for it is a.
truism of observation that something unusual, the ignotum of the·
proverb, has far more terrors for all animals than what one might term
a natural danger, or one arising through some agency to which they are·
accustomed. The sound sense of such a theory of animal nerves is·
most acceptable and in strange contrast to the difficulty many observers·
feel in bringing themselves to take anyone seriously who attributes to·
the trout a rigid, rational examination of a fly, though it is not hard to·
conceive of a fish being blindly and irrationally afraid of something out.
of the usual about a fly. None of us know what impressions remain
on the tabula rasa of the troutish brain, but they seem nevertheless·
to have some sort of power of association, which appears to be more·
physical than mental, even admitting the materialistic aspect of all
thought when regard is had to the strange relationship of mind and
matter.

Fear of a small unusual thing is perhaps more due to "nerves" than.
to lack of courage. I tried an experiment of this kind with a lion..
The great beast looked at me with majestic calm. I flashed a white·
handkerchief from my pocket, and he gave as startled a leap as the
average old maid on the mention of mice or "firearms." On this·
analogy it has always appeared to me that the putting of a trout down
is due more to nervous excitation than to any actual fear, much less
fear of a rational kind. It is with regret, amounting almost to positive·
aversion to the task, that I feel myself compelled at this point to utter·
a protest against the hypocritical assumption of angling virtue and the·
unwarranted arrogation to themselves of angling superiority in skill and
in knowledge, which certain Purists have of late displayed. This·
hypocrisy and arrogance are so wholly opposed to the latitudinarian
spirit of angling toleration that the Purists referred to have only them-·
selves to blame if such truth as really underlies their contentions, and
the much useful information as to the habits of fish and of their insect
and other food contained in their dogmatic assertions are alike dis-·
regarded by the older school of anglers and dismissed as "new-fangled
and absurd fads." If a more modest and less superior and dogmatic
tone were adopted, I feel assured that the most conservative of anglers.

would give the dicta of even the ultra-Purist his careful consideration with the result that the false being rejected by a process of reasoned elimination, much that is useful and much that is true would be added to the knowledge of fish and their ways that is of common and equal value to both schools of angling thought.

Certain Purists have, however, formed themselves into an exclusive society, in which mutual admiration, hypocrisy, sophistry, pharisaicism, and dispraise of the barbarian are strangely blended with the exercise of mechanical angling skill of the highest kind, a minute and painstaking study of entomology and of the habits, moods and humours of trout *under certain conditions of existence.* This Order has produced a sort of angling aristocracy self-elected to the highest place, but absolutely without a title to that proud eminence whether founded on the right of might or on the special deeds written on the face of difficult waters—deeds which all other free-men under the Great Charter of the angling kingdom would willingly recognize. Everything that is not "the thing" is condemned by the Purist as "stale, flat, and unprofitable," and all anglers who are not members of the society are mere ignorant barbarians, the scoff of the scoffer, the "publicans and sinners" of this new-created world of angling Pharisees that "thank God they are not as these men." Note how some of them treat the "reasoned fear" which I have mentioned, and which led me unwillingly to enter this protest against the usurpation by the oligarchy of all the high places. One of them will tell you how he happened on a small grayling feeding in a clear place on tiny flies of a particular colour. He assumes the "smutting" grayling and narrates how he failed to kill him, not because his skill or his gut were at fault, or because the water was clear and the conditions against the most consummate mechanical precision and power to deceive for doom, but simply because he did not possess a fly of exactly the same colour as the flies on which the grayling was feeding—and this though the difference in the hue must be minimised by the bell of air surrounding the lower portion of the tiniest fly when in the water, and may only be perceptible when the fly is submitted to microscopic examination—two facts to which the same Purist will be certain to draw your attention when desirous of emphasising another phase of his superiority to the ordinary angler. Another of his irritating assumptions of virtue is the affected and hypocritical manner he adopts towards any trout under 3lbs. He pretends to despise all fish under that weight. Now though I own to having no love for small fish and confess that the catching of 100 loch trout running three to 1lb. gives me but little pleasure compared with the joy afforded by the capture of half-a-dozen big fish —whether these are difficult to raise and hook or difficult to play and land, or both—yet it is for me not a matter of congratulation but of the very keenest regret that, having drunk too deeply of the blood of giants, I am grown blasé and have lost a joy of life similar and akin to the sweetest memory of a man's angling career—the memory of those rare nights of excited and exulting anticipation, when we lay awake in the places of youth and listened to the steady pattering fall of rain which promised a spate on the morrow in the burn, and a full creel of small fish with, mayhap, a leviathan, and in moments of the greatest optimism a two-pound sea trout fresh from the sea as the highest top-gallant of expected joy.

Another of the Purist's phases that is widening the breach, is the trait which makes him tell the world that all patterns save his own were rejected by rising fish. He will excuse his failure by declaring that we now "hackle" our flies too heavily, and will make his lack of success a theme for singing the praises of one of the guild and for declaiming on the prodigies of skill his "brother" would have performed had he enjoyed the opportunities of the *dies irae* he describes, in the expecta-tion, of course, that the said "brother" will in turn take up the trumpet and sound a similar note of high-swelling praise. Another and still more startling phase of the Purist's assumption of superiority is shewn by his claim that he is by the use of the dry fly making a high order of intelligence hereditary in trout,* a process of education which will no doubt eventually result in some angler showing trained trout at one or other of "the halls," going through a performance illustrating the raising, hooking, and landing of fish grown grey in cunning. All this one may, perhaps, forgive the Purist. When, however, he carries science to the verge of pedantry and tells us that we have no business

---

* One would have thought that, by parity of assumption, a cod hook in the gullet would have been a much more educative argumentum ad piscem than the prick of a tiny fly or the sight of a fly not quite accurately dressed, and lacking something of the real Simon Pure. Punch's irate angler who threw his fly-book in with the words "choose for yourselves," was sketched with prophetic eye. The hour has come and some of the men.

as sportsmen to use a certain fly because it is not an imitation but a deadly fancy, and that trout will not take an imitation because it is scientifically and microscopically imperfect, we resent his autocratic dictation, doubt his sincerity, and are inclined to ask very pointedly, do trout travel not merely in schools, but live, move, and have their being in aquatic universities? How is it that we find an ultra-scientist admitting that a fancy fly like the Pink Wickham will often prove fatal to a trout or fish feeding on tiny flies beyond human imitation, unless, indeed, a pike scale laid flat on a tiny ooo hook can be called an imitation of the pin point "smut?" On the last analysis, however, the use of any kind of fly is justifiable, provided one employs it in a sporting way on gut just sufficiently fine to make the conditions of the contest between man and fish equal, or rather in favour of the fish. I yield to no man in my admiration for the skill of the "dry-fly" angler; no one can value more highly than I do the light which he has thrown on angling entomology; though I hold the Pharisee of the school in scorn, I have made this protest against his exclusive arrogance much more in sorrow than in anger.

To resume, however, the line of thought which the phrase " reasoned fear " in relation to the rejection of a fly by a trout suggested, it may be pointed out that one consideration leads to another in a question of this kind, and it may here be observed that if the dry fly " sails " down the stream just as the natural insect does after hatching out in the water, and so appears to the trout natural by reasoned inference, why should a trout take presumably by the same process of reflection, a wet fly dashing about the stream in a manner in which no fly does dash, much less the half-drowned or wholly dead insects the wet fly is supposed to represent? It is all a matter of education, says the "dry fly" angler. I regard it, on the other hand, as a question of irrational impulse due to the sensation either of existing hunger or of hunger stimulated by the sight of an appetiser in the person of the little dainty object. The difficulty of arriving at a satisfactory conclusion is as difficult as solving the old problem of the Idealists and the Realists. The observations do not agree. At one time trout will only take imitations of natural insects behaving naturally, at another they will only take these same imitations behaving unnaturally, and at yet another time under the same limita-

o

tions as to behaviour they will only take an obvious lusus naturæ in
the shape of a gorgeous fancy fly.

This last aspect of the question is certainly in favour of the Sensational explanation, yet the "association of ideas" difficulty remains.
That association of a kind exists no one disputes. It is nowhere better
illustrated than on the Matlock Bridge length of the Derwent in
Derbyshire. There trout rise in front and behind and all around the
noisy passage of trippers' boats through the river. In rivers along
whose banks run much frequented paths the fish show no great fear of
a human being on the banks. For these reasons of a similar and
parallel kind, I venture to think that it is because a thing is unusual that
it alarms a trout. Such a proposition involves a very nice distinction
between reasoning memory, which is due to association and abstract
conception, and unreasoning memory, which is merely physical suggestion
of neurotic and optic origin. Still it is not impossible to quote further
examples of apparent association of ideas in trout, the association, it
must be observed, being due not so much to abstract conceptions of
danger as to its direct sensational suggestion or, in other words, to
similar sensations awakening similar impulses. Conversely it may
appear that an overmastering sensation or appetite may drive all natural
caution or fear out of a trout. In an earlier chapter I gave two
examples of this apparent overcoming of the terrors of the unknown by
the pleasures of the known, and amongst the examples of apparent
association of ideas in fish and of the exercise of the mnemonic
faculty now to be quoted another and still more striking example of a
similar "mental phase" will be found.

On a certain Derbyshire canal, along whose banks I was in the habit
of frequently passing, I observed on several occasions that, though pike
and other fish lying in the shallows would suffer a barge to go noisily
past them, with the rope swishing and dashing on the water, and the
horse crunching the gravel on the bank above where they were lying, yet
that whenever my footstep—without the accompanying noise and
tumult of the barge—grated on the gravel path the fish instantly scooted
from the shallow to the deep—a tremulous wave marking their rapid
course, as a sort of index of their fearful haste to be gone. Why the
fish should have acted thus I have never been able to satisfy myself.
As a matter of fact, the barge was infinitely more ominous of danger

(the canal "bargees" being notorious poachers) than the tramp, not of one, but of a thousand foot passengers. Yet it was of the latter that the fish were afraid. Those who believe in the reasoning power of fish will at once say that the barge, with its concomitants, was an every hour occurrence, to which the fish had got used, while the occasional foot passenger was, on the contrary, an unusual sight, which, therefore, had upon the fish the invariable effect anything strange has upon animals. While prepared to admit that this explanation is very probably the correct one, it may be just as well to examine the bearing of an analogy drawn from a different sphere of animal life. I refer to the behaviour of grouse on stooks, premising, however, that there is no comparison between the intellectual or brain power of a bird and a fish. Grouse, when feeding on stooks, no matter how wild they may be on the adjacent moors, will much more readily suffer themselves to be approached by a man driving a horse and cart coming to lift the sheaves, than by a solitary individual advancing on foot, whether he is or is not armed with a gun being quite immaterial. Now, whether the indifference to the approach of the horse and cart is due to previous experience of the innocence of their intentions, or to the fact that the power to grasp the idea of a horse, a cart, and a man is beyond the intellectual capacity even of the grouse, the fact remains that a walking man causes far more alarm to grouse amongst the stooks than would a Jubilee procession of carts proceeding quietly and in a normal and ordinary way without shouting and noise. A similar remark applies to that most suspicious and most wary of birds—the wild goose, which is so superior to the grouse in intelligence that if the latter know where the butts are, and occasionally regulate their line of flight accordingly, the former can tell you the names of the shooters.

A wild goose can assuredly be much more easily approached on pony back than on foot, while I have frequently literally kicked them up out of potato patches in spring, and have approached within a few yards of them when loch fishing from a boat. It would, therefore, appear that there is nothing which an animal, consciously or unconsciously, regards with more dread that a man, pure, simple, and unadorned in the sense that is applicable to my present subject. He comes in his most questionable shape when he comes in his simplest guise without disguise, and it is an undoubted fact that animals are more afraid of

man than they are of other animals, even of those who prey upon them
habitually. This leads me to the conclusion that my friends the fish of
the canal were irrationally more afraid of a human footstep, because
ominous and solitary, like the single knock of Cromwell upon the door
of the Woodstock Inn, than they were of the noise and tumult of
passing barges. That there is safety in numbers seems to be a rule
that animals unconsciously apply.*

I will give another illustration of this apparent association of ideas,
which came under my notice in a certain stream on the West coast of
Scotland. The stream in question was a mixed one, a stream, that is
to say, containing salmon, sea trout, and trout, and ran through a rich
and fertile country. One day, when idling on a bridge over it, and
gazing down in a deepish hole below, I happened to throw into the
water a bit of some bread with which I had been regaling the hens in a
neighbouring yard. The salmon naturally paid no attention to it, but
as it was being carried down stream and gradually disintegrated to float
away in detached pieces, a trout tried it, and finding it good, speedily
swallowed it, while several of his fellows, attracted by his actions, swam
up and attacked the minute particles of bread that had been detached
from the main piece. On observing this, I sent down another piece,
and at once the trout that had eaten the first piece and found it good,
made a dash for it, followed by many of his fellows. He failed,
however, to secure it, for a fish higher up stream, evently grasping the
situation, flashed up and underneath the bread, seized it, and thus
became the bread-winner, just as the first fish with a boiling rush
swirled up for his prey only to find it gone. As it happened, the gain
of his friend was no loss to him, for I at once got a large supply of
bread and tried a number of experiments with the pellets.
First of all, I made a handful of bread pellets and threw them in.
This caused no particular excitement, as there had been some considerable interval between my throwing of the first two bits of bread and
the deluge of pieces. When, however, one fish began to feed, a sort of
bread riot arose. The feeder began dashing first at one pellet and then
at another, gobbling them up like a greedy hen (hungry hen is a mis-
nomer, for hens are always hungry), and making hay with a vengeance

---

* This peculiar trait is often attributed to the inability of animals to count—the
conception of number being an abstraction of which certain animals are said to be
incapable. The statement as to the mutual fear of animals is a generalisation.

while the sun shone. This roused his fellows to emulation, and, as I have said, a sort of bread riot ensued. The sea trout joined in the scramble, while a perfect armada of ducks set forth from some reeds. where, like a Spanish fleet of to-day, they had been lying hid from mortal ken, to investigate the cause of the excitement agitating the fish world. Now ducks are supposed to eat live fish, and the trout should therefore have been afraid of the ducks, and should have left to them the remnants of the feast. As a matter of fact the trout cared "not a wag of the tail" (which I venture to think is a phrase of the Lingua Trutta) for the ducks, but would dash up under their silly noses, or rather beaks, and would snap up a morsel just as it seemed certain to be translated into duck. Single pellets dropped at intervals would be followed by a rush of all the fish and the ducks towards the morsel, and the splutter which fin and feather made in their endeavours to be there first was very human. The salmon, however, were quite indifferent. They lay low and gave no sign. By keeping up the practice of feeding for a few days one had only to stand on the bridge, and if no trout were visible they would soon begin to appear, while a few pellets seemed to draw the fish from both above and below the bridge. Now all this would seem to point to a certain amount of power of associating a man with bread to eat, and to argue a limited kind of ability to form an abstract conception founded on a very materialistic form of sensationalism. I desisted from feeding for a couple of days, and the charm ceased to work. The sensations were no longer excited, and the association between my presence on the bridge and bread to eat became practically non-existent. There was no memory apart from the appetite gratified, which is precisely what one would expect in an animal without a brain cortex and a fish is the only vertebrate without one.* This experience naturally tended to confirm the position that your trout can only associate ideas through the direct excitation of his senses.

Now though the facts I have already adduced are of the very greatest importance when one comes to state a philosophy of the fly based on the Sensational theory of fish life, yet there are other facts which one cannot afford to ignore and which may very well be of as great moment in proving that the trout, if carnivorous, is also omnivorous, and an optimist of the first, as he will be of the last, water.

* This view is now pretty generally accepted as anatomically correct.

It must, indeed, have often struck even the casual observer of fish and their habits that the lures employed by anglers for their capture are frequently of a singular and anomalous kind. The purists who would debar all save "dry fly" men from the category of scientific anglers maintains, as we have seen, with a rigid exclusivism that his lure, the dry fly dressed and made to sail in imitation of the real insect in form, colour, and actions, represents the highest form of angling art, because it deceives the trout by holding the mirror up to nature. Yet even his aim is to find what will "kill." His pride is to deceive the trout to its ruin, and to record in history writ on many waters the rise and fall of salmo fario who have, in very human fashion, been persuaded that what appears to be good really is as good as it appears to be. The first and final criterion of his philosophy is that the imitating of nature is such a sincere form of flattery when applied to trout, that it and it alone can lull to sleep the suspicions of the trout and make him rise obsequious through one deceived sense to the safe gratification of another. Yet it must be observed that the natural law, in the popular sense, underlying the one title in the declaratory constitution of his angling kingdom, though apparently in accordance with facts, is in reality opposed to them. The purist does not recognise the trout's multiform appetite, but simply one manifestation of it. If one were to dare in a dry fly stream, acting with a fuller recognition of the same principle of natural law, to deftly present other food than a cocked ephemerid to the troutish notice, your purist would abjure this application of his principle as an outrage on nature—a caricature, if you will, and not an imitation and faithful picture of what to the trout is natural food, though it never drops from nature's table into the ready mouths of the least fastidious children that her broad bosom nurtures.

This apparent paradox is a truism. There is not a fish that swims which has not its natural food, yet there is not a fish that swims which is not omnivorous. Experience shows that this is true of all fish, from the cod that will swallow a bunch of keys or a bunch of mussels to the salmon, who with all his ocean strength dashes through the green and swirling tides in pursuit of the dainty herring or falls an ill-advised victim to a red and boiled prawn, threading an unnatural course through the depths of some slow-gliding pool in a manner no prawn, dead or living, has ever been known to do, since the first progenitor of all anglers threw out his line in the virgin waters of the young world. This forgotten hero, whose name I have ascertained was A. Priori, must assuredly have developed ideas of his own in the matter of lures. Possibly he may have sat shivering in his cave, if a trout fisher, when the sullen East hurled forth its blasts to shake the primeval forests, and dull skies of leaden hue sent his heart instinctively down into where his boots should have been. No doubt he discussed with Mrs. A. Priori and all the Minor Hypotheses the comparative merits of flies dressed with megatherium fur and pterodactyl feathers, and of those dressed with a mastodon body and ichthyosaurus scale. Antedeluvian historians are silent on the point, and as it was countless æons before the American Press Age, when this primeval angler exercised his wiles, to declare that he did all these things would be to palm off a changeling on that sorely tried mother, necessity.

One may, however, feel assured that the most primitive and least observant of anglers, whether in fresh water or in salt, would soon discover that though fish, after the fashion of their human captors, like some things better than others at all times, and prefer particular things at particular times, yet are in the main omnivorous. Your fish is, in truth, a first-class optimist and materialist rolled into one, whose philosophy is summed up in the comfortable phrase, " Whatever is, is good to eat." A fish, in fact, resembles the hero of a very long story, which I shall endeavour to compress into brief compass. An angler, wearied and hungry, arrived at daybreak at a lonely Highland hostelry. He ordered breakfast as a matter of course, and the good wife said, " Whaat will you hev ? " " Ham and eggs," said he. These, however, were not to be come by, and the excuse given was a plausible one, wound up by " but say what you'll hev, just say what you'll hev." The angler suggested all sorts of things, each suggestion being less pretentious than its predecessor, but each was met with a negative and an excuse, crowned with a bold " but say what you'll hev, just say what you'll hev." In despair he at length asked for some whisky. Then a look of stern reproach came into the landlady's face, and in rebuking tones she turned on the Sassenach and said, " Why did you no' say what you'll hev ? " and then tripped off and brought him a liberal measure of whisky, which, as a matter of fact, was all there was in the house.

Now the fish is in a precisely similar predicament to the hero of this story. Salmo fario may prefer the troutish equivalent to ham and eggs for breakfast, but if he is hungry and there is nothing better (or worse) to be come by than what corresponds to whisky, why he will have whisky. The main thing is that he wants and will have something.

The recognition of this principle involves the deplorable conclusion, as a general axiom, that the trout which rises to a floating fly, thrown far and fine over him as he lies in clear water, takes that fly on precisely the same principle as a blundering bonito or assinine albicore, rises and seizes a rag-adorned hook bobbing in and out below the dolphin-striker of a vessel ploughing the tropical seas. This primitive lure consists merely in a bit of white rag tied to a big hook " busked " straight on to a stout quarter-inch rope. This is fastened to the martingale below the flying jibboon in such a way that when the vessel rises with the lift of the sea the rag jumps out of the water and bobs in again as the vessel falls away, and thus resembles a flying fish disporting itself in the creamy, yeasty foam spurned in endless lines of white from the plough- ing stem. Such a crude lure is essentially an ocean fly, and is exactly analogous to the " dry fly " because it imitates nature, the flying fish being fond of playing in this kind of way about the forefoot of a vessel, a fact that is well known to the bonito and albicore, fish that take their quarry, from that quarry's nature, with all the dash of a " rainbow."

What applies to very primitive flies applies also to very primitive " spun " lures, and surely it is not more anomalous for a bit of rag to represent the fly than it is for a patent log to pose to the shark as a phantom minnow. Personally I have never killed a shark in this way, nor have I ever seen one seize a patent log,* though I have often wondered why they did not do so. My venerable friend, Mr. E. L. Layard, whose long and honourable career in the diplomatic service in southern regions has given him a very wide experience of the fish of tropical seas, assures me that sharks do take patent logs, and in a private letter cites one experience in particular during a voyage on board one of our old-time frigates, in the course of which several patent logs were

* I have frequently observed sharks swimming just behind patent logs, and remember catching one such swimmer with a bit of "spun" pork. He took the latter at once and gave rare sport.

1.—New Zealand Spinning Lure, made of wood, lined with shell cut from the "Haliotis" or "Venus Ear" shell. Length, 3½ ihch; greatest width, ⅝th inch; depth, ½ inch. Curved so as to spin. Barb and point made of human bone, tied to the shank with native thread. This hook had a fringe of feathers round the base of the bend.

2.—Solomon Island Hook, made of tortoise (i.e. turtle) shell, softened so as to bend by a process, known to the natives, which makes the hook very strong. It is 3½ inches long by ¼ inch broad, and has a piece of pearl shell cut so as to resemble a fish "busked" on to the back. It must have been an attractive lure for the hook and pearl fish are scratched with teeth marks.

3.—Solomon Islands Lure.—The shank is made of a kind of jade, a pale yellow and semi-transparent stone. The point is formed of bone and has no barb, while the hook is eyed—after a sort, the hole or "eye," being drilled by means of the mid-rib of a cocoa-nut leaf rubbed between the hands and fed with fine sand and water, after the stone has been heated and a drop of cold water has caused scaling by the sudden cooling. The "feather" in this case is a tuft of hair, and the length of the hook is 3¾th inches, and its diameter ½ inch.

5.—This represents one-half of a Spinning Lure, 5 inches long, made on the Fiji native plan. The other half was bitten in two and carried off by a fish.

4 and 6.—These are specimens of (1) South Sea Island and (2) Ceylon Tackle. Both, it will be observed, are cunningly "guyed" so as to relieve the strain.

It may be mentioned that these hooks and lures are now rare and have been super seded by "trade" hooks.

Primitive Lures and "Flies."—Sketched from the originals.

ruined by the sharks ! Nor is this all that Mr. Layard's name suggests by way of illustrating the question under discussion by those many examples which the world of fish affords, with that happy analogical latitude is one of the charms of speculative "anglology." I have mentioned the primitive angler and his lures and have spoken of him with respect as Mr. A. Priori. There is no necessity so to describe him. Thanks to Mr. Layard's kindness the hooks and lures of the primitive angler lie before me, or at least the hooks and lures that were used by certain South Sea savages before the white angler discovered them. These hooks and lures are as instructive as they are interesting. Some of the former are on the cross-thorn principle, still used on our South-East coast by anglers "ledgering" for flounders, while others are exquisitely carved in mother-of-pearl and bone and are in every way efficient eyed-hooks ! The lures, however, are more interesting. They are as truly imitations of fish, the material out of which they are carved being bright mother-of-pearl, as the most up-to-date of imitation spinning baits. Moreover, they are constructed to spin, and are swivelled and otherwise singularly well adapted for their purpose. A few of them suggest "flies" of a primitive kind, and all are, as I have said, singulary suited for the end they have in view, namely by their resemblance to something edible, to tempt fish to their doom. When to this similitude to food in situ, is added the life-like resemblance to food which they bear in motion, I am back again at my starting point and can only repeat that the dictum, whatever is is good to eat, really explains all the apparent anomalies in fish lures, even though some baits are natural and some are unnatural. A worm, a dry fly of suitable pattern, a May-fly, a caddis grub, are all natural baits when naturally presented, and fish take them, and die, I hope, with a clear conscience and in the knowledge that their appetite, if it has shown them to be greedy, has not proved them as foolish as fain. Present these lures unnaturally, and they are no longer natural baits, just as joints of beef and mutton do not, outside of a Drury-lane pantomime, grow in kitchen gardens on cabbage stalks. Wasp grub is another natural bait, so long as it does not swim up stream, and is most natural when it drops off a tree, while the same may be said of a young frog when it hops off a bank with a hook in it.

What, however, of a prawn boiled and prepared, that salmon often take
with avidity, of bullocks' pith and brains, so fatal to your winter chub,
of cheese paste, loved of the same, of creed wheat that tempts the
September roach to his doom, of the prepared bread paste of the Lea
" poler," of cherries and boiled potatoes for carp, of prawn and anchovy
paste and of that cross between a cow's tail and an old wife's red
" mutch " called a pike fly, and other lures of an anomalous and unnatural character ? They are all taken because they either are or
appear to be good to eat and are merely quoted because they are instructive analogies.

What then is the final conclusion to which all this points in the case
of trout ?   The answer to that query may be thus summarised.   A trout
does appear to associate danger more readily with some things than
with others, and this in itself argues a certain power of reasoned
memory, which is strange in an animal said to possess no brain cortex
—the alleged seat of mnemonic power.   As, however, a trout's vigilance
is differentiated by its sensations in being, by its appetites, impulses, and
instincts, in the broadest and narrowest sense of these terms—and
varies far more with habitat and the altering conditions of existence,
such as high or discoloured or low and clear waters, lake or stream, in
the same fish than it does in the fish of different rivers, a trout's
education is not a question of reason but of sensation, and is dependent
for its degree upon those circumstances which appeal to the sensational
in fish.

If this final conclusion can be held to be justified by the facts I have
adduced and the analogies I have utilized from fish life in general, then
the philosophy of the fly may be said to be based on general or
eternal principles which may vary in their realization according to the
special circumstances of their realization.   One is forced to recognize
that circumstances make a difference in the sensations produced by
certain flies whether this difference be due to the mere external
appearance of the fly or to its mode of motion.   By this philosophy of
the fly alone can we not only evade acknowledging the existence of
educated trout in the fullest sense of the term, but can at the same time
attribute the apparently educated condition of the trout of certain
waters to a perfectly intelligible cause.   The theory, moreover, in no-
way derogates from the claim of dry fly fishing as practised to be

considered the highest development of angling art, since it accords to
the floating flyman the task of betraying the most superlative dexterity
in avoiding the giving of a trout alarm through his sensations under
circumstances which are most likely to make him see an ignotum pro
terrible in every shadow and something unnatural about every fly.
Nay more. It not only preserves, when the conditions alter, the
optimism of the trout in the matter of food, but admits all anglers
with the fly, each in his degree and the loch fisher with the rest,
within the sacred circle of the elect. Finally, it emphasises what
appears to be the trend of thought on the subject, namely, that
the fact that trout occasionally in some waters, invariably in others,
take small moving objects, which as truly and sometimes as nearly
imitate aquatic insects as do the most exact imitations of
true flies, is a sufficient justification for the use of flies, framed
in imitation of such insects, being termed scientific angling.
As the loch fisher with the fly almost invariably, but not exclusively,
uses such imitations and uses them, as I shall presently show, in an
even more natural kind of way than does the stream angler, it is
obviously of some moment in the settling of an old-standing, but always
"sportingly-waged," strife to have this point settled and the mutual concessions which it involves amicably granted. Of the philosophy of the
fly, as I have stated it, it can at least be affirmed that it is not a
philosophy based either on exceptions or on observations narrowed to
a restricted field. It is broad-based on a recognition of the eternal
principles of fish life not merely in the stream and lake but in the wide
waters that wash the world ; and while thus a philosophy of limitless
range, it is declaratory and realises that within the narrower waters of
rivers and lochs, certain circumstances must be recognised, if the laws
formulated are to bear a declaratory character and do justice alike to
the skill of the far and fine school who tempt trout to their doom on
the shallows of sun-lit waters by holding one kind of mirror up to
nature and the loch fisher who on the broader, darker, and deeper
bosom of the lake holds up another but not less true mirror to nature,
as he must read her, to reflect the moods of her children and catch the
inspiration of those lessons that have won for angling the proud title of
the contemplative man's recreation.

CHAPTER XVIII.

The Philosophy in Practice.

The practical application of the philosophy of the fly as stated obviously involves, as the theory is a compromise, a recognition of the dual character of "flies," of "flies," that is to say, as we know them either as imitations of known ephemerids* or known aquatic insects, or as fancy flies that resemble no insect, aquatic or otherwise. If, therefore, one takes any series of loch flies and determines to use that series, the list of flies thus chosen will, in terms of the sensational philosophy of the fly, divide itself into three varieties of flies, which may be classified under the following heads :—

1.—Flies that represent "flies" in the popular sense.
2.—Flies that represent aquatic insects.
3.—Flies that represent "hybrids" in the popular sense, and may be
    (a) Fancy aquatic insects.
    (b) Fancy "flies."
    (c) Fancy hybrids with some of the features of both.

Now it is obvious that on the last analysis the distinction drawn embraces only two varieties of flies and that for purposes of angling classification, it might be sufficient to divide flies, into surface flies and subaqueous flies.

The value in use of such a division becomes clear when one considers that it secures a classification for angling purposes of flies that may and should be used as "first dropper," or "bob" flies, flies, that is to say, that can be fished high, and flies, that are second, third, or tail flies, which may and should be fished deep. It may be observed that the sensational theory of the fly in its practical application really amounts to the laying down of the axiom that the more natural or imitative a fly is, and the more natural the manner in which it is brought under the notice of a trout, the less likely is that trout to be alarmed by the necessary discrepancy between the appearance and movements

---

* The phrase is used in its popular sense.

of the most cunningly contrived and cleverly presented imitation and the
real Simon Pure. This is the general principle underlying the theory
which admits, in accordance with the irresistible deductions drawn
from angling experience, that trout take and always have taken imitations of "flies that fly," made to behave in a manner in which they
never do behave or, in other words, in a most unnatural manner. Dead
flies or half drowned flies do not swim up stream or sail either in the
eye or close to the wind in a lake, but nevertheless we know that both
in streams and lochs trout take our winged messengers of death, whose
vitality thus displays itself in a triumph over the grave. The explanation given of this apparent inconsistency in troutish behaviour is that the
drowned or dead flies are not taken for the flies we intend them to be
taken for, but for aquatic insects of an indeterminate and by us, if not
the trout, an unclassified kind to which, by the motion we impart, we
give a deceptive character. As this explanation is fully in accordance
with the sensational theory of the fly, which attributes an optimism to the
trout in the matter of food summed up in the dictum "whatever is, is
good to eat," and only assumes as a condition precedent to its exceptions
a rousing of sensations that run counter to the main impulse, it must be
accepted as wholly satisfactory.

As I have already observed, however, to return to the main classification of flies, the endeavour of the practical angler must be to confine
his varieties of flies, as far as possible, to imitations of natural insects
and flies, while the principle on which the use of these flies or insects
must be based is that they must be made to act as naturally as possible—
aquatic insect imitations being worked low, and "fly" imitations being
worked high.

When out on a loch the most careless observer cannot fail to have
been struck by the fact that all flies on the water, whether dead and
drowned, or half drowned, or merely held prisoner in its grip, necessarily
travel down wind. Though this fact is thus writ so very large on the
water of all lakes, there is no truth that has been so largely disregarded
by the loch angler who is content to accept the traditional methods, and
does not seek to elevate his sport into an art and a science and, therefore, pro tanto enhance the pleasure to be derived from the pursuit
and the study of his pastime. Of so great importance do I esteem the
recognition of the simple fact just cited that I have no hesitation in

attributing any success I may have achieved as a loch fisher to a recognition of the principle involved as a modifier of my methods and as one of the bases of my general plan of campaign. Strictly speaking all loch flies that are imitations of flies and not imitations of aquatic insects should be worked down not up-wind, whereas by most anglers they are worked nearly up-wind irrespective of their imitative character. When a "cast," as usually happens in actual angling, carries imitations both of aquatic insects and of flies, the degree of departure from the natural motions of the lures is obviously not so great, and can by the exercise of care be reduced to a minimum by varying the working of the "flies," so as to recognize the proper principle of motion that should be applied to each kind of lure. I shall, of course, explain the application of this principle when dealing with "casting" and the various methods of fishing different varieties of lochs. At present I merely state the theory of my plan so far as it is necessary to the elucidation of the principles regulating the selection and use of certain flies for loch fishing.

Now, it is obvious that if our aim is to limit our list of flies as far as is possible to flies that are imitations of natural insects which fly over or swim in the lake, or in a word are eaten by the trout, it is clear that we must choose "flies" that occur in nearly all lakes. Now the most common water insects are the fresh-water shrimp (strictly speaking a crustacean), and the various varieties of water beetles, though the latter from an actinic point of view may be under normal circumstances, classified for practical purposes as embracing only one variety. Whether loch fishers have or have not been actuated by any definite purpose in the matter, whether they have consciously or unconsciously given practical recognition to the sensational theory of the fly, it is certain that in making the "teal and red," or "teal and claret," or "teal and black," and the "heckum peckum" standard loch patterns, they have shown a wise discretion of choice worthy of the most deliberate and reasoned application of the lessons of observation to practice. Familiar as are these patterns, theirs is the familiarity of long use that should breed not contempt but respect, for they are essentially imitations of the natural food of the trout, and even in lakes where the shrimp is not found, the "teal and red," under the exception I have already noted and which applies with equal truth to many wet flies when used in rivers, can still claim to be a natural imitation of a darting insect which the trout takes for what it appears to be, something alive and of the insect order, and therefore good to eat. Both flies, however, should be used in a natural manner, and as both represent aquatic insects, in the sense I have already explained, they should obviously always be used as tail flies— or at the worst as third droppers, the ideal position for both on the same cast being "teal and red" as tail, and "heckum peckum" as the fly next to it.*

So firm is my faith in these two patterns, so assured am I that, fished in their proper position and in a proper manner, they are the two most deadly loch flies in existence, that if I were condemned to the hard lot of angling for loch trout from April to September and were sentenced to six months hard labour on the lakes that lie between Windermere in the South and the lochs of Ultima Thule in the North, and between Loch Leven in the East and the Wilds of Connemara in the West, and further were ordered by the court to restrict my flies to two, I should be content with "red and teal" and "heckum peckum." Nor would I keep the court waiting for a decision. My choice would be instantly and finally made. There is, of course, a tendency to mistake the most taking fly for the fly that being most often in use is most often presented to the trout when in a taking mood, and therefore very naturally kills most fish. But this possible fallacy is not illustrated by the loch fisher's most faithful servants the "teal and red" and the "heckum peckum." They kill occasional trout when other flies kill none at all and in lochs where large trout only are found and one has to wait, for a feeding fish, as the dry fly man has to wait, there are no flies which tempt to their doom more "marked down" and specially angled for trout than do the two flies in question. Nay more. The latitude, which the sensational theory of the fly admits, is well illustrated by another excellent quality these flies possess. When loch trout are on the move, or in other words are questing under the overmastering impulse of hunger or superabundant life and activity, they are naturally not very particular in the matter of flies, so long as in pattern

---

* The "Heckum Peckum" as it represents a corixa—an insect which can and sometimes does fly, and one which is under the necessity of coming to the surface to breathe, may, of course, be fished rather higher than the "teal and red." To sink and raise it is to "move it" naturally, for when the corixa is coming up to breathe it is, like a seal, in its most defenceless state—a fact which the trout may well know. I presume that the reader is aware that a corixa with a broken oar is quite helpless. This note refers only to uninjured corixae.

and size they are fairly reasonable. When, however, the fish are either
not hungry or lethargic and are not on the move or are keeping low a
fly of great visibility under ordinary conditions of light, will often tempt
them to rise, when a fly that is not visible and is, therefore, not a
temptation cannot afford the predisposing cause necessary to produce
the desired effect. As both the "teal and red" and the "heckum
peckum" have this quality of visibility, even in this aspect they are
better flies than any other patterns. Their proper dressing will be found
in the list of loch flies set forth in the course of this chapter.

Though I have thus sung the praises of these two patterns, it is
obvious that they very far from exhaust the list of indispensable patterns of sunk flies which the angler should possess.

Angling is such a complex subject that whenever one appears to have
completed a fairly satisfactory general survey of a particular item, some
after-thought arises. In this case the rule holds good, and I may
here mention a peculiar habit of loch trout suggested by the two flies
with which I have been dealing. In some choice and quiet corner of
a lake on one of those glorious summer days when loch fishing not only
affords its highest joys, but also demands the greatest measure of skill,
I have frequently observed that feeding trout, while ranging up and
down, like ceaseless sentinels and vigilant warders, some yards of shore
under the shady boughs, now and then sucking in a specially tempting
fly amongst the hundreds at their disposal, will nevertheless almost always take an artificial fly as presented and invariably show a marked preference for, an active keenness with regard to, such a fly that is in strange
contrast to their lazy indifference to the rich feast spread on the bountiful table of nature. When one attempts to solve this mystery of mood,
the light that comes illumines the old and reveals new beauties in angling not as the art of killing fish but as the science of those stepping
stones to higher things. The trout, this warder of the mere, that stands
spear in hand keeping his ceaseless watch and ward over the stronghold
of the stout fin, the choice pasture won by the might of lithe activity and
the courage of blue blood, illustrates in every phrase of his mood the
psychology of desire—the lust of nations and the striving of man against
man and of man with himself. The easy morsels that lie to his hand
are not worth taking, in part because custom has staled their variety, in
part because they are already the spoil of his spear and bow, in part

because no rival can dispute possession. But this darting lively trio or quartette that suddenly sweep across his ken as he moves with stately motion to and fro, these may be the spoil of another and are themselves a challenge to the Alexander of the lake—an object of temptation because novel, an object of desire because the sword may flash over their mastery, the red maze of rival war have to be trodden before they are made captive of the appetite that has led the trout prisoner. If Aristotle had been an angler, he might well have been a wiser man. But even the angler pure and simple, who throws all lessons of his art to the winds save those that enable him to bring trout down to the grave with blood has in this trait of trout a very instructive object lesson. The fish obviously takes the moving, lively, artificial flies simply because they are lively or life-like, and are behaving in a natural or tempting manner. It is an old trick of the scientific sea-trout fisher with the fly in lochs to take advantage of this peculiarity and when fish are rising short, as I shall show when dealing with that aspect of my subject, a little extra movement deliberately and carefully imparted to the fly will often convert a merely inquisitive fish of a particular type into a taking fish.*

It must not be supposed that because I have thus devoted so much space to singing the praises of the "teal and red," and the "heckum peckum" as imitating the shrimp and one of the corixae, these two flies exhaust all that is excellent by way of imitation in so called "flydom." On the contrary, though there are no flies which equal them in all-round excellence and invariable deadliness, there are just as many flies which may be used with effect on lochs as there are flies which can be and are used with excellent results on our rivers. I do not desire, however, to involve myself in a discussion of the admittedly intricate problem whether flies fished wet that are imitations of flies that fly are or are not taken by the trout for imitations of the flies which they are intended to imitate. The sensational theory of the fly evades that speculative issue if it does not satisfactorily explain the reason why trout take certain imitations of flies behaving in a way the originals never behave. The avidity with which trout take such flies varies with their mood, and it is very possible—and indeed probable—that a rise of the

---

*This trick of the trade is also useful when large fish are coming in hesitating fashion in a calm and the rise is as long-drawn as that of a dimpling dace.

P

natural insect of which the fly used is an imitation merely acts as
a predisposing excitation of appetite and occupies as surface bait an
exactly analogous position to ground bait. That this is true of the
loch, a series of experiments I made during the past two seasons enabled me to establish to my own satisfaction. On a certain lake which
contained only large and well-fed fish, three particular varieties of flies,.
to wit, the green drake, the grey drake, and the red ant were specially
abundant. The former, as sometimes happens, were present in greatest
abundance during the pride of the day. When a special burst of fly
would rise like a yellow snowstorm and go fluttering down the breeze
and the lake was covered with these proud Argosies and flaked with their
wrecked predecessors, occasionally a rise of trout would follow. During such a rise, it was, however, the exception and not the rule for the
fish to take a green drake. As a matter of fact during such rises I killed
all my fish on a large zulu fished very high. Similarly when the loch
would, owing to a sudden squall or some other reason, be suddenly
sown with a cloud of red ants that distributed themselves over its surface, the fish would again be excited to rise, by the suggestion of food,
though but few of the flies would be actually taken. During such a
rise most of the fish I killed were taken on the " teal and red " or "heckum
peckum," or indeed on the " sunk " flies I happened to be using, but few
or none were taken on the " bob " fly.* In the evening, however, when
the grey drake came out at a period of the day corresponding with the
general feeding time of the trout, that fly was taken by every trout that
rose, and was not only the predisposing cause of the rise by the idea of
appetite it suggested to the trout, but was the very object of that appetite, which nothing else could satisfy. The inference I drew from
this experience, after it had been repeated sufficiently frequently to
show that it was a rule and not an exception that I was observing, was
the very natural one, that when trout are merely excited to feed by a
rise of a certain fly not co-incident with their natural feeding time, they
will, at least in lakes, take any fly and will take that fly best which re-

* This view has been slightly modified by my experience while these pages were in
the Press. I had not at the time referred to designed the Red Ant, whose dressing
is given. This June, however, during a rise of "Alders," I killed 8 trout (12¾lb.
with the "Red Ant." The rise was confined to a calm spot and was entirely produced by
"Alders." It lasted some three-quarters of hour, and was so localised that not another
rise was seen that day on the loch. For some further remarks on the points touched on,.
vide the chapter on "Moods of Loch Trout."

sembles most closely in movement the fly that is the predisposing cause of the " move." I use the phrase " move " advisedly, for to set a trout in motion, or in other words, rouse him from his lethargy, is to wake him up to a sense of the presence of food or of the fly—a fact that may result in his being tempted to his doom. On the other hand I came to the conclusion that when the feeding hour of a fish has arrived—and it is to be presumed that appetite has its seasons in trout as in other animals and may suit itself to the opportunities of its gratification—and a rise of a particular fly occurs, then that fly is almost exclusively taken by the trout and is the proper fly to use.

It follows, therefore, from these observations of what are facts of nature—and the conclusion is absolutely in accordance with the sensational theory—that unless the fish are feeding on a particular fly to the exclusion and rejection of all other flies and forms of food, then any fly will kill, providing it is not too outrageous a lusus naturae, while its deadliness will vary, first with the degree of its divergence from or adherence to the mode of motion of the predisposing fly, and secondly the mode of motion of the fly which it is supposed to imitate. Even when it imitates no living thing in appearance, the mode of motion remains still of the same importance, as certain considerations already stated conclusively show.

I do not, as I have already indicated, propose to discuss the wider problem of why trout take imitations of natural flies behaving unnaturally. It is enough to know that they do take them, and take them too in terms of the sensational theory because they appear good to eat, and the hungry trout, mistaking them for what they are or appear to be, does not stand and examine.

To return, however, to the imitative aspect of loch flies, it is obvious that save under abnormal conditions and when fishing for small and ever-hungry fish, the fly that imitates the natural food of the trout will, when naturally worked, not only kill the greatest number of fish and secure the largest and presumably the most cautious, the best fed and most fastidious specimens, but will also tend to the production of a more scientific and instructive style of fishing with higher ideals and more scientific aims. A system of fly-selection that reconciles the utilitarian in results with the scientific in ambition is obviously a satisfying system because it hits the golden mean and combines, as it were, the pursuit of geology with the discovery of gold nuggets by way of reward for the virtue displayed. It is on this principle that I now submit a list of loch flies with their dressings, which I have divided into flies that are to be used as first droppers and flies that are to be used as second, third or tail flies. The latter are either imitations of natural aquatic insects on which the trout feed or are flies that might be aquatic insects on which the trout would feed were they like the famous sky-blue horse removed from the category of the lusus naturae. The former are either imitations of flies found on all waters, or are merely winged creatures that represent themselves and may appear to the trout to be good to eat. Finally certain of the flies are patterns selected merely for their visibility and power to tempt when all other patterns have failed.

"SUBAQUEOUS" FLIES.

1. Teal and Red. Tail, three or four long strands of red cock twice or more the length of the main fly; body, red silk or red wool ribbed with silver; wing, teal finishing with a black tip; hackle, red furnace dressed to fall close under the fly lengthways.

2. Improved Teal and Red. The same as the above without any tail, but with some long purple strands dressed just to overlap the teal wing.

3. Heckum Peckum. Tail red cock, body same as teal and red; hackle, red cock; wing, greeny-black feather from mallard, as glossy as possible.

4. Improved Heckum Peckum. Same as above, body greenish herl of peacock. This is not a fancy fly.

5. The Crow Zulu. Tail, red ibis; body, black ribbed with silver; hackle, black; wing, blue crow, as burnished as possible.

6. Woodcock and Red. Same as Red and Teal, save for its woodcock wing.

7. The Tadpole. This fly must be dressed on long shanked hooks of the "Salmo Irritans" type. It is simply an imitation of the tadpole. My dressing is a thick hackle at the head of the hook, bunched so as to resemble the tadpole, and two long strands hanging loose, and either a silver or a hurl body. It is, in one sense, a fancy "fly" and its use is only recommended as a last resource. It is certainly a more sporting lure than a trolled minnow.

8. The Cardinal. Tail, red ibis; body, red ibis, ribbed with silver or gold; wings, red ibis; hackle, furnace.

9. The Red Stuart or Improved Cardinal. Tail, golden pheasant; body all silver; wings, red ibis; head, peacock hurl; hackle, red ibis. Another variety (dressed very small) is: tail, red ibis; wings and hackle, red ibis; head, peacock hurl; body, half silver, half peacock hurl, the silver being next the head.

10. Any of the flies usually used in river fishing as wet flies.

DROPPER FLIES.

1. The Zulu. Tail, red worsted or Indian crow; body, black silk, silver ribbed; hackle, black, with a suggestion of green.

2. March Brown. In all its forms.

3. Cow Dung Fly (cinnamon and gold). Wing, landrail; body, all gold; hackle, yellow. The "all gold" is better in lochs than down or wool.

4. The Blue Upright as usually dressed.

5. Black and Silver. Wings, coal black; body, all silver; tail, golden pheasant.

6. The Red Ant. Body, red silk; legs, red hackle; wings, blae, dressed one pair at the head, the other pair at the tail of the fly. The second pair may be reversed; this dressing gives the appearance the fly presents on the water.

7. Any fly that is used in rivers in its season and occurs in lochs, including the Grey Drake, dressed with Egyptian goose wings and a yellow silk black-ribbed body, or staw, and the house fly* which the black and silver fairly imitate.

While I was engaged on this chapter I was naturally interested to note that the "Field" with that great journalistic insight which characterises the editing of its angling columns, had instituted a sort of plebiscite of favourite flies. The voters were limited to three flies, and amongst loch flies selected apparently as first choice the claret and mallard. I quote the words of the article answering the result of the plebiscite, premising that the authority of the voters is not stated—a matter of moment, for in angling witnesses must be weighed not numbered.

---

*For the dressing of this and other patterns, vide the list of sea-trout flies in a later chapter.

"Next coming to loch flies, the feature of the discussion was the almost unanimous opinion that in loch fishing the well-known claret and mallard held much the same position as the Jock Scott did in salmon fishing. The opener of the discussion recommended a claret and mallard for general use, a zulu, owing to its strong contrast of colour, for very dark days or dark peat-stained water, and a rather lightly coloured red bodied palmer for clear water, on bright, breezy days. The next speaker said the best loch flies were the teal and red and the zulu. This was followed by a recommendation to use the mallard and orange, the claret and mallard, and the March brown. One who had had some experience in Norway spoke of the value in that country of the teal and red, the March brown, and the coachman. It was interesting to note how several of these experienced fishermen gave evidence of their faith in local patterns, while others declined to allow them any special virtues, alleging that the local patterns often arose from the limited resources of the local fly-dresser, who would, if he could get nothing better, dress his body with a bit of wool torn from the nearest hearth rug or carpet, and, if needs must, make a black wing from a rook or crow. This suggestion of using black wings may seem far fetched, but, as a matter of fact, black is used in a few fairly well-known patterns, and local anglers who have to study economy often dress their own flies in this fashion."

It will be observed that claret and mallard does not occur on my list for the simple reasons that I have never found it a specially attractive fly for brown trout, though an excellent sea-trout fly, that it is an imitation of nothing unless a very incorrect one of a red ant (this position is not specially important save in the sense already indicated) and finally that after comparing the results obtained by using it and the other patterns to which I have given preference, those other patterns enjoy a most pronounced ascendancy. The second point that strikes me in this up-to-date expression of what is presumably popular opinion is the preference given to dark flies for use in dark waters and on dark days, and the recommendation that bright flies should be utilised on bright, breezy days and for clear waters. It is totally opposed to my experience on lochs which tallies with that of Franck, gathered by a study of salmon rivers. Franck, who may fairly claim to be the first of all tourist-anglers, recommends a dark fly for bright day and, by implication, for bright waters and a bright or gay fly when the day—and

presumably the water—"is promiscous and dark occasioned by smooty
and discoloured clouds."* Franck, it is true, is not referring to lochs, on
which his experience was singularly unfortunate and in which he seems
only to have fished with set lines, but to rivers, so that his evidence is
of more archaeological and analogical interest than practical value. At
the same time as he was a keen observer—his descriptions of salmon
when spawning and of the places he visited are wonderfully accurate—the
fact that he differs on this point from most of the modern authorities on
salmon fishing is not without significance. Had he been writing of
lochs, the opinion he states would have been entirely in accordance
with the lessons which experience has taught me. I leave the subject
at this point to resume it a little later and pass to the next thought suggested by the extract from the " Field" which I have given. I am
struck by the fact that no reference is made in the choice of flies to the
season of their use and presume, as I am warranted in presuming,
that the reason for this omission is to be found either in the fact that a
season enduring from May to the end of August is assumed, or it is taken
for granted that the angler will find that season in loch flies is a matter
of no moment. I scarcely pause to examine this statement—as I shall
shortly be referring to the question of season as it affects loch flies, but
will content myself with pointing out that whichever alternative be
adopted as the explanation, the result is retrogression, a lowering of the
scientific standard in loch fishing and a consequent loss of much of its
inner charm. Finally I am struck by the opinions expressed on the
subject of local flies. These may be summarily dismissed. Local flies
are mostly legacies of chance successes with nondescript flies on abnormal days, when the fish have been so keenly mad for food, so bent on
seizing all that moves and appears to be good to eat, that they will rise
at a bit of wood or a piece of cork in the eagerness of rivalry to be there
first. Moreover it is impossible in the matter of local flies to ignore
the well ascertained fact which I have so frequently mentioned, that
trout do not always stand and examine, and even in rivers habitually take
wet flies that are abnormally unnatural because being imitations, they
utterly depart from the natural habits of those imitations. It is on this
analogy a safe presumption that local patterns are taken by the fish on
what may be termed the omnivorous principle already explained in

* Northern Memoirs, p. 158, et seq.

dealing with the " Philosophy of the Fly." The fallacy that underlies faith in local patterns is, I may say in concluding this lengthy digression, the self same error which underlies the advice of the guide book, " trout are partial to a grey wing and a red body," or some other imaginary "favourite" fly. There is no such fly as a specialised favourite fly. In lochs all flies that are favourites are general favourites, though it may happen that on certain lochs a fly becomes a favourite with a reputation simply because the trout are ready risers or because tradition having assigned an attractiveness to a certain fly that fly is most used and has, therefore, most opportunities of finding the trout in a taking mood and hence of adding to its hereditary fame as a killer. It is on precisely the same principle that a Trentside salmon angler, if such a being still exists, who has killed one salmon in the course of his career from boyhood to old age, will declare that the spinning bait with which he secured that sample of the rari nantes in gurgite vasto is the one and only lure of that nature worth using for the king of fish by the man of experienced wisdom.

I have already indicated—and the list of flies submitted not as exclusive killers, but as those my experience has justified makes it doubly clear—that the ideal cast consists of a shrimp imitation as tail fly, a corixae imitation as second fly, and an ephemerid imitation as "bob" fly, or as it is called in England first dropper. From this it would appear that I prefer to use three flies to four. The inference is natural and it should be pointed out that the use of four flies, though a matter on which the angler can please himself, is nevertheless not a practice that prudence justifies in the majority of lochs. It certainly adds but little to the basket on lakes frequented by large fish and is positively disadvantageous in such lochs, if something abnormal in the way of rises should occur. It but rarely happens that four trout of any size rise at once and it still more rarely happens that when they do, all so time their rise by chance, that all are hooked. On the first occasion on which I ever fished that large fish pond, Loch Leven, I rose four trout at once, but hooked none. On another occasion, however, when angling in a certain Hebridean lake I rose, hooked, and landed four fish from ¾lb. to 1¼lbs., but the incident was exceptional and my success was largely due to good luck. As a third example—though in mentioning it I am intruding on the very distinct art and science of sea-trout fishing in lochs with the fly—I rose a shoal of sea-trout and hooked, when using three flies three fish all over 3lbs. I landed only one and had no control over the fish at all simply because their antics were so extraordinary that I could scarcely hold the rod for merriment. Had I been fishing with four flies I should have hooked four, and had I been fishing with six flies, six fish would have established a temporary connection. They were lying off the mouth of a burn close in by the shore. It is, therefore, not desirable to use four flies, even on the low ground that one fish at a time is the most satisfactory fishing. There is, however, an exception to this general rule. When fish are not rising there is a possibility of four flies proving more attractive by force of numbers than three—providence on such days being on the side of the big battalions. Finally it is obvious that in weedy and reedy lochs the chance of fouling is increased by the use of four flies, while there is a much greater risk of your hooking another and smaller fish when playing a large one and thus losing more than you gain by the addition of a fourth lure to your cast. On the whole, therefore, three flies, under the exception noted, appear to be the best number to use, at least in lakes boasting fish of a good size. These flies, as already noted, should, in terms of the general principle on which loch fishing with the fly is based, occupy a position in the cast determined by the character of the real or imaginary insect—swimming or flying—which they represent. The bob or first dropper fly will obviously present the most marked departure from the natural condition under which such flies are presented by nature to the trout. It is, of course, true that many flies that fly, I use the phrase for the sake of clearness, go skimming over the surface of the water kissing it here and there. Such flies are, I believe, known as "flutterers" in Ireland and possibly in certain localities out of the Sister Isle. It is true also that trout will rise at imitations of such flies. When they do so, however, it is usually only during a short season or, as already indicated, when their natural feeding time coincides with the placing on the board of this particular form of food. Presuming, however, that the skilful angler could imitate the fluttering insect—flies with automatic wings and mechanical interiors fitted with machinery being the obvious triumph towards which the imitative evolution is tending—or could when working its cunningly made presentment impart to it the dancing motion, there is no doubt that large baskets would result. He must, however, impart the appearance of life to the aquatic insects that are its attendant harbingers of doom,—subaqueous things that move and live, being, as a rule,* more tempting to the trout than dead dwellers beneath the waves—and, therefore, his "bob" fly must more or less adapt its movements to those of the other two and, on the whole, much more important flies. At the same time it is not wholly impossible to sacrifice a little of the effectiveness of the deadly twain, for the sake of the fly that is supposed to imitate the surface insect in form and colour and, as far as possible in movement. Observe what that movement is. A fly floats on a loch. It is not alternately sucked under, hurled to the surface and twisted round and round in the eddies as it is in a river. It may, it is true, be occasionally overwhelmed by a wave when these run high or it is drowned and waterlogged, its least attractive condition within my observation to good loch trout on normal days.† Its general motion is steadily down wind in its direction and undulating in character. It corresponds in fact to the onward motion of the waves, and responds to the impulse of the wind. Sometimes it is true its motion exactly corresponds to that of a vessel hove to some six points off the wind. It lifts to the rise and fall of the sea, and while making leeway appears to be fighting against the force that is driving it to leeward. This is, perhaps, more pronounced when the wind is blowing straight up and down a loch, in which case the direction of the wind and of the waves will not exactly correspond, the waves deviating from the true direction of the wind by a point or two to the "shoreward," to invent a new compass term. In any case it is obvious that the appearance you desire to give to your bob fly is that of a fly floating in the proper direction and behaving in a natural manner, so that if it is amongst half a dozen of the real Simon Pures floating through danger to death, it will appear to be one of the doomed. This may be drawing too fine a distinction, but it is nevertheless in accordance both with the morality and utilitarian expediency of loch fishing, and even in the assumption that the former is arbitrary, the latter is necessarily declaratory, because based on the facts of observation and experience.

---

*An injured minnow is, perhaps, one of the exceptions indicated by the saving clause, "as a rule."

†Vide on this and kindred points the chapter on "The Moods of Loch Trout."

Hitherto none of the ordinary flies—whether floating or wet, and I have experimented repeatedly with the former—have fully adapted themselves to the requirements of the effect desired to be produced. In the course of writing this chapter, however, I received from Messrs. Allcock a dozen specimens of flies called " Baker's patent dapping flies," which appear to me to contain the solution of the difficulty and to furnish the kind of artificial fly desired. Mr. Baker's ingenious contrivance is primarily intended as a dapping fly, and I presume for use in rivers, but it appears to me that flies, built on a similar plan and of a similar pattern, will prove the most deadly first dropper flies that were ever used in that position on lochs containing trout worth catching, not only for their size and quality, but also for their "play" and fastidousness. The hook (the fly is not dressed on it) may be very small as it is passed through the body of the fly which can be moved in any direction and will, therefore, in a loch respond to the motion of the waves.* If thrown well up wind in a light breeze or allowed to drift down wind under a carefully controlled restraint, as the boat is kept moving slowly up wind—in a manner I shall have to describe when dealing with casting—or, if, in a word, used in such a way as to represent as nearly as possible the natural movement of the fly as circumstances will admit, this ingenious invention will, I feel certain, solve the difficulty I have indicated.

Mr. Baker's fly contains precisely the idea that has often shaped itself in my mind when actually fishing and noting the defects of both floating and wet flies used alternately in the vain endeavour to secure the imitation of nature desired. I cannot, however, pursue further the purely imitative or quasi-imitative application of the philosophy of the fly as stated in the preceding chapter, and must pass to certain other aspects of the question. I have already pointed out in several passages that precisely in the same manner as, and not to a greater degree than, river trout take the fly that are imitations of natural flies behaving in an unnatural manner, so loch trout take winged flies made to act as only subaqueous insects act. This fact justifies a few observations on the use of loch flies in general. In the first place I have already incidentally mentioned the question of season as affecting possibly the expediency, and certainly the morality of selection. It is

---

* I found on actual trial that the flies raised many fish but were rather poor " hookers."

obvious that if the loch fisher is to keep before him the scientific and
pro tanto the instructive ideal at which modern fly fishing, in its moral
aspect, aims, he cannot afford to wholly neglect the suiting of the flies
to the season, so far as it can be said to affect the reasoned use of his
lures.   The degree to which it will do so, depends, it is clear, upon the
duration   of   that   season,   so   that   in   certain   lakes   in
which   the   trout   cease   rising   to   the   fly   after   a
certain date the question will be of less moment than in other
lochs in which the trout are in condition as early as March and as late
as September, and continue to take the fly with most admired regularity
for nearly one half of the year.   As I have seen loch trout rising in Islay
in December—a sight that must be still more common in Rum and
Colonsay—it might even be said that there are lakes in which short of
a close season and the cowardice of conscience the angler might be
forced to unite a study of summer with one of winter flies.   The consideration, in its serious aspect, is not, however, one peculiar to the
lake.   The seasonal aspect of flies is common to lake and river and
just as on the river so on the lake certain flies, of which the March
Brown is the chief, appear, so far as effectiveness is concerned, to be
always taken, and hence to be always in season, though naturally they
are more deadly at their natural than at their unnatural period.   I have
already indicated that in lochs trout do not always take most keenly
flies that are in season, and that they frequently take other flies acting
somewhat like the flies in season, when the latter merely occupy the position of appetisers or suggestive and predisposing agents.   Finally I
have said that within my observation the fly in season is most deadly
at the natural feeding hour of the trout, particularly when a rise of that
fly and the feeding time correspond either by chance or by reason of
their occupying the position of cause and effect.   The size of the flies
used, or, to speak correctly, the size of hook on which the flies are
dressed is obviously a matter of some importance.   Most anglers use
too large flies and it is difficult to see why the size should be made, as
often happens, to vary with the size of the lake for natural flies and
aquatic insects of the same species are the same size in all lakes, while
the size of the wave can be a consideration of no moment in
lakes in which trout take the "fly" in all its forms at all, or, in other
words, feed on the insects, winged or aquatic, which we intimate.   The

biggest wave that ever rolled will not prevent a trout seeing the smallest fly that ever floated; in fact, if use goes for anything the eye-sight of trout accustomed to stormy waters should be proportionately keener than that of trout in calmer waters whose waves do not "bury" the prey. Nature, as we know, is an ideal economist and soon enables animals to develop organs as well as instincts necessary to the sustaining of their being. Fish at great depths are black and blind; those kept in darkness are either purblind or blind. Possibly this difference in visual power does not exist in trout; but of this we can feel certain that any fly, however small, can be seen and that its visibility depends more upon its colour than its dimensions. We may, therefore, dismiss the dictum that large flies should be used in large lakes as meaningless so far as their attractiveness to the trout is concerned. It may, of course, happen as in the case of certain Irish lakes that the trout, when large, rise only during a brief three weeks or so, when, that is to say, the May fly, or whatever name it may receive, is on the rise. I confess to a strong desire—which the exigencies of daily journalism will never, I am afraid, suffer me to gratify—to visit one of those lakes and to tempt the fish on calm nights with very small flies. No doubt my efforts would result in failure, but if the lessons of the fish pond go for anything, they teach conclusively that your big fish is not a gross but a very dainty feeder when food is abundant and rich, and once in condition, will pick and choose only such morsels as suit his fastidious palate. I presume that lake trout which rise to the natural May-fly make that carnival the poor man's Christmas of their year—a period supposed by the poet to cheer his heart for a full twelve months. For the remaining eleven months and one week, I presume that they eat something even if in July's pride it be only something dainty. That is the rub. Patience might kill traditional belief. There are in Scotland a few, but not many, lakes holding good fish, in which, though there is no carnival, it is popularly believed to be next to useless to fly-fish after a certain period, generally the middle of May. There being nothing in the environment of such lakes to justify the local belief which was apparently based merely on the traditional tenets of the district anglers, who prefer, I may mention, trolling with the natural minnow to fly fishing, I set myself on two or three occasions to trying very small flies on one of these lakes. As it never does yield big baskets, I soon satisfied my-

self that the local idea was wrong, and killed some trout up to 3lbs. and
rose one very large fish of between 5lbs. and 6lbs. to judge from the
full view of him I had. There are obviously, therefore, traditions not
only as to the trout of certain lakes not taking the fly at all or only during a certain season or only of a certain size, to wit large, to which it
is just as well not to give any adherence until experiment has verified
their accuracy. I do not refer so much to some of the Irish lakes,
which have presumably been satisfactorily tested, as to certain Scottish
lochs and to the flies used upon others, whose season is not in doubt. I
am a firm believer in small flies and have invariably killed my best
baskets by using very small flies in those very lakes, for which large
flies are locally and generally recommended. The larger the fish and the
more plentiful the feeding, the smaller should be the fly, is a very safe
maxim, to which there may no doubt be some exceptions, more apparently satisfying than really so, when all the circumstances are analysed
attending the capture of a heavy basket on large flies. Big fish do not
want a big mouthful on waters where the fly is plentiful, but big fish
may take a large fly on waters where the fly is scarce and variety is a
presumptive desideratum. Personally I never use a fly dressed on a
hook above No. 12 on the Limerick scale, and cannot conceive why any
larger hook should be used for ordinary trout, unless, of course, one is
compelled to imitate a large natural fly, in which case necessity justifies the abuse. If salmon will occasionally take trout flies* when they
reject salmon flies; if the largest fish in our rivers feed on " smuts," mere
pin points incapable of human imitation, even when dressed on a ooo
hook, and big sea-trout will take finely dressed flies on No. 14 hooks,
it is obvious that the trout one can reasonably expect to catch in the
majority of our lakes do not need a large fly and are, in fact, usually
angled for with flies that are two large. I presume that many anglers
regard not merely the " raising " but also the " holding " power of hooks
as a determining factor in the size of the fly to be used, but again I
reply that if I can kill 3 trout weighing 18½lbs. in 38½ minutes of
actual fishing in a loch in a dead calm casting over rising fish with
flies on No. 13 hooks, it is obvious that there is not much amiss with
their holding power, especially as one of those fish happened to be a

---

* The largest salmon ever captured with the fly on Loch Lomond was, I believe,
killed by Mr. Hamilton Maxwell, on a trout rod and a trout fly.

10lb. fish. And even if there were, it is clear that if sport is to be determined by the difficulties overcome and by the handicap allowance the angler is willing to give the fish, then the smaller the fly and the finer the tackle the greater is the sport. I confess that short of the pleasure of being in the haunts of nature and studying her life, I can find but little joy in killing some dozens of 3 to the lb. fish on ordinary loch tackle, unless there be a chance—and this is one of the charms of lake fishing—of some leviathan coming to avenge his brethren, and win or lose an Homeric combat. The angler who desires qua angler to drink the cup of loch fishing that is most intoxicating will angle with fine tackle both in lakes where fish are large and stiff and in lakes in which they are large and natural obstacles are fairly plentiful. He will not sacrifice thereby expediency at the shrine of morality. He will not only kill more fish, once he masters the difficulties, but he will also derive an incalculable increase of pleasure from the chivalrous combat. Non cuivis adire Corinthum and the best hope of winning it is to suit the tackle to the conditions of the lake of small and "easy" trout. Let your rivals continue to kill their hecatombs, if they can, by the "slashing" methods of strong tackle. They are learning nothing and advancing to no ideal. Use small flies and fine tackle; master the delicate art of the vis major; study the fish and their habits and watch the life of the lake and let science carry the long names down the wind so long as you know the things themselves. Later you may take up the delightful task of knowing the insect world by name as well as by sight and in any case you will at the least have reft from the loch one of the joys it can give and be none the poorer.

Finally, there remains the question of colour in flies, which, as I have frequently indicated, is a more important factor in producing visibility than size. On the colour of the material used to manufacture flies, the ethics of loch angling have not, apart from the imitative and hence instructive aspect of the fly question, placed any very severe limitation. It is justifiable to use any imitation of any known insect, winged or otherwise. When these imitations fail then the ingenious can devise lusus naturae that might be ferae naturae. Most of the grayling flies used in the North of England belong to this class and custom has so justified their use, that though some of them, such as "Bradshaw's fancy," are confessedly called fancy flies, yet all of them are standard patterns. In lochs the use of such flies is not only justifiable but even occasionally advisable.* Such a fly is the improved Cardinal, called by some tackle makers the " Red Stuart " by reason of the fact that in its improved form I gave it a new lease of life. With this fly in various sizes it is possible to kill salmon, sea-trout, chub, dace, grayling and lythe and saithe. I have killed all these fish with it and once came as near killing a grey mullet as inducing a fish to come up and examine a fly may represent. It is, however, a better sea-trout than brown trout fly. Its attractiveness appears to be due to its colour and it does best in dark lochs on dark days and in the evening. I prefer it dressed with a silver body, and both for brown trout and salmon the peacock hurl addition is desirable. It is not, however, a great salmon fly, but it has more raison d'etre than the all black and all white flies used by a certain salmon angler and also salmon slayer in the north, unless tradition has bequeathed an untruth. The quality in fancy flies in loch fishing is visibility, and they are of service mostly on bad days or when trout are in a peculiar humour and the angler is puzzled.

Finally, I would point out that there is a tendency in Scotland to dress loch flies far too " rough." Such flies are more attractive to sea-trout than brown, and they are, moreover, apt to be soft and easily reduced to shreds. Fine bodies are much to be preferred for brown trout and are almost as necessary in some lochs as small flies and fine gut. Some further points in connection with flies will occur in the course of the next chapter dealing with the moods of loch trout—a subject that admits of a good deal of speculative discussion and one, therefore, of more than usual interest.

* It is, of course, quite possible to use the dry fly in lochs, but as it can only be of service in a calm or at the most in a very gentle breeze, amounting to little more than a ripple, any remarks on its employment may be left over until I deal with loch fishing in a calm. It may, however, be stated that the dry fly can only, as a rule, be of service on the loch, as on the river when fish are rising, and that on no occasion have I ever been compelled to use the dry fly to kill a particular fish. Its use is thus not necessary, and is only justified because it varies the sport and affords an interesting experiment.

CHAPTER XIX.

The Moods and Humours of Loch Trout.

In our degree we all track with fresh feet the ancient mazes, and of no subject for thought can it be said with greater truth than of angling that it is difficult to decide where facts end and speculative inferences begin to reign. The reason of this is not far to seek. Fish are still as truly the masters of their own mysteries fenced by the inviolable world of waters and the elemental fiat of Nature's procul este as they were before ichthyology essayed to penetrate the secrets of the wondrous life that lies beneath the deep and of which a single drop of water is the epitomised reflection. Some light has, it is true, been thrown by the generous lamp of modern science on much that was dark in the world of fishes, but the inner mysteries, the secrets of moods, the marvels of growth, the multiform shapes, the variations in colour that put even the rainbow's flitting form and changing hues to shame, these are still, so far as exactitude of scientific definition, of known cause as distinguished from effect, are concerned, a speculative heritage for the heirs of the ages. We see, it is true, much that is obvious in the running brook, but we scarcely see it with the clearness with which the geologist has preached the sermons of stones. He assumes an infinity and through all the years that have rolled down the steep descent of time can win no summit that is not a rock of faith set above the mists of reason. He studies effects that time has waxed old to produce and stands on the one firm spot amidst the roar of chaos watching the evolution of order by steps he can trace but of the date of whose foundation stone, he can affirm nothing. The student of fish, on the other hand, has to study an order that is without a key to its growth save those inferences from facts, which are themselves vague and often speculative. The geologist can in a word be inductive; the student of fish is almost wholly the slave of deduction and his premises are largely assumptions. So true is this that it is difficult to decide

Q

whether fish problems or the facts of fish life are like puzzles of which
the component parts can and must be made to fit or are mere kaleido-
scopes that illustrate the beauty of the ever-changing yet perfect symmetry of all the designs of nature, of which we appear to catch the
truth only to find that by a sudden and subtle movement of her forces,
the whole aspect of the picture she presents has altered. So far as the
world of fish is concerned, it is certain that though anglers, each in his
own humble way, have observed many facts of fish life that would in
all probability have escaped even hundred-eyed science, the true "all-
seeing cycle " of to-day, yet that by far the deepest mysteries of moods
and their natural retro-action on habits remain yet to be discovered.
It is true, as I have already shown, that environment as the chief
moulder and the prime maker of appetites, is a very excellent and very
safe guide to certain habits, but even environment, studied in all its
aspects, is scarcely able as a didactic agent to solve all the problems of
piscine phychology or to assign to every mood its proper material cause.
All the truths yielded by a study of environment are mere generalisations,
generalisations, it is true, of incalculable importance, but still generalisations. We know, for example, that in a good environment—in a lake
over which each day the horn of plenty is emptied, lusty trout of fastidious appetite will be found. That is the generalisation. But this truth
hardly aids us in solving the mystery of moods within moods, or why
at one hour these same fastidious trout appear to have lost their leading
characteristic and at another appear to have acquired a double measure
of the abstinence of the epicure, and to have assumed the virtue of an
asceticism that strikes a balance with the equal heaven of which trout
are the heirs.*

Yet we are not wholly without some dim light to illumine these dark
places of speculation. The fish-farmer has in a measure come to our
aid. He has verified, as most of us had assumed, that trout are, like
other animals, most excellent barometers and respond with all the readiness of an aneroid near the centre of a cyclone, to those subtle at-
mospheric changes of which we finer animals, being more mind than
matter, are for the most part wholly unconscious, unless, indeed, nature

---

* I killed in June, 1899, a very fine trout with a huge horse-leech in its mouth. It
took an ordinary fly. An hour or two later, had he survived, this trout would have been
" smutting " as his fellows were.

has vouchsafed us those most undesirable of personal weather bureaus, rheumatically-inclined limbs.

Fish-farmers have, in fact, so far solved the problem of moods in one of its aspects that they have been able to lay down the general rule as absolutely true of fish in captivity, and therefore, ex hypothesi, true of fish in a state of nature that in cold weather fish do not feed with the same degree of avidity as they do in fine, warm, genial weather.

The " common sense " of this rule is obvious. Nay, more. It is so consistent with the sensational theory as to the feeding habits of trout— moods are specialised habits—that it is necessary to point out the correspondence of the rule and the theory. Trout feed in terms of the theory when there is a predisposing cause—an excitation suggesting and creating appetite, which according to the moral leanings of the observer, may either be called a tonic or an appetiser. They feed, however, with the keenest and most absorbing appetite—then the over-mastering impulse—when times of hunger co-incide with times of plenty, when, that is to say, not only is there a desire to feed independent of the suggestion of food, but the predisposing cause that is the suggestion is also present. Now in the longest and most natural period for cold weather to occur, namely winter, there is, as a rule, but little of the material predisposing cause in evidence, or, in other words, food is scarce. Nature being provident, has out of this specialised environment, evolved a mood or habit, for the line of demarcation between the two is not clear, and has endowed trout with the faculty, common to all animals similarly situated, of doing without. When, therefore, the season of food comes round and heat, the handmaiden of summer spreads the board with all manner of delicacies, plentiful as luscious, born of sunshine and caloric, the trout, following the same wise economic provision of nature, eat their fill and soon leave behind all traces of the lean abhorred monsters that were their winter-selves. Winter, however, leaves some traces of the habits of its environment. When the cold winds blow and the sullen East or the biting North hurl forth their blasts and a winter sleep falls on the life of food, when each living thing even the most minute as well as those that he who runs may see, feels the chill that arrests all motion, that kills the joyous life of the sun-dance, and ends the fluttering from fastness to fastness, the trout with the surface suggestion gone, gladdens no more our hearts with those rings of swirling yellow eloquent of feeding fish, but becomes either a sulker in the weeds or beneath the stones or a questing hunter seeking his prey in its lairs and hiding places.

How true all this is to the facts of nature as we find her it seems scarcely necessary to prove by examples and yet experience on this point is so instructive that one cannot afford to ignore it. The value of such experience to the practical angler is that he can find a definite cause for his lack of success and can moreover replenish his stock of hope by studying the effect of temperature on fish. If cold, as a rule, "puts fish down" then he finds his consolation in the fact; if any change for the better in the weather will put fish on the rise, then he has his new source of hope. That both these conclusions are justified the following experiences will help to prove.

One April day, in 1890, I was fishing Milton Loch, in South Uist. The wind when I commenced operations was N.E., moderately strong and cold. As it fell away the sun grew hot and strong, and the trout began to show all over the loch, but they would not take my flies. Suddenly it fell calm, or nearly so. At once they began to take, and, when a gentle breeze from the west sprang up, they took greedily for the ten minutes or so during which it lasted; every cast I got a fish or a rise. Shortly, however, the cold grey north-easter asserted its sway, and not a fish would move. This is only one of many instances; but could any proof be more conclusive? The joyous burst of sunshine seemed to reach the hearts of the trout, and made them anticipate delicate morsels in the shape of flies; while, when the grey north-easter swept once more over loch and moor, its cold and cheerless blast bred despair of delicate and toothsome fare in the troutish breast, and hence they kept to the bottom, because there was but little to be expected and no suggestion of food on the surface.

There are, however, no rules without exceptions, and as it is the exception that must give us pause whenever we are apt to wax vain glorious over our triumphs as readers of the riddles of troutish moods. Two of these exceptions may here be noted amongst many that might be cited. In Loch Guirm in Islay one April day I fished for several hours on the weather shore where the water was clearest and the sand had not been stirred up by the strong wind that was blowing. A day of ordinary angling duration yielded me some eight trout and about seven o'clock, as the wind was chill and blowing strongly and the sky was clear, hard and cold, I thought it the part of wisdom to seek the seclusion of home. A certain curiosity made me cross the loch and enquire of a party of three rods who had, in defiance of the traditions of the loch been fishing the lee shore, how they had fared. I found them in the midst of a most abnormal rise of fish, for everywhere, in spite of the cold night, the hard sky, the biting wind, the drumlie loch and the absence of flies and hence of any predisposing cause, trout were rising with such keenness of purpose, such abandonment of appetite that I added 42 fish to my basket in an incredibly short space of time. It was not fishing, but slaughter, and all that was required to kill fish was a measure of mechanical accuracy in striking, playing and landing them. Now read merely in the light of its own apparent facts this experience would appear to be directly opposed to the experience first cited and the generalisation of moods which it illustrates. On the contrary, when all the circumstances of the case are stated, it is only at the best a modified exception to the rule. The day in question was the end of a phenomenally long and a particularly hard winter, and in its warmer periods had really been the first day of spring and the harbinger of many fine, genuine spring days worthy of the best traditions of that season of hope. No doubt though human bodies did not respond to the coming life of the revolving year that was in the air, yet the barometric persons of the trout nobly answered the subtle invitation and the great rise was thus not only the prologue to the omen coming on, but also, as that prologue was felt by the life of the lake in general, the result of an awakening of the old appetites by material suggestions of the coming feast as unseen by the eye only studying the surface of the lake, as the approaching climatic change was unfelt by the body which should have been that eye's watch tower.

Sometimes, however, great rises occur without my apparent reason at all, during which all the trout in certain parts of the lake seem quite mad, for they boil and spume on the surface with fierce boisterous rises and yet are not feeding and will take nothing. I saw last year two such commotions—they appeared to be battles—on a certain lake which holds only large fish. On the first occasion there was a steady curl on the water, but there were no flies. Suddenly, however, when I was fishing in shore I observed straight out from where I was casting a great many of these spluttering rises which gave the loch in that quarter the same appearance on a small scale as a shoal of saithe or lythe might have done. They appeared, to my fancy at least, to be engaged in something very like a battle, because two or three rises would follow in quick succession near the same place, and they appeared to be caused by different fish. The presence of an otter also occurred to me as a solution, but I did not see the tell-tale head appear once, though I kept my eyes fixed on the spot. The very next day I fished the lake, I saw a similar sight, but the rise was closer in shore, and so many fish were moving that had they been rising at the fly or for feeding purposes, I should certainly have killed some of them. As it was none of these fish paid the slightest attention to my flies, and when I went right in amongst them appeared to move off a bit and renew the fierce rising with which they made the water boil again. It occurred to me at the time that for some reason or other a number of the fish had been rendered in a bellicose mood and that I had witnessed a battle royal without being able to see the details of the fight.

An actual trout duel which I witnessed during the ensuing September confirmed this opinion. The stream in which the duel took place is in part artificial, and the portion in which it was fought is fenced off so that the fish cannot escape. Into this fenced portion, over 2,000 trout of different kinds—rainbows, brown trout, and Loch Leveners—and varying in size from ¾lb. to 1½lbs., had been put some months before. The duellists were two of these fish. One was a female brown trout, and the other was a female rainbow, a species that has a great reputation as a fighter at certain seasons. I first noticed the fish through a fierce commotion and turmoil very similar but on a smaller scale to what I saw on the loch, that was going on in the smooth water just above where an artificial waterfall marked "the torrent's smoothness ere it dash below." On approaching the hurly-burly of the waters, the cause of their troubling became clear. The female rainbow was at that moment making a series of determined onslaughts upon the other lady trout, who, to prevent the charges getting home, was displaying the agility of an indiarubber fish, while watching for a chance to adopt the excellent tactics of changing a retreat into an attack.

Presently there was a lull in the battle, and both fish, as if by mutual consent, paused for breath. They lay parallel to one another, about six inches apart, as near the surface as they could get, and as close to the barrier as possible, presumably with the object of having their respective rears protected.   In this, as will presently appear, they showed themselves masters of tactics and wonderfully intelligent generals—especially for animals who are supposed to possess no brain cortex, and hence no memory, in the strict sense of the phrase. Suddenly Mrs. Brown Trout swept swiftly round to the rear of Mrs. Rainbow, and made a series of lively dashes and little grabs at the point where the tail joins the body—technically known as the wrist.   Mrs. Rainbow was, however, equal to the occasion.   As Mrs. Brown grabbed, Mrs. Rainbow's head went down and her tail up.

Then suddenly changing defensive into offensive tactics, she swept round in her turn and delivered a series of vicious attacks on Mrs. Brown's rear, which compelled that fish to fly and circle round until the water foamed again.   For over an hour the same tactics were pursued, the bouts varying in viciousness and fierceness according to the duration of the rest between the " rounds," when each fish, so to speak, retired to its corner to recover its wind.   At last I went right down on the fish and tried to separate them with a stick.   It was of no avail. The moment they were left to themselves they were at it again as hard as ever.   Darkness finally shrouded this curious duel, but as the shades of night fell Mrs. Rainbow seemed likely to be the victor, for Mrs. Brown's attacks were growing less frequent and more feeble, and she scarcely ever dared to leave the vicinity of the barrier which protected her rear.

It may be mentioned that for animals thus to lose all their sense of caution and of fear at the approach of man when the battle rage is on them is nothing new.   A case of two king-fishers who were fighting so fiercely that they suffered themselves to be caught by the hand was recently reported in the South of England, while, robins, blackcock, capercailzie (shyest and most wary of all game birds), pheasants, and other birds frequently exhibit the same warrior scorn for man when engaged in battle with their peers in plumage and rivals in love.

Here then was a practical example of what must often occur in the loch and give the angler the mistaken idea that he has seen a feeding fish rise or many feeding rise according to the number of the combatants and the extent of the battle.   The bellicose mood is obviously not one to be desired, for during its continuation the fish are intent only on pummelling one another and have not the slightest interest in flies or anything else of an edible nature. It has only one possible advantage. It may be the means of demonstrating to an angler the presence of fish and on a bad day the sight of fish, whether one can catch them or not, acts as a renovator of hope and an inspirer of further effort.

Nor will the loch fisher fail to occasionally encounter examples of trout that physicalise the moods or habits, called "bulging," "tailing," and "smutting." It is however, a most exceptional circumstance to find the trout of lochs, peopled for the most part by fish of a small size, displaying either of these three irritating, but extremely interesting phases. On the other hand in lakes abounding in large fish—and the number of lakes in which all the trout, from the angler's point of view, are large fish, is very limited—it may, with approximate truth, be stated that the trout display all three moods with even greater frequency than do the fish of the majority of rivers occupying the same position on the scale of angling waters. It is, in fact, such a common occurrence to find large loch trout rising and either not feeding or feeding on "something" which the angler cannot match, that in certain lakes, any of these three moods may more truthfully be described as a habit —a permanent trait of regular occurrence which varies only in the degree and intensity of its display. Of the "bulging" trout—a trout, that is to say, feeding on the nymphae of certain flies, before they reach the surface, the loch fisher need not have the same respectful fear as the "dry fly" angler. The reason is not far to seek. The loch-fisher fishes as a rule with his flies sunk and if he uses certain patterns, he must necessarily present to the trout subaqueous food. For example, if the trout be feeding—and the false "rise" is always localised to certain reaches and is never universal—on May flies on their way to the surface, a sunk May fly will sometimes take fish, though on an average of occasions the "red and teal," and the "heckum peckum" are, even under such circumstances, by far the most effective flies. Another and much more irritating form of "quasi-bulging" I have already described. It occurs without any apparent predisposing cause but, differs from the true "bulging," in so far as there is no remedy for its tantalising effect. It is interesting to watch and affords ample scope for much pleasing, but scarcely profitable, speculation. It may happen at any period of the day, but is of most frequent occurrence, a short time before the beginning of the evening rise in lakes in which that thrice-glorious event is of certain occurrence.

I have seen occasional examples of both the true and the false "bulging" even in lakes holding comparatively small fish, and have already recalled one of many Hebridean instances of the former, during a change of a very light wind from North-East to West and just before a burst of sunshine warmed water and moor lying in shivering greyness beneath a sullen dome of leaden hue. Of "smutting" trout, again, not only will the lake fisher meet with many examples in lochs holding only large fish which are in the habit of rising to the fly, but he will also find that, as in the river, so in the lake, the raising of such fish is possibly a matter of chance and assuredly a feat only to be accomplished by the exercise of unwearied patience and the steady trial of one fly or of many flies. So far as I am aware, no satisfactory explanation has ever been given of why trout suddenly develop an exclusive love for small pin-point flies and resolutely decline to look at any other kind of fly—artificial or natural. Our leading entomological anglers, especially those who study fish in clear shallow water, must have more and better opportunities of observing the cause and effect of fish moods than the mere student of fish in lakes can have—even though the education of the latter has not been confined to lochs, but has extended over rivers of the North and of the South. It is, therefore, a somewhat remarkable fact that the chalk-stream angler has been content to state the facts of this mystery of mood, without attempting to solve the problem underlying these facts. In attacking this and kindred questions, the best plan appears to be to throw all prejudices to the winds and to give full play to the imagination—which is merely reason in a fancy dress. Acting on this plan I proceeded on the hypothesis that the "bulging" trout and the "tailing" trout are the fathers of the "smutting" trout, or, in other words, that "bulging" and "tailing" are the preliminary stages to "smutting," the causes which produce the effect known by that inelegant, but expressive term. Now "tailing" fish are necessarily less frequently observed in lochs than in rivers, for the very simple and obvious reason that lakes are deeper than rivers. They are quite as numerous, however, even if one does not see them save in shallows and by reed beds. In the absence of direct ocular proof there is, however, the internal evidence, which an autopsy reveals or the external evidence which trout, as a rule, are willing to afford by ejecting food after capture. The field of my investigation was purposely limited to a single loch, not only because in a matter of this kind the lessons of one lake are necessarily the generalisations one would have to deduce from a study of many lakes with their unavoidable, even if only apparent, exceptions to the rule inferred from the noted cases, but also because a study of large trout in a good environment of easy plenty and of large trout only, so situated, could result in any light being thrown on a mood, that presupposes and must presuppose the existence of the conditions outlined as necessary to its production and display. It may happen, and under certain conditions will almost invariably happen, that even smallish loch-trout, say fish averaging three to the pound, will refuse every known lure, but I can recall no lake in which small trout when on the rise display the malignant "recusancy" of the "bulger" or the "tailer" or the "smutter" in lakes and rivers holding large and well-fed fish.

Taking the "tailer" first, I endeavoured to record as many instances as the big, fastidious fish would permit, of days on which it was obvious by an examination of the food ejected or contained in the gullet or stomach that the trout had been feeding on shrimps, snails, tadpoles, and even horse-leaches! Having noted during the day the nature of the food contained in, or ejected by, the trout, obviously the next step in the process of confirmatory observation was to note whether or not on such days "smutting" characterised the only assured rise of the day—the evening rise—and to what degree the "smutting" responded to the degree of "tailing" which had been indulged in—presuming that the intensity of the latter feeding mood could be roughly estimated. One example of recent occurrence may suffice to illustrate not only the connection between the cause—"tailing"—and the effect—"smutting"—but also the process of confirmation to which the hypothesis was subjected.

In June of the present year in the lake selected for experimental purposes, I fished diligently on a certain day from 9 a.m. until 3.30 p.m. without a rise, and I saw only occasional fish break the surface in the shallows. These were undoubted "tailers." Finally, at 3.30 I rose, hooked and landed an exquisitely shaped and beautiful trout of just

over 2lbs. It came at a red-ant—the fly then on the water in greatest.
abundance—with the fierceness of a tiger. On being landed it ejected!
a huge horse-leach about 3 inches long and as black as the proverbial
Sathanas. The old order was resumed until about half-past seven, when
there was a sudden and rather localised rise. I happened at the moment
it began to be within casting distance of the scene of the chief troutish
activity, and in consequence my flies were at once sent over almost the
first fish that rose. For a short time every fish over which I cast took
the fly and I landed four, and had the rather novel experience (in this
lake) of raising and hooking only very lightly other two. Up to this
point all went well. The fish were not "smutting." Suddenly, however, they began to display this mood and not a single fish that rose,
whether quietly, in which case he merely put his nose up, or noisily, in
which case he "boiled" like a salmon, would condescend to look at
my flies. I tried "dry fly" and "wet fly," small flies and big, fancy
flies and, in fact, ran the whole gamut of choice, but all were equally
vain. A rise of midges soon made their presence felt and it was these
pests in conjunction with the previous "tailing" that had obviously
produced the fastidious mood. Other and previous experiences of a
similar nature had fallen to my lot in the same lake and the conclusion
appears to be unavoidable, even if it be not yet wholly justified by a
sufficient number of instances, that indulgence in a surfeit of animal
food, shrimps, tadpoles and so forth is, when conjoined with the
presence of the predisposing agent—some minute fly—the cause of
"smutting." If experience on a lake can be any safe guide to the river
fisher, another and equally necessary conclusion to be drawn is that at
the very beginning of a "smutting" rise and before the immediate cause
of the rise has had time to consolidate, as it were, the mood or prejudice the taste, trout will readily take ordinary flies of a much larger
size than the pin-point called by the generic name of "the curse."*
     My observations of the effect of "bulging" agree in every way with
the effect produced by "tailing," whether inferred or seen or both, and

---

* When these pages were in the press Mr. J. W. Blakey informed me that he once
killed a smutting grayling with (1) "smuts" in its gullet, and (2) 97 Limnea Peregra in
its stomach. The latter was the only food in the stomach, and very few of the shells were
broken. The fish had indulged in a regular gorge on this food. This grayling took a
Double Palmer. The facts of this case furnish strong confirmatory evidence of the
general accuracy of the theory.

though the number of instances I have noted is limited, the effect has invariably followed the cause.

One is scarcely called upon to prove a negative, but negative evidence is often the most convincing proof. It is somewhat curious, therefore, that the angling conditions of the day immediately succeeding the one to which I have already referred should have provided precisely the kind of negative evidence desired. It was a bright, hot, calm day. Little airs were breathed now and then out of the heated stillness and with the earliest of these there was a slight, but marked, rise of May fly. I began operations when the last fly of the rise was yet fluttering in the air and when an odd fish was still responding to the predisposing cause. I was forced to use a rod to which my hand was a stranger and the one and only fish I succeeded in raising—and I rose him the second cast—was a fish that had just taken the last fly already referred to. He came to a sunk May fly of a pattern recommended to me by Mr. J. W. Blakey, the Editor of the "Angler," who is an exceptionally keen observer of troutish moods, and in consequence adopts the wise plan of suiting his feathered lures to the occasion, as all opportunists should do. The fact that this fish came to a sunk May fly or a May fly fished wet clearly showed that had the rise of fly continued, the trout would probably have begun to "bulge." As a matter of fact the rise ceased and only an occasional May fly at long and irregular intervals, burst from the lake and went fluttering over its surface, playing at the very gates of death the old, old game of many a sun-kissed day with the grim overlord and his vassals and retainers, the trout that lurk below and the gulls that hover above each fatal reach. As surely as a fore-doomed May fly rose, as surely it flew, floated and fluttered to the dark inn. Yet was death wayward. A fly might win a hundred yards in safety; it might traverse only a few yards of the stricken field before the doom of the deep was meted out. It was a weird, uncanny sight to watch—this epitomised picture of the chance and change of life in the wider world. There is no shadow of the coming event thrown across the sunlit path of the May fly. It is sublimely unconscious of its doom. A cynic would have longed for some one with whom to wager on the length of the road to death each occasional May fly would succeed in traversing; to an optimist each drama of death would have suggested certain problems in Greek Anthology, of death as a sleep made welcome by faint dreams of the roar of old ocean on a western beach, of the vanity and nothingness of things—a lapse to pessimism banished by some idle musings on the true inwardness of nature worship, of the higher Pantheism, the cradled slumber of Heliodora on the bosom of the kindest of all mothers, the Earth, the promised bliss of the Eleusinian Mysteries and the wondrous frame of mind that has enabled some men to see the comic side of death and to smile not in death, but at the idea of the end of thinking being—the utter night that may, and in one aspect, must descend over the horizon of consciousness when our little life is rounded with a dreamless sleep or a sleep in which dreams may come—the worse of the two evils if Nirvana is heaven, and Shakespeare misinterpreted the coward conscience.

These reflections were, no doubt, justified by the occasion, but strictly speaking, they were only magnificent and not angling war. I essayed, therefore to imitate the May-fly fluttering on and off the lap of death— now kissing the surface, now floating in peaceful trust, anon sailing up a few feet into the gladsome air and finally dropping to its doom. As it is only when the May fly lives, moves, and has its being that it has any attractiveness for the loch trout, this was high policy. The fish, it is true, take the fly below the surface as it comes up or, in other words, "bulge." A very sure sign that they are so feeding is an occasional wild, hurtling, quivering leap from the water that lacks all signs of playfulness and is so instinct with business that it cannot, once seen, ever be mistaken; but, as a rule, it is the living and moving May fly that tempts the fish to feed. The spent fly, dead and floating a bedraggled wreck shorn of all life, has no charms for the loch trout faithful to the traditions of his high born race. A fish of the baser sort, some lank malignant, may seize such lifeless prey, but the sporting fish holds it in high scorn as mere garbage, for he is a born hunter and his food must be the very spoil of his spear and bow.

For an hour or more the drama continued. By high noon the lake was apparently lifeless. Nature lay asleep in the sun. And her sleep was long. She slept until the shadows began to creep up in the East and a red glow flushed up in the West—a glow that was caught by the hill-tops, that stained the heather a deeper red and was reflected by the lake until the water by its further shores gleamed violet in the

calm, like the smooth surface of a crescent-shaped amethyst. And with
the shadows and the blushing farewell of the day came the rise—the
rise of fish that had not fed all the day, that had neither "bulged" nor
"tailed," but had slept with nature and responded to her mood. Theirs
was the hunger of a healthy breakfast appetite destined not to be
tempted from its waking meal, by the pin-point delicacies of the evening
before and assuredly unblunted by the grosser fare eaten at irregular
meal-hours during a running feast that lasted the livelong day. The
fish, as a matter of fact, rose steadily and regularly and I only ceased
to kill an occasional specimen (one of my captures is figured on page
24) when darkness and the imperious calls of personal hunger sounded
the cessation of hostilities.

The only inference which can be drawn from these and similar experiences is that when fish have been "bulging" and "tailing," they
will either not take at all or will "smut" if the predisposing cause be
present. In the absence, therefore, of any more satisfying explanation,
(1), of the "bulging" and "tailing" mood or habit—for according to
the intensity and frequency both are displayed, "bulging" and "tailing"
may be either a mood or a habit—and, (2), of the "smutting" mood or
habit—under the same reservation—the explanation which I have
outlined and illustrated may be accepted as based on personally observed facts, while the inference from these facts is the only logical
and possible inference. That the explanation traces all these moods or
habits and their retroactive influence the one upon the other to material
agencies and hence to specialised environments, is, it need hardly be
pointed out, the only consistent method of reasoning which the sensational theory of fish life admits of being employed. It is, for that very
reason, highly probable that it contains if not the whole truth, such a
measure of the truth, that its claim to be a satisfying explanation will
be hard to rebutt.

I have already indicated that trout are excellent barometers, but why
they should be so is a question that must be classed amongst the as yet
unanswered and perhaps unanswerable problems. The fact is, however,
of some use to the angler, for it readily accounts for bad days when
conditions are apparently favourable. Most of, indeed all, the weather
rules are subject to exceptions, but for any divergence there is generally
a possible explanation. The very best sport is obtained in the great

majority of lakes in fine, settled weather, possibly because it sets up a
certain amount of regularity in the rise of flies and a corresponding
sequence of moods in the trout, while most coming or actual climatic
changes for the better appear to have a subtle influence on the fish and
to predispose them to rise apart from any more apparent cause.

There is one climatic condition, namely, the depression before an
approaching thunderstorm, in which loch trout are thought to be un-
willing to rise.   In the general case this may be true; but again we are
met with the mystery of troutish humour, for within my own experience
I can recall a few very notable exceptions.   In Loch Guirm in Islay, in
July, 1896, I could not get a rise until just before a thunderstorm and
during its continuation, while, after it was over (a period usually favourable) the trout would hardly look at the fly.   In Loch Dhu, in
Perthshire, in the spring both of 1888 and 1889, it was during a heavy
thunder-plump, and before and during a thunderstorm, that I was most
successful; while an angler who has frequently fished Loch Dochart
told me that the largest basket which he ever secured in that lake was
killed, for the most part, under similar conditions.   The effect of
thunder on trout depends, so far as my observation warrants me in
laying down any rules, on the general nature of the weather
preceding the outburst.   If it has been warm and fine, or, in other
words, favourable as a whole for loch fishing, and the trout have acted
in a manner consistent with the weather, then thunder usually puts
them down; but they will, by way of compensation, rise freely after the
air has cleared, and very freely, if it has been an afternoon storm, followed by a fine, fresh, exhilarating evening, with a   pleasant   little
breeze.   In spring, however, when thunder is often preceded by rude
and boisterous weather, a thunderstorm during its various stages will
generally act as an exciting cause and bring fish on the rise, while in
summer and early autumn, if the weather has been cold and stormy, the
loch angler may find that a thunderstorm if it is the harbinger of good
weather or the change following on bad, acts as an exciting influence towards making loch trout rise, while on the other hand, when the
thunderstorm is caused by a lengthened period of fine warm weather,
it has a depressing effect, which will last for a time, dependent either
upon the duration of the storm itself or the quality of the weather which
is to follow it, the bad effect being the more prolonged the worse the
subsequent weather.

I have, in these remarks, on a rather speculative subject, confined myself for the most part to those generalisations which experience has suggested. The subject is an almost inexhaustible one and as habits are in one sense merely long continued moods, or in other words, the humours, in the old sense of that phrase, induced by very special conditions of environment, I shall be able in the succeeding chapter, on the habits. of loch trout so far as they affect angling for them, to add something, perhaps, of a more definite nature, to those somewhat speculative generalisations already set forth on the moods, or transient, as distinguished from permanent, habits of trout in lochs.

CHAPTER XX.

The Habits and Habitats of Trout in Lochs.

Habits being the results of general environment as moods are the products of "specialised" environment it is but natural to find that the trout of different lochs have different habits which correspond, more or less approximately, to the differences in their respective environments and arise in precisely the same way and from similar causes as do the varying moods of trout in the same loch.

If we were in a position to invade the secret places of any loch and could for a week keep an observant eye on its denizens and their food and methods of securing it we would assuredly be able to build up a much more exact history of the habits of trout, so far as these habits affect the angler than we are at present in a position to do. Much of the evidence on which our conclusions are based is circumstantial, some is hypothetical and our reasoning is largely by analogy and by inferring causes from the observation of effects rather than by deducing effects from known causes. It is even difficult, as I have pointed out, to distinguish a mood or transient habit from a permanent characteristic in the form of action. Nevertheless the generalisations are not unsupported by specific instances not only of how habits are acquired, but of how habits affect what we term "the nature" of the trout as a sport-yielding fish. Environment being the moulder of habits and a question of food, and in a lesser degree of "housing" we would expect trout frequenting a lake like Loch Stennis in Orkney to display very different habits to the trout of a small upland tarn. Invaded as Loch Stennis is by the salt wash of the tide, and abounding, as it does, in all those forms of food that go to the making of great fish, we would expect to find a race of trout inhabiting its spreading waters of giant size and quick growth. Nay more. As we know that Stennis is of the blood of ocean and the bubbling spring, we would expect to find its trout possessing some of the characterictics or habits of the salmon when

R

in the sea and in the majority—in fact nearly all—of our large lakes. We would, in other words expect the trout to display a marked partiality for the grosser kinds of food, for there is no question that the sea has a debasing influence on the feeding habits of fish—a fact that might point to a semi-ethical foundation for the virtue of abstention displayed by the salmon in fresh water, if one were seeking a principle of piscine metaphysics. In any case we would expect to find that the trout of Stennis were bottom and "animal" feeders and not fish with a marked habit of rising to the fly. Experiment would at once verify this expectation, but would at the same time present us with a fresh, but by no means insoluble problem. We would find that, though trout over a certain size, did not, as a matter of habit, take the fly, yet that up to a certain size they did take it with an avidity and a constancy varying with their approximation to or divergence from that size. There is here an inconsistency more apparent than real, which the facts of the case on further analysis would help us to solve. Environment being the creator of habits we would naturally turn to the earlier environment of the smaller trout of Stennis and in a lesser degree to the difference in their environment and that of the larger fish in the lake, premising so far as the latter is concerned, that though fish within the same environment are de jure commoners of water, de facto the blessings of environment fall to the strong fin, just as in the world of men and in all the animal kingdom they are the spoil of the fittest, whether "fitness" springs from brawn and muscle or brain and reason. If, therefore, we enquired into the early environment we should find that it was not in Stennis itself but in its tributary streams that the babyhood if not childhood of the fly-taking fish was passed. Knowing as we do that the habit of taking the fly can be created and fostered in trout by the cultivation of a condition of existence prompting and necessitating the taking of the fly, it is an easy and an irresistible conclusion that the fly-taking habit in the smaller Stennis trout is a legacy of their earlier environment. Nay more, we know, in spite of a peculiar local belief that the trout of Harray are sickened by salt water very much as the coarse fish of the Norfolk Broads undoubtedly are,* that the troutish

---

* The roach which occasionally frequent certain tidal reaches of the Thames in which the water has, presumably, a flavour of salt, do not appear to be effected by it. The effect of salt water on coarse fish appears, in fact, to be a matter of custom. In the case of trout, its effect is hygienic. It never does harm, and is usually beneficial.

population of Stennis is regularly added to by immigrants from Harray, who for some time will continue to display the fly-feeding habit acquired in their earlier environment. Further in the case both of the natives and the immigrants,* their existing environment, whether considered topographically or merely from the point of view of its distributed blessings, is actually conducive, by the limitation it imposes on the safe gratification of the appetites it creates by suggestion, and by the necessities to which it gives birth, to the growth of the sensational association of ideas to which the earlier environment gave rise, between a fly and something good to eat.

It is easy to see, therefore, why the trout of Stennis until they attain a certain measure of size and strength are not made citizens in the right of the richer blessings of the lake, and commoners that feed "above the salt," at its richly but unequally spread table. Compelled therefore, literally vi et armis to seek humbler and safer quarters, the old habit of their first environment continues to be kept from falling into desuetude by the necessities of their present conditions of existence.

We have here, therefore, not only an explanation of why trout in all lakes where bottom feeding is plentiful and surface feeding scarce, do not take the fly as a matter of habit, but also an equally satisfactory solution of two other problems, namely the varying avidity for the fly shown by the trout of the same lake at different seasons of the year and by fish of different sizes during the season when the fish are surface feeders. The degree of partiality displayed by the fish for the fly, whether during the whole season or an ascertained period of the season, will, however, depend upon certain other considerations. The first and most obvious of these is the proportion which surface food in the form of flies, in the popular sense, bears to subaqueous food, while obviously the character of that subaqueous food must largely affect the striking of the balance between "rising" and "non-rising" in the angling as distinguished from the strict sense of the phrase. It is obviously, in other words, not absolutely necessary that trout should feed on ephemerids or any other form of winged fly that flies, to secure for the angler the assurance that he does not offer his imitations in vain. If, for example, a loch be people by the corixae in any of their thirty or

* Practically all the Stennis trout may be said to spawn and to be born and bred in the tributary burns of Harray.

more forms, some of the trout in the lake, and indeed all the trout in
the lake, other things being equal, will feed on them with a steady
avidity amounting to a confirmed habit born in the fish through environ.
ment as soon as it is able to master the corixa. Now though the corixa
is a water insect that swims about propelled by its oars, yet it rises
to the surface to breathe, and hence must often be seized when near or
actually on the surface by the trout. Moreover a trout is by no means
a fool in the matter of sensational wisdom and will probably discover
that when the corixa goes to the surface, it is in its most helpless,* because most breathless, condition and falls, therefore, at such a time an
easier prey to his vigilant rapacity than when with lungs charged and
in possession of its second wind it can make a life or death race, if nothing of a fight, with a fish beyond the fry stage. It is obvious, therefore, that no amount of subaqueous feeding of this nature will make
fish resolutely refuse the fly or develop a habit opposed to the interests
of the fly-fisher.

It is at the same time true that the presence of this sort of food in
great abundance, while it does not create the habit of absolute abstention from surface food in the angling sense, yet tends to foster the
habit of bottom feeding. In any particular lake in which the condition
of existence just referred to prevails, we will find that its effect upon
the fish in the direction indicated will vary with certain other conditions,
of which not the least important is the topographical condition of
depth. The presence of immense numbers of subaqueous insects of
the corixae family would obviously in a lake abounding in shallows,
much more in one possessing no deeps, have the very opposite effect
upon the trout of that lake than to create in them the non-rising habit.
On the other hand, if the lake consisted, as most reservoirs do, in
deeps and was characterised by the absence of shallows, even the fact
that the corixae rose to the surface, presuming they would thrive in
such a lake would scarcely create the rising habit in the trout to
the same extent as in a shallow lake. Viewed absolutely depth is
we know inimical to the cultivation of the fly-feeding habit if only because deep waters are not the best homes for water-born insects.
There are, moreover, other conditions which one cannot afford to overlook. Two of these are the number of burns or rivers falling into a

* The corixa is, of course, most helpless when it breaks an "oar."

lake and the abundance of non-fertile shallows that afford shelter, if they do not afford much food, to the small fish in the lake, presuming that we are dealing with a lake holding good fish. Apart from the fact that the number of tributaries falling into a lake materially affect, as spawning beds and nurseries, the number of its inhabitants, it is clear that as they never afford under natural conditions the same feeding as the lake itself, the habits acquired in these tributaries will very largely influence the habits of the trout when they seek the wider and richer waters of the lake. In the burns and rivers the trout will assuredly develop the fly-taking habit and this they will continue to display in the loch in a degree varying with the predisposing excitation of their sensations. A similar process of reasoning enables us to arrive at the conclusion that according to the number of poverty-stricken shallows not frequented by the larger trout of the lake, save when the shadows fall and the predatory cannibalistic appetite asserts its sway under the evil influence of the powers of darkness, so will the fly-taking habit be induced in the trout, to be continued as before in accordance with the duration of the exciting cause.

If this general reasoning be correct—and I think its conclusions are logical and based on sound premises, we would expect to find that lakes of unequal feeding grounds, of barren shallows and fertile bottoms of a depth not sufficient to preclude fly-fishing, and into which many or some streams fall, are generally those in which the trout display the fly-taking habit and may be taken by the fly.

On the other hand we would expect to find, that, apart from spawning and other considerations, lakes of absolutely or approximately equal quality all over their extent, boasting few or no barren shallows and fed by few or no tributaries will contain, other things being equal, trout less disposed to rise to the fly than those of the first class of lake.

Loch Leven is an example of the first class of lake, and amongst others that occur to me at the moment of writing Loch Ardnahuidh in Islay is an example of the second class. The question is clearly an important one if we are to make the cultivation of environment a problem to be solved by the design of ascertained models of excellence from the lowest angling standpoint and not one, dependent for its solution, on a fortuitous combination of circumstances. I pass, however, to the consideration of certain other conditions which affect the habits of loch trout as fish yielding sport to the fly fisher. Before, however, enlarging upon these conditions, it appears to me to be necessary to ascertain the ideal at which it is proper to aim. Angling ideals vary, but all fishermen are at least agreed that the habit of taking the fly is a necessity to sport with the fly; where they differ is in stating the degree to which that habit should be created, while the ultimate standard of excellence resolves itself into what may fairly be termed a question of education in so far as it affects the methods, lures and gear to be employed in the capture of trout by the fly. It is very obvious that if we could make our lakes by artificial means, whether considered topographically or in relation to the habits of their denizens or both—and the latter is the proper position, but little better than large fish ponds affording a " straight forward " and uniform surface on which to work a fly, we would reduce angling to a mere question of mechanical skill of no very high order, and would, in fact, secure not anglers' but duffers' paradises. Natural lakes of this character exist on which the tyro can kill good, and the skilled angler better, baskets, but it is the difficult or what I term the sporting lakes that give the greatest pleasure because they not only demand skill of hand, but also necessitate hard thinking of the most delightful and mind-resting kind for the man whose brain through all its convolutions of grey matter carries the great burden of these days of ceaseless activity and competition that sleeps only on its feet. I assume, therefore, that the ideal lake of to-day is the sporting lake; that the ideal lake of the future, when our waters are made to bear the harvest commensurate with their natural fertility, will be of the same character; and that the habits of the trout of the lakes on the margin of cultivation in the days to come will be of less moment than are those of the fish of the easy lakes of to-day, save as negative evidence. At the same time as all science—and loch fishing can when considered in all its aspects claim a share in the universal heritage of knowledge—is complementary, it is scarcely possible to ignore the habits of the fish of any lake, no matter what its character as a home for trout may be. We must, therefore, from this consideration, admit the trout of all lakes as witnesses in the question of general habits.

Resuming accordingly the general question, under the presumption leading to this digression, there is the question of cannibalism to be considered as a habit created by environment, or in other words by the existence of conditions predisposing towards it. Now there is a popular belief, based to some extent on fact, that only certain trout in any lake or indeed river, are confirmed and inveterate cannibals and that other trout in the same lake never display what is erroneously called the cannibalistic instinct, but is really the cannibalistic habit. The most common explanation given of the existence in certain lakes of large fish only is that they are cannibals and eat their fellows and hence have the field practically left to themselves.

Now, the cannibalistic habit being like all other habits the result of environment, it is necessary before giving adherence to the above general proposition to examine the conditions under which the habit is most likely to arise as well as the limitations which, on the one hand, the habit will necessarily by its exercise impose on itself, and, on the other, will have imposed on its exercise by the topographical and other conditions of existence in any lake. The popular belief is—and to this popular belief fish-farmers have given the approval of their experience, that fish located in a pond or lake where feeding is scarce will attain unequal sizes corresponding to their opportunities or to that same natural tendency to be a "big fellow" or a "little chap" displayed far more frequently by men than animals. These big fellows or big bullies— for courtesy is lost on the fish in discussing their night side—take to eating their fellows and their size and strength growing by what it feeds upon, a sort of oligarchy of the strong fin is set up after a reign of cannibalistic anarchy and we have the cannibalistic habit.

I would, at this point, draw attention to a very important fact. This theory, though it is not so stated by its exponents, really rests on a very solid substratum of indisputable fact, which they take for granted. I refer to the indubitable truth that all trout are cannibals. Though this is true, it does not necessarily follow that all trout are cannibals to the same degree. This brings us back to the point at which we started, namely the position that the development of the cannibalistic habit is entirely a question of environment. Nor does the habit satisfactorily account for the fact that certain lakes appear to be entirely given over to large trout, to whose presence and inferred cannibalism, we attribute the absence of small trout, while we presuppose their existence with delightful inconsequence, by calling the big denizens cannibals. This position of approbate and reprobate involves such an

obvious contradiction in terms, that it is clearly impossible to trace the
absence of small fish in all lakes in which none are taken and very few
are seen merely to the predatory habits of their fathers, mothers and
other relations.

If, for example, we take a lake of the class to which I have frequently
referred, a lake, that is to say, with many tributary burns or sheltering
shallows or both, and by experiment discover that it contains only
large fish, it would be rash to draw the conclusion that the absence of
small fish in the lake itself as distinct from the burns was due to a
ceaseless predatory internecine war waged by the big fish on the small.
Trout from the egg to the alevin and from the alevin to the fry stage
have many enemies who are more natural foes than the giants of their
own race. It is, in fact, not too much to say that they are born in
danger, cradled in peril, make their first and every succeeding movement before the eyes of ambushed foes and are, in a word, ever " within
the danger " not only of living enemies but of the forces of nature in
all their many forms.

In such a lake, therefore, it would be rash to blame the midnight
prowler on the sheltering shallows for the whole bill of mortality. That
" stark moss trooper " of the lake may or may not always be the ugly
villain of unconscionable mood that he has been painted; but even if
he were it is doubtful if his presence in force can always be held ac-
countable for the slaughter of the innocents. To their other foes, not
less to those who share their environment as to those who pay it occasional, and perhaps regular, predatory visits, may be attributed the
long roll of casualties that are never tabulated. If in such a lake we
found that aquatic beetles abounded, especially those of a warlike and
predatory nature, whether in their larval or in their perfect form, we
would be justified in placing on their shoulders with a double curse for
their crushing, the burden of the yellow trout's early doom. These
tyrants of the lake when still resembling rather an animated pair of
hungry pincers than anything less cruel of purpose will lie in ambushed
guile like the stealthy eel and will pounce on fish at all stages of babyhood, from the wobbling alevin in his perambulator sac to the fry of an
inch and a half long who has discovered the sweet savour of life and
the glory of that unfettered dash which is the high top-gallant of piscine
joy.

One class of beetles when they come to fly and leave the degenerate condition of mere ambushed hunters for the free sweep of an ancient Scythian or modern Dervish, become as fierce as the winged-serpents of Herodotus, the most unconscionable animals in the range of fiction just as certain female spiders illustrate de facto the true meaning of a devouring passion, and are the queens of this class of animal in the domain of fact. These winged-monsters wage ceaseless war and to them, in lakes where they abound, as much as to the midnight prowler the scarcity of youngsters must be attributed.

The caddis fly in its larval stage is another deadly foe, which appears to be even a worse enemy to young fish than are the water beetles in their larval condition, so that its presence in abundance in any lake must be taken as another certain cause of a high rate of juvenile mortality.

Though the above examples of living dangers are far from exhausting the list of foes who lurk, unseen by the casual observer, beneath the spreading waters of the lake, they are sufficient in themselves to account for the infant death-rate of any lake without presupposing the canni-balistic trait in adult fish.

When to their terrors are added those of the corixae to very small fish, of leeches,* of eels to fish of all sizes, of birds, of temperature and of gales we have, according to the circumstances of each case, sufficient causes of death to account for the absence of small fish even in a lake of the class referred to without taking the cannibalistic habit into con-sideration at all.   The eel, to take one only of the instruments of death, is a far more predatory and cannibalistic fish than any trout that ever swam.   Happily nature has not given the eel the unquestioned mastery over even very small trout which its lithe activity would suggest that it possesses.   Abounding as the eel does in most lochs, his depreda-tions appear to be for the most part confined to trout in the very earliest and most helpless stages of their existence.   I have already noted how even congers and large fresh water eels find it no easy matter to corner, kill and devour salmon and grilse and have only to add to my observa-tions on the point the facts of an extremely instructive trout-hunt by eels which I witnessed in a large pool in an Orcadian burn.   The water

---

* Whether leeches attack small trout is doubtful, but a recent writer in the " Field " records the fact that on a Continental river nearly every fish which he killed in a certain reach had a leech adhering to its gills.   Large trout eat leeches, and I have already recorded the case of a trout that ejected one after landing.

was extremely low, and the pool, some fifteen yards long by some seven
or eight across, was currentless and isolated, there being a mere trickle
of water entering and leaving it. The small trout were, therefore, prisoners and the eels of which there were several appeared to have them at
their mercy. The water of the pool was very clear, and at no place more
than two feet deep, while the day was bright and very favourable for
observing this lesson in the survival of the fittest. The trout, fish from
an ounce to 2½ ounces in weight, were obviously quite conscious of their
danger and all their movements betokened a wary watchfulness and a
total absence in móments of supreme peril of the influence of that fascination of terror with which snakes are supposed to hold birds and
pike make prisoner roach in the bondage of the resigned despair of
assured doom. The eels certainly chose the best places for ambush
that were available, and the patient maliginity of purpose with which
they waited was unworthy of a better cause. The trout did not suspend the main business of their existence. They quested for food or
lay still looking for it. Whether stationary or in motion their eyes
were never shut to the dangers of their position. If they passed close
enough to the eel's lurking place the latter would deliver a sudden onslaught, with a darting motion I could scarcely follow, but which the
trout could calculate with unfailing accuracy, for by a quicker dart and
a defter turn they would elude the blow which they could not parry.
When throwing concealment to the winds an eel in concert with another
eel followed one particular trout from place to place until the hunt
was fairly up, the run was of short duration. I watched the pool with
patience for two hours or more, but only once did an eel come near
securing its quarry. This narrow escape of the trout was due, I think,
to my failing to keep myself as closely concealed as I had previously
done, and to the alarm I gave the nearest fish which almost ran into
the open mouth of an ambushed eel. This experience—which I
brought to a termination by catching all the eels—convinced me that the
trout is not only a very wary, a very watchful and a very plucky fish,
but also that he is quite a match for the eel once he attains a certain
size and acquires the faculty of independence and the power to look
after and act for himself. In the lake, in which the whereabouts of the
ambushed eels cannot be so well known to the trout, fish may occasionally fall victims to eels, but it is a fair assumption, that save when he

is deeply engrossed in feeding and his vigilance is, therefore, relaxed, the trout keeps such a keen eye on all lurking dangers that the eel can only secure an occasional triumph.   How hand-reared trout would fare is another matter.

To resume, however, the general question of the cannibalistic habit and its effect upon the feeding habits of the trout, so far as these affect the angler directly or indirectly, it may be noted, in terms of the general premise that environment is the creator of habits, that in deep lakes or in lakes with a prepondence of deep water over shallows, the trout both large and small being necessarily compelled to consort more together than in lakes presenting greater inequalities in depths or more numerous and more varied shallows, will naturally tend to develop the cannibalistic habit to a degree commensurate with this difference in topographical and sociological environment.   The extent, moreover, to which the habit will be developed must necessarily also depend upon the quality and quantity of the food otherwise provided.   In such deep artificial lakes as the majority of corporation reservoirs, it is obvious that the absence of spawning beds must necessarily arrest that propagation of species which is a sine qua non to the development of the cannibalistic habit, while in all lakes the same limitation is imposed upon its display once the war of extermination has reached a certain period and the unhappy hunting fields are either devoid of game or objects of the chase are so rare, that the hunters perforce grow attenuated and are compelled to seek fresh grounds, if they can make the journey, or perish if they cannot, where they are unless they develop other traits under the pressure of the necessity of environment and in terms of its limitations.

By the somewhat devious paths that we have tracked through the mazes of the problem from the observation of the gladiatorial combats fought in the arena of the fish pond between fish and fish, between fish and beetle, alevin and coixa, to the combats and chases of the wider battlefields and hunting grounds of nature, we are beginning to emerge from the labyrinth of perplexing issues and side issues to a somewhat clearer appreciation of the truth underlying the facts which the consideration of the question has brought to light.   The importance of the cannibalistic habit to the angler is so obvious that the reason why it is so needs only to be stated to be accepted.   The habit means not only poor fish, but fish that will not rise to the fly and appear to justifiy the use of the minnow. Further it necessarily implies a diminution in population and finally, in alliance with other foes, the total extinction of the race. Happily nature has provided her own remedy for the disease. There is no natural lake in Great Britain whose environment is such as to necessitate cannibalism save in isolated cases, which are the result of a fortuitous combination of circumstances of a precisely analogous character to those circumstances which convert a good sheep dog into a sheep worrier when once it has tasted of the blood of sheep.

To illustrate both the rule and the occasional exception it will, therefore, be necessary to cite some examples.

It is a well-known fact that the large trout of certain lakes are cannibals or, at least, are not in the regular habit of taking the fly though they occasionally do so. These large trout are in most British lakes known by the specific name of Salmo Ferox, while on the Continent where they occur in greater frequency and in a larger number of lakes, they are also described as specific fish, though obviously more truly varieties of the same fish produced by differences in environment. The so called bottom-trout of Lake Constance—the grund-forelle to give it the title distinguishing it from the schweb forelle, or surface feeding trout, is a notable example, though for our present purpose the Salmo Marsiglii found in certain mountain lakes in Austria and Bavaria is a much more instructive fish, not only because of its habits and the great size to which it attains, but also because under the name of the Great Bavarian trout, this or a kindred fish is now being bred by some of our fish-farmers.* As it reaches an ordinary length of three feet and a weight of from 20 to 25lbs., while a large specimen may turn the scale at from 50 to 65lbs, this trout is evidently a fish that requires a liberal diet and is moreover the type of fish which for that very reason is certain to be a cannibal. It is not surprising, therefore, to learn that when young they frequent the feeding grounds of the roach in the lakes in which they are found, and pursue them until the small fishes seek, as is their wont, the shelter of shallow water. Nor is it surprising that when they attain a size of from 25 to 30lbs. fish weighing only from ½lb. to 2lbs. will satisfy them. It is interesting to note further that this

* Some fish-farmers sell the Salmo Lacustris, which is, de facto, the same fish.

large species of trout does not need any great depth of water to wax big and strong, provided he has plenty of food. Now here we have obviously a typical cannibal which illustrates the cause of cannibalism rather better than he does its commonly accredited effect, if, that is to say, we presume that the cannibalistic trout has special characteristics of external feature when found either in lakes in which all the fish are cannibals or in lakes in which the cannibal is the exception, and not the rule. The latter assumption is, we know, erroneous, while the former is not necessarily constant and must at the best be a question of degree of development of the habit as well as of the age and perhaps the sex. of the fish.

It is, however, clear in terms of the law of environment and apart. from special circumstances which may modify the opportunities of any environment in the case of certain fish living within its limits, that big, fish must necessarily require a larger share—" the portion of a man "—of the blessings of an environment than do smaller fish. Even if the division of the spoil is unequal and favours, as it is certain to do, the large fish, it is an unavoidable conclusion that it will not favour the big fish to such an extent as not to place him under the necessity of supplementing his portion by preying on his fellows. Food has to be taken vi et armis ; it is not given in the lake save when it is presented. by the course of events precisely in that fishy form, which means not, indeed, the creation, but the cultivation of the cannibalistic habit. Once acquired, the habit is never lost on the " tasting of blood " principle to which I have already more than once referred. Now as it is a well ascertained fact that from its very earliest days of independent. feeding a trout will always seize to see if it be good to eat anything that. moves, it is obvious that this trait will not be lessened but enhanced by the cannabalistic habit, though it is highly probable that larger objects will alone excite the impulse, a fact which if evolution means anything, may very well be accompanied by a decrease in visual power, sufficient, apart from all other considerations, to account for very large trout declining to notice a fly. The considerations which I have advanced seem, therefore, on ground of expediency to warrant the use of the minnow in certain lakes. By doing a little harm, one may thereby do a great good, since not only will the lake be rid of certain fish that keep its stock down, but the offspring of these cannibals will be—

curtailed in number, while the chance of the lake being largely peopled with fish with the hereditary defect of their sires will be greatly diminished.

That the cannibalistic trait, as an exclusive appetite is too readily attributed to the trout of many lakes at all times and to those of some lakes after a certain period in the season, and that to a greater or less degree it is a characteristic of all trout are for me commonplaces of knowledge, which angling experience has proved and observation of fish in the ponds of farms has amply verified. On the last position I have already dilated at some length, but on the other propositions, it is necessary to offer a few observations, as the facts are of singular importance to the angler. First as to the cannibalistic trait as a characteristic of all trout, my experiments were made in actual angling during a particularly fortunate season when I was able from March to September to spend almost every day on the lakes, save those devoted to the river and the moor and coverts. I trolled with various sizes of minnow over both the deeps and shallows of a loch in which the trout ran from ¼lb. to 1lb., but were, as a rule, about 5oz. in weight. I found that while fish of all sizes took the minnow (and in some cases there was not much to choose between lure and lured), the fish in the central and deeper portions of the lake, fish, that is to say, of poor general quality, took it with a greater avidity and boldness than did the fish either frequenting the shallows or haunting the debatable water between the two. It naturally struck me as a remarkable circumstance that fish of a very small size should seize so large and formidable a prey as the minnow must necessarily have appeared even to a hungry fish, but the circumstance was no more remarkable, when one further considered it, than the fact that very small par should seize a salmon fly or sticklebacks, so small that one will continue to cast without observing their presence on the hook, will take a fly dressed on a No. 10 hook, as they frequently do in certain of the Hebridean lakes. My experiments when carried out in other lakes had precisely the same results, and there was no other conclusion possible, but the one which I drew and which accords with the observation of the feeding habits of trout in rivers, that even a large fish if it appears to be disabled, will tempt a trout not much larger than itself to make a predatory onslaught on it with a view to securing a meal. No doubt the initial onslaught is only intended in the case of small fish attacking injured fish nearly as large as themselves, to reduce the wounded fish into possession. If this be so, it is not the least remarkable fact attending the onslaught that the attack is generally delivered on what is the usual point of onslaught in battle between sound fish, to wit, the wrist.

I noted further the instructive fact that on days when there was a large rise of natural flies—and on one of the lakes in which my experiments were conducted there was a phenomenal rise of " March browns " nearly every day—the fish either took the minnow with the same avidity or they resolutely declined to take it all. They never took it with greater avidity when the cause predisposing them to feed was present, while the days on which it had the effect of making them fly-feeders or takers of the artificial fly far exceeded in number those days on which it made no apparent difference at all so far as partiality for the minnow was concerned. Using the minnow for the purposes of experiment is, however, a very different thing from using it in lochs for the mere purpose of securing a few trout by its means. Before proceeding, therefore, to further discuss the general question at issue, it seems desirable to dismiss its special aspect raised by the mention of trolling and the use of spun lures in lakes.

In the first place the use of the minnow to keep down the cannibals— present and to come—may well be justified on a somewhat wider principle than is embodied in Clough's ironical expansion of the Commandment

> " Thou shalt not kill, but needst not strive
> Officiously to keep alive."

for if ever killing even by immoral as distinguished from illegal means is justified it is when one wages a war characterised by slaughter grim and great amongst fish which are not only useless from a sporting point of view, but positively dangerous to future sport.

Even trolling for such fish is justified, if the angler can take them by no other means, though here we have a fine example of the accuracy of that best of proverbs " use does not justify abuse." An angler is placed in a position of temptation when trolling with the minnow in a loch and is apt like Lucifer " to fally greatly," a phrase which exhausts temptation as the great relative circumstance which ever forbids codified punishment and is the key note of justice. To place an angler on a lake

and to bid him go troll as a moral agent with an ameliorating mission,.
is necessarily to tempt him to pursue the same path to power, when
he has discovered the assured and easily won successes to which it leads..
Now as the aim of scientific angling is to reconcile expediency with morality, policy with honesty and, in a word to cultivate a moral utilitarianism, I may here interpolate a few observations on a method of using the
minnow, but little practised in lakes, but which not only in a measure-
saves the situation but is in some lakes even more deadly than the-
time-honoured plan of dragging a spun lure after a boat in precisely the-
same manner as one " whiffs " for lithe or careers before a breeze when
after mackerel with the gear of the professional sea-fisher.   In my salad'
days I held more than one lady in high esteem—when lady anglers were-
scarce, who could pour into my admiring and awe-struck ear the tale-
of a two pounder killed in Loch So and So.   I elevated these dames to
sublime piscatorial heights and wondered with the simplicity of the ever-
ambitious child, if the glorious day would ever dawn, when I too would
carve my name deep on the temple of angling fame as the hero of a:
two pound fight.   When knowledge does come, wisdom does not linger,.
whatever the poet may say to the contrary, and these ladies were-
brought down in most summary and ungallant fashion from the pin-
nacle of my fancy when I discovered on experiment, first that pike, and'
secondly that trout, even two pounders, could be taken by unwinding
a ball of string, attaching a blue phantom to the end and dragging the-
whole primitive concern through the lake.   Nor was there any necessity
to retire to pray like an Homeric hero, to a place " where there was
shelter from the winds and the gods might hear."   The " evil doom "
of one or other of those gods was on the fish and not on their would-be-
slayer.   Fortune smiled on my efforts and so easy did the whole pro--
cess appear that not even by the exercise of my inflated juvenile fancy,.
was I able for a single moment to regard myself as a conquering hero.
The hereditary and acquired sporting instinct was too strong within me·
to make any mistake between the water and the wine of loch-angling in
the least degree possible.   Shortly after the fall of the ladies and my own
disillusionising, the capture of a great female trout, of how many pounds·
weight the lapse of time and the absence of living witnesses forbid me to
state, completed the lesson.   It fell a dishonoured victim to a dead parr·
ruthlessly impaled on a pike hook of sturdy brass sold at the easy rate:

"A STERN NECESSITY": MALLOCH'S INGENIOUS LOCH TROLLER.

of one penny. The whole fastened to some stout whipcord and thrown out into a backwater to work out its evil and salutary destiny.

Henceforth for me the trolling rod was out of joint.*

If, therefore, the loch fisher must use the natural minnow, either in his character of a legalised executioner or as a sportsman, desirous of varying his methods or of overcrowing evil fortune after hours of angling darkness, he should not condescend to the ignoble method of trolling until at least he has put other plans of attack in operation. With a Nottingham or a Malloch or Cummins or Hardy reel specially designed for the purpose of spinning or even with an ordinary reel used in the Thames or other " coil " style, it is just as easy to spin in a lake as it is a river. The last occasion on which I essayed this method, I killed eight fish in about half-an-hour and killed them with almost as clear a conscience as if I had been using fly.   It was in a difficult loch on a particularly stiff day during the course of which not a single fish rose. At the same time the last resource was not put in practice on a true sporting loch—a loch, that is to say, in which the trout are surface feeders and can always be killed by patience and skill and a steady regard to fish feeding under the boughs and in the shallows. There is here in gremio a very useful hint to many of those past masters of the art of spinning, who are found on Trentside and on the banks of the Thames and other English rivers.   If some of the most skilled "spinning" exponents of Nottingham, Newark, and Sheffield would only essay the practically virgin field, so far as the spinner is concerned, of Scottish and Irish lakes I feel assured that they would achieve success, revolutionise the methods in use and work a very desirable moral regeneration, whether they angled for pike and perch in winter, for trout and " ferox " in summer, or salmon in spring.   It requires neither skill nor fine tackle to hook and land loch trout when trolling, and even the capture of the lordly ferox (I preserve the popular distinction for the sake of clearness) is merely a matter of time, of patience, of employing the proper

* I feel certain that Mr. P. D. Malloch of Perth—an angler who has drunk deep of the blood of giants and is imbued to his finger tips with the sporting cacoethes—must have felt many a pang of conscientious regret when he was designing that ingenious contrivance whereby rods may be fixed when trolling to the stern of a boat. Mr. Malloch's contrivance is justified by the necessities of Loch Tay—otherwise it is a diabolical, if not an infernal, machine. How it would have pleased a certain worthy, now on the other side of the Styx, who trolled Loch Leven with a forest of rods, the while he sipped an occasional glass of '34 port in luxurious ease !

S

lure and of putting in practice a certain measure of topographical know-ledge as to the deeps and shallows of any particular lake. It is true that trout, salmon, and ferox, even when hooked by trolling do give sport after a sort, but the method of hooking is so opposed to all the canons that to dignify it by the name of an art, much more to devote space to describing it save in words that damn without even faintly praising, would be to essay two tasks of equal vanity. The angler with a mission is, as I have already said, justified in trolling if he cannot otherwise secure his prey owing to its habits or his own deficiencies. The trout angler without a mission never is justified in putting this method in practice. There is open to him the more sporting method of spinning from the boat as he would from the bank, and if my own results—and I rarely put it in practice and have but indifferent skill—are a reliable guide to its deadliness, then he will find that not only is it a better method on moral but also on utilitarian and expedient grounds. As the reconciling of morality and expediency and of honesty with policy is the aim of all angling, no higher or better argument could be advanced in favour of the method I have indicated as the proper substitute for the conservative and pernicious plan of trolling, the refuge of the duffer or the casual angler who is not a sportsman.

There are, moreover, certain lakes, and at this point I resume the general subject, in which the habits of the trout seem to invite the alternate utilisation both of fly and minnow, lakes, that is to say, in which up to a certain period of the season, usually with the 1st of June as an extreme limit, the trout do not rise with the same freedom as during March, April and May. Of these short-seasoned lochs in local belief and practice, Lochs Ard and Vennachar are perhaps the examples best known to the majority of anglers. In any case they are typical of a certain class of lake, in which the trout take the artificial fly with a decreasing avidity from 1st May to 1st June, and on or about the latter date are said to practically abandon taking it at all by the so-called local "experts." The basis in which this belief rests is the assumption that after a certain date, dependent naturally on the climatic conditions, the trout become bottom feeders and, ex hypothesi of the lure employed for their capture, namely, the minnow, turn cannibals—after a sort, to use the most expressive phrase quoted by the immortal Bailie. The local belief sets up a rather rigid exclusivism and the rule of both lochs may be codified in the dictum "The fly is of no use; only a trolled bait will kill, and of trolled baits the natural minnow is by far the best."

These two lakes afford, therefore, an instructive object lesson in the effect of trout habits upon the methods employed in loch-angling, and are of particular interest not only in the matter of the cannibalistic habit in general but also with regard to its special display as a seasonal characteristic. My experience on both lakes, limited in each case, but more particularly in that of Loch Ard, indicated no increased avidity for the minnow during the reputed season of cannibalism, ground feeding and "fly" antipathy, but merely a decreased keenness for the fly, at no season in Loch Vennachar save on special occasions very marked, which corresponded in all essentials, mutatis mutandis, with the results of my previous experiments with the minnow amongst the free rising trout of certain other lakes whose seasonal characteristics in the matter of taking the fly were somewhat different and will be shortly noted. Possibly the limited number of days on which I observed Loch Ard may have been specially favourable to fish rising, as there was a large quantity of "fly" on the water, but in any case, it was made clear that even allowing for exceptional circumstances, there was no rooted aversion to the fly, but merely a diminution of keenness for it, proportioned to the greater or less degree of suggestion measured in terms of its abundance or scarcity. In Loch Vennachar, on the other hand, I observed precisely the same state of affairs, only the diminished avidity for the fly was less marked as a constant characteristic than in Loch Ard. As a matter of fact I killed in Vennachar heavier fish than had ever before fallen to my rod in its waters, and rose a fish of such great size that the startled cry it forced from my undisciplined boatmen made me miss a very easy chance from a taking fish of the most pronounced type.

In spite, however, of what I observed and have here chronicled, there was no escaping the fact that the environment of the loch had altered with the season and had produced a corresponding change in the feeding habits of the fish quite appreciable by the fly fisher.*

* For the purpose of illustrating the principle involved I might, at the least, have included the adjacent lake, Loch Achray. Area for area, it holds far more fish than Vennachar, which is a lake sadly in need of stocking and capable of carrying a large head of good fish. In a recent June, I drove past both Loch Achray and Vennachar on a

Into the causes leading to this change it is, perhaps, unnecessary to inquire, but they were briefly these. The increase in the vegetation had naturally tended to increase the quantity of purely subaqueous food, from tadpoles to the most minute organisms, while the spawning time of the pike and the perch in the lake—the presence of these fish giving rise to a special condition of environment—was contemporaneous with that of the minnow and its greatest abundance in the fry and other stages of growth. These are circumstances special to the season and suggest something very different to cannibalism which, in the strict sense, only arises when a fish devours its own species—as unhappily all fish do.

I arrived, therefore, at the conclusion that it was not cannibalism but the abundance of subaqueous food of all kinds, which, relative to its quantity and the number of flies on the surface, altered the character of the fish of these lakes so far as the angler was concerned.

The general inference I drew from all the facts as already stated was that cannibalism, as a general trait of all trout, is as much a characteristic of fly-taking trout as fly-taking is a characteristic of cannibalistic trout, and that the cannibalistic habit in trout so far as it affects the angler is a question of degree and not of kind, dependent for its display on the special rather than on the general conditions of environment.

As this is tantamount to saying that the feeding habits of trout in lakes do not differ from those in rivers, it is obvious that if we can justify the use of the parr and eel tail and other lures of that kind in such rivers as the Don and Findhorn after a certain period in the season, then the use of a spinning lure that is spun and not trolled is equally justified in certain lakes after, but not before, a full but unfruitful trial has been given to the fly. As there is no condition of weather in which trout in lochs cannot be persuaded to rise to the fly, this concession is obviously limited to that season and to it alone, during which the special conditions of their environment render the trout of certain lakes more of a bottom and less of a surface feeder than during another and earlier portion of the season. To kill off the cannibals and thereafter to

---

very fine calm evening. I noted 50 fish—and they were good fish—rising and steadily feeding in Loch Achray for one I saw on Loch Vennachar. On neither lake, however, was there any sign of marked antipathy to the natural fly.

cultivate an environment yielding surface food would be perfectly safe reforms; the former must do positive good; the latter can assuredly do no harm, and is likely to be beneficial since the tendency to rise or otherwise is directly dependent upon the relative abundance of surface and bottom feeding.

I pass now to an examination of the question of environment as it affects the fly-taking appetite of the trout of lakes which either afford the same or obviously different conditions of existence, but all of which are essentially fly waters. For this purpose I will select Lower Bornish in South Uist and Loch Coil-a-Bharra in the Crinan district of Argyle as lakes holding large and stiff trout, while as typical examples of the opposite class of lake Lach Yarehouse in Caithness and Loch Lossit in Islay may be selected. Taking the last two first the difference in environment and general character and hence in the trout in both these lakes is so small that it may be ignored. As a consequence of this similiarity of environment, their habits so far as the angler is concerned are practically indentical up to a period of the season that may be put down, on an average of years, as the 15th June. Lossit trout owing to the difference in latitude are earlier in condition and take the fly with such avidity up to the date mentioned that a bsket of 100 is by no means anything out of the usual. On the other hand after a certain period in the season, when, that is to say, the vegetation attains a certain growth, the trout become most confirmed bottom feeders, though there are no minnows in the lake and the question of cannibalism does not intrude. In Yarehouse, on the other hand, the growth of vegetation is much later, and hence the loch fishes right on to the middle or even the end of September and begins, in fact, to be at its best when Lossit is approaching its worst. Now the wise man who follows lamb and green peas North can attain his heart's desire in September and can even in that month enjoy a "crowning dish" of raspberries if not, indeed, of strawberries, for the simple reason that the season in the North is late. This lateness is of some importance to the angler when one considers both its effect and its cause. As to the effect, a loch in which the growth of vegetation is early ceases, as a rule, to be a fly water not when the trout have been put in condition by feasting on flies, but when with the growth of the vegetation the excess of fly to bottom feeding is being gradually diminished, until the law of demand and supply beginning to

operate the supply of both fly and bottom feeding is in excess of the
requirements of the trout in the lake which are now in high condition
and, therefore, only disposed to feed sparsely and on what is handiest,
though on occasional days displaying a partiality for the fly. We see
precisely the same trait exhibited by river trout when once they are in
condition and the season advances—a fact which by analogy seems to
point to the common affinity of trout and salmon through their feeding
habits when by an assimilation of the effects of environment they are
both in the same condition. It is obvious from this consideration that
in lochs situated in early-seasoned districts the angler must be content
with poor results after a certain date which varies, but is ever coin-
cidental with the arising of the conditions already outlined.

It is equally clear that no amount of personal effort can
overcome what is essentially a condition imposed by nature.
It is, in fact, foolish to waste time angling in lakes where the habits
of the trout are so clearly seasonal that they can be dogmatically defined. There is, it is true, one possible remedy for this defect, if it be
a defect in a lake, though I am by no means sure that the result of an
extremely interesting experiment I was able to make a few years ago,
would be attended with the same result in all lakes more or less resembling those under discussion. It was, moreover, an experiment not
always practicable, but as it is eminently instructive in its character as
an example of the general effect upon angling of altering environment
I will give the facts briefly. A certain West Highland loch out of
which a small burn issued and into which several small drains emptied
themselves had no great reputation as a fish-yielding water, though it
enjoyed considerable fame as a fish-holding water. It lay by the road-
side, and in consequence was frequently laid under the tribute of a cast
and a fish—generally of some ½lb or so—by the passing angler. It
was in part artificial and the trout were stiff. I first tried it at its
normal level from a boat with no great success. Then through the
kindness of the factor, who made it convenient to order some repairs in
the drains below the lake, the burn was dammed up for a day or two
and the level of the loch was raised several feet, until, in fact, a full
loch was produced. My first hour or two on the loch yielded some
30 trout, some as heavy as 2½lbs.—a size never before approached—
while the fish rose with an avidity at the fly wholly opposed to their

time-honoured and very clearly established reputation. So long as the loch was kept high, so long did the sport last. It was, in fact, clearly proved that the loch not only contained very fine fish in great abundance, but that the raising of its level—a topographical change of environment had altered their feeding habits to such an extent that from a " dour " non-fly-taking race they became a quick and lively people willing to rise with an obsequiousness that from some points of view marred the pleasure of killing them.

Waiving the question of somewhat hypocritical asceticism, which the last remark suggests, we have here an extremely interesting practical application of a truth which is undoubtedly accepted, in theory at least, by most pisciculturists and practical students of fish. Whether, however, similar means would produce similar happy results in all lochs, much less in short-seasoned lochs, remains as yet to be proved, but the experiment can at least be tried with perfect safety in all lochs in which it is possible to put it in force and on whose trout the conditions of existence impose the habit of ceasing to take the fly with any keenness after a certain period of the year has been reached.

As to Lochs Coil-a-Bharra and Bornish, it cannot be said that the environments of the two lakes are the same, or that they approximate in any way, save in so far as the food supply in both lakes is practically unlimited. They differ, however, both in their topography and in the nature of the food supply. Coil-a-Bharra is surrounded by woods and rocks; Bornish lies on the Machar-land without a single tree, save a monkey-puzzle, nearer its shores than the Isle of Skye. The water of Coil-a-Bharra is a beautiful tea colour; that of Bornish though tinged with brown is an exquisite shade of bright greeny-grey. Bornish has no deeps.; Coil-a-Bharra has many; the bottom of the latter abounds in great rocks and stones between sandy beds, while the decaying branches of the trees all round its shores fall into the water, and vegetation, extraneous and growing, is abundant in certain reaches only. As a consequence of its surroundings fly-life and surface food are abundant, while shrimps, the corixae, and tadpoles abound. There are, however, no minnows or other small fish. The fly life on Bornish is normal, and the surface feeding is limited. It abounds, however, in subaqueous life and sticklebacks are numerous. The consequences of these differences are peculiar, as the angler on both lakes will find to his cost. Bornish

is fishable all over, and is in consequence an incomparably easier lake
to fish than Coil-a-Bharra, though it is at the same time a fine sporting
water. Its trout through their great activity—a legacy of their more
direct descent from the sea-trout—are extremely difficult to control,
and when in their primest order, which appears to vary with the day
rather than with the season, both extremes excepted, will lead the most
skilful handler of a fish a merry dance and give him not a few anxious
moments before they are finally encreeled. In such a lake trout are
irregular risers and may, in terms of some causes I have never, outside
of the weather conditions, been able to formulate, either rise well or ill
or not at all. Owing to their environment they are, in other words, fish
of most irregular habits in the matter of fly-taking. On the other hand
they take the fly from April to September and are in practically the same
condition in the latter half of April as they are in the first half of
September.   Another peculiarity—and it is a common characteristic
of all such lakes—is that the fish rise anywhere and have no apparent
habitat save the habitat of reach, the guide to which in cases when the
eye is not the director must be found by experiment or by local enquiry
in trustworthy quarters. Coil-a-Bharra is by reason of its environment
almost, save in one or two of its reaches, a " shore " loch. Owing to the
abundance of surface food the trout are fly-feeders. Nevertheless they are
not to be taken by simply trying for them even in a breeze. In consequence of its configuration a breeze but rarely strikes all portions of the
lake, and hence there are always portions of it calm even in a
strong breeze. The fish, however, if they rarely come on the rise more
than once a day are always represented by feeding fish at some point or
other along its shores. When feeding, fish in a lake of this kind range
up and down a fixed portion of shore and may be angled for so long
as they are on the feed. Sometimes as when casting over a rising trout
on a dry fly or other stream, it may take the angler from 10 to 20 minutes
to persuade even a feeding fish to rise; but when he does rise, and the
same applies to Bornish trout, business is meant and short rising is uncommon. In lakes of these two types fish continue to rise the whole
season and the lessons which they teach to the angler is very obvious.
On lochs of the Bornish type one never knows, as a rule, when a fish is
going to rise or where a fish may be, and should, therefore, search every
inch of water, while in lakes of the other class, the proper plan is either

VICTORY AND FAILURE: SNAP SHOTS OF LEAPING SALMON.

to confine one's attention to rising fish or to fish every spot on their shores which appears likely to be the habitat of a fish.*

This last observation leads to the question of habitat in lochs, both as regards special fish and the fish in the lake in general.

The rules as to the salmonidæ in lakes as a whole, is capable of being axiomatically stated as follows:—Salmon have both a general and a special habitat; sea-trout have a general but no special habitat, and loch trout have both a special and a general habitat. The meaning of the phrase "general and special habitat" is that not only do fish display a special partiality for certain portions of a lake, but that each individual fish has a favourite feeding spot, while on the analogy of fish in rivers, each may have a favourite resting place or lying ground. When I come to deal with salmon and sea-trout lochs, I shall refer again to their habits in the matter of habitat, but in the meantime confine myself to a few observations on the habits of the loch trout in this particular. That loch trout have a general habitat or rather general habitats, in the sense already indicated is a commonplace of knowledge, which a very brief experience of any lake soon enables even an angler out on a loch for the first time to discover. These habitats may or may not be obvious to even the experienced eye on certain lochs unless, indeed, fish be rising, but at the same time the lochs on which the general habitats are invisible to the eye studying the bottom of the lake are comparatively few. When they are invisible owing to the colour of the water and the lack of rising fish (trout it should be observed occasionally rise freely off their usual feeding habitats and in deep water)† the angler must either consult his boatmen, if he has one with him, or he must consult a chart of the lake, or failing that must test the depth and nature of the bottom with his oar and judge of it otherwise by the configuration of the shore. As a rule, however this difficulty does not arise save in strange and very unfrequented waters, while when it does arise it is usually easily overcome, especially in comparatively small lakes. It seems scarcely necessary, therefore, as the matter is a very simple one, when the habitats are visible, to do more than point out that as a rule feeding fish are found in water varying from 10 feet to a few inches in

---

* In lakes like Coil-a-Bharra, and in Coil-a-Bharra itself, there are a few reaches in which fish rise, even in deepish water, and may be seen feeding.

† This trait is most frequently in evidence during the evening rise.

depth, both being extreme limits, over either a sandy, grassy or stony or mixed bottom, while between the shallow and the deep where it slopes abruptly down is as favourite a place for feeding loch trout to take up their position as it is for sea-trout. The habitat will vary to some slight extent with the height of the lake, which should, therefore, be noted, but when every inch of water is searched within certain limits, in the manner set forth in a succeeding chapter, this position is only material in so far as it may save some minutes which might be more profitably employed. Near reeds and off the mouths of burns are good places in most lochs, but they are not invariably better than other spots, and, in fact, the latter are sometimes of very little value, for the loch trout is by no means dependent for his meals, save in lakes of rather poor feeding, on the chance morsels a poverty-stricken burn may wash down to swell the bill of fare of the lake. When, however, a burn discharges its superfluous waters near, but not at, a specially excellent feeding ground or general habitat, it is extremely probable that a few fish will establish a special feeding and resting habitat at or near its entrance to the lake, while their watch and ward will occasionally be shared by unwelcome guests from the adjacent pasture. When such guests are present the chances for and against a few fish are about equal. You may find either a rivalry for the fly that means death to fish, or you may find the fish in one of those bellicose moods noted in the previous chapter.

When the burn rises in its last pool to the dignity of an arm of the lake, it is generally a sure hold for fish, but as often as not they are but poor risers.

It requires the educated " fishy " eye to pick out the special habitat, which in the case of bays and reaches cannot, of course, be detected unless the bottom be visible or rocks and reeds occur. Precisely the same kind of observation and reasoning from observation as guide the eye in a river must guide the angler in keeping a careful eye on such spots and the process of education is perhaps as unconscious as the training of the eye to detect fish and judge the depths in flounder-spearing.

In the case of shore lochs a cultivation of this form of opportimism is as necessary as is the development of the quick eye which can detect not merely the faintest break, but even the glimmer of a fish below the surface. The latter faculty may, perhaps, be as natural a gift as the

power to see a hare two fields off which some keepers with the eyes of
a hawk seem to possess, but it is very certain, if I may judge from
my own experience, that fish are frequently killed in spots where this
glimmer has caught the eye. As to the first mentioned power, it is
so largely a matter of education and observation that it is easily acquired
by anyone possessed of average intelligence, though some, no doubt
from wider experience and greater natural gifts, possess and cultivate
it to a greater extent than others. I call it the "fishy" eye, and when one
considers that seeing necessitates the use of the brain as well as of the
eye, if the sight is to become a conscious possession and turned to
profitable account, the phrase may be accepted as defining and covering
the whole process. Further it may be pointed out that the best school
for training the kind of eye desired to be produced is not the lake, but
the river. The lessons learned on the river are, in fact, the lessons that
should on this as on other points be applied to the lake, by the angler
who would conjoin the killing of fish with a study of the reason why
he succeeds in raising, hooking, and landing each particular fish. Finally with regard to the habits of loch trout it may be remembered as a
generalisation that loch trout occasionally roam the lake in an apparently
aimless kind of way and often swim high when changing pastures. The
angler who remembers this rule is too apt to merely keep his flies trailing
behind the boat on the "off-chance" of killing a fish. Fish so killed are
murdered. The ethics of loch fishing demand casting or a suspension of
hostilities. The wise man in a lake will, however, never cease fishing
except to observe some interesting fact worthy of attention, or when his
physical powers put the veto on his turning a pleasure into a toil. The
advice of the Scottish laird who advised his son "aye to be putting in
a tree, when he had nothing better to do," on the ground that "they
would aye be growing when he was sleeping," is very good advice,
mutatis mutandis, to the loch fisher, for even when he is shifting his
quarters he may rise one of those wandering fish known to the boatmen
of certain lakes as "mad 'uns."

CHAPTER XXI.

An Explanation, an Analogy and an Apology.

" Schoolmaster to little boys and tailor to the clouds " is a vicarious estimate of Milton made by Charles II in a critical mood,* and indicates even a worse fate than being the prototype of all that is mute and inglorious, whatever the proverbial philosopher of the common-place may urge to the contrary in that headline morality, which marks the graves of mighty thoughts murdered. All who essay to wax didactic on an art that necessitates the possession and the use of skill—innate or acquired—tempt the same fate as did " the schoolmaster to little boys and tailor to the clouds, which he furnished with suits of black lined with silver at no other expense than that of sense."

Per contra, one may be more glorified by being mute on those practical details which no dogmatic maxims can wholly impart and which must be supplemented to be valuable in use by the lessons of personal experience and laborious hours in the field of sport where alone the spurs of mighty men are won.

To make my meaning plain I will draw an analogy between athletic prowess in general and that particular manifestation of it, which the angler displays, whether his skill and endurance be hereditary gifts cultivated by practice or acquired powers the result of a persevering and industrious exercise of the imitative faculty. In doing so I would point out that the environment of men gives them precisely the same general and sporting character as it gives to fish. The other day a London tradesman was reminded of the fact that he had never seen wild flowers growing by receiving a present of a box of these sweet nestlings of nature. It was also related of a metropolitan parson that, on persuading one of his parishioners to take a country ramble, the latter asked on seeing a plough lying idle by a hedge row in a field " what that strange

---

* I say " vicarious," because the criticism is one which Scott puts into the mouth of Charles II., as one in keeping with his character.

looking thing was?" Environment makes the man and the sportsman-
what he is, and not only imposes limitations on natural powers but
creates aptitudes which are as truly products of environment as are
the specific differences of the fish with which we have been dealing.

William Wallace and Robert the Bruce, for example, would, without
doubt, have been most excellent forwards had they not been born some-
600 years before their time. Rob Roy, by parity of reasoning, would
have excelled in goal as an exponent of the Association code, for he had'
arms of such abnormal length that he could garter his hose below the
knees without stooping; while there is little doubt, if the non-maidenish
quality of his upper limbs prove anything, that the apocryphal Roderick
Dhu would have been the prince of hard and low tacklers, with the grip-
of an octopus and the litheness of an adder. But would they have
been great cricketers or great anglers?

As Rob Roy has a descendant of cricket fame in the field, Gregor
M'Gregor, who possess in his length of arm one of the many physical
qualifications of his ancestor, it is safe to assume that the red-headed
Highland hero would have been an excellent wicket-keeper, with the
eye of an eagle, an aptitude for taking balls wide on the leg side and
possibly three inches of dirk for the trembling umpire whose decisions
failed to please the Scottish Robin Hood. Wallace might, as a smiter,
have placed Bonnor as wholly in the shade as he did the famous Red
Rover of the Channel; and Bruce might have made the ball corruscate
with a brilliancy before which Jessop and Thornton would have had
to pale their ineffectual fires. All this is delightfully "a priori" reasoning. We can safely assume the iron muscles, the enduring frames, the
keen, educated eye, the wrist of steel, with the suppleness of a Damascus or Andre Ferrara blade, the activity of the mountain cat, the will
to do, the power to dare, that make for greatness in the world of ath-
letics and sport, where the qualities of great men are the qualities of
great warriors—unless that competent authority, the hero of Waterloo,
was a poor judge of the merchants, the hewers and carriers in the trade
of war.

This preamble is intended to introduce the great truism that though
the physical and mental qualities of the athlete and sportsman are the
same in all ages and all climes, the form in which athleticism and sport
as a legacy of war, realizes themselves in time and circumstances, both in

the individual and in the nation, is wholly dependent upon the latter, interpreted in the widest sense of which it is capable. The average Englishman of to-day is not the average Englishman of the days of King Richard Cœur de Lion. Nor from the point of view of muscularity is he the equal even of the average Englishman when the good Queen Bess commanded both bows and bills. But the English athlete, save perhaps for the quality of enduring each dire inclemency of rough fare and rougher quarters, is probably the superior of the English bowman and yeoman—a finer animal because of superior intelligence and method.

In the Scotchman and in the Highlander, this general as distinct from specialised descent from a rude physical robustness is not so marked. Mentally he long ago lost the last traces of his savage ancestry thanks to certain very provident measures of the Stuarts, and a certain natural poverty which compelled the cultivation of shrewdness, the making of ends to meet, and a sustained indulgence in the great world game of "beggar-your-neighbour;" but in the losing of what was the worst part of his hereditary nature he stuck with a highly characteristic tenacity to its utilitarian strength, and remained on the average more of a man of brawn and wiry muscle than his Sassenach equal.

In his athletic and sporting development he displayed this same physical conservatism, conditioned by circumstances over which he had no control. A great footballer even in the days of "the wisest fool in Europe;" a great golfer of unassailed supremacy when the links of the Kingdom of Fife, the Inches of Perth, and the Park of Stirling had never flashed back the sunlight from a scarlet coat that boasted a Saxon owner; a dour, dogged runner when the wheel of time rolled him on to the running path; a wrestler fit to hold the ring against the might of Cumberland; a yachtsman that beat the Corinthian mariners of England at their own peculiar game when the mountain breezes from a thousand Ben-na-Darchs were joyous in the white-winged competing armadas and a champion in other fields of athletic fame, he never was a man who could take a bellyful in the ring; much less has he ever been—and this is more germane to the matter—save in rare and isolated cases, exceptions that prove the rule, fit to compete with the giants of cricket, the Titans of the green sward, of whom the turfy swell of England's romantic meadows has born so plentiful and apparently inexhaustible a crop.

Yet the question can be, and must be, regarded from other points if one best of the sons of England, who have not only been born but also made, conceding a liberal allowance of that adaptability which generations of cricketing sires must have made an hereditary trait—a traditional instinct in all English boys worthy of the name who first saw the light in districts given over to the worship of the great goddess Cricketania. Those who have read " Old Ebor's " delightful talks with old Yorkshire cricketers, those men who literally fought their way to cricket fame, know well the trait to which I refer. It is bred in the bone.*

Yet it can be otherwise regarded, and it must be so regarded if one would understand why the Scotchman, with all his adaptability for success in whatsoever his hand findeth to do, has never climbed to the cricket altitudes where are the seats of the mighty wielders and trundlers, the immortals that live above when at last they sleep below the green turf on the far side of the great boundary amidst the crowd of the unnumbered dead. An Englishman in most districts of England has not a Scotchman's infinite variety of recreative pastimes. The physical conditions of his country—its sport-yielding crop, so to speak—is more limited. Cricket topographically, and, in some sense, geographically considered, is his natural pastime. It only needed a beginning to become the national game, the game in which nature found her own compensation, and created that outlet for the physical energy of the leisure moments of youth which was bound to find expression, when war ceasing to be a trade, peaceful industry was unable to exhaust the full, flowing stream of manhood, of manly ambition, that was its best, but not its only profitable legacy. Cricket needs a soil on which to flourish, and is, like all pastimes, most likely to flourish where nature places on it the imprimatur of its approval. Let me illustrate the truth of this dictum by an appeal to what I may term an exaggeration of one aspect of the Scottish case. I refer to the primitive cricket played in the Faroe Islands. In those islands of the North men live, and can only live, on slopes, simply because there is no level ground, and a meadow is unknown. Yet they play cricket—after a sort. The bat is a piece of wood, and the ball is made of two sheep horns. The game is called

---

* Mr. Pullin's book should be read by everyone. I know no work which better illustrates the true journalistic mean between facts and comment on facts.

"Sheeps dogs," and was probably a sport of the Vikings, and has not advanced since these lusty pirates "caroused in seas of sable beer," and sent down over after over with a ramshorn ball to a half-naked giant wielding a bat as big as a galley's stem! Such lack of development is perfectly natural, not extraordinary. The conditions were all against the game, and a Faroe Island team is never likely to visit our shores, though, as whale hunters and expert cragsmen, they would give any English eleven, even with "W.G." at their head, a long start and a beating.

Now, Scotland is not a Faroe Island in any sense of the word. Nevertheless, the physical conditions and general circumstances of Scotland are "pro tanto" equally against the development of the game of cricket to the extent to which it has been developed in all save the "least cricketing" counties of England.

Now what is the cause? Some cricketers—and these the best—are born, others are made; Scotchmen have the aptitude for cricket, but the racial idea is against developing it, if only because, in spite of the antiquity of Scottish cricket clubs, most of which are far older than any of its football organisations, Nature has placed barriers in the way, and given many compensating joys, firmed by custom into prescriptive habits, for that unrealised cricketing ambition for which Scotland still in its heart of hearts yearns, but for the realisation of which it declines to scorn other delights and live the necessary laborious hours.

Now what is true of racial characteristics as the result of environment, not only in the wide arena of life but also in the narrower lists of sport, is as applicable to angling as it is to cricket, the sport I chose as an illustration of how aptitudes are developed by circumstances until the become hereditary traits. The average English angler is born the heir to a fair domain of placid smooth-sliding rivers crowned like Mincius "with vocal reels" and of clear limpid waters that shed like meek Cephisus a scanty tide.

The Scot—"Lowland and Highland far and near"—is, on the other hand a son of "the land of the mountain and the flood," born to a heritage of "sweeping vales and foaming floods" and an endless succession of lakes great and small, of every kind and variety, all holding trout in greater or less plenty and necessitating a very different racial or characteristic style of angling than do the rivers of the South, though as has already been pointed out the Scottish loch and the English river have many features that are common to both. In spite, however, of these common features, and the increasing custom of stocking ponds, public and private, and reservoirs with trout that are in many instances descended from loch trout, and the consequent increase of loch fishing after a sort in England, it is obvious that English anglers as a whole have only the same opportunities of developing the loch fishing "idea" as Scottish cricketers have of perfecting themselves in the essentially English game of cricket.

Heredity and locality, if the two can be separated, must count for something in angling as in cricket, so that one would naturally expect the man, born amongst the lakes and sprung from a race of anglers who have for generations angled in their spreading waters to have not only more natural skill in fishing them but also an inborn aptitude, a correspondence of spirit to their mood, which will make him a more successful student of the mysteries of their life and of the art of overmastering by the angle the fish great and small, wise and simple that people their deeps and shallows.

Yet without laborious hours of toil that is a pleasure, even this natural aptitude cannot bear fruition much less that form of fruit which one can pluck and hand to another as a very apple from the tree of knowledge. Though cricket was never learned from a book, nevertheless advice from skilled cricketers dispensed to all the world in words, is an excellent aid to practice. It corrects errors in style and imparts new tricks, and affords to the student of tactics an endless field for the use of his eyes, the exercise of his cunning and the display of his reasoning powers. It is, nevertheless, doubtful if any angler, however great his own knowledge may be, can impart to his fellow anglers useful lessons of practical value, save those which can be inferred from his observations of the quarry and it is still more doubtful if mechanical skill can be imparted by any teacher. Angling is, however, less of an exact science than cricket, whose mysteries lie on the surface—a positive of attack—a negative of defence that can be seen, and short of accidents of a chance, be provided against. It is a game played against an unseen team—a team of moods and without fixtures. Your opponents are a subtle, a deep, a mysterious race whose secrets are fenced by an elemental rampart, bristling with difficulties.

T

All, therefore, of a useful didactic character any writer can hope to impart is, in the first place, such facts or what have appeared to him to be facts, with regard to the habits and moods of the particular fish or fishes about which he is discoursing; these he must leave to his readers to appraise by comparing their accuracy or inaccuracy with their own observations, past and to come, bona fides being in all cases understood; whatever alteration these facts may cause in methods will obviously be proportionate to the degree of accuracy in his observations ascertained to exist by the comparative method already referred to. If this comparison results in the correction of an error in method which may ab initio have been a prejudice, or based on reasoning from false premises, the value of the lesson in facts is obviously considerable, for it is the result of personal and impersonal experience viewed in relation to the angler who puts it in practice. In the second place a mere setting forth of methods, as the applied and practical results of observation, must be read in the light of the facts of observation that have preceded and are the bases on which these methods are founded. It is with this apology and explanation that I venture to wax didactic in the succeeding chapters in which I shall adopt the method of the writer on economics and take certain hypotheses as granted, which the reader who has had the patience to follow me so far can, or should be, in a position to supply in their proper places. Finally, I would point out that what is true of cricket and every other department of sport is true of angling, and, therefore, of loch fishing. Certain anglers are born, others are made. The former can hope to make themselves assuredly perfect by opportunity and practice; the latter can only expect to attain a certain measure of skill and are far more dependent upon the lessons of others than are the born anglers. Nor can one afford to overlook the fact that the born angler is an observer and a student—a man who uses at once his head and his hand—a co-operation of mind and matter which distinguishes all the great exponents of any pastime.

CHAPTER XXII.

How to Fish a Trout Loch: The Method of Casting.

Angling genius consists in an infinite capacity for taking pains. If, therefore, in loch fishing with the fly the angler is content to follow the traditional methods, he had better confine himself to that most simple of all lakes, the lake which readily admits of the old drift method with the boat broadside to the wind and one angler in the bow and another in the stern, each in the right of the water lying to the right or left of an imaginary line drawn at right angles to the centre of the boat and extending down wind to the end of the drift or to the lee shore. My theory of lake fishing, even in such a loch as this, and Loch Leven is its typical representative, is based on the principle that a lake is merely an overgrown currentless pool, which must be attacked on precisely the same plan as one would attack a pool in a river. This being so, you must ask your companion to step ashore. If he refuses to go, throw him overboard; if one is going to enjoy the freedom of the lake and unfettered action and to put one's thinking machinery in motion, one must not be tramelled by the rights of another, but must be absolute skipper of his own craft, and have no one to consider but himself. Still keeping this categorical imperative of the resemblance between lake and river in view, it is obvious that the streams from the kintergarten of the burn to the university of the limpid river—the meek Cephisus of scanty sun-dried tide, are the best possible educators for the loch, since they are better schools for the training of the fishy eye than the lake, with its greater apparent, but not greater real, uniformity of " spots." The error into which loch fishers of the traditional school fall is thus to treat the loch as the sea, though the latter by no means wholly deserves, from a sporting standpoint, to be summarily dismissed as the true paradise of the duffer. At the same time to initiate an angler into the mysteries of the craft in a loch, is to introduce him to an apparent uniformity wholly uneducative to the fishy eye which does not reflect the lessons of the river. For my own part I was, while still a toddler in the angling nursery, a burn fisher who paid stolen visits, which cost me dear, to the river, and for another long period a river fisher pure and simple. The lessons I learned on burn and river I carried with me to the lake and applied them in every kind of way. A non-adherence to this principle— the very basis and root idea of successful loch fishing, may possibly explain why certain clever river fishers—even men educated in the dry fly world—whom I have met on lakes, have signally failed to do their mechanical powers justice, and have reduced their genius by the chalk stream to the level of the dullest understanding, when standing by the shores or afloat on the surface of a loch. They have approached loch fishing—and probably the prejudice is begot of the "purist" mind, imbued either with the idea that there is nothing to learn or that there is everything to learn. Both frames of mind are equally fatal to success. The former begets a confidence that is the father of carelessness and has resulted in many a rude awakening; the latter induces a spirit of dependence on boatmen and natives—a reliance upon the experience of others that may be, and often is, misplaced, and is assuredly opposed to the principle which makes for greatness in angling and is the basis of all success in the art. The loch fisher must, therefore, rely upon himself and supplement his skill acquired on the river by personal observation on the lake, by the comparison of lake and river and the noting of their differences, and finally must verify the facts of lake life as stated by others by ranging them along side of the facts of his own personal experience.

He will find if he does so, that in straightforward loch fishing, in drifting, that is to say, over known lies, where fishing water is of uniform excellence, his success will depend upon the observance of two general principles, the method in which he works his flies and the great extent of water he covers and small area of water he misses.

In a river he would cover every inch of water with the fly and would fish it slowly and deliberately, an aim he would be helped to achieve by reason of the fact that he was master of his own motions and the regulator of his advance. Nor would he consider it conducive to sport if he

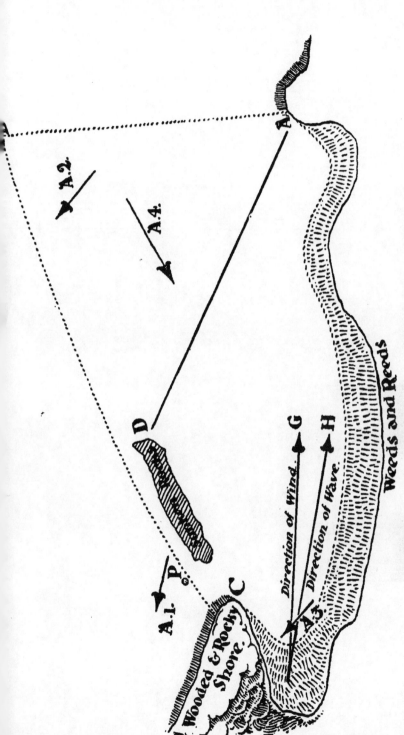

How to Fish a Bay—General Theory of "Attack."

Dotted Line is Boundary of Fish-holding Area.

had to fish a pool, and at the same time regulate his movements by the movements of another. This broad fact points to two conclusions. It shows, in the first place, that a man should be alone, and in the second place, that the drift method is not a satisfying method, unless, indeed, one be alone or the wind be very gentle.* Both conditions must, strictly speaking, be granted before the drift method can be pronounced even moderately satisfying. It is obvious if one must cover every inch of water that the proper plan is to have your gillie constantly at the oars and to adopt, when fishing in a breeze a reach or bay known to hold fish, some method that will secure as nearly as possible the desired end. Nor is it less material, in this the simplest style of loch fishing, that one should cover all the water possible on "good" days as on "bad," for on the former our "bag" will obviously depend upon the reaping of the full harvest as it will on the latter on neglecting no opportunity to pick up the stray straws. To secure the desired end is clearly a question rather of navigation and boat management than of angling skill, which must necessarily vary with the circumstances of the case. I refer to the subject in a later chapter when dealing with sea-trout fishing, and will here content myself with a mere statement of the principle illustrated by two examples. Let us suppose that the angler is fishing a bay of the following nature—premising that I am describing a portion of a certain loch and that the picture is drawn from life and is not a product of the imagination. The bay in question begins at a rocky point, of which, for some fifty yards out, fish lie within an area of which lines drawn from A to B, from C to F, and back to A would be the limits. If G be the direction of the wind and I had reached the point C, having fished the wooded shore as marked, my probable plans of campaign in a light breeze and a strong breeze respectively, would be as follows. First in a strong breeze; after some careful casts off the point C, where the boat, being under the shelter of the rocks and trees, could remain stationary until every inch of water was searched by varying the length of the cast, I would direct the gillie to place the boat in the position P, with her head in the direction of the arrow marked

* I am aware of the difficulty of obtaining a boat to oneself in Highland lochs in the height of the season, but the fact no more invalidates my contention than does the fact that a crowded hotel may necessitate sleeping on a billiard table with half-a-dozen others prove such a sleeping place to be a more comfortable couch than a single bed of down.

A1, and by holding her against the wind would cast over every inch of the water above and to windward of the sunken rocks in the chart. I would repeat the same operation a little nearer the rocks until every inch on the other side of the rocks and a little out from them had been fished, continuing in each case as far as the limit of the line between B and C and B and A. I should then, after the second crossing, work down from B to A, keeping the boat's head in the direction marked by the arrow A2, which would land me off the point, where I would, still holding the boat against the wind, search all the nooks and crannies about A, including the little bay. Next I should work up from A to C in a series of gentle zigzags, and should, on reaching C again, fish the point, and work round towards F, where the head of the boat being kept in the direction of A3 I should work slowly down the reeds, casting out and in, searching in the latter case not only every inch of the water adjacent to the reeds, but also all breaks in them and each tiny bay. Finally, I would take the line from A to D, and would cast on both sides of the boat, whose head would be kept about two points of the wind and in the position A 4. In a very light breeze I should pursue practically the same tactics, with this difference, that as it would be easier to keep the boat head to the wind and to follow a definite course which would divide the water into layers, I might fish it in straight sections after exhausting the immediate resources of the sunken rocks. This somewhat bald description of my method in fishing an actual portion of a lake with which I am familiar may, perhaps, serve to illustrate the principle which I have been endeavouring to state. I need hardly point out that apart from covering far more water than he can do by drifting pure and simple, the angler by adopting the above plan secures the enormous advantage of always being to windward of his fish; strictly speaking, he is sometimes to leeward, but he is always able to secure the windward berth of a fish because the boat's head is to the wind —for example as in position A 4—and hence is ever able to make a cool and deliberate second cast over a fish he has risen and missed. When drifting and fishing with a companion a fish missed is usually a fish lost, for if the boat be not at once over it, the cast which will tempt a second rise is usually a hurried and flurried one, unless the other angler is good enough to suffer a cessation of his casting. In any case time must be lost to secure the position, and with the lapse of time and the turmoil of securing the position for a fresh cast, its value and the opportunity generally vanish.

Loch fishing in a calm, I regard as a separate branch of the sport and have so treated it, but loch fishing in a breeze, gentle or strong, along a shore where the fish lie in some places close in and at others for a certain distance out from it, falls within the scope of my present subject. "Shore fishing," in this wide sense, I shall have to refer to again when dealing with sea-trout, but in the meantime, still keeping the principle of covering as much water as possible in view, it must be clear that a mere straight drift along a shore close in or at some little distance out from it, according to the nature and depth of the water, is an even less satisfactory method than when fishing bays and reaches. With two anglers in the boat one must suffer, and the inshore rod will kill all the fish save when water is being traversed in which the fish lie some distance out from the shore. Even when there is only one angler in the boat the drift method cannot possibly yield results fully commensurate with the possibilities—looking at the question from the utilitarian point of view, while from the "moral" standpoint, no angler who has but half-searched water and has not exercised his ingenuity in the widest sense of the term, can feel wholly satisfied that he has taken the greatest degree of pleasure out of his pastime and combined recreation with an interesting and instructive study of tactics and trout habits. Each likely spot on the shore, by stone that rises above or sunken rock that lies below the surface must be noted and fished with care; each inch of likely looking water under a bush or the overhanging boughs of a tree must be carefully searched, and the "fishy" eye must miss nothing.

Once more it is obvious that the problem of covering a maximum amount of water, resolves itself into one of navigation or to speak by the card, of mixed navigation and angling. I will again illustrate the principle by an example once more drawn from the realities of lakeland. The shore in question is of this character. For some four hundred yards its steep sides are covered with rocks hurled in confusion to the water's edge, while from amongst these spring many trees whose boughs everywhere over-shadow and weep and wave over the water. This portion of the shore is only fishable close in. Then comes a bit of wooded shore with a shingle beach. This lasts for some distance, and the water opposite it is fishable for forty yards out, being some four to six feet or more deep with splendid feeding ground and shelter. Then comes a mixed variety of shore, reeds and weeds, and rocks and stones showing above and under the water, while a small burn finds its way in at one point and here and there occur sunken roots and masses of fallen branches. In some places the water is fishable for some 40 yards out; in other places only close in, while the best spots are those affording shelter. Now let us suppose that a moderate breeze is blowing down the shore and that the angler is at A about to begin operations. Before describing the plan I should adopt it may be pointed out as the chart shows, that the direction of the wave will not be quite the same as the direction of the wind, waves, when the wind blows straight down a loch, always inclining towards the shore. This fact is of more importance than appears on the surface, for in fishing the shore, say, from A to B the direction of the boat's head must be such as to secure a position that will be about two points off the course of the resultant arrow placed between the arrows indicating respectively the directions of the wind and of the wave. This may be roughly represented by P1. and the boat will be kept and worked up the shore as nearly as possible at this angle to it. The angler will face the wind and use the undercut cast, working his flies mostly up against the wind so as to keep his line taut. This method he can, of course, vary as he sees fit and as the course of events justify. He will leave no corner unfished, however close to the shore and will pay particular attention to every likely looking hold. On reaching B, he will work right across to E, the line joining E representing the path of the boat, while he will cast in the direction of the wind so as to cover the water near the line BE and within BEF. He will then work from E to G, keeping the boat's head to the wind and may then fish the line between G and H in the same way; next he will take the line H to I, then those from M to I, M to N, N to J, J to O, O to L, L to K to F, finishing by coming inwards a little inside of BF, but finishing near B. He will then work up from B to C as he did from A to B. This is the theory of his attack; obviously, however, he will not be able to adhere to it in practice with the same minuteness as on

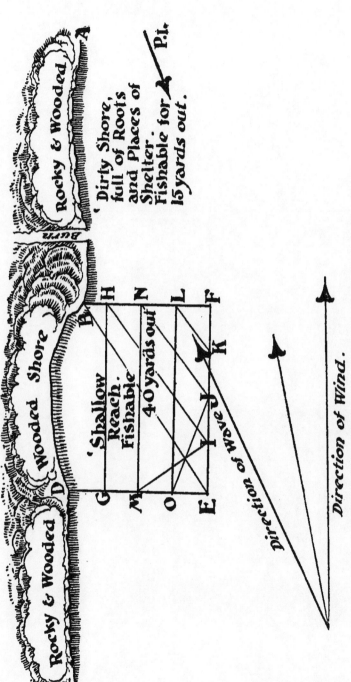

Rocky & Wooded

Rocky & Wooded

Wooded Shore

BURN

'Dirty Shore,
full of Roots
and Places of
Shelter.
Fishable for
15 yards out.

P.L.

'Shallow
Reach.
Fishable.

40 yards out.

Direction of Wave

Direction of Wind.

How to Fish a Shore—General Theory of "Attack."

paper, but in any case he will fish every inch of water. The angling "averages" are not, fortunately or unfortunately, published every Monday and at the end of each season, like those of cricket. Even if they were they would, if viewed apart from the circumstances of their making, be still more misleading than are cricket figures. All first class cricketers play on an average of seasons on the same and on the same variety of wickets, fiery, baked, slow or fast. But all anglers do not fish in the same lochs; nor when a certain number of anglers fish the same waters do they always fish them under similar conditions. Nevertheless the returns extending over a whole season are a pretty safe guide to the efficacy of methods, for I prefer to leave the question of personal skill out of account. If, therefore, the above method of fishing a loch, as a general plan of campaign, has enabled me to regularly secure better results than other anglers fishing alone on their own plan, then obviously when method is opposed to method, the method just described is entitled to take first place. Further, if fishing alone be a condition precedent to the success of the above method, and by fishing alone I have secured better baskets than the aggregate baskets of two rods fishing together, then the onus of proof in favour of my method becomes overwhelming. If, on taking the results of a whole season, it be found that the baskets of the angler fishing alone and on the above plan far exceed, on an average being struck, the combined average basket of two rods fishing together on any other plan, then the method is vindicated and its comparative efficacy is placed beyond dispute. If a succession of seasons be taken and their results aggregated and compared, and the result once more is that the angler pursuing the above plan comes out a very easy first, then obviously he has solved the problem of the proper plan on which a loch should be fished. I have already been under the painful necessity of recording personal figures to prove the accuracy of this contention by facts which are stubborn chiels and need not, therefore, do so again. There remains, however, the question as to how the flies should be worked, but on this I need scarcely condescend at any length. The chapters dealing with the "Philosophy of the Fly" and with the application of that philosophy have already indicated with sufficient clearness the general principle involved. If that general principle be kept steadily before the angler, he will naturally give his flies, first, that movement most natural to the component parts of his cast, of which the two (or three) rearmost members are always those whose interests must be his primary care, second, such variation in motion as may be suggested to him by the angling conditions of the moment, or may appear calculated to give his "fluttering" ally a chance to show how trout are killed. On this point it is impossible to offer useful advice without entering into a wealth of detail that might be confusing and would scarcely be profitable. There is but one point, however, which should be noted and to which I have already referred. I allude to the fact that flies float shorewards under the impulse of wind and waves. This fact the angler should occasionally recognise and endeavour to imitate, especially on a stiff and difficult loch or on bad days. In light breezes it is quite possible to cast up wind, and in all breezes it is possible to make your flies personate the doomed originals they copy. As an example of the difference this sometimes makes I am compelled to quote one of those personal experiences which I would fain avoid, but it is such an instructive lesson in the difference in results achieved by difference in methods and of suiting methods to the occasion that I cannot refrain from quoting it.

On a certain loch I had as my companion an angler of the older school, who, I daresay, had killed more fish by far in his day than I had landed at the time when we angled together. He fished with a long line and on the traditional plan. But he caught no fish; nor did I when I based my plan of campaign on his. I speedily gave it up, however, used a short line and started what was a sort of "dapping," that is to say, I tried to make my flies move exactly as the natural flies on the water were moving, which an occasional trout was taking. By this means and other little variations I killed 15 fish the first day and 25 the second. His total catch was one. But this faculty of observing and of drawing inferences appears to be a gift.* It assuredly adds pleasure to the sport for even when many of the inferences are erroneous, the pleasure of proving them to be so is in a measure to

---

* I can never forget, in this connection, the strange tale which a famous specialist, known all over the world, told me of his first introduction to dry fly and almost to angling. In a certain dry fly stream, which happened to be running in full volume, he observed that the trout were taking the flies off certain leaves in the stream. He caught one of these leaves, passed the hook of a fly resembling the fly which the fish were taking off them through the leaf, and by this means took some three brace of fish and earned the reputation, everybody else being "blank," of having used worm ! He had, as a matter of fact, only used his head.

share the thoughts of mighty men in a humble kind of way. It cannot be doubted, however, that such a faculty once possessed should be diligently exercised, and if not possessed in any marked degree is well worth cultivating. Our pleasures are the serious matters of life on holiday, and a week of unconscious hard thinking on a loch not only gives the usual wheels of the brain a rest, but consolidates the whole mechanism and strengthens most of all the sources of all power and success, the faculty to observe, deduce and persevere until, as in angling, finis coronat opus.

CHAPTER XXIII.

Raising, Hooking, Playing and Landing.

That prince of panders, Chiffinch, left the world better than he found it by the altitude of a good phrase, "the moment of projection," which very happily describes the period in practical angling when a trout gleams yellow by the fly. From time immemorial this stepping stone to the final crowning mercy of capture has been called a "rise"—a phrase on which custom has set the imprimatur of its approval, but which, nevertheless, is not in all cases a correct definition of the actual movement of the fish from the position in which it sights the fly to its locating of itself near it by one of the most graceful examples of the poetry of motion in the animal world. The manner of a loch trout's coming to the fly very obviously depends upon a variety of circumstances. Of these the chief are the depth of the water, the nature of the light, the presence or absence of rival claimants, the distance at which the fish is from the fly at the moment of sighting the prize, the quick or slow movement, possibly the pattern of the fly and the depth to which it is sunk, the character of the bottom, the colour of the water, the general habit and particular mood as well as size of the trout, the force of the wind and the size of the wave and the nature of the loch in general and of the particular spot at which the fish is tempted for doom.

All these circumstances affect to a greater or less degree the manner in which a loch trout will thrill the angling heart. It would obviously involve the drawing of too many nice distinctions and the laborious condescension upon an excess of bewildering details, to attempt to describe the effect of each and all of these conditions upon the character of what is termed the rise. Moreover it may be questioned if the stating of these effects would convey any practical lesson or even information that cannot be much better learned on the loch—the finest and most beautiful school in nature.

It is, nevertheless, necessary to point out the effect of some of the circumstances I have mentioned upon the method in which a loch trout takes the fly. I will first illustrate by examples the effect of depth,. location, and the colour of the water, three circumstances that generally operate together in producing the effect referred to. Casting in some very clear water about a foot in depth and close by the shore near a stone surrounded by other and smaller stones, which together appeared to afford a likely habitat for a trout, I observed a fish leave the shelter of the largest stone and swim in leisurely, but evidently purposeful fashion after my tail fly. I at once removed it from "within his danger" to see what the trout would then do. He became frantic with eagerness, changed his sober gait for that of a swift-pacing gannet sweeping to catch a lost shoal of herring. I threw the fly in his neighbourhood, and the moment he spied it, every fin quivered and after a brief but visible poise, he swept with the gyrating tremble of a well-aimed torpedo full. on his doom. On another accasion while fishing in some two feet of water in a discoloured lake I noted the sudden apparition of a ghostly thing in the shape of a trout coming up in slow, hesitating fashion at my tail fly, until, as I judged, it was within a foot of the prize; then it suddenly changed its slow-pacing, uncertain motion for a movement of almost incredible velocity. It was, however, an easy matter to rob him of his prey, and after a boil and splutter on the top, he began swimming about in small circles, ranging close and not wide as the trout in the clear water had done, looking for his vanished prize. Presently he sighted it and hung for a moment as if watching it; then. he practically stalked it, or, at least, approached it stealthily and sucked it in with great deliberation.

We have here obviously a most instructive example of the effect of the colour of the loch, the trout's location, and, in a lesser degree, of the depth of the water, upon the manner in which trout take the fly. In both cases the fish came slowly at the fly when it was first observed.. The reason of this slowness was not, however, the same in both cases. The trout in the clear shallow water was absolute master of the situation. He could afford, being alone, to secure his prize at leisure ; on the other hand, the trout in the discoloured loch had three reasons for not moving fast; at first he was doubtful as to whether he had or had not sighted a prize; when he became assured that he had done so, he obviously made up his mind that a stealthy advance was best in a watery fog, while, finally he, too, was a beatus possidens in the fee and.

usufruct of his habitat, and his supremacy was undisputed. When the fly vanished, both behaved in a manner perfectly consistent with the conditions of the hunt. The distinctions which I have drawn, if somewhat "nice," are not without practical value. Obviously in the case of the first trout, the method of working the fly which would have made the assurance of his taking double sure, would in the light of his subsequent conduct have been to impart just sufficient additional speed to the motion of the fly to secure the arousing of the keen desire for what may be lost, the intensity of appetites, noble and ignoble, being in trout as in men, as often as not conditioned by the ease or otherwise with which desire can be gratified.

In the case of the second fish a policy of masterly inactivity was evidently the most likely to achieve the common end.

I have mentioned these examples amongst many that could have been cited with equal appositeness, not so much by reason of their practical and direct value as lessons, as by reason of their indirect value as examples of the kind of facts the loch fisher must observe and the inferences he must draw from them, if he would not only kill fish but also make sure of extracting the greatest degree of pleasure and of instruction out of his sport. The last is by no means the least important gain, for the nature of the subject learned, so long as it is not purely technical, is of much less moment from the educational standpoint, than is its power to promote the "insitam vim," or in ordinary language, to develop brain muscularity and the power to put the thinking muscles to their best use. When the brain goes into training, interest is the best of all aids to knowledge and climbing from fact to inference ceases to be a conscious labour.

This aspect of sport is so often overlooked that I offer no apology for pointing it out, especially as angling, above all sports, affords opportunities for this unconscious training of the mind for fishing in the great and troubled stream of life, above which frowns a perfect twilight forest of rival rods. And even if one places too high an estimate on the general as distinct from the special value of such observations and deductions as those cited, one can, at least, claim for the sport which gave rise to them that it rests the wheels which the serious business of life has worn or clogged.* Their character, as well as their direct

* In the course of conversation Mr. Forbes Robertson once told me that he took to cycling in London, when specially brain-fagged by the cares of production and study of

and indirect value, thus not only justify their stating, but warrant me in passing to a more general statement as to the nature of the varieties of ways in which a loch trout takes the fly. I can safely leave the teaching of the subtleties to the tuition of experience on the lake itself.

Before, however, describing these rises and the way in which they should be met, certain preliminary observations on the question of skill seem necessary.

Nothing trains for war, but war, and your master of theory of tactics must be an opportunist and a student of circumstances. A knowledge of habits and moods may be imparted and the faculty of observation may be cultivated through the inspiration of the observations of others, but opportunism and the application of even mechanical hints are essentially the products of practics. If you accept, for example, the theory of how to hold a golf club when about to drive, you will be forced to attempt, inter alia, to keep the grip of your left hand loose and to avoid letting your thumb lie along the club. But ask Vardon how he drives, and he will probably tell you that " it came natural to him," and that he does not know whether his left hand is loose or tight; he simply " addresses " himself to the ball in a manner natural to the occasion, and which suits the aptitudes of those forces constituting his physical genius and the subtle correspondence of hand and eye. Jessop, Thornton, and all natural hitters smite their hardest and truest when in their best health, and when the occasion suffers them to realise their peculiar powers—again due to the correspondence of hand and eye in producing a resultant force directed by a perfectly unconscious process of dynamic method. It is even doubtful if the best " scientific " batsmen could do more_than tell you that certain balls should be met on principle in such and such a way. The execution as designed is not wholly dependent on the excellence of the intention. Stokes and other long·drop kicks will probably tell you that their greatest individual achievements were due to the sudden unpremeditated and almost wholly involuntary seizure of an opportunity and the instant answer of a free sweeping leg acting under the dictates of mind and eye to propel by a perfectly natural and wholly unreasoned method the ball of battles some sixty odd yards between two posts eighteen and a half feet apart, parts, simply because his mind got a rest through the necessity of concentrating his attention on the guidance of his wheel through the maze of traffic perils. " Palinure's unaltered mood " ship-wrecked that worthy.

and over a bar ten feet from the ground. Of shooting, other than with
the rifle, precisely the same holds good, and the best sot is the man
who never consciously' aims and has no method whatsoever, which he
remembers when birds are coming down wind as if all the fiends from
heaven that fell were on their track and had pealed the banner cry of
hell, the proud-swelling, death-dealing whistle of an infernal hawk into
whose person the evil souls of a thousand birds of unconscionable mood
had been compressed. Possibly of all sports billiards most nearly approaches to angling in the blending of the display of opportune skill
with reasoned intention and definite plan. Such, at least, is the impression left on the spectator after watching Roberts make a big break
which show design, but not the slightest trace of hesitancy, in its execution. What is true of skill, special and general, in all sports, under the exception noted in the case of billiards, is true of angling, and if in describing the three commonest varieties of the loch trout rise, I am forced to
wax didactic in setting forth the corresponding " strikes," my remarks
must be read in the light of these preliminary observations on the unconscious character of the skill, much more a gift of nature than acquired, by the exercise of which they must be met. My theoretical conception of the " strike " so called will, moreover, be stated at the same
time as the varieties of rise, for as the rise and " strike " correspond in
time and are practically cause and effect, it would be impossible to
describe the " strike " without also describing the rise that led to it.

The most common rise of the three is when the trout swirls half-in
and half-out of the water, and takes the fly when the swirl is half-com-
pleted. This is the ordinary rise. The proper way to meet it is to
strike when the fish is felt, and never before. When one is fishing his
very best and missing few or no fish, his strike is invariably late-delivered
and deliberate. Once wild striking begins, many fish are missed, and
missing fish " grows by what it feeds upon." The motive power in all
single-handed fly-fishing is confined to the elbow joint, the wrist, the
fingers and the thumb.* The strike is essentially the joint work of the
wrist and thumb. In working the flies the forefinger will rest on the line
and the thumb will lie vertically on the rod ; an increased pressure of
the thumb produces an almost, involuntary and very slight turn of the

*As in skating, cricket, shooting and other sports, the " swing " of the body has to
be reckoned with, but to attempt to assign to the body its share in the " rythm of
motion " would be to confuse.

wrist. This tightens the line without any jerk, and produces just the degree of force necessary to the occasion. Many fish require no striking, for a fish almost invariably turns on taking a fly—in fact, in the very act of doing so, and in nearly all cases goes down with its head first and with its weight pressing down on the barb in such a way as to drive it home. It will be observed that the theory of the "strike" just stated appears after a study of the actual movements in angling to express the "strike" drill through which I unconsciously put myself, or am put by a rising fish.

This theory differs essentially from that of anglers of much greater mechanical skill—a circumstance which further explains the reason why I referred at some length to the unconscious exercise of certain powers on no ascertained or fixed plan by practical exponents of other sports. It further shows that the best method is either the one which custom has firmed into habit, or certain personal characterictics and aptitudes render proper. Many expert anglers strike from the reel, while others, whose claims to a position in the front rank cannot be disputed, appear to "check" the line when striking. Amongst the former is Mr. R. B. Marston, and amongst the latter is Sir Edward Grey. In stating their views both these writers are referring to their method of striking when using the dry fly, but I presume that the fact in no way affects the general principle involved. Mr. Marston bases his practice on the ground that when you get hung up in casting there is less chance of a snap following the sudden arrest of the rod when your finger is off the line and the reel is free to give than when the line is de facto fastened between the reel and first ring by the restraining finger. Though, as a rule, there is very little chance of your being hung up when fishing a loch, yet it does sometimes happen on lakes with trees growing down to and overhanging their shore waters, while there is always the chance in lake fishing of catching on a reed or on a rock—evil fates that may be quite as disastrous to the loch fisher as are boughs, grass, tall poppies, and other natural objects, which are things of beauty at all other times, to his brother-angler by the riverside. As to the strike proper, the trout-executioner's coup de grace, Mr. Marston, on precise'y similar dynamic grounds, would have it delivered from the reel. I differ from him, but only on the ground that it is a matter of use and wont as well as of temperament. Deliberate self-control is, on the last analysis, the

U

secret underlying successful striking, when it finds expression in an opportune setting in motion of just the necessary degree of force to meet the circumstances of the rise.   In this aspect, therefore, the strike may be held to occupy the same position in angling, as the " throw forward " does in shooting.   In other words its rules do not admit of codification, but only of generalisation on ascertained principles, the chief of which may be said to be the cultivation of control.   The morality of the strike is thus summed up in the categorical imperative " Thou shalt not strike," which, when interpreted, means that your intention not to strike must be honest, whatever your actual practice may be.   By adhering to this general rule of conduct you will cultivate the habit of striking late, and hence of striking with what may be termed, by a pleasing licence, unconsciously deliberate purpose.   It is, at least, certain that more loch trout are hooked than are missed by late striking, while it is equally certain that more trout are missed by too quick striking than by late striking, or by not striking at all.   That a fish may be missed by not striking or by delaying the strike, a few self-sacrificing experiments which I made in the season of 1898 appear to satisfactorily prove.   I had some difficulty in securing a reach of a loch suitable for the purpose of the experiments, but at length I found a beautiful little tree-cradled bay where the water was perfectly clear and about four feet deep.   The next difficulty was to persuade a trout to rise, while, of course, I had to trust to chance that the fish would rise in the proper kind of way, would come, that is, to the fly from a point beyond it and take it down with him in such a way that I could note what happened.   After one or two failures I, at last, secured just the sort of rise desired.   The fish, apparently one of the normal weight of the trout in the lake (1½lbs.), came deliberately up to the fly, his head being towards it and towards the boat.   He turned as he took the fly and went almost straight down. The line was nearly taut, and I had the greatest possible difficulty in keeping the old angling Adam from yielding to the temptation.   I succeeded, however, in restraining this legacy of another bite, with the result that when the fish had sunk some three feet down, he opened his oracular jaws, shot the fly out with great force,* and presented me

---

* Trout, sea-trout and salmon seem to put this power in practice with a degree of rapidity indicated by the order in which I have placed them.   Fishing in a West Highland salmon river, my rod in making a cast came against a tree which prevented the further working of the fly.   At that moment a salmon took it and held on to.   He sunk with it

not only with an exception to the golden rule of the happy mean in striking which I had endeavoured to cultivate, but also with a very interesting and instructive lesson in the often unsuspected and unnoted means of defence against our guile in which Nature has thought fit to panoply her cold-blooded children. There was no question here as to how the fish was holding the fly. It had disappeared and his mouth was closed. Whenever he felt what a very bony and insipid member of the insect race he had secured, he rejected it with the same hasty scorn as the official lobster-measurer throws an undersized crustacean to the mercy of the deep. As it is only human to strike, and such exceptions as that just noted are as rare as the virtue of complete abstention from striking, the only rule of conduct appears to be the one already laid down. The cultivation of the habit of self-restraint in striking is absolutely necessary in sea-trout angling in lakes, as I hope to be able to show when dealing with that branch of loch-fishing so far as it differs from that now under discussion.

The second common variety of rise may be defined as the " springing " rise or the " rolling " rise, the term applied varying with the height to which the fish ascends in taking the fly. The trout jumps clean out of the water, and either (1) carries the fly with it in the jump, or (2) takes it just as the jump is completed and it is reentering the water.

The cause of jumping in the first variety of the " springing " rise appears to be speed begot of greed, while the leap in the second variety may be due to the fact that trout occasionally endeavour to drown natural flies by coming down on them. The rises can be distinguished from one another, for in the second the trout lingers longer in the air, with a view to steadying its aim. To meet such a rise no strike is necessary, for the turn, in the first variety, will send the barb home, and the descending impetus, in the second, will be sufficient to accomplish the same end. If the angler strikes a fish that has taken the fly before leaping, he will put a strain on it in the air, with the usual result, while in the case of a fish that is going to take the fly by coming down on it, he will simply snatch the fly from it, or, alternatively, produce the same effect as if he struck far too forcibly. All this is evident,

---

very slowly and held it a very long time before "spitting" it out. I saw the whole operation. A trout or sea-trout would have ejected the fly much sooner.

and experience is constantly verifying it. The "springing" rise is rarely the method in which heavy fish take the fly, though not only large brown trout, but also the very heaviest sea-trout occasionally give the angler a "rolling" rise which is a modified form of the "springing" rise. When large trout come up in this way, the whole of their bodies are never out of the water at the same time, though every part of their body is out of the water in turn during the rise. The rule in this case is the same as in the first rise of this type, and so far from any strike being necessary, it is a fatal error in judgment to strike. The third variety of rise is the rise below the water which is of most frequent occurrence in the two extremes of loch-angling conditions—a calm or a strong breeze. As a rule the best fish rise in this way. Not only is this so, but trout which give the angler this kind of rise should never be missed. They are feeding fish and not merely fish which happening to see your fly, prove themselves opportunists. I kept a careful note of the nature of the rises I received from 30 loch trout running from 1½lbs. to 2½lbs., which I had observed feeding close in shore, and for which I angled systematically and purposely after the plan of the dry fly angler. In every case the rise was so low and quiet that in some instances only the very slightest bubble indicated the sucking in of the fly, while in others there was no break whatsoever until the fish was hooked. Then it was the break of a hooked and not of a rising fish. This kind of rise requires very careful timing, and a cultivation of the telepathic sense of arrest transmitted by the sucking in of the fly to the whole frame and the response of the "striking" portions of it to the transmitted order.*

To the successful meeting of all the varieties of rise noted, the same general rule of self-restraint may be held to apply, but practice can alone confer the acquired mechanical skill this attitude of mind tends to create, while it is equally certain that the insita vis of natural angling ability can only be cultivated by education based on the same recognition of " the psychological." Into what are termed, or may be termed, "wild

---

* The long-drawn-out rise in a dead calm, when a big fish follows the fly for some feet, is fully described in the chapter dealing with the same aspect of sea-trouting fishing, as this chapter covers in the case of loch trout. This present season (1899) I experienced many examples of it, and extraordinary good fortune in meeting it successfully. As stated supra I regard the successful meeting of this rise as the most difficult feat in the whole domain of sport, for it involves the exercise of the maximum of self-restraint and of mechanical skill.

rising," and "short rising," it is scarcely necessary in the case of loch trout to enter.   No skill can avail the angler if a fish rises wildly and misses the fly.   When fish rise wildly, the wise angler resigns himself to the inevitable, and does not allow the fact to disturb his equanimity or ruffle his temper to the vanishing of all that coolness which is of the very essence of success.   " Short rising," in the strict sense, is not so marked a characteristic of loch trout as of sea-trout.   No doubt many loch trout " move " to our flies without our observing the fact, just as many salmon are rendered restless by the passage of a fly and betray their uneasiness by a movement more or less pronounced.*

In   the   chapter   on   " Moods "   I   have   described   certain varieties of the non-feeding rise, while I recur to the subject of short-rising in dealing with the trait as exemplified by the sea-trout.   There is, however, a rise peculiar to certain waters—the rise of a fish flashing out of the green mystery of weed and taking the fly, which merely requires watching to be successfully met.   The fish startles the angler and generally slackens its pace just before reaching the fly.   It is this pause which is fatal, for the angler is apt not to make allowance for it.   If no fish be struck until felt or seen to take the fly, very few will be missed and the cultivation of restraint is on the last analysis, and, as already pointed out, the surest indirect means of ensuring direct success.

Having thus in a more or less satisfactory manner succeeded on paper in raising and hooking our trout we have still to reduce him into real, as distinguished from constructive, possession.   Here again I am forced to generalise, to set forth principles of conduct and not rules of action, at least in circumstances of an ordinary and not a special character.   In water in which such seen dangers as reeds or such seen or unseen perils as weeds, do not exist, there is practically no drill-book giving the normal exercise of playing a fish.   You can be told how to play a " yorker," if you can get your masters to agree upon what a " yorker " is ; you can be instructed in the negative art of keeping a rising ball down,

---

*There are few better situated pools in this country than that just above Hoddom Bridge, on the Annan, for observing the restlessness, of very varying degree, which the passage of a fly over the surface occasions amongst salmon lying in a pool.   Some interesting experiments, illustrative of this trait amongst sea-trout in lochs and ditches, are recorded in a later chapter.   It may be mentioned that both in the case of salmon and sea-trout the angler is sublimely unconscious that he has moved a fish at all.   As a matter of fact, in any river or lake carrying a good head of the migratory salmonidæ fish are moved in every pool or on every reach on the very worst of days.

but the instruction will not give you the skill necessary to meet such balls in practice any more than our old friend, the advice to hold your left hand loose will enable you to send a golf ball into the next county. At the same time there is a much greater measure of exactitude in these things than there is in the possible movements of a fish ; the cultivation as well as the exercise of the delicate art of the vis major, positively or negatively considered, in playing a trout, the knack of yielding and and standing firm, of appearing to humour, while in reality you lead, of persuading rather than forcing the direction of the rushes necessary to exhaustion, and, in a word, the tactics of battle between those mighty opposites, angling man and hooked fish, necessitate the combination in the highest degree of the suaviter in modo with the fortiter in re.

In most sports and in nearly all occupations, from riding to beating an egg, from billiards to the slicing of orange peel for the " original " marmalade, precisely the same sort of combination of lightness of touch and strength of grip both of mind and body distinguish those that are born skilful.   Nevertheless there are certain principles of conduct which may almost be called rules when one is playing a loch trout in open water.   The first and by far the most important of these is to play the fish with the boat, presuming always that he is of sufficient size, activity and strength to necessitate skill in playing him at all.   The secret of the successful playing of a fish—apart from the thwarting of his special tricks of the acrobatic order—is to keep control over him ; and to keep control over him you must be parallel with him. If you allow him to rush away to windward while you drift to leeward, the likelihood of your bidding a long farewell to any fish save one that is very firmly hooked is directly proportionate to the distance you suffer him to put between you.   The old rule of playing a fish to windward, while the boat drifts along is a legacy of the mistaken policy of the loch—the dual control with apportioned spheres of influence, but it does not favour the ultimate dissection of the " yellow corpse " in posse while mutual concessions are in the angling, as in the diplomatic world, made with a rose in the extended, a birch rod in the hand held behind the back.   A masterful fish will, of course, take the law into his own hands and compel a suspension of hostilities, and I recall a case of this kind in which a Yorkshire doctor was dragged about a loch for the best part of an autumn day, while a London angler in the stern sat like patience on a monument smiling at grief and praying for that very break which would have cracked the heart of the tyro being played by his first big fish. I presuppose, however, an angler fishing alone and having, therefore, only his own interests to regard. On this hypothesis, it is, of course, with a gillie at the oars, always possible to follow a fish not slavishly but only so far as is necessary to keep him parallel with the boat, and as near to it and, therefore, as much under control as possible. This by no manner of means deprives the angler of the pleasure of the rush. He enjoys the rush of a salmon which he follows in a river, but he is very careful not to let the rush carry the fish beyond control.*

Two other principles of conduct that may be called rules may also be stated, and they apply to the playing of all fish, whatever be their size.

These two maxims are, that the strain on the fish should be uniform and steady, while the "jump" should be always anticipated. As to the former, how much strain to put on is a question of circumstances; if the fish have tender mouths and are hooking lightly, the strain should not be so great as when they are rising boldly and freely and hooking firmly, though, at the same time, when fish are hooking lightly, it some times pays in the end to get them near the net as quickly as possible, and a persuasive strain may be risked. This persuasive force is "the rub." It can only be acquired by experience, and never is properly acquired unless the angler possess a "gentle hand." To play a lightly-hooked fish too long is to risk its almost certain loss. As to the jump, it is the most dangerous of all methods of effecting an escape put in practice by the trout. The rule may be stated as absolute that a fish always gains ground when it jumps. The angler must, therefore, "give" to the fish as it is in the air and until it re-enters the water, but the moment it does so, the strain must be at once renewed, for a jump is . usually followed by a headshake which the fish will keep up as it goes down and which is one of its strongest means of defence.

Not the least interesting fact connected with the playing of loch-trout is that the trout of different lochs while all putting in practice the same general plans of escape, yet give preference to one plan over

---

* Some further and fuller remarks on this playing of the fish with the boat will be found in the chapter dealing with "Playing Sea-Trout."

another. In one loch jumping will be the favourite plan; in lochs of which this may be predicated, a fierce rush is usually the prelude to the jump. In another loch deep-boring with the head down and the tail up conjoined with head-shaking and a striking of the gut with the tail is the favourite plan. There are no lochs, however, in which one plan is used to the exclusion of the othres, while the method employed to escape doom and regain liberty varies in the same loch with the period of the season, the nature of the day, the character of the reach in which the fish is hooked, and the part of his person in which the hook is located.

Feeding fish in the fullest sense, especially if hooked in a calm—and this applies with greatest force to large fish—almost invariably jump the moment the hook goes home and the restraining influence is felt, while fish hooked in deepish water, though they may give one jump, are certain to bore deep and indulge in head-shaking and tail-striking. Fish in dark-coloured lochs do the same,* while fish in clear lochs keep high and trust to surface acrobatics. Heavy well-fed trout in a loch rich in bottom feeding seek the deeps and put the former plan in practice; trout possessing an excessive strain of the imigrant usually display a tendency to employ the latter method. These are generalisations drawn from experience. They are not rules that can be formulated nor do they admit of dogmatic statement. In all cases the angler must expect the unexpected and be prepared to meet and master it.

Lastly there is the danger of reeds and of weeds; my remarks on how to avoid these allies to the fish and aids to a sporting finish I shall defer until dealing with the playing of sea-trout.

The ultima ratio of loch angling, the landing of the fish should be accomplished by the angler himself holding the stock of his landing net under his arm in the manner shown in the plate "Landing a Two-Pounder." That picture is, however, a little misleading as the boat should have its head up in the wind, especially, when a large fish is being landed. The method I put in practice is, however, fully described in the chapter dealing with sea-trout fishing, for it is of more importance to the angler fishing regularly for large fish than to the

* The trout of the Rowan Tree Loch, near Invarary—the favourite loch of the Duke of Argyll in his sporting days—afford an exception to this rule. They are the gamest fish for their size, which I know, and though the waters of the loch are very dark, the trout jump repeatedly. Other exceptions to the general rule could also be quoted.

A LAZY DAY: LANDING A TWO POUNDER.

loch trout angler who can rarely hope for many captures over 2lbs. in weight. It may, nevertheless, be pointed out that the style advocated is as truly the most sporting and the most profitable method the trout fisher can adopt, as it is the only satisfactory and the only safe system for the sea-trout angler to follow.

If in playing a fish the angler aims at keeping him under control and at anticipating all his movements, and does not suffer him to run to windward or away at angle of 45 deg. to the boat, he will lose but few fish unless those tall allies, the weeds, come to their aid. Finally, if he nets the fish himself to leeward over the stern, he will find that fewer escape at the supreme moment, not only because the operation is generally more skillfully and quietly performed, but also by reason of the important fact that the hand holding the rod is in greater sympathy with the hand holding the net and with the fish—whose final enmeshing is the crowning mercy of angling battle.

CHAPTER XXIV.

PIKE AND PERCH LOCHS : CANALS AS TROUT HOMES.

Pike and perch do not occupy the same place in the esteem of the Scottish angler as they do in that of his English brother, and in a. lesser degree the Irish fisher, but I can scarcely do justice to lakeland without pointing out how much and how unjustly Scotland, as a land of lakes teeming with pike and perch, has been neglected. Some years ago I wrote in the " Field " two articles on this subject one of which was entitled " Scottish Lochs and Pike," and the other " Primitive Pike Fishing."

The first of these articles was, I believe, officially noticed. by the Scottish Fishery Board, as it contained certain recommendations as to the best means of exterminating pike in lochs, and some rather pointed criticism of the methods actually employed. The second article was of a semi-humorous character and, as far as I can remember, drew a touching picture of the essential simplicity of the Scottish pike in the matter of lures and tackle. I have copies of neither article, but it is within my recollection that one of the methods of extermination urged was the use of a hang-net for pike, in union with the system put in practice by "splash-netters " after sea-trout in the romantic silence of Highland sea-lochs, when :

> " Midnight o'er the moonless skies
> Her pall of transient death doth spread."

As the matter is one of some importance to those having trout lochs infested with pike, I may venture on a description of this poaching and illegal style of taking sea-trout which can be applied to pike-haunted reed-beds. Briefly its " modus operandi " is this. Sea trout lie right on the shore at night—the time of their feeding being the 'mirk' hour and the place the extremest shallows—the latter fact accounting for their rising on lochs right among the breaking waves. The net is shot round the shore in a semi-circle. Inside the circle the boat moves while the water is splashed with the oars, and the fish driven out to strike the net, their dash being often marked by a phosphorescent glow and their strike by a similar quiver of fire from the net. Then comes the excitement of lifting the latter, a kaleidoscopic mass of dripping and shivering lines of light, and the unmeshing of struggling bars of silver or some lusty five-pounder who wants holding. Queer things get into the net, some of them by no means pleasant, but these are incidents of the sport and as you are generally poaching, and if you let your net rest, or land yourself, or draw the net on to the shore, you must be breaking the law, they are the bitters that go with the sweets of wrong doing. Now obviously this method if put in practice against pike would be much more effective than any other style that could be employed.

The principal object, however, which I had in view in writing the articles for the " Field " was to advocate the claims of Scottish lakes as pike and perch waters and to urge upon English anglers the advisability of aiding the war of extermination by allying their sporting forces with the cruder and less sporting methods practiced in Scotland for the capture of pike. The majority of Scottish pike anglers are not lovers of the sport, neither do they pursue it at the proper season, so that there lies open to English anglers the rare privilege, in these days of crowded ways, of pursuing their pastime in what are practically virgin waters, or waters, at the least, to which no man comes to angle after the October leaf is sere, much less when it is the sport of "chill November's surly blast." Many English anglers now go to Ireland expressly for pike fishing. Some at least of the stream that sets West might with advantage turn Northwards, for between the Tweed and John o' Groats there are no fewer than 108 lochs which contain pike in varying abundance, but of uniform excellence. These pike lakes are distributed all over the country, and are "Lowland and Highland far and near." All or nearly all are situated amidst scenes of great natural beauty; many of them are richly dowered with the gifts of boon nature. Of these lochs, Loch Lomond, Loch Vennachur, and Loch Katrine are perhaps the chief, though they are by no means the best from an angling point of view.* In Wigtonshire there are a fair number

* Curiously enough the last two of these three lakes yielded not a single pike to a party who devoted a week to them last Christmas. They tried every means—trimmers, trolling, live-baiting, but Lochs Achray, Vennacha and Katrine refused to yield a fish. The circumstances were, no doubt, exceptional, and the failure must be taken as unusual.

of pikeing lochs, some of which contain fish up to 30 lbs., while in romantic Invernessshire there are many lakes affording as good pike fishing as can be had in the United Kingdom.* If you desire to angle for monsters greater far than have ever haunted the midnight couch of the pike-fisher breathing the Irish air, you can penetrate to the head waters of the Spey and in a lonely tarn cradled far up in the silence of the bens, can essay to catch or be caught by a fish of 140lbs. which lurks, according to local tradition, in its deep abiding places. If you are a sporting prophet or would inherit a corner of the mantle of Thomas the Rhymer there awaits for you the catching of the magic pike of Loch Usie in Ross-shire, and the extracting from its belly of the legendary white pebble which will give you the powers of the seer. In the Hebrides there are only one perch and two pike lochs. The two latter are very small sheets of water in Islay, one a mere pond, while the only perch loch is also in the same inland. The perch were introduced by a former Campbell and take the fly greedily. In Sutherlandshire and in Caithnessshire the pike is unknown—a fact which may account for the excellent trouting the lochs of these counties afford. Loch Leven, however, famous as it is for trout, can fairly dispute pride of place with any of the English lakes as a water yielding sport to the perch fisher, while all over Scotland splendid perch fishing may be obtained in lakes whose names and fame, for this kind of sport and its kindred pastime, pike fishing, has been dwarfed by the superior charms of the salmon, trout, and sea-trout lakes and rivers. If the English angler brought his experience and tackle to bear on these waters at their proper season, he would reap, I feel assured, a rich harvest which is now suffered to run to seed.

Scottish pike lochs were not thus neglected in the old days. I find, after a little research, that the earlier tourist-anglers devoted far more attention to the splendid pike of the Scottish lochs than their successors

---

* There is in Kenmure Castle the head and shoulders of a pike said to have weighed 72 lbs. Of this fish most persons interested in pike have heard, but a story connected with its capture is not so widely know and is well worth telling. It was killed by the keeper, who was a great character, of the late Lord Kenmure. His lordship, himself also a bit of an eccentric, used to chaff this keeper and taunt him with never catching anything "bigger than a sprat." On the day on which he killed this pike, John, the keeper, staggered into the drawing-room of Kenmure Castle, with the pike over his shoulder, and flopped the great beast down on the carpet with the words "There, ye can gang an' catch the next sprat yersel'."

have done. Possibly the pioneers carried with them more of their English predeliction for all-round sport and were less affected by the craze called fashion than are the men of to-day. In any case both Franck and Thornton were keenly alive to the charm of variety in angling. Both had drunk deep of the strong wine of salmon fishing, yet neither despised the pike. Indeed they fully recognised that in a pike loch there were even greater possibilities of monsters beyond the wildest dreams of ambition than in the salmon and trout rivers or lakes. The pike, whether deservedly or undeservedly, enjoys an evil reputation and to this fact as well as to the circumstance that its maximum growth is unknown, must be attributed the eerie fascination of pike-fishing in waters said to contain fish of fabulous size, incredible age, desperate ferocity, unconquerable strength, and diabolical malignity. Franck does not chronicle his experiences amongst Scottish pike with any degree of minuteness for a reason which will presently appear, but there is no doubt that the size of the pike which he encountered in the Scottish lochs impressed the ex-soldier of Cromwell, for he says : " but in the lough you shall find him there o'er grown, sometimes to an amazing bigness." He refers, it is true, to pike " that have measured a yard and a half " taken out of the Loch of Minever, which I take from his topographical references to be either Loch Monzievaird or the Lake Mentieth, but he does not condescend upon particulars. Nor is he much more explicit when he refers to the fine perch and by implication to the pike of Lochs Loundy (Lundie) and Pitloil in Furfarshire. The reason why is obvious to the reader. He encountered by " the fatal loch of Pitloil " " a large and lusty hare (but they call her a Maukin) sitting upon a large and gritty stone washing and furbishing her face with her feet." This hare turns out to be a witch—Franks with great caution calls her " a mortal demon "—and he loses two dogs and we lose, something much more important, to wit, all details of the fishing.

Happily, Thornton is more explicit.. That prince of sportsmen pot-hunters—a class utterly condemned by Franck in the memorable words " mercenary slaves that murder all they meet with and hunt like otters to accommodate the paunch "—loves to linger on his experiences amongst the Scottish pike, fish for which he had an intense admiration. He confirms what I have said about Loch An-Spey and its monster pike and declares that he has heard of the capture of a fish of 106 lbs.

and vouches for one of 40 lbs. His own greatest triumph and most thrilling experience as a pike-fisher in Scottish lakes ought, if quoted at length, to cause quite a fluttter in the English dovecots and send a whole host of pike-fishers to the waters of the far North. The great triumph was secured in Loch Alva or Alvie in Invernesshire. After killing a fish of 20 lbs.—whether with rod or trimmer is not stated—the Colonel found one of his "fox-hounds," for such is his name for trimmers, missing. He lost the pike on it, a fish of some 20 or 30 lbs. but hooks another "an absolute wonder," which pulls the boat about the lake for an hour and a quarter. He was finally landed, two of the servants being sent into the water to assist at the operation. The Colonel in his joy "ordered all the signals with the sky-scrapers to be hoisted, and the whoop re-echoed through the whole range of the Grampians." He says that he never saw "so dreadful a forest of teeth or tusks" as were in that pike's jaw, gives its length at five feet four inches from eye to fork, and "estimates" its weight at between 47 and 48 lbs., his scales and weights not being equal to the task of weighing him. "There may," he naively says, "be larger pike, but I cannot credit the accounts of such until I receive more authentic information." We can afford in these later days to be more generous of our faith. The Colonel evidently killed, "more suo"* a monster of monsters, whose descendants to this day cry aloud—through me, their advocate— for some angler-warrior of the South, of whose steel they are surely worthy, to come and meet them in the watery lists of the North.

Another matter which may fairly be claimed to fall within my subject is the question of fly-fishing in canals. I am not in a position to quote statistics but to judge from casual experience the number of canals in this country which hold trout must be very limited. No doubt there are few or no canals in some of whose reaches an occasional trout is not to be found, but on the whole trout are not so common in canals as they might be, considering the by no means insuperable objections which may be urged against the stocking of these waterways with trout. The principal of these objections no doubt is the very considerable poaching which prevails amongst bargemen. For the most part the water of our canals is pure enough to carry trout, while as many of them are fished

---

* Thornton has a habit of varying the weights of his fish. He call a big perch killed in Loch Lomond 7 lbs. in one page and 7½lb. in another.

by ticket, there is no reason, even when allowance is made for the higher temptation, why poaching should be more rife amongst the trout than amongst the coarse fish which are the usual objects of the canal angler's quest. Apart from poaching, there are many canals which could carry a fair head of trout, and if our friends the rainbows and fontinales have ultimately a verdict "for doom" pronounced against them, our canals would be the very places to stock with the large surplus population of these fish, thrown by reason of their condemnation on the fish farmer's hands.

Fly fishing in a canal, either with or without a breeze, would be precisely the same as loch fishing. On canals, moreover, one could more readily use the dry-fly than on lochs. In the latter the total absence of any current takes away from dry-fly fishing one of its essentials, for on still water a fly only floats, it does not float down, and to drag it is to risk a departure from nature. In a gentle breeze in a loch, you can make a dry fly travel with the wind, and to a certain extent can therefore imitate a fly being carried on the surface. This method is really "dapping." In fact in loch fishing, save at the mouths of burns, you can only use a dry fly by casting it "very dry" beside a rising trout and letting it float for a second or two motionless. If the trout takes it, you can catch him with a dry fly, but you do not take him by dry fly fishing in the strict sense. I have always found a very small wet fly, fished far and fine and well sunk, far more deadly than the dry-fly or even a floating May-fly, when that is "up." In a canal it would however, be more often feasible to fish dry-fly, because there is often sufficient current to float it along in a natural kind of way.

If, however, all our canals were like the Crinan Canal in Scotland, our failure to stock them with trout would be an angling crime. The canal in question is in the matter of water and feeding precisely the same as an ideal loch. Moreover it abounds in trout of all sizes from a few ounces up to 9 and 10 lbs. It is never, however, systematically fished by any save local professors, who, for the most part, use primitive gear, and the bait which Adam, as the first gardener, would naturally have employed. There is a very comfortable inn at Cairnbaan, about half way up the nine miles of the canal, and I venture to think that if some patient "Thames trout" or other angler used to being content with "laborious hours" spent over the capture of a few big fish, were to put

up at this inn and conscientiously work the various locks early and late
with a spinning bait, he would kill some very heavy fish.   On the
whole our canals appear to be as worthy of cultivation as our lakes and
reservoirs, and certainly deserve, at the least, this brief notice in a work
devoted to lake-land.

CHAPTER XXV.

SALMON AND SEA-TROUT LOCHS.

There are very few persons who if asked to name the "Iron Duke's" father would reply correctly "the first Earl of Mornington." Similarly there are not many persons who can answer with any approach to accuracy a question as to the number of lochs in Scotland holding salmon and sea-trout. All who essayed a haphazard answer to such a question would name a number far in excess of the figures which a loch census of an accurate kind would furnish. Considering the number of Scottish lakes that are connected either directly or by tributaries of a fair size with noted salmon and sea-trout rivers, or that could be so connected without any very serious difficulties having to be overcome, there are comparatively few lochs in Scotland affording salmon and sea-trout fishing to any kind of lure and still fewer which offer the fly fisher any reasonable expectation of sport. When one comes to compare, relatively to their land and water area, the number of lochs on the islands not only holding salmon and sea-trout, but also giving assured sport with the fly, with the number on the mainland, it becomes abundantly clear that the theories advanced in an earlier chapter, first, as to the reason why salmon do not take the fly in lochs, and secondly, as to the true home of the sea-trout being the waters of a land of estuaries, are capable of being vindicated by an appeal to statistics of a somewhat different character to those given in the chapter referred to.

As to the first of these theories, there are, it is true, at least three notable exceptions to the general conclusion arrived at that in large deep lakes salmon seem to revert with a regularity modified by special conditions of environment, topographical rather than dietary, to their habits while in the sea—a period of existence during which they are essentially predatory fish and cannibals in the widest sense of the term. The three exceptions to which I refer are Lochs Lomond, Awe, and Shiel.* None of these lakes can, however, be described as first class

---

* In Lochs Eck and Shiel salmon are usually taken trolling. I advisedly exclude Loch Eck from consideration.

W

salmon waters. It would, moreover, be inaccurate to assert that their salmon show that almost exclusive partiality for the fly displayed by the fish of the small Hebridean lakes, while it is at the same time a most instructive circumstance that in Lochs Lomond and Awe the salmon captured with the fly are usually taken either with flies that are somewhat erroneously described as sea-trout flies, or with lake-trout flies in the popular and catalogued sense of the phrase. A much more instructive fact, and one that opens up a wider field for conjecture, is revealed when one considers the topographical environment of these lakes in the special aspect of the means of access by which salmon win their way into their spreading waters. All three lakes are connected with the sea by very short rivers. Of these rivers one at least has a special environment. It is polluted, and has been polluted by the same cause to a greater or less degree since Colonel Thornton killed those salmon chronicled with a sigh of regret for the vanished greatness of the Leven in the chapter dealing with the " Evolution of Loch Fishing." Franck, who visited Loch Lomond, in the time of Cromwell, does not mention pollution, but opens our eyes to its disastrous effects by thus referring, in his usual inflated manner, to Loch Lomond and its effluent. " The smiles of the weather prognosticate that we shall reach Dumbarton in very good time, when we may redress and refit such tackle as shall serve to accommodate both our art and exercise; for near to those famous and flourishing ports glides a rapid and peremptory river, that gulphs forth of the bowels of Loemon,* replenished with trout, and, beyond all measure, of incomparable salmon (if I calculate right) where we may sport to-day and to-morrow too, provided the season serve to our purpose." After a disquisition on " such solitary entertainments as the angler most delights in "—within which, by the way, he includes " a multiplicity of boggs," " lofty domineering towers that storm the air upon two stately elevated pondrous rocks " and " exquisite perspectives " in whose " uniform piermonts " a " disproportion " cannot be traced—he succeeds by a reference to " Neptune careering on briny billows " in getting back to the lake side and matters mundane, or, to speak by the card, earthly, since worms are his subject. Thereafter

---

* Franck's spelling of the names of places is as worthy of a housemaid as was the orthography of Claverhouse, but his topographical accuracy is wonderful.

the anglers separate and one using the minnow, the other the fly, secure between them some trout "that would make a cockney's teeth stand a-water and spring a leek," and seven salmon, four of which were "newly tickled to death with a fly." As the fly fisher had previously announced his "purpose to attempt the head of Loemon," it may be assumed that they were killed in the lake. If so, it is the earliest direct reference to the killing of a salmon in a loch with the fly that I have been able to discover and records a feat not often, if ever, accomplished in these days—the killing of a salmon from the shore in the Queen of Scottish lakes. No particulars are given and there is no mention of a boat being used. From these extracts it would appear that not only was Loch Lomond a very fine salmon and trout lake in the 17th century, but also that the salmon took the minnow and fly indifferently both in it and in its connecting river, the Leven—a fact which the evidence of Colonel Thornton seems to corroborate. In any case it is clear that the fish were in the habit of resting in the Leven in the days of Franck as they rest to this day in the Awe, and it is a fair inference from this fact that the modified avidity with which Loch Lomond salmon take the fly may be in some degree an hereditary trait due to this old condition of topographical environment and its resultant habit of "resting." Moreover it must be observed that both in Loch Awe and in Loch Lomond the great majority of the salmon caught with the fly are not fish that can be proved to take up their regular abode in the loch for a fixed period. In the case of Loch Awe many of the fish taken with the fly are fish on their road to the Orchy, while a considerable proportion of them are fish that have rested in the Awe; very few if any are fish of a fixed lake habitat, special or general, in the sense already explained. In Loch Lomond the same rule holds good, save in so far as it is modified by the special change in topographical environment due to the polluted state of the Leven, which only permits of safe-running when in a flooded condition and absolutely prohibits any resting in its pools, save the rest that merges into the long sleep and a grave on the riverside. There still remains the special question of the short connection between the lake and the sea. On the analogy of the Hebridean lakes and their connecting estuaries I should be willing to accept this peculiarity as a circumstance of topographical environment presenting features sufficient to account for the departure of the salmon of the waters in question from the general habits of the salmon in lakes and to warrant the dictum that topographical environment may so modify the habits of the salmon as to assimilate these habits, in a degree, proportionate to the altered environment, to the habits of the sea-trout. It may be noted in support of this contention that the estuaries or tidal lochs into which the superfluous waters of Lochs Awe and Lomond find their way, are in the one case, a long arm of the sea, which is almost a salt-water river so fierce and furious is the rush of its green and swirling tides, while, in the other case, the effluent finds its way into the long, brackish estuary of a river once famous amongst the salmon streams of Scotland. In the former tide-swept arm of the sea, far-winding Loch Etive, the fly-fisher to this day can secure excellent sport with sea-trout, by using precisely the same lures in precisely the same manner as obtains in the saltwater rivers and tidal pools of the Hebrides, while in the latter, though history is silent on the point, I have no doubt that similar sport was obtained in the days whose chronicles lie in the dust of old oblivion. Read in the light of these apparent, rather than real, exceptions to the theory of environment as affecting the taking of the fly by salmon in lochs and giving due weight to the absolute, as well as the relative disparity in numbers, between, not only the lakes frequented by the migratory salmonidæ on the mainland, but also those in which they afford sport to the fly-fisher, and those of the island fulfilling both conditions, the following figures, for whose general accuracy alone I can vouch, are not only interesting but instructive. On the mainland the number and angling character of the lakes frequented by the migratory salmonidæ appear to be as follows:

Salmon only.		Salmon and Sea-Trout.		Sea-Trout only.		Total.
1st Class.	2nd Class.	1st Class.	2nd Class.	1st Class.	2nd Class.	
7	11	7	24	1	10	63

The lakes of the islands holding migratory salmonidæ—(including, all the islands from Shetland to Arran) appear to be as follows:

Salmon only.		Salmon and Sea-Trout,		Sea-Trout only.		Total.
1st Class.	2nd Class.	1st Class.	2nd Class.	1st Class.	2nd Class.	
—	—	23	16	39	43	121

These figures as given are admittedly not very safe guides. In the first place I can only guarantee their general accuracy. Absolute ac-

curacy a special tour of inspection could alone have secured. In the
second place many of the lakes placed in Class II amongst the island
lochs, would occupy a position in Class I amongst the mainland lakes.
In the third place every lake on the islands can, with fairness and
accuracy, be described as a lake not only affording sport to the fly fisher,
but also as one in which the fly is either the only lure possible or in
which it will kill 100 fish to one falling a victim to any form of spun
lure. On the mainland, on the other hand, very few of the first class
salmon lochs are lochs yielding sport amongst salmon to the fly, Lochs
More and Stack being the most prominent fly waters, as Lochs Tay and
Ness are the principal spinning or rather trolling waters. Finally, an
appeal as to class may be made to the statistics of both the mainland
and island waters in the case, at least, of sea-trout lakes, or of lakes in
which sea-trout are taken either with the fly or otherwise. These statistics can be either of a personal or impersonal character. First I turn
to my own ledger and find that taking the last 70 "days" recorded
therein on "island" sea-trout and mixed lochs, I killed entirely with
the fly 836 sea-trout, 1,116¼lbs.—a record I do not think I could have
approached on any series of mainland lakes, though possibly one which
a more skilled angler could equal, if not beat, on Loch Stack. On any
of the best sea-trout lochs in the Hebrides, such as Loch Roag and
Voshmid—certainly on the former, it would be by no means impossible
to kill over 2,000 sea-trout with the fly in 70 days, if I am to judge by
the fact that in two days I killed 109, weighing 191lbs. As to impersonal statistics I find by reference to the Scottish Fishery Board
Report of the season 1890, that the aggregate number of sea-trout—
how they were taken is not specified—killed by anglers fishing from
ten hotels on the mainland having the right of angling in sea-trout
lochs was just over 400. In the same season the anglers fishing from
the Lochboisdale Hotel, South Uist, killed 1,036 sea-trout weighing
1,113¾lbs.,* in the open or hotel sea-trout lochs.

Nor are the detailed figures for the best of the
lakes less instructive and convincing. One loch alone
yielded 409 sea-trout weighing 458¼lbs., while another
produced an aggregate capture of 283 fish weighing 356¼lbs.,
so that the take on the first of these lakes actually beat the aggregate

* See p. 127 infra.

take from the lochs of ten mainland hotels, and the two together made
any comparison between the relative productivity of mainland and island
waters impossible.   If I had been able to obtain the necessary statistics from the other islands for the same season and had aggregated the
total captures of sea-trout in North Uist, Harris, Mull, the Lews,
Orkney and Shetland, I feel assured that I could have set at least 4,000
fish against the beggarly array of 400 produced by mainland "hotel"
waters.   I apologise to the hotel keepers in the right of such waters.
They have other and compensating advantages in the way of sport to
offer their guests.   Moreover the truth is great and must prevail, and
I cannot afford to sacrifice facts necessary to the elucidation of my
subject for fear of giving unintentional offence to any of those best
of all hosts—the Highland hosts of to-day, whose defence I recently undertook in the columns of " The Angler."

The intention, which I had in view, in making these preliminary
observations on salmon and sea-trout lochs, must now be plain. I
desired to emphasise several conclusions drawn in a previous chapter.
Those may be briefly summarised as follows, and cannot be overlooked
in any didactic statement based on experience of the best methods of
angling with the fly for sea-trout and salmon in lochs.

(1) The sea-trout is essentially an estuary fish and is found in greatest
abundance in lochs lying in a land of estuaries, and in greatest abundance in such lochs when they are tidal.

(2) As a consequence of this estuary environment, and hence of estuary
roaming, the sea-trout has no special and only a general habitat in
lakes, a trait that varies in its display with the character of the lake,
and is most pronounced in tidal lakes.

(3) The sea-trout being a shore feeder in deep estuaries and a ranger
with a tendency to shore feeding in all estuaries, will be found in
very shallow water when feeding in lakes with rocky shores of a
quick descent to deep water, while in shallow lakes they will be
found all over the lake to an extent varying with the colour and
height of the water and also with the nature of the bottom and
the general topographical peculiarities of the lake.

(4) Salmon being ocean roamers without a general ocean habitat retain
their ocean feeding habits to a degree corresponding with the size of
the lake, and take the fly, under certain exceptions, with an avidity

conditioned in its display (1) by the length of their run from the
sea, (2) by the size, depth and general character, topographical and
dietary, of the environment, and (3) by the degree to which special
conditions compel them to approximate their habits to those of the
sea-trout—conditions found to prevail in certain of the mainland
lakes in which salmon take the fly.

(5) Salmon in small lochs, in which the conditions of existence, approximate those prevailing in the average Highland river
of the smaller class take up, as in such rivers fixed habitats—a trait which can be proved by the fact that many instances
could be quoted of salmon hooked and lost by "breaking," the angler being caught in precisely the same spot a day or two days or
more afterwards with the lost fly in their mouths.   It is, moreover,
an effect of environment which is consistent with the general theory
as to the reason why salmon take the fly in certain lakes and not in
others, and take it in all the island lakes.

A very little consideration will enable the angler to see the important influence these conclusions must exercise on his method of fly fishing.   It is clear that he must fish for both salmon and sea-trout with
the fly in lochs in precisely the same manner and that the habits and
habitats, special and general in the case of the salmon, general in the
case of the sea-trout, will only influence his expectation and not his
manner of using the fly nor the kind of fly nor gear generally which he
will employ.   In a mixed loch, a loch, that is to say, containing both
sea-trout and salmon, the angler will, as a rule, raise more sea-trout
than salmon.   Hence as a general principle of policy he will best consult his own interests by using sea-trout flies, even in lakes in which
heavy salmon are occasionally taken with the fly.   As I hope to show
in the succeeding chapters, the "sea-trout fly" need not be a large
fly, nor even of the size usually called "sea-trout size," much less need
the angler use salmon gut, though strongish tackle is permissible even on
moral grounds in very weedy and reedy lakes, until, at least, the angler
acquires the art of playing heavy fish under difficult conditions and
from and with the boat under all circumstances.   In certain localities
the angler will never have very large sea-trout to play.   In the Lews,
for example, the sea-trout run small.   The fact, however, in no way
affects the general position, and the angler can use when fishing from a

boat precisely the same kind of rod, the same size of flies, the same quality of gut and the same general gear from Loch Lomond and all the lochs East and West of it to the most northerly loch of Shetland lit up by the rays of the midnight sun. In clear lakes infested by reeds and weeds—though from my point of view these, add within limitations, to the sport because increasing the difficulties—he should on ethical grounds use rather finer tackle, other things being equal, than in reedy and weedy lakes in which he is occasionally compelled to exercise the vis major in rather determined and Philistine fashion. I may, therefore, summarily dismiss the question of "outfit" for sea-trout and salmon fishing with the fly in lochs so far as it differs from that for trout fishing. If the angler is strong enough to use a 12 foot single-handed rod—for a single-handed rod is a sine qua non to proficiency—that is the proper length of the rod to use. As to the style of rod the angler must suit himself, but it is, at least, politic to have a rod that combines power with lightness, and can not only throw a fly far and fine, but also hold a heavy fish. Mr. Burrow, of Preston, has just built me a steel centre built-cane rod of 12 feet, which, though still a weapon innocent of blood, will, I think, when the hour of battle comes help me to drink deep of the stern joy-cup of warriors.* If the angler cannot use a 12 foot single handed rod, then a light thirteen foot double-handed rod is the next best size, and after that a single handed 11 foot rod. In the one case what he gains in power, he loses by inability to stick to the casting point and to fish "fine," while in the other what he gains in fineness and ability to keep on casting, he loses in power in playing. These are, of course, mere generalisations and will vary in their display from angler to angler. On the size of rod to be used in shore fishing—a style that robs loch fishing of its special character, though offering joys of its own by way of compensation—I do not condescend, for reasons stated in another chapter. If the angler plays his fish from and with the boat 40 yards of line are more than ample, save for those emergencies whose facing and overcoming are not the least of the charms of angling. The rest

---

*A very excellent and very cheap rod, suitable in every way for sea-trout fishing in lochs, is sold by Mr. Miller, of Leeds. It has a whole cane butt, while the other two pieces are a judicious mixture of greenheart and hickory. Heavy salmon have been landed on a 12 foot rod of this kind. It unites great power with lightness, and came well out of the tests to which I subjected it.

of his outfit will be the same as for loch-trout fishing, the fineness or otherwise of his tackle being left to his honesty as a sportsman, when policy does not teach him a lesson which explains the "true inwardness" of the familiar proverb.

Before proceeding, however, to state the methods I employ in fishing sea-trout and salmon lakes, it appears to me necessary to devote a further chapter to the description of certain habits of the migratory salmonidæ in lakes which have fallen under my observation, and the inferences which I have drawn from these facts.

CHAPTER XXVI.

HABITS OF THE MIGRATORY SALMONIDÆ IN LAKES.

The rhapsodist is justified of the sea-trout. Of all the salmonidæ that frequent the lake he is the "fiery Rupert" whose desperate charge is of the very essence of warlike activity—whose rush is so fierce, wild and unexpected that often when one fancies him to be dashing impetuously on a bed of reeds, he appears suddenly away to the right or left in a strategic position which promises even greater safety to himself and threatens a long farewell to the angler. To his brilliant activity—for that rather than strength, is his leading characteristic—even the lordly salmon must yield pride of place, while that sober fish, the bull trout, even in his prime, can no more be compared with him than can a heavy cart horse be matched against a race horse. His first rush in a strong breeze as he dashes through the waves and makes the line hum like the bow of Odysseus, when battle was in the air, and the reel scream as if a demoniac trout were careering through a lake of dreamland, or the water of fancy that gleams by the couch of the salmon-fever patient, is the high top-gallant of angling joy. The quick turn and mighty jump, the dash to right or left or straight charge back on the boat, the desperate stand outside the reed-bed, and the last battle wearied efforts are themes to which a bard of martial lay could alone do justice. And in the yielding to fate, there is often a resignation that is as noble as his fight—the desperate resignation of those who die with their face to the foe in the last stand on some stricken field.

Compared with the fiery chivalry by which the sea-trout proves himself a match to rushing Mars, the salmon of most lakes and certainly of the Hebridean tarns is a mere plodding mercenary—his fight that of the unit in a plump of stout spears set in serried stubbornness to withstand the tide of war. Over the bull trout no moan need be made. He is a "dour" but never a brilliant fighter. Those who know the sea-trout best, love and esteem him most. He is most difficult to hook in a calm, but he is hardest to land in a gale and there is no point of view from which he may not be regarded as the most sporting fish of the salmon kind.

I have already dwelt at some length on his general habits, which, so far as they affect the angler, are in all lochs of a peculiarly accommodating kind, for not only is he a greedy feeder and keen riser under favourable conditions, but he is also the least easy of all fly-taking fish to tempt to his doom, when the conditions of that difficult character prevail, beloved of the sportsman and student of fish and their ways. The sea-trout thus not only affords sport to the tyro, but also to the expert, though in his mastering in certain lakes, experience and skill, are absolutely necessary to success. There is, for example, a certain Hebridean loch which teems with large sea-trout and is fenced on all its sides with beds of tall reeds, and is crossed towards one end by another stretch of these rustling allies of fish. In this lake, unless favoured by exceptional luck, even the most expert anglers, used to killing sea-trout in wider and freer waters, have found their skill and experience, gained on those other fields, of no avail in waging this special kind of fishy war. Anglers who have slain salmon in hecatombs in Tweed and Tay have in this lake been beaten by the first rush of a fish they could not control save by an exercise of vis major which the tackle they were compelled to use would not stand. Dry-fly men have been bewildered by the rush of some giant fish to whose ways they are unaccustomed, and have regained their heads only in time to mark a white splutter gleaming amongst the distant reeds and to see their broken casts dancing a merry heys in the Hebridean breeze.

How these slings and arrows of misfortune may be avoided, I hope in the succeeding chapter to show, but in the meantime as a preparation for battle, will first note certain habits of the three " friendly foes "— salmon, sea-trout and bull trout, when they make the lake their home.

My statements are based on personal observation, and some of the habits noted have never, so far as I am aware, been chronicled by any writer on these interesting fish.

I have already indicated that the sea-trout is essentially an estuary roamer and not a fish that makes, as the salmon does, long and indeed marvellous journeys by sea.* This characteristic of the

* Somewhat remarkable proof of a negative kind of the sea-trout being an estuary fish is afforded by the present condition of the rivers flowing into Loch Fyne. That

sea-trout, if maintained as a habit after he enters the lake, is one of considerable importance in practical angling. If, in other words, the sea-trout wanders about lochs and can be called a restless, questing fish within the limits of a certain area, then obviously the angler who fails to hook a sea-trout when he rises, should not act on the assumption that the fish will remain in or about the spot where he first came to the fly, even if he allows only an interval of a few minutes to elapse between the rise and his next cast. Much less should he act on the assumption that an hour afterwards he can again cast over the same spot—no matter how apparently localized it is—with any reasonable expectation of raising the same fish, though without doubt he might have an equal "chance of a fish " as he had when making the cast that rose the fish which he failed to hook. I do not here touch on the advisability of at once casting again over a sea-trout that has been missed —a point to which I refer at a later period—but will confine my remarks exclusively to proving that the sea-trout carries with him into the loch, the same general restlessness that characterises him in the estuary and is indeed the leading feature in his eminently active nature.

In the first place, then, this ranging in the lake can be proved by the experience acquired in actual or "experimental" fishing. I have frequently risen large sea-trout at a certain, well defined spot, say beside a large stone standing out of the water at the side of a point running out into the lake, but I have never on allowing any appreciable time to elapse, succeeded in again raising the same fish at the same spot. This evidence is perhaps not very convincing but it is only a minor link in the chain. It may also be urged that it is impossible for an angler to identify a fish he has risen, save by the locality. The weight that must be attached to such an argument depends upon the character of the lake and the experience of the angler. As to the first, it is obvious that the experience is of more value in a lake not frequented by great numbers of large sea-trout than it is in a lake in which large sea-trout are numerous and rise freely to the fly. As to the second, it may fairly be claimed for the angler with a very highly trained eye,

---

longest of all Scottish sea-lochs is a kind of estuary. It is harried perpetually by nets— trawl and drift. If the habits of sea-trout were the same as those of the salmon, one would expect both fish to suffer equally. As a matter of fact, the sea-trout has been the principal victim. He "stays at home," and is caught. The salmon ranges, and more of his race escape. In consequence, the Loch Fyne rivers are better salmon than sea-trout streams.

that he detects differences and focuses the pecularities of fish just as a shepherd knows each of his sheep by sight, or a cattle dealer can identify a beast, with singular accuracy, out of a herd he has seen only once.   But corroborative evidence of another and an analogical nature is not lacking of the accuracy of the statement, even if it rested on no more certain ground than an inference drawn from experience.   The evidence is afforded by the habits of the salmon and in a lesser degree of the bull trout in this particular respect.   With regard to the salmon, I cannot curiously enough, speak from personal experience save of a negative kind.   In other words I have never killed a salmon in a loch with the fly after first missing and then resting him for a sufficient time to prove that he had remained where he originally rose.   Numerous cases have, however, occurred in which anglers have raised, hooked, and been broken by salmon in easily identified spots. To these spots the "broken" anglers have returned an hour, a day, or even a week after, and have raised, hooked, and killed the fish originally risen with the fly lost still adorning its jaws.   I recall two such cases on lochs in which I was fishing at the time of the final triumph. There is, therefore, no necessity for further specifying the circumstances which were as stated.   As to the bull trout, I have frequently killed specimens of this fish in the identical spot in which they have been originally "raised."   The inference is obvious.   Both salmon and bull trout are proved to frequent the same spot and to have a special habitat in a lake ; if, therefore, the sea-trout had such a habitat and were not a restless roamer, he too would be captured under circumstances similar to those in which salmon and bull trout are taken, by returning to and casting over the spot where they were first seen.   As, however, the sea-trout never is so taken, it is clear that the fish does not take up a special habitat in lakes.   The chain of evidence slowly being forged grows even stronger when one considers the estuary habits of the sea-trout and the effect those habits have, not only on its condition, but also on its migrations from and to waters, in which through their topographical character, it has perfect freedom to exercise what I may term its natural appetites and instincts.   I have already shown that the sea-trout, when living in its most natural or best environments, roams out and in of the tidal lochs, now taking a trip to the estuary, now returning to the lake.   It is this fact which accounts not only for certain waters of the kind indicated affording sport among fish in perfect condition from February to November, but also for the varied condition of sea-trout actually taken in the tidal way. I have captured perfectly black sea-trout in the sea in August, a very clear proof that the fish had descended from the loch with the tide in the very same way as he ascended with the tide and possibly for the very opposite reason. If, therefore, the sea-trout be a restless fish in his general character, it is scarcely possible, especially in the absence of proof to the contrary, to avoid the conclusion that he is, at the least, a sufficiently restless fish when in the lake to warrant the conclusion that he has no habitat. Nor is this the final proof of this characteristic. The habits of the sea-trout in salt-water rivers are essentially those of an opportunist—a nomad who follows his food and only establishes himself in a fertile region so long as it bears the kindly fruits of a soil that needs no tilling. It is true that in such salt-water rivers giant fish sometimes take their stand facing the green rush of ebbing or flowing tide, as motionless and inert as if they were the guardians of the promised waters, overflowing with plenty, that lie above and below the place of their sentinel watch. This apparent exception to the rule, for these fish, I frankly admit, appear to maintain such a position in the salt water river for two or even three days on end with a most "uncanny" suggestiveness, may, however be explained on two or three grounds. They are usually sea-trout of the very largest class and occupy choice feeding spots in the river which only fish of their size and strength could hold. Moreover they rarely invade the loch-like parts of the salt-water river, while in the last place—and this reasoning has a Hibernian and not a Hebridean flavour—I have always suspected that these so-called sea-trout were either bull-trout or salmon, an occasional specimen of the latter fish being taken on the coasts of the "exclusive" sea-trout islands.

Even if the above facts were not considered to supply proof of a sufficient convincing kind, there remains the strongest and most unassailable evidence of all—the evidence of personal observation—the conclusive testimony of the eye. On a certain deer forest, jealously guarded from the stray intruder, lies a small and semi-artificial lake, which at one end has a clear bright granite bottom, interspersed with sandy stretches and with patches of a little green plant growing between the stones. This lake is frequented by both sea-trout and salmon. Of the latter I never saw a specimen in the water and presume that they lie at the other and deeper end. Not so the sea-trout. On a calm, clear, bright day, if I took up my station at a convenient point for observing, I would generally be rewarded by the sight of a sea-trout or two crusing about not in companies and shoals as small trout do in mountain tarns, but in solitary state. Sometimes the fish appeared to have no special object in their journey but even in such cases it was instructive. There were various little arms in this lake with islands, and in these arms the bottom was of white sand. I have seen a fish swim up, circle the bay, going in by one channel and out at the other and so pass upwards and onwards on his constitutional. At other times I have noted a fish hunting the loch, literally quartering the shallows and so manifestly questing that the dullest eye could see that he was seeking what he could devour. There no doubt are periods during which a sea-trout rests in a lake, as all fish rest and as sea trout lie in a river, but such fish are not feeding fish, and are not of the same interest to the angler, since the point I desire to emphasise is that when feeding, the sea-trout in lochs hunts and quests and does not remain in one spot waiting for food to turn up.

Nor is the character of the food eaten, or to use angling language, taken by the three migratory salmonidæ in lochs where they afford assured sport to the fly, less interesting than their habits and methods of securing it. I know of only one lake, and it is a small and semi-artificial one, in which salmon will condescend to take the worm, but in this respect the habits of salmon in very small lakes do not vary much more than in very small rivers. In the Sorn, in Islay, for example, salmon do not take the worm, whereas in the Laggan, the only other salmon river on the island, they take it with fair avidity. In the Aray, again, salmon are very partial to the worm, whereas in the Add a river with an exceptionally long estuary which finds its way not into Loch Fyne like the Aray, but into the Atlantic, they appear to be wholly indifferent to it. In pools below certain lochs in Harris salmon will take scarcely any lure, much less will they look at a worm. The habit of taking the worm is, in fact, of irregular though not wholly indeterminate occurrence; for the few lakes in which the salmon are captured by this ignoble lure are usually but little better than large river pools, and in time of heavy rain have an appreciable current. The circumstance is not without significance to the angler because it indicates that in certain lakes, in lakes, that is to say, in which the salmon rise freely to the fly, the fish throws off in a more marked degree than do the salmon entering rivers the habit of taking food of gross quality, eaten by the salmon in the sea. The salmon of these same lochs affording sure sport to the fly fisher are, it must be observed, much more gross feeders than the sea-trout when in the estuaries. Hebridean salmon—for as already stated it is in the Hebridean lochs that by far the best sport is obtained with the fly—are not infrequently taken in the sea on flounder lines—most primitive and coarsest of all' gear—baited with that very gross bait, a square or strip of herring. They are also taken occasionally on a similar bait from pier-heads and even off the rocks. Sea-trout never are so taken, and when in the estuary are killed exclusively with the fly or with some spun lure.

It is obvious, therefore, if salmon, on entering such lochs, but rarely take the worm and change their feeding habits in so marked a degree in the matter of quality of food, that small flies are much more likely to tempt them to rise than are large. This inference is borne out by the experience of actual angling, and far more fish are killed on sea-trout flies than fall victims even to small salmon flies. Sea-trout again never take the worm in Hebridean lochs and tidal pools, though an occasional fish may be taken by this lure when heavy rain has sent down the burns in flood into lochs boasting such tributary streams. This rule is subject to a limited kind of exception in lochs connected with the sea by very short rivers or genuine burns. It is, therefore, not surprising that a good many sea-trout are killed in the voes of Shetland at the point of exit of the burns connecting these estuaries with the lochs above. In South Uist I made repeated experimental trials of the worm, both in the tidal reaches of the How-more and in the ditch at the head of Loch Roag, and in that connecting Lower Kildonan with the sea, but the only fish secured were eels and a few flounders. The sea-trout were utterly indifferent to the worm, though in the Roag ditch, where feeding was poor, no natural fly fluttering on the water or purposely placed on it was suffered to go very far without being snapped up. This obvious daintiness on the part of the sea-trout is only what one would expect in a well-fed fish blessed with a richly endowed environment of easy access, while it is a simple inference to trace the known partiality for the worm shown by sea-trout in rivers to the absence of that very plenty which is the cause of the daintiness displayed by sea-trout in tidal pools or even in tidal lochs in which the feeding, at the worst, is usually better than in rivers—at least for fish garrisoned with fat and stored with energy against the days of compulsory and economic famine. The angler has certainly every reason to be thankful that the feeding habit of the sea-trout is as I have described, for it ensures sport, not only with the fly but also with small flies.

Salmon, at least in lakes where they rise to the fly freely, do not take the prawn—a trait which is consistent with the greater daintiness which a lake environment of a particular class induces. Nor do sea-trout. I have tried prawn where I knew sea-trout were lying in great abundance, but neither in tidal pools, lakes proper nor ditches—tidal and non-tidal—have I ever succeeded in persuading sea-trout to take the prawn. At the mouth of burns they were quite indifferent, and all methods in lakes were equally futile. Last year I essayed trolling the prawn in Loch Dhu, near Inverary, in the endeavour to discover if the sea-trout and salmon of that semi-tidal lake differed in this respect from their Hebridean brothers. So far as my experiments went, the result was the same—no offers and a complete indifference.

The " homing " instinct of both salmon and sea-trout frequenting lochs is as strongly marked as it is in river fish. In the case of salmon running up rivers of any length to lakes, this is precisely what one would expect, while the question of length of connecting river as affecting the habit does not arise in the case of sea-trout, for so far as I am aware there is no sea-trout loch of any note with a long connection to the sea, while it is clear that the sea-trout being an estuary and not a sea fish can scarcely fail to return. The trait, however, must be regarded as a very important factor in the life-history of the salmon even when viewed as a lake-haunting fish and in spite of the fact that no lake boasting a lengthy road to the sea, with the exception of Loch More, contains salmon that rise freely to the fly.

In the case even of sea-trout the " homing " instinct may become an important trait when the fish has a choice

X

of lakes all emptying their superfluous waters into the same estuary, or of lakes forming a chain above an estuary. It is also possible to conceive of a case in which some change of environment of a topographical character within the lake itself would drive the fish away from their original estuary to seek a new estuary and a new connecting lake. As to the first of these possibilities, a rather instructive example of the effect of a topographical change of an artificial kind on the " homing " instinct of sea-trout,* under circumstances uniting the first two of these conditions, came under my observation in one of the Hebrides. A certain sea-trout loch of unsurpassed excellence had a fine ditch at the end furthest from the tidal influence. Up this ditch immense numbers of sea-trout were in the habit of running a certain distance, and in it they took the fly freely. Some half way between the ditch and the sea another and smaller ditch ran up to another loch, which in turn had a burn flowing in at its head. Half way down the tidal pools another ditch ran up to another chain of lochs. Now the artificial topographical change in the environment introduced into the lake was this. A barrier was placed over the mouth of the favourite ditch which completely stopped the way and prevented the sea-trout running up it. The consequence was that hundreds of sea-trout gathered in the part of the loch in the neighbourhood of the ditch and gradually acquired a restlessness which is frequently displayed by the migratory salmonidæ when delayed in tidal waters against their will, and is the very antithesis of the nomadic questing habit because putting a veto on its indulgence. This restlessness—an uneasy discontent has generally a reflex influence on the " taking " habits of the fish; nor was such an effect lacking in the case under notice. The fishing fell off though the number of fish showed no decrease for some time. Eventually, however, the fish resented this arbitrary curtailment of their liberty as nomads of the estuary and lake and many of them either ran up to the loch above with the free burn, or descended into the tidal pools and ascended by the other ditch into its connecting loch, the fishing in which was, in consequence, much improved. The loss would, of course, have been a serious one had the three lakes belonged to different owners. Finally, in reference to the "homing" instinct it

* Some further remarks on the "homing" instinct will be found in the succeeding chapter.

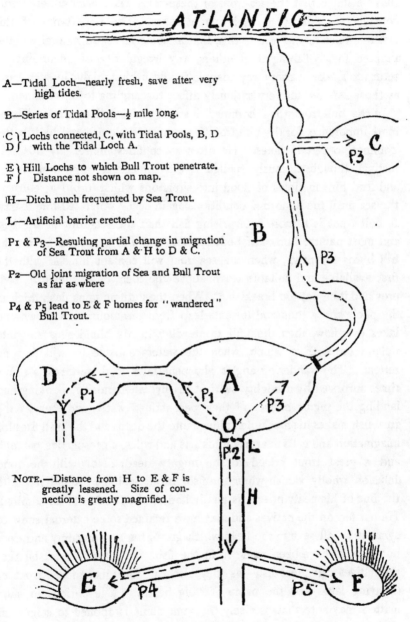

A—Tidal Loch—nearly fresh, save after very high tides.

B—Series of Tidal Pools—½ mile long.

C ⎫ Lochs connected, C, with Tidal Pools, B, D
D ⎭ with the Tidal Loch A.

E ⎫ Hill Lochs to which Bull Trout penetrate.
F ⎭ Distance not shown on map.

H—Ditch much frequented by Sea Trout.

L—Artificial barrier erected.

P1 & P3—Resulting partial change in migration of Sea Trout from A & H to D & C.

P2—Old joint migration of Sea and Bull Trout as far as where

P4 & P5 lead to E & F homes for "wandered" Bull Trout.

NOTE.—Distance from H to E & F is greatly lessened. Size of connection is greatly magnified.

TOPOGRAPHICAL ENVIRONMENT AND MIGRATION.

may be stated that the sea-trout of these three lakes each adhered with considerable fidelity to their parent lakes. The importance of this last reference to the trait is this, that as some lakes are naturally better adapted for fly-fishing than others, any irregularity or uncertainty of return to a lake in every way adapted for fly fishing might, in such cases as those referred to, very seriously affect the angling to be obtained.

In the bull-trout the "homing" instinct varies in intensity and is of more imporance, for the bull trout is not a desirable fish and he is better confined to certain lakes. He often so confines himself by this very instinct, though curiously enough it will sometimes carry him too far and lead him in times of flood into situations which forbid a return to the sea until the abnormal conditions again occur which led him astray. A bull trout is a more enterprising fish than the sea-trout in the best and most natural homes of both species, and will penetrate far up the hill burns to spawn, when the sea-trout will content himself with the first available and suitable reach above the loch, or in the loch itself provided it be not too brackish.*   When the autumn rains flash thick in the pools and a thousand torrents leap from the mountain's crown and lakes over-flow, then the bull trout will win his blundering way into upland tarns, from which, when the waters subside he will find no retreat. The wandering angler who penetrates to these tarns is sometimes surprised by a mighty swirl at his fly, when raising, hooking and landing the pigmy natives of their peat-stained water, and sees, as the great fish makes his first sullen plunge into the deeps and the rush fires his imagination and calls to arms all his arts and wiles, a prospective triumph and a great trout added to the mighty dead. Nor will the fond delusion wholly vanish when the fish, bronze-coloured and dyed with the hue of his peaty prison, is finally laid on the heather to be admired. He has fed on the natives and may have retained some external show of symmetry—all save in the head which grows big and ungainly and does not seem to have been made to fit the fish. It is for this reason that the natives call these fish—as they also call the tuberculosed trout of decaying lakes—by the name of "big heads." The curious in such matters may note that precisely the same name is applied to somewhat similar fish in Sweden, while in Italy a fish with a big head and a wasted

---

*A very slight proportion of salt water is fatal to the ova of all the salmonidæ—a fact which strengthens the contention that the salmonidæ had either a mixed or fresh water origin.

body is known as a Quixote, or wanderer, though the fish thus described is not the eriox. It is perhaps still more instructive to note that in one lake in Finland the bull trout is said to have become land-locked, (there is, however, some doubt as to the specific character of the fish in this apparently parallel case) and to display the same tendency to become wandered, while he also developes the " big head."

A short time after capture these fish become slimy and flaccid, while at all times their flesh is tasteless and insipid. They are best utilized for baiting lobster-creels with an apology in Lobsterese pinned to their broad, square tails. The importance of this characteristic in the bull trout is of obvious advantage to certain sea-trout lochs whose angling reputation may be maintained by the fact that once the bull trout establishes himself in a lake, he adheres to that lake, while of all lakes he prefers those from which he can penetrate into the uplands with that enterprise which is his one and only virtue. It further accounts for two rather puzzling facts. One occasionally—I might almost say frequently—kills bull trout in August differing so markedly in condition that the only possible explanation is to be found in the inference suggested by the facts as stated. The poor-conditioned fish are probably escaped prisoners as they are usually taken after heavy rains. Corroborative evidence of a circumtsantial nature is not lacking. I have observed in a certain tidal river and loch famous not only for sea-trout, but also for bull trout, that the latter fish had its "good" and "bad" seasons. While the sea-trout did not appear to vary in number, bull trout always seemed to be most numerous when a dry autumn and hard winter were followed by a fine spring. Conversely, when a wet autumn and open winter were succeeded by a cold dry spring, the bull trout showed a marked falling off. At least one rose and saw rising much fewer specimens of this, the least desirable, of all the salmonidæ. The inference is obvious. The prisoners made captive by the "tarn-traps" were more numerous in a wet autumn than in a dry autumn, while if a dry spring succeeded the trapping, the term of imprisonment was indefinitely lengthened.

The bull trout's rise is as characteristic as his play. It is low and sluggish, and the sport he gives is simply that of a strong, slow fish. It lacks all activity and all purpose. He never takes the fly very freely.

Nor, it must be confessed, can the salmon in most lochs in which he takes the fly be compared with the sea-trout as a sport-giving fish. He degenerates in condition much more rapidly, and as he never, even in tidal lochs, appears to keep himself in condition by short visits to the sea, he speedily becomes black, or rather coppery in hue, and in peaty water takes on a greater amount of that mucus, seen on all salmon long in flesh water, than do fish in rivers.* Personally I prefer one sea-trout to a bag of these salmon, when they have been "up" for any length of time. His "homing" instinct, it may be observed, is the same as in rivers. On this point I may mention that some years ago Lord Dunmore, in the course of conversation, told me of an interesting experiment which he made in two of the best lochs in North Harris, before he sold that famous forest and sporting estate to the father of Sir Samuel Scott, and carried away the price (£160,000) in his pocket in bank-notes! My recollection of the facts is as follows:—Thirteen salmon caught either in Loch Voshmid or Loch Scurst were taken from the loch in which they were caught, and after being duly marked were placed in the other loch. Before the end of the season some six or seven of the fish were taken in the loch in which they had originally been captured and which was obviously their natal water. Some interesting experiments have lately been made in Norway as to the "homing" instinct of river salmon, and they seem to establish beyond dispute—pace an odd Norwegian salmon being reported as taken in the Tweed—the mysterious power a salmon has of finding his native place. The Harris experiment set forth above seems not only to establish the fact that salmon—loch-born, loch-reared, and loch-frequenting—have precisely the same power and are characterised by the same habit, but also warrants the inference that Loch Tay salmon are literally Loch Tay salmon with "peculiarities" in the matter of lures traceable, as already indicated to their environment.

Finally, in this connection, it may be said that in mixed lochs the angler may expect most sea-trout where he would look for most brown trout, that is to say, in shallow, sandy, or stony reaches, while he will

---

*An occasional exception to this general rule occurs in the case of salmon frequenting Loch Dhu (a tidal loch) near Inverary, but, judging from its topographical environment, this is precisely what I should expect. Such fish must be carefully distinguished from compulsorily delayed "back-enders."

expect to find most salmon over rocky bottoms with those holes and
lies occupied by salmon in rivers.   In the Hebridean lakes salmon lie
in such places, and as a rule they occur where points jut out into the
loch.   Where there is no water of this character, salmon are fond of
lying by the reeds and under shelving banks when the water is deep
enough or dark enough to conceal them.   The former is likewise an occasional " spot" for a sea-trout, but near reeds it a bad place for the
angler to hook a fish who is at all afraid of his quarry—a feeling, or at
least something akin to which—let us say, respectful awe mingled with
stern joy, I confess often to have felt, especially when a giant sea-trout
of broad blue back, belly of gleaming white, and sides of flashing silver
is pursuing his meteoric course towards the rusling sanctuary.

Before   passing   to   a   brief   notice   of   sea-trout   flies,
and   setting   forth   the   results   of   some   experiments,   it
may not be uninteresting to chronicle the fact that so
far as my personal experience of the sea-trout warrants me in
laying down any limit the fish does not seem to attain a greater size
than 10lbs. in those districts which appear to be his natural home.   I
have already quoted some statistics* which seem to support this contention.   The largest true sea-trout I have ever killed was a 10lbs. fish—a
" springer" of excellent shape, that fell a victim to a No. 13 fly on a
calm day, and was killed by casting over him where he had risen.   On
consulting my ledger, in which I have kept a faithful record of my captures, to discover the proportionate size of sea-trout in Hebridean
waters, I decided to take as the fairest plan 1,000 sea-trout killed with
the fly on successive occasions.   The following was the result:

2lbs. and under.	2lbs. to 3lbs.	3lbs. to 4lbs.	4lbs. to 5lbs.	5lbs. to 6lbs.	6lbs. to 7lbs.	7lbs. to 8lbs.	10lbs.	Total.
834	79	32	26	16	9	3	1	1000.

The figures show that 55 out of the 1,000 sea-trout, or rather better
than one in 20, was over 4lbs.   The general figures quoted in a previous
chapter gave 1 in 16, but the discrepancy is easily explained on two
grounds.   I killed may small fish in the tidal waters, while I shrewdly
suspect that not a few of the fish entered as sea-trout in the general
returns were bull-trout.   My figures include sea-trout only.   The ordin-

* P. 127 infra.

ary, as distinguished from the average, size of sea-trout is as near as may
be 1lb., and the chances are that 10 fish, if fairly weighed, will bring
down the scale at from 14 to 18lbs.*   No doubt in some lochs fish which
are called sea-trout may attain greater weights, but as I have never met
with or seen a true sea-trout exceeding 10lbs. in waters which appear to be
their natural home and certainly exceed all other waters in productivity,
it is scarcely probable that the sea-trout of the natural home will be
beaten in weight by sea-trout in the lochs of other and less "natural"
districts.

The patterns and size of flies to be used both for sea-trout and
salmon in lochs are obviously matters of some importance as well
as of interest.   For my own part, though I have no great love for salmon fishing in lochs with the fly, when angling for sea-trout of a large
size is to be obtained, there does not, apart from this purely personal
but very natural predeliction, appear to be any very pressing necessity
for drawing a very clear line of demarcation between sea-trout and
salmon flies for loch fishing, whether they be regarded from the point
of view of pattern or of size.   As to size the salmon, as already pointed
out, appears to assume the virtue of a dainty abstemiousness when he
enters lakes in which he condescends to rise to the fly.   This being
so, there is no necessity for using a large fly to tempt him to his doom.
Sometimes, indeed, as in the case of the largest salmon ever killed in
Loch Lomond with the fly, small flies appear, even in lakes whose
traditions favour a fly corresponding to their billows in size, to take not
only the best-conditioned but also the heaviest fish.   Moreover one
will raise far more sea-trout than salmon in the majority of mixed
lochs, and on an average of days,† hence it is high policy to use sea-
trout flies, even in the old sense of the term.   Further a rod, line, cast
and fly that will kill a big fresh-run sea-trout will land any salmon that
ever entered a loch to afford the fly-fisher an opportunity of proving his
skill.   Lastly on ethical grounds one must use the smallest flies, that
will raise fish, and the finest tackle that will successfully stand or be

* A basket of 11 fish will probably contain 10 fish weighing 10 lbs. and one fish
weighing from 4 lbs. to 8 lbs.

† When there is a chain of lochs frequented by sea-trout and salmon, the smallest of
the three or four lakes is usually the best for salmon.   The Lacisdale Lochs in Harris
afford an example of this fact, which is quite in accordance with the theory that the
smaller the lake the more freely, as a rule, do salmon rise to the fly.

made by skill to stand the strain of playing and the storm and stress of battle.

While it is true, that the salmon will take all flies that the sea-trout takes, it is certainly not true that the sea-trout will take—at least with anything like the same avidity—flies that may prove fatal to the salmon. This leads me to state certain facts—observed in part by deliberate experiment, acquired in part in the course of angling experience. The broad distinction between the salmon and the sea-trout in the matter of flies appears to be this. The salmon, while occasionally feeding on natural flies, is not in the regular habit of doing so; the sea-trout, on the other hand, is in the habit of doing so, though the trait varies in its intensity as well as in the manner of its display with the conditions of environment. I have already instanced a case in which salmon were proved to be rising and feeding on small flies in a river precisely in the manner the common trout does. I have also cited a case in which sea-trout came to be fed with bread and devoured pellets of it when thrown to them. It was also stated that the salmon in the hole continued to lie low and were in no way excited by this unexpected advent of extraneous plenty. A somewhat similar indifference on the part of the salmon seems to prevail regularly in the loch under the exceptions noted. It may, of course, happen as was once recorded of Loch Tay salmon that the fish will rise at snowflakes which they mistake for feathers, by an error similar to that into which the Scythians in the district of Elis are said by Herodotus to have fallen—a fact, or otherwise, which gives the ancient writer an opportunity of pointing out the singular resemblance snowflakes bear to feathers. It is obvious, therefore, if the sea-trout in lochs is a fly-feeder, a fish, that is to say, in the habit of taking natural flies and the salmon is not, that pattern is of more moment when sea-trout are being angled for than when salmon are the objects of the chase.

My earliest efforts to discover the favourite natural fly of sea-trout were made in a water singularly well adapted for observation and for experiment. It was a ditch varying in width from ten to fifteen yards. The water was dark and it was very full of sea-trout, of which, when a strong breeze was ruffling its surface, I had killed over 50 (ten were between 4 and 5lbs.) the day before making my initial experiments.

On the day, however, on which I made the experiments
there was no wind, and a strong bright sun was
shining from a clear sky. I first tried a fly closely resembling the
cinnamon fly. As it touched the water a big fish made a huge lounge
at it and missed, while it had barely travelled a foot when another
monster made a similar error in aim. A small fish that may have considered his chances nil, made a more deliberate rise and secured the
spoil. He had barely incorporated it, when two or three more fish showed
near where it had been. Now as the fish were refusing or rising short
to the wet fly, this little experiment, a small thing in itself, had established two facts, first, that sea-trout feed on flies, and, secondly, that
the dry fly may often prove deadly in such ditches—and they are not of
common, though scarcely of rare occurrence—when the wet fly fails.
Unfortunately at the time of which I am writing, some 12 years ago, dry
fly fishing was in its childhood, or, at least, was an art about which so
little was known in Scotland, save through the angling columns of certain papers, that I had not such a thing as a floating fly in my possession
and could not, therefore, make an actual experiment by suffering a fly
to float over the fish. On my succeeding visits I was in precisely the
same position, and as I have not had the chance of fishing any of these
ditches since 1891, the opportunity of testing the dry fly is still to come.
I put in practice, however, a quasi-dry fly style. In other words I tried
a trick which I had learned in river trouting.* I put on a fly imitating
as closely as possible the fly at which the fish had risen, cast it dry on
to the opposite bank or reeds and allowed it to drop off. In this way
I killed some 13 sea-trout, but missed thrice as many. These ditches,
may, therefore, be fished with the dry fly with success and should prove
most excellent training grounds for the ambitious tyro desirous of rising
in the angling world.† Another consequence of the experiment was the
selection of the cinnamon fly as a pattern for a sea-trout fly, while its
location on the cast as a bob-fly—to be used on bright and calm
or calm days was also fixed. I next tried a fly resembling an Orange
Stinger, but this was taken with rather less avidity, and it appears on

---

* The trick referred to was no doubt the origin of dry fly fishing proper. I was a boy
when I first put it in practice with deadly effect.

† The facts of this experiment may be quoted with advantage in any argument with a
believer in, or, at least, with an advocate of, the existence of "educated trout."

my list with a blue or a black body in preference to a pale pink, though
it may be dressed in all three colours.   I also found that the fish rose
freely to a fly resembling a March Brown, and also that they took that
fly when fished " dry " in the sense already noted, while a fly resembling
the " Shining Black Silver Horns " was also taken.   These flies all figure
in the list given later and are all assured killers, though I have no
doubt that use has given them an extrinsic value in my eyes.   After
all, however, the principal fact that I was establishing, was that sea-
trout in lakes—for the ditch was simply a narrow arm of the lake—feed
on the natural fly and seem to prefer some flies to others.   The latter
point remained to be further verified, first, by a trial of a variety of
flies under similar conditions, and secondly by examining the mouths
and gullets of fish taken in the lake.   The former experiment was a
matter of time, and it was decided in the course of fishing with flies of
various sizes and patterns.   The result of this experience was the
selection of the dozen flies given.   As to size it did not take me
long to discover that sea-trout, even in a whole gale, will take small
flies—small, that is to say, relatively to the size usually called sea-trout
size—with the same avidity and equal accuracy as in a moderate ripple
or even in a calm.   I venture to express the opinion—and am under
the impression that I have already done so in an article in the " Field "
entitled " Small Flies for Sea-trout," which appeared in 1892 or 1893—
that the greater measure of success attending the anglers in South
Uist compared with the success achieved by anglers in other districts
is in some measure due to the use of small flies, whose
claims both by precept and example I had urged.   Sea-trout will, of
course, take a larger fly in a gale than in a gentle breeze, but there is a
limit to their complacency in this direction, and as the use of small
flies combines angling policy with angling honesty, in the sense I have
frequently indicated, it is neither expedient nor virtuous to use flies
larger than No. 9 (on the old scale) while Nos. 10, 11, 12 and 13, Nos.
10 and 11 being the standard size, appear to be the proper sizes of
hooks to have the flies dressed on.   As to the fly I found most frequently in the mouths of sea-trout it was, mirabile dictu, the common
house fly in all his unadorned simplicity.   How he reached his grave
was simple enough.   It appeared to be in two ways, one of which would
be of most frequent occurrence on cold or stormy days and late in

the season, while the other was of more or less
regular occurrence and varied with the mood of the
fish as prompted by the presence of the flies. It is a well-ascertained
fact that late in the year or on cold days the house fly and the blue
bottle are frequently overcome with the cold and drop on to water or
land, as the case may be. This fact accounts for their presence in the
mouths of the sea-trout. I was for a time puzzled by a peculiar habit
of the sea-trout which I observed in a certain lake. They would jump
clean out of the water twice or thrice in quick succession. At first I
thought that the jump was due to the pursuit of a big fish. The discovery of the house flies put quite a different construction upon the
jumping, and gave it a reasoned purpose. It generally happens when
one studies fish and their ways that corroboration of the
inference drawn from observed facts is not long lacking. In this instance it was speedily furnished by a singularly instructive fact from
which there was no necessity to deduce anything. The facts were
too clear and plain. One side of the loch was bounded by machar land,
the rest was the heritage of the moor. On this moor great numbers
of heather bees were found. Towards evening these busy insects, their
day's work done, were in the habit of winging their honey-laden way over
the lake. They would often fly low and in a breeze, when unfavourable
and necessitating "beating," would tack across the loch about a foot or
two feet above the surface. Sometimes they gave way and fell in the
lake. In all cases a touch with the rod point would cause them to do
so. As they fought their way over, the sea-trout would leap out of
the water at them. Here then the mystery of the leaps was fully explained. The jumping at the bees afforded most ample and satisfying
corroborative proof that the trout I had previously seen jumping were
in pursuit of house flies, objects too small to be noted at any distance.
Just as the bees fell into the water in a breeze so did the flies, so that
both in cold and breezy weather, the sea-trout had house fly au naturel,
as a regular item on their menu. Nor did this exhaust the corroborative
evidence forthcoming. An angler to whom I narrated the facts as set
forth above told me that he hooked and killed in the loch a sea-trout
which took his fly when dangling in the air. The trout jumped out of the
water about a foot and a half to seize it. A day or two afterwards while
playing a big fish, a small sea-trout made a leap at my "bob" fly,

but luckily failed to secure it. In the end I tried the "waving in the wind method" of fly fishing, and succeeded in "jumping" fish, though so far as I recollect I did not kill any of the ambitious acrobats. As to the preference of sea-trout for certain colours, apart from the tints used in imitating certain flies or water insects, some remarks on this subject will be found in the chapter dealing with "Loch Fishing in a Calm." I content myself with stating that red, yellow, green and blue appear under certain conditions to have a varying degree of attractiveness for the fish, in fancy and in imitation flies, red and green being perhaps more constant favourites than the other two, and the first mentioned the chief favourite of all in calm weather. It is, however, with diffidence that I submit the following list of flies, because it is quite possible that a very much better one could be prepared. At the same time they are proved "killers," and as that is the best general quality a fly can possess, such patterns as are excluded, may console themselves with the reflection that mine is the blissful contentment of ignorance of their merits.

"BOB" FLIES.

1. Zulu. As already given.
2. Cinnamon and Gold. As already given.
3. Black and Silver. As already given.
4. Red Ant. As already given.
    pink silk tinsel, ribbed with narrow silver; tail, tippets; hackle, red furnace.
    pink silk tinsel, ribbed with narrow silver; tail, tippets; hackle, "red furnace."
6. The "Jumper." This may be dressed in any of the following ways:
    (1) body, green peacock hurl, close; wings, blae; head, brown silk; hackle, black cock. (2) Wings, very light blea, as fine as possible; body, grey silk ribbed with green; hackle, fine and led all the way to end of busking; head, brown silk. (3) Wings, coal black, with two strands of golden pheasant overlapping them; body, half silver half green peacock hurl (next head); head, brown silk.
7. The Guv'nor. Day and afternoon.
8. The Coachman. Evening fishing.
9. The March Brown.

TAIL AND SECOND DROPPERS.

10 Teal and Claret, Teal and Red, Teal and Green—the last being a better fly for salmon than for sea-trout.*

11 Woodcock and Green. Wings, woodcock; body, emerald green mohair tinsel narrow oval silver ribbed all the way; tail, tippets, golden pheasant crest or red worsted; hackle, black cock. Alternative wings, teal or mallard (white tip), but woodcock is undoubtedly better than either. There is no more deadly sea-trout fly under ordinary conditions.

12 Heckum Peckum. As already given.

13. Red Stuart. In all its varieties—the all red being the best form for evening fishing, and the red with half silver, half peacock hurl body, or all silver body for angling in a calm.

14 Woodcock and Red Same as above with a red silk body. This fly dressed very small is the best fly for "day" fishing in a calm.

15 Woodcock and Blue and Yellow. Wings, woodcock (from wing feather); body half-blue (next head) half-yellow mohair, ribbed with narrow oval silver; tail, golden pheasant crest or a tippet; hackle, black cock.

16 The Yellow Ogre. This is a pure fancy fly, and its "idea" is based merely on the partiality of sea-trout for a yellow fly. It may be dressed as follows: wings—which should be long, thin and entwined —dark olive yellow, with two or three strands of golden pheasant over topping them; hackle, red cock; body, brown silk; tail, three tippets.

17 Grouse and Yellow. This is my favourite tail fly. Wings, grouse; body, dingy yellow, or half-yellow half-red mohair; tail, red worsted, if yellow body, red ibis if half-red, half-yellow (red next head), tinsel, narrow oval silver; hackle, red furnace dressed full.

18 Grey Hen and Purple. Wings (mottled), from common grey hen (farmyard), or from grey goose; body, purple mohair; hackle, bright green (taken well up amongst the wings), tinsel, gold oval finished with a tip at tail; tail, red worsted. This will be found a much better fly than it looks; it is very unorthodox, but is specially good in brackish water. Dressed small, the wings should be grey (unmottled); body,

* In some rivers the "Teal and Green" and "Teal and Yellow" are regarded as the best flies for salmon and sea-trout. In the Shira, for example, these are the "favourite" flies.

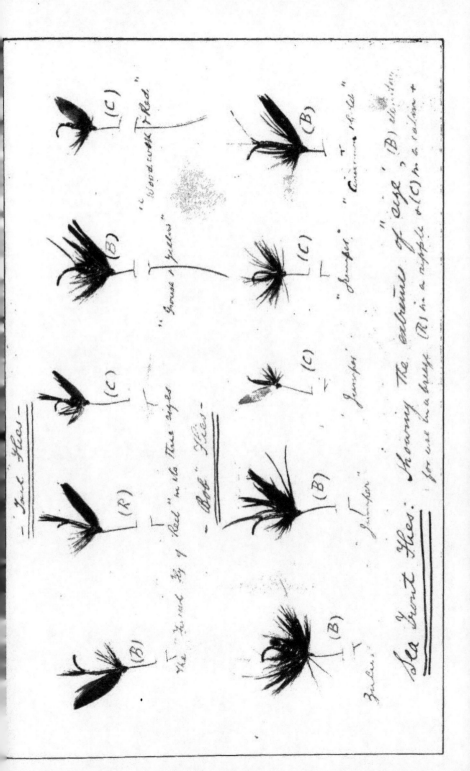

- Tail "Flies -

The "Tail Fly" q "Red" in its three sizes

(B) (R) (C)

Zulu

- Bob" Flies -

"Jumper" "Jumper" "Jumper"

(B) (C) (C)

"Grouse & Yellow" "Woodcock & Red"

(B) (C)

"Connemara Black"

(B)

Sea Trout Flies. Showing the extremes of "size". (B) denoting
for use in a bright (R) in a ripple & (C) in a calm +

plain purple; hackle, red furnace; tail, yellow worsted—hardly the same fly, but a variety which is very effective.

The angler may, in addition to the above patters, occasionally find that salmon flies dressed trout size have very great attractions for the sea-trout, but it scarcely ever happens in ordinary weather that the fish show an exclusive preference for these quaint flies over the more orthodox patterns submitted. In saltwater rivers and in tidal pools, the same patterns may be used as in lakes, while it is advisable to have flies dressed on hooks a size or two larger and to employ stouter gut for angling in the first of these three varieties of water.

CHAPTER XXVII.

The "Migratory" Madness: Lessons of an Artificial Sea-Trout Loch.

The world dearly loves the salmon and the sea-trout, and there is a fascination about the migratory salmonidæ which the common trout may not match—a fascination partly due to sentiment, partly to the genuine merits of the fish, partly to the hold which they have over the angling imagination. Lie abed o' night, near a salmon and sea-trout stream, and listen with thrilling expectation to the steady patter of falling rain, rain which promises a porter-hued water on the morrow, and you will vision the livelong night gleaming bodies of silvery white fresh from the mysterious life, the free wandering of the green tides of ocean, that roll up with heart-throbbing power near your fly and burst away with a force that appears irresistible, a speed which exhausts motion and defies the cold and formal accuracy of figures. And if your sleeping place be not in a land of rivers and foaming floods, but in a land of lakes invaded by the salt wash of the kindred sea, and you can see from where you lie the mystery of a high tide creeping up in silvered silence beneath a full harvest moon right to the portals of the loch, your imagination must be vain if you cannot vision below the burnished sheen of the broad and slowly spreading shield of moon-lit water, sea-trout in their hundreds swimming for doom into the lists set against the morrow. These are the poetic or imaginative aspects of the migratory salmonidæ—the pleasures of hope—as the sport they give is the prose—the joys of realisation—if there be anything prosaic at all in salmon and sea-trout angling.

View it as you will, so masterful is the fascination that all men who angle are ambitious to possess salmon and sea-trout waters, and to convert waters not boasting such "game" into waters where they will abound and "be fruitful and multiply." Sometimes the fascination becomes madness, madness born of such strong sentimental yearnings.

for the migratory salmonidæ that wise and prudent men will give in their adherence to the most visionary and reckless schemes for the conversion of the most unsuitable of waters to waters that may hold the world's desire in the form of fish.

There is, for example, a most notable scheme on foot for the restoration of the very ancient glories of the Thames as a salmon river—an ambition so noble and a project so fascinating, when the fancy is allowed free play, that prudence, knowledge and experience have been thrown to the winds that vex Greenwich and the Isle of Dogs, while on grounds of sentiment alone it has received the cordial approval and promised aid of men who must know how vain is the dream and Utopian the scheme when subjected to the fierce light of dispassionate criticism and analysis. How difficult it is to convert even an unpolluted water not holding migratory salmonidæ into a water of the same description, only those fully know who have essayed to alter and improve waters already frequented by such fish. First there is the mystery of the homing instinct—a trait on which, even as displayed by the pigeon,* an animal whose life history and habits are ascertained and ascertainable, experts do not care to dogmatise. It is a fact of nature to whose mystery Nature holds, and seems likely to hold, the key. Of this, however, we may feel assured that knowledge and experience of " home " can alone create the homing " instinct "—a term I use with the diffidence of little knowledge, and with the humility of one standing under the shadow of a barrier-problem. If, therefore, the making of a salmon and sea-trout river depends, as it does and must depend, on the presence in its future fish of this homing instinct and if, in turn, this homing instinct can only be created and fostered to full vigour by experience and knowledge of and residence in the river to be converted or ameliorated, it is obvious that your migratory fish must

* It may be noted in the matter of the homing instinct in pigeons that a " squab " or young pigeon (or a bird in a stage corresponding to the fry stage in fish) before it has its feathers, may be taken to any loft and will there develop the homing instinct for that loft. When it has reached the " squeaker " stage, has its feathers and is able to fly, and has flown to and from its loft, it is practically impossible, in the majority of cases, to create a new homing instinct for a fresh loft. Sometimes, it is true, that by long confinement, through mating or through a mere freak of fancy the pigeon loses its homing instinct for the old loft and acquires a new homing instinct for another loft ; but this is exceptional, and the facts, as already stated, form an accurate generalisation. In any case, it is possible to attempt the education of a pigeon and impossible to educate fry, while no comparison between the intelligence of the two animals is possible.

Y

live from babyhood to the smolt stage in the river itself. Reared in
any other environment, the homing instinct cannot be present for
there is no place save the home desired to be the home which can
create it, if the instinct, quoad the water to be ameliorated, is to have
any utilitarian value. To place smolts bred in strange waters in the
estuary of a river is merely to throw yourself on the mercy of chance,
and to violate a natural law which is not only above chance, but will
avenge its violation. Secondly, there is the question of topographical
environment, which may be the artificial ally of the categorical impera-
tivè of the law of nature already referred to, and in itself must always
illustrate the equally unavoidable operation of another law of nature not
less truly declaratory of a principle, modified in its different realisations
by the special conditions of each case. It may very well happen, as
those who have tampered with the natural conditions prevailing in
waters frequented by the migratory salmonidæ are aware, that any
imposition of fetters or any curtailment of the perfect liberty—the jus
plenum spatiandi, of migrants may be, and often is, resented by those
free children of river, lake, estuary and sea to a degree, and in a manner that mean detriment to the waters and desertion of them as a home
by the fish. I have already cited an instance of this and a study of
the chart " Environment and Migration " will clearly show the lesson
which that case taught. To convert a water into a salmon and sea-
trout water, an appearance, at least, of perfect liberty to come and go
must be given to the fish, while to secure their coming, the manner
of their going from the water for the first time to the sea must be
that of free natives going on a marine holiday for their health, and not
that of prisoners confined in cells suddenly ushered into the bewildering freedom of commoners of the world of waters. It is, perhaps, easier
to create new salmon and sea-trout waters than to ameliorate existing salmon and sea-trout waters. But the most difficult task is to restore the
former glories of waters once deserving to be called homes of the
migratory salmonidæ, but now fallen from that high estate through the
operation of causes which continue to exist in almost unabated vigour,
or have lost their power for evil in one direction only. In Colonsay
and in Coll, for example, there are no sea-trout and salmon rivers or
lochs, but it might, and probably would, be a comparatively easy matter
to make the latter, provided one gave recognition to the natural laws

governing the migratory salmonidæ in carrying out the necessary architectural, building and stocking operations. Everything would be under the arbitrary control of the fashioner. He would have only a positive task to perform; no reforms to make, no abuses to abolish, whether of pollution or of construction. He would make his lake and its sea connections and superior spawning streams on approved and certain plans. The de nóvo character of all the works would make the task comparatively simple, while when the stocking period arrived he would begin with ova placed in the spawning beds, so as to secure a percentage not only of truly native but of truly natural fish, while he would supplement these with fry at various stages of growth, placed in the proper places for wild fry to be. He could then stand and wait in perfect confidence. He has made a perfect home on natural designs for his coming migrants; he has stocked that home with natural fish and he has merely assisted nature; he has not defied and run counter to her laws.

When one leaves the virgin waters of districts still presenting the same external features as they did when the world was young and civilisation had not begun its devastating march, the task of restoring rivers and lakes still haunted by the migratory salmonidæ to their former glory, or of re-peopling with such fish waters that have become totally depopulated, assumes a magnitude which renders it always a difficult and slow, in some cases an impossible undertaking when regard is had to the uncertainty of success, the immense expense, the conflict of interests and the comparatively incommensurate reward. To take natural pure rivers, like the Add in Argyleshire, the Barr in Kintyre, the Lacisdale in South Harris, and dam them up and artificially create a lake like Loch Jorsa in Arran, Loch Fincastle in South Harris, and Loch Dhu near Inverary, lakes formed respectively by the waters of the Jorsa, the Lacisdale and the Shira being gathered in basins partly natural, partly artificial, and by so doing to reproduce on a smaller scale lakes of a topographical environment similar to lakes like Loch Awe, Loch Lomond and others of that class, is obviously a very different undertaking to restoring rivers like the Thames, the Trent, the Don and the Deveron, and lakes like one of those mentioned, Loch Lomond, to their former glory as waters haunted by the migratory salmonidæ. In virgin waters you are a builder merely, and if you build

on the lines dictated by the natural laws governing the migration of
the anadromous salmonidæ, you can safely leave to Nature the com-
pletion of the task. When, however, waters have, through causes
which still continue to operate, become either totally depopulated of the
migratory salmonidæ, or depopulated to such an extent as to place
them very low on the scale of such waters, then, before re-stocking is
advisable, or positive amelioration is possible, many reforms of a preliminary character have to be carried through. Pollution has to be
checked and the process of purification is slow; weekly close times
have to be regulated and prolonged; cruives, dams and weirs have to
be removed or improved; net-fishing and poaching have, the former to
be curtailed, the latter extirpated, and many other equally heavy tasks
have to be performed, all of which are essential and mean time and
money. When these are finished only then can the first step in the
direction of positive amelioration be made. Up to this point reform
in its progress would pursue the same paths whether the water to be
restored carried no migratory salmonidæ or a sadly diminished head of
these desirable fish. From this point onwards, however, supposing it
were attained, the process of restoration would be pursued on different
lines. In the case of waters already carrying migratory salmonidæ
Nature could be left to work out the salvation of her children, whereas
in the case of waters devoid of such fish, artificial stocking would be
necessary. An example or two may illustrate the enormous difficulties
which have to be overcome before a position admitting of positive
action whether on the part of Nature or of man can begin. Loch
Lomond is connected with the sea by a polluted river. To purify that
river would cost thousands of pounds and disturb all manner of pre-
scriptively vested commercial rights. The purification of the Leven,
would, however, when accomplished necessitate the greater task of
purifying the Clyde, if the expense of purifying the Dumbartonshire
stream had to be justified by the results obtained. The Trent affords
another example of the same difficulties and of the conflict of interests
that would necessarily arise. De facto and de jure from Shardlow
downwards the Trent is a navigable river, a commercial highway. The
passage of fish is blocked for commercial purposes; its main waters
and its tributary streams are no longer of pristine purity. The river,
in a word, has ceased to afford a proper topographical environment

for the needs of salmon. As a consequence Trent salmon are practically an extinct race. They are victims of the higher needs of civilisation. The Thames affords another example of the same process of
deterioration at a later stage. The deterioration is, in fact, completed,
and the Thames is no longer in any sense a fit home for the migratory
salmonidæ. It is a new river and its old glories, in this respect, are gone.
To attempt, therefore, to restock such waters is to defy natural laws.
The old conditions of existence must be restored in their entirety before
the migratory salmonidæ can find a suitable home and the old glories
once more reign. To the degree that it is possible to restore the old
conditions to that degree will any attempts to restore those
ancient glories be crowned with success. To place smolts, reared
elsewhere than in the waters which are to be their future homes as adult
fish, in the connecting estuaries of such waters is, as I have already
indicated, a method which can only result in failure, because wholly opposed to the facts of nature and the laws of nature declaratory of those
facts. Such an experiment failed dismally in the Trent; it will fail in
the Thames; it must fail everywhere.* The homing instinct in all
animals is the growth of environment; as such smolts will never have
had any experience of the only environment which could specialise that
instinct, it cannot possibly be awakened in them when, at the expira-
tion of their first ocean sojourn, their nature calls aloud for a fresh
water environment. The special, as distinguished from the racial habits, of fish are almost wholly independent of heredity; and of special
habits the homing instinct in its localised aspect is least of all an
hereditary trait. There is a certain degree of looseness in the way in
which I have expressed this great truth, but a very little consideration
of the life-history of the migratory salmonidæ, and indeed, of the salmonidæ as a family, will enable any intelligent student to see that so

* Nothing is more remarkable than the uncertainty—I do not care to say ignorance—
which seems to prevail as to certain traits of the migratory salmonidæ. For example,
only the other day, in giving his evidence, a leading pisciculturist stated that the infallible
distinction between a migratory and a non-migratory " trout" was that the adipose fin
of the former was yellow and of the latter red. As a matter of fact, the adipose fin of the
Galway sea-trout up to 8 or 9 inches is always pink-coloured, while I have frequently
observed variations in the colouring of the adipose fins of migratory trout in the Hebrides.
We are woefully ignorant as to the chemistry of colour in fish, whether the colour be
temporary or permanent. In frozen salmon the fins are often yellow. This is due to a
chemical change, and, for ought we know, temperature may be one of the causes ruling
colour in fish.

called hereditary traits are, as the products of the environment, liable
to change by any alteration in the conditions of existence which produced them.* Natural laws vary in their realisation according to the
circumstances of their realisation. It is the principle underlying the
law which alone remains constant. So-called hereditary traits quickly
vanish under the influence of the unnatural environment of the fish-
pond. Even the homing instinct responds at once to altered conditions,
especially if these conditions are altered for the better. That the
latter position is justified a very interesting experiment recently made
in Harris, to which I have already (Foot Note p. 128) referred, seems
most conclusively to prove. On the West side of that island there was
a long narrow ditch-like burn which rose in a very small lake called
South Lacisdale—a lake of only some four acres extent and reputed to
be the smallest natural salmon and sea-trout loch in the world. The
angling area of this small, but famous, salmon tarn is, owing to the presence of reeds, weeds and shallows, limited to about two acres, and
to that portion of the lake to the right of a line drawn from the small
isolated bed of reeds lying off the top-shore in the accompanying picture to a point just inside where the road disappears in the said picture
behind a knoll. The fishable portion is, in fact, the water to the right
of the reeds. Its area is so restricted that in the old days and prior to
the experiment under notice being made, the salmon and sea-trout were
crowded to such a degree that they became restless, and save on rare
days, baskets commensurate with the fish-holding reputation of the loch
were extremely rare. The picture of the loch figured gives a very excellent idea of the appearance which it presents after heavy rain. Both
loch and effluent are flooded. As a consequence of this neither the
reeds which limit the angling area nor the peculiar configuration of
the pools below the loch in ordinary weather are faithfully depicted.
One of these pools is about 40 feet long by 20 feet in width, and in

*A very fine example of a so-called hereditary trait, which is in reality and in terms
of the law of evolution an environment-born habit or faculty, is afforded by the " creeping
perch " of India. This fish can travel on land, creep up plants and exist for very long
periods out of water. It has developed these special powers—the last is to a certain
extent not a peculiar possession but one enjoyed by our perch and other fish—through the
necessities of its environment, for in its native home, the ponds in which it lives, are liable
to be dried up. It would be an interesting experiment to breed fish from the two
specimens now at the Zoo, and to note how long a period would elapse before under
altered conditions—including an assured supply of water—these fish began to lose their
special environment-born faculties.

ordinary weather it is practically a lochan which serves the purpose of an overflow meeting-place much affected, like the rest of the ditch, by the salmon and the largest sea-trout. It will be noted from the picture that the loch is a considerable distance from the sea and that its topographical environment is in this as well as in other respects, very different from the topographical environments of most of the South Uist sea-trout lochs. Its connecting link finds its slow and tortuous way through a long reach of moor to the sea and under the old and original conditions passed through a natural basin and finally, after a series of tidal pools amongst sands, at low water made a gentle, and at high water a fairly impetuous and rock-fretted, re-union with the parent sea. Whether Lord Dunmore and Mr. Thomas Wilson, his factor, drew the same inferences from a study of the habits of the migratory salmonidæ in Hebridean waters as I have set forth in the chapter on "Salmon and Sea-trout Problems," or whether the mere adaptability of the basin already referred to suggested to them the making of it into an artificial sea-trout loch, I am not in a position to state. The fact remains, that had they drawn these same inferences and desired to give them practical effect by constructing a sea-trout lake calculated to relieve the congestion in South Lacisdale and designed in such a way as to recognise the laws governing sea-trout and salmon existence, they could scarcely have conceived, planned and made a lake more in accordance with the lessons of those inferences, or one more declaratory of the facts of nature. The lake in question is about 10 acres in extent and completely fills a natural basin, which lacked almost the whole of one side—the side next the sea. This defect has been artificially remedied by the construction of the wall at the extreme sea end of the loch. One part of this wall, which will be easily recognised in the accompanying pictures of the loch, is about 100 yards long, 20 feet broad at the top and 24 feet at the base, while it varies in height, according to the configuration of the ground, from 12 feet to 14 feet. It is built, as will be seen from the plate depicting the point of exit of the superfluous waters of the lake to the sea, of dry stone boulders. Near the point of exit (for the breastwork is not continuous, thanks to the presence of natural barriers) the wall is on the sea side only some 9 feet broad at the base, tapering to 3 feet at the top, while on the loch side it is 6 feet broad tapering to 2½ feet at the top. The centre is packed with a clayey silt—

almost equal to clay. At the landward end of the loch the eye will catch two points of similar configuration. It is in the little bay just behind the point furthest from the eye that the Lacisdale "river" finds its way into the loch, while it makes its exit to the sea just where the barrier meets the natural sea wall at the extreme right hand corner of the loch looking towards the sea from the landward end. The mode of exit from and entrance to the loch are clearly shown in another plate. To the right hand of the exit—and the picture, it may be stated, represents the exit not only at low tide but after a time of great drought—part of the breastwork at its lowest point is seen, while to the left the natural rock barrier is figured. The overflow channel is about 24 feet broad at present, but is to be enlarged, as a heavy flood in 1898 went over the breastwork, whose stability stood the severe test to which it was thereby subjected. How far the loch is tidal—and for all practical purposes considered in relation to the habits of the sea-trout it is a tidal loch in the proper and "South Uist" sense of the phrase—may be gathered from the following facts. At neap tides the sea reaches half way up the overflow, a condition which, mutatis mutandis, precisely corresponds to the average conditions prevailing in most South Uist lochs under the same presumption of tidal rise. Ordinary spring tides, again, just reach the top of the overflow, when the loch is at its normal level and invade it when wet weather is con-joined with spring tides—a condition which again corresponds with the state of matters prevailing in South Uist, under the reservation already noted. At very high tides—whatever be the height of the loch, the sea rises above the overflow and pours for a few minutes into the loch, and thus once more affords another "South Uist" condition. At low water and half tide, the Luskintyre Sands, which lie below the loch, and through which its superfluous water find their way to the sea, are ex-posed for about two miles—a condition which corresponds to the con-ditions prevailing on the Howmore river in South Uist at low tide, all as already described in the chapter dealing with the "Salmonidæ in Brackish Water." It may be observed that immediately below the over-flow a very fine pool is being worn in the sands by the rush of water. This pool is some 100 feet long by three feet deep and is a most desirable adjunct to the loch, especially in spring, for it is in such pools that the sea-trout loves at that season to rest and it is in them that he often affords the best sport, when in a taking mood. In full flood, it may also be mentioned, the water rushes through the overflow almost up to the top edge of the breastwork and pours down on to the sands, spreading over them to a distance of some 50 yards. The overflow has been very judiciously chosen and is formed of a spoon-shaped hollow in the natural rock. It required a little blasting to complete its natural suitability for the purpose in all states of water. This was secured by blasting the overflow in such a way as to make one part of it—that at the extreme right—a little lower than the rest. A continuous flow of water was thus secured as will be seen from the plate, which depicts, as already stated, the overflow after an exceptionally long period of dry weather. The cost of the whole undertaking, I may mention for the benefit of those contemplating a similar work, was about £200.

Interesting as are the facts of this experiment, the consequences are doubly so. When the facts were first laid before me, I came at once to the conclusion that the sea-trout would take up their home in the artificial loch, while the salmon—and no doubt some of the sea-trout—would continue to ascend to the pools and the loch above. I came to the further conclusion—based, be it observed on a study of Hebridean waters in a state of nature—that the artificial loch would afford sport amongst sea-trout practically throughout the angling year. Both conclusions appear so far to be justified to the very letter. The salmon are continuing to ascend to the upper loch; the sea-trout are making the artificial or "tidal" loch their home, while the spring fishing has been good and promises to be better.

The significance of this experiment is overwhelmingly great. Nothing could show more clearly, not only that the sea-trout is an estuary fish, but also that the homing instinct differs in its general as distinguished from its specialised display. Viewed as a whole the homing instinct of the migratory salmonidæ may be, and indeed is an hereditary trait, so long, that is to say, as the experience of environment is present and remains constant, construed in terms of general environment. In this aspect the homing instinct is merely the general instinct for a fresh water environment shown at certain periods in their life by the migratory salmonidæ—an instinct due to the imperious necessities of the fish as an animal bound by the fetters of sensational entity. In its specialised aspect a particular water will by the operation of the same subtle, inexplicable mnemonic impulse of sensational growth be selected by the fish, and that water will always be the water in which it has passed the earlier portion of its life as a fresh water fish, whose habits during that period are conditioned by a fresh water environment, and whose necessities at a certain stage, make it a migrant to the sea. In the case of the sea-trout—standing as it does in closer proximity to the common trout in the chain of evolved species than the salmon—the sea migration is more limited, both as to its distance and duration than is the migration of the salmon, whose wanderings are so wide that for him the boundless ocean is reduced to the dimensions of a field of " four plough gates." Finally, and for precisely the same reasons the homing instinct of the sea-trout is less strongly marked than that of the salmon within, that is to say, the limits of his native environment viewed as a whole. In a South Uist case I showed how the migration of the sea-trout was appreciably altered within the limits referred to by an artificial barrier, while in the Harris case a similar result has followed a topographical change of a different, because ameliorating, character. The change, moreover, has in no way affected the homing instinct of the salmon which continue to pursue precisely the same line of migration and to occupy precisely the same places as they have done, since the history of the water has been recorded.

The value of the Harris experiment as a general lesson in the habits of the migratory salmonidæ is immense. He who runs may read it. Properly construed it should, when read with the other facts to which I have drawn attention, be the death blow of all such visionary schemes, based on sentiment and opposed to sense, as that now mooted with regard to the Thames.

CHAPTER XXVIII.

How to Fish a Salmon or Sea-Trout Loch.

Fishers and well wishers to the game, who have endured the preceeding pages will not at this period in the subject anticipate any further disquisition on the habits of the sea-trout in lochs, so far as these affect the angler. It is necessary, however, to the proper stating of my methods of fishing sea-trout lochs to distinguish the different varieties of lakes into which such sea-trout lochs as I have fished appear to invite division. The line of demarcation is not always very sharply defined, some lochs presenting features common to the two main classes of sea-trout lochs and, therefore, necessitating a triparite division. The division ignores the question of colour, but on the whole the "shore" lochs are usually darker in colour and more peat-stained than the fishable "all over" lochs, to invent an ugly but expressive phrase. Ignoring, therefore, this consideration sea-trout and salmon lochs divide themselves naturally into

(1) "Shore" lochs, lochs, that is to say, in which the taking fish lie right amongst the waves as they break in foam amongst the rocks and stones with which the shallows are usually plentifully supplied.

(2) Shallow lochs of almost uniform depth in which the sea-trout are found all over the loch, but in which they are also taken close in shore.

(3) Lochs presenting both these features and having deeps and shallows as well as lying grounds near the shore.

The first two varieties of loch are of most frequent occurrence in the Hebrides, where, as a rule, the "shore" loch is a larger lake than the "all over" loch. The third variety in the usual type of sea-trout and salmon loch found on the mainland.

The proper method to adopt in fishing a "shore" loch has already been foreshadowed in the chapter dealing with the fishing of a trout loch. It may, therefore be briefly stated with the explanation, that it is the method which I have found most effective in a strong breeze—

the " climatic " condition in which such lochs generally yield most fish, and in one aspect, therefore, most sport.

Manifestly in a shore loch, if there be two anglers, the inshore rod would always have the better chance, if the " drifting down the shore " method were adopted; while the leading rod would, by parity of reasoning be in the better position, if the " working up-wind " style be favoured.   In such a loch, therefore, if in no other, there should be only one angler in the boat.   Let us suppose that the shore in its general line lies north-west, and that the wind is blowing with considerable force from that direction.   There will then be a fair wave all along the shore, which will tend inwards towards the shore and break all along its length.   Starting at the extreme end of the shore, the head of the boat should be kept about three to four points off the wind, and the gillie pull slowly up against it.   The angler will then seat himself on the board running across the boat with his face and body towards the wind, and will cast inwards with a short line, not more than twenty feet in length.   As he is casting against the wind to some extent, he must make use of the underhand cast, a kind of cut, which will sweep his flies as low as possible, both rod and line being almost horizontal. The fingers in making it will be uppermost, but the moment his flies reach the water the wrist should be turned (the back of the hand will then be uppermost) so as to keep the line taut.   The point of the rod will then be worked in towards the boat, never being elevated above 45 degs. and often less, according to the force of the wind.   The object of all   this   is   to   keep   the   line   from   bellying,   and   to work the flies up and across the general direction of the wave.

The following rough diagram may illustrate my meaning:—A is the direction of the wind, B of the wave (which has always a tendency towards the shore), C is the direction in which the boat's head should be, D is the angler, E1 and E2 is the rod, and L the line, while M is the direction which the flies should take, generally speaking, in their course through the water.   The angler should cast as frequently as 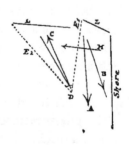 possible; indeed he will find that quick and frequent casting is necessitated by the adoption of this method.   Every inch of water where, in

A MAINLAND TIDAL WATER. THE "DHULOCH," INVERARY.

Thornton (p. 247, 1804 edition) thus writes of this water:—"A lake called Loch Dow, at the influx of the tide abounds with both sea and freshwater fish; and I am well informed, that salmon, pike, herrings, trout and whitings have been taken together in the same haul of the net." As a matter of fact, at the present day, salmon, sea-trout, yellow trout, tidal trout, lythe, cod and flounders are caught in Loch Dhu or "The Dhuloch," pronounced locally "Duloch."

this class of lakes, a feeding fish may be, is searched; rod and line are always under the angler's control; while, in the event of a fish missing, the angler, being always to leeward of the fish, can cast over him again.

As, however, no wind in any loch can blow along every shore, another method must be adopted to suit other circumstances; but such methods are only variations of the above, and all rest on the same general principle—cover as much water as possible. If, for example, the wind be blowing right on to or at right angles with a shore, the head of the boat should be kept slightly up in the wind, so as to diminish the

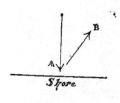

leeway, as in the diagram, A being the direction of the wind, and B the direction in which the boat's head should be kept. The angler will, in this case, fish with his face towards the stern, and cast inwards. He should vary as much as possible his method of working the flies, now sinking them, now keeping them high,

now across the wave, now more with it, as may appear necessary; but he should never lose sight of two principles—cover as much water as possible by frequent casting, and never allow either your line or your vigilance to slacken.

As in a trout loch, so in a sea-trout loch a keen eye should be kept on likely spots, which include in shore lochs the mouths of burns, all stony points and particular rocks, and speaking generally, the line of water between the points of small bays if, that is to say, the configuration suggests two shelves or ledges or rock that run towards one another across such a bay—a not infrequent formation found in many lochs.

In the second class of loch it is, of course, possible to fish "two in a boat" with far greater chance of success than in a shore loch, and that, too, without adopting the "drift" method which leaves the loch half-fished; but here, again, I must advocate the solitary method, because the angler has to study himself only, and can, therefore, use his head. The proper method to adopt in "fishable-all-over" lochs is to work them zigzag, up-wind, with the boat's head about four points off the wind's eye. The accompanying rough plan of what is certainly, for its size, the best "open" or "hotel" sea-trout loch in Scotland may serve to illustrate my meaning. In this loch the main body of the fish roam in the irregular four-sided figure which would be formed by joining the points A, B, C, and D, between A and C being the choicest line on an average of years. Starting from D, the dotted line would represent the probable coarse of the boat,* while the arrow heads represent, roughly speaking, the direction in which its head would point; for instance,

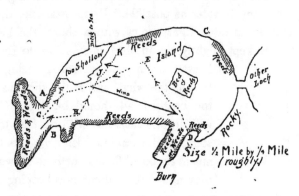

between G and H the head of the boat would be off the shore while the boat was going past the point. The object is to secure as slow a passage as possible, so that all the water may be carefully searched. The angler would, in this case, cast towards the shore, using the common form of cast; from D to E, on the other hand, the low cut already noticed would be the most paying plan. Of course, the direction in which the boat moves can be varied as the angler pleases, but in all cases he will find that he obtains far more rises by zig-zagging the boat about the loch, always keeping it sufficiently far up in the wind to necessitate the constant use of the oars, than by any succession of drifts before it, whether he uses an anchor or stone to stay its progress or not— a method which is as clumsy as it is superfluous. The varying of his position, as he sits on the board, and the kind of cast, ordinary, switch, undercut, etc., to adopt to suit the circumstances, are matters of detail, which will readily suggest themselves in actual fishing. In a breeze of wind I usually fish such lochs with a short line, and, though I may cast in the ordinary way, almost invariably work the flies in the manner described in treating of the underhand cut in fishing "shore lochs" up-wind. The line is kept under better control—a fact of great importance when a fish rises.

* The loch figured is Lower Kildonan, South Uist.

In lakes of mixed character and large extent both methods may be employed, while it is a better policy to confine one's efforts to banks and points where fish are known to be, than to wander or drift over miles of water good, bad, and indifferent. Having found a good bay in which there are fish, the angler should thoroughly search it, working the main portion of it in the manner advised in connection with " fishable-all-over-lochs," and the reeds and shores, according to their line relatively to the wind, in the manner described when treating of " shore" lochs. Let us take a typical example. In Loch Lomond you may fish round some famous point for salmon and sea-trout and get no rises, though you carefully search all the water twenty times. The twenty-first may be fruitful both of rises and fish. I have had cause more than once on Loch Lomond to regret having abandoned some known hold of salmon just five minutes too soon. Precisely the same holds good with regard to all large lochs on which it is very easy to be on the wrong spot at the right time, not so much by the irony of angling fate as by lack of method.

CHAPTER XXIX.

Raising, Hooking, Playing and Landing Sea-Trout.

Like their brethren of the mere, the common loch trout, sea-trout rise in a variety of ways of which the three most common are: (1) the rise below the water; (2) the ordinary rise when the trout swirls round the fly, half in and half out of the water; and (3) the "jumping rise," when the trout springs clean out of the water, or nearly so, and either (a) takes the fly as it (the trout) leaves the water, or (b) takes it as it re-enters the water.

"The rise below the water" is common even on stormy days, and must be met by refraining from striking. In the case of heavy fish the rise proper, if it comes at all, is usually preceded by a wave against the wave, very easily noticed when the eye becomes trained. The fish, though below and never above the water, is often seen, and this adds another difficulty to the situation. The fish must be allowed to take a good hold, and the fly be worked as though no fish were visible. The angler will feel a kind of nibbling at his fly, and eventually a steady pull; then is the time to strike firmly, but quietly. Easy in theory, this is very difficult in practice, and that man of iron nerves is yet to be born who can meet with cool, unwearied patience and invariable success this or indeed any other kind of rise.

The temptation to strike is almost irresistible, and self-restraint is even more necessary to success than in striking brown trout. For example, you have been fishing for an hour with unremitting zeal, and no rise has rewarded, no capture crowned, your efforts, when suddenly from the shallows by some rocky point something long and gleaming shows with jaws agape for your fly. You are startled into a quick strike, and the disgusted fish sinks to rise no more for an indefinite time. Had you continued to move your flies and not been startled into an impatient and ill-timed strike, you would have been enjoying a gloriously crowded ten minutes—one of those periods which make an angler's life worth living—instead of vainly attempting to pose before your gillie as a moral instructor in the philosophical method of meeting and meekly bearing with unmurmuring patience "the slings and arrows of outrageous fortune." This superlative zeal is, however, a fault of nature, which experience cannot wholly eradicate.*

Another peculiarity about the sea-trout rise—which applies with equal force to salmon—it that the angler must discriminate from the character of the rise between the advisibility, on the one hand, of immediately casting over the fish again, and, on the other, resting it for a little. As the sea-trout has no habitat, when one has decided on a rest, it should be of short duration. There may be no fish to cast over if you rest him too long. A salmon, on the other hand, having a habitat may be tried for with some reasonable hope of success, even after a long rest. In the case of small sea-trout the angler need not hesitate. He cannot lose or gain much in any case, and the smaller sea-trout are usually most accommodating in giving the angler a second chance. If the fish be a 4lb. or 5lb. fish he should, however, exercise some judgment. It is little or no use casting again over a thoroughly wild fish unless one can detect an unusual amount of eagerness to take in the rise. There is, apart from the one infallible guide which I shall shortly mention, a subtle distinction between the "wild playful" and the "wild taking" rise, which is not easily described. The only feature I have noticed as distinguishing the one from the other is, in the case of the playful, a movement from near to away from the fly with an upward tendency of the head, as if the fish were more interesting in the scenic surroundings of the fly than in the fly itself; while in the case of the "wild taking" the movement is from "afar towards" the fly, with a downward on the fly tendency of the head, as if, conversely, nature's beauties had no charm compared with the edible qualities of one of Nature's most evanescent children. The distinction is somewhat subtle when read in cold print, but in practical fishing, it appeals to the angler as being rather more than merely specious, for the greed is manifest in the one case and the indifference equally clear in the other.

The one infallible guide, however, which can at once enable the angler to discriminate between a taking and non-taking rise, whether

*A big sea-trout when missed is, if he rises again, very apt to come short just as a salmon will. He "bells" up below the fly. Lack of energy and "lowness" are the leading characteristics of this second rise.

z

wild or quiet, slow or quick, tempestuously eager, or calmly deliberate, is the mouth. I know of nothing so capable of being dogmatically laid down in angling as the rule, that if a sea-trout comes with jaws agape at your fly he is a taking fish; whereas it is equally certain that if his mouth be shut, however active he may seem, however eager he may appear to be, the rise is not a taking one, but a " short " rise, which may, however, under certain circumstances be converted into a taking rise. Of course, whether a fish rising with his mouth open will come again or not depends upon other circumstances, but that the rise was "meant" there is not the slightest ground for doubting. If the fish has risen high out of the water, with his head towards the angler, the chances are that he will not come again. He seems to see something that alarms him, the " ignotum " which plays so prominent a part in fish life; but if, on the other hand, the movement be parallel to the boat, then by parity of reasoning, the probability is that the fish will once more gladden your heart by rising. If then the rise betray genuine eagerness, it is better, as a rule, to try again at once, and in any case the safer plan, apart from the question of habitat, is not to let more than a few minutes elapse between the first rise and your attempt to produce a second " offer." These conclusions are, I need hardly say, inferences drawn from observed cases, a record being kept of the nature of each rise and the result of attempts at securing a second or even a third offer. I cite two only of many cases. I rose close by the shore to a " Zulu " as " bob fly " a sea-trout of about 5lbs. He came clean out of the water in a graceful curve intending to take the fly as he went down. The curve of his rise was away from the boat. I struck him when I should not have struck at all. He rose a second time the curve of his rise, also clean out of the water, being parallel with the boat. The third time he came up towards the boat. He declined to rise again. This last rise would, of course, have proved nothing, because it would scarcely have been reasonable to expect a fish to keep on rising in this acrobatic style to suit my purpose. The first two rises were, however, instructive. Shortly after raising this fish I rose another which came up very slowly and must have seen the boat. He rose with his head towards it. In any case nothing would tempt him to come again. After observing, as stated, a number of similar rises to the first, being followed by a similar effect and of similar rises to the second rise being followed by a similar consequence, the conclusions as already stated were arrived at in the usual manner. The rise peculiar to calm days I describe in its proper place, but the question of short rising may here be discussed and dismissed. It has long been a questio vexata. The reason of this is not very far to seek. It is found in the fact that one is too apt, on days when rises are frequent, "hookings" rare, and captures still rarer, to blame one's own want of skill rather than the caprice of the fish, to place the inaccuracy on the wrong shoulders, and generally to rouse a storm of indignation against oneself as the true cause of misfortunes which in reality have their source in the uncaptured, not in the would-be capturer. The matter may be summed up thus. Sea-trout assuredly do rise short, and this short rising does most undoubtedly rouse anything but benignant feelings; hence annoyance displaces skill, and the misfortune of short rising "grows by what it feeds upon."

The short rise is difficult to describe. That you do not feel the fish is not an accurate description. In many cases you not only feel, but also foul-hook the fish, the explanation being that it touches your gut in its "roll"—the question of hooking or not hooking depending on its proximity or otherwise to your fly, and the angle of the hook or the position of it relative to the body of the fish.

In fact, the short rise is indescribable because of its very variety. At one time it is a lazy low swirl, with little or no life, with a hanging dubious tendency as though the fish had just enough vitality to energise a rise without having sufficient strength of mind to come to a decision one way or the other; while at another its appearance is full of life that is too sportive to imply even a danger of death—a sort of Waltonian vita non janua mortis. It is a difficult matter to explain, so let me call in the surest guide in such matters—experience. It certainly will not lighten all the dark ways of troutish caprice, but it ought at least to help us to elucidate in some degree the mystery.

I take three days of a certain season vividly impressed on my memory. On the first I killed forty-seven sea-trout, but the rises I had were so numerous that I cannot pretend to estimate them. Now, what was the nature of the day? Occasionally I had a steady curl, but never a good breeze, and every now and then almost a calm, while the rain descended with untiring energy in solid sheets. Every variety of the " short " rise was exemplified that day, but by far the most common form it assumed was the low, lazy swirl.

I blamed the weather for the short rising; it was dull, heavy, and depressing, and the fish were manifestly affected by it.

The second day was precisely similar. I had many rises and killed a few fish in the morning, while similar climatic conditions to those of the first day prevailed; during an hour or so, however, in the afternoon, when the mist lifted, and the breeze came away steady, the sport was glorious. I had fifty-seven sea-trout, but quite one half of them were killed during the hour of so when the mist lifted, for when it came down the short rising began again.

On the third day very different conditions prevailed. I was not fishing nearly such good water; but still the sea-trout were large and plentiful. The weather was bright and warm, with a nice little steady breeze, which caused a good curl; yet something ailed the day. In one short drift I counted twenty-five moves from the bottom; but only one fish (3½lbs.) took the fly. I could see in the clear light each fish as he came to the fly, and could note every movement. The fish seemed to rise out of nothingness in a dim shadowy way; then their bodies became clearer and more sharply defined, though still retaining the spectral look they had at first presented. Their movement was slow and stately, almost ghost-like. There was almost no break in the water, only a gentle undulating movement from the rise, though occasionally a fish would suddenly energise a swirl. A fish doing so never rose twice. The slow rising fish did, however, and it seemed almost as if each fish had made up its mind to display so much energy and no more, but whether that energy was expended in one rise or in two seemed a matter of no moment.*

The explanation of the so-called short-rising on the third day is not, I think, far to seek. The light was exceptional and it is highly probable that had it not been so, quite two thirds of the fish I saw would have escaped my observation. A fly we know makes a salmon uneasy when it goes over him and there is no reason why a sea-trout as a fly-taking fish should not move further than a salmon often does without being noticed. Why they should move thus far and no further is a matter of mood, and the fish is as clearly entitled to its moods as is the angler.

As to salmon rises. A salmon, as a rule, rises in the same way as a

---

* Some of the fish just left the bottom and came up a foot or so.

large sea-trout, that is to say, it rises low and slow. Its rise must, there-fore, be met with a correspondingly late-delivered strike, if indeed any-thing more than a mere tightening of the line be necessary.

Once hooked the playing of both fish will vary with the loch and the place in the loch where the fish is hooked. In a "free" loch, or in an open part of a reed-girt loch the initial movements of a sea-trout may vary, whereas as a rule a salmon acts in very much the same manner in all cases. He will give you some sluggish rushes varied by boring, but in no case will his movements necessitate a different line of action than will those of the sea-trout. I confine, myself, therefore, to the latter as the more difficult and dangerous fish to handle.

In the first place if lightly hooked a sea-trout will often not run at all, but will simply lash on the surface of the water and escape at once. If, however, he is well-hooked or hooked in a place that reminds him of the fact that he is hooked, or as soon as he realises the strange new position in which he finds himself, a fresh-run fish makes a strong sweeping burst, usually ending in a leap. This is not invariably the case, however. Sometimes the fish commences his struggles for freedom by making an angry and astonished plunge to the bottom. This is followed by a slow grating sort of movement, then a gradual gathering of way, suddenly accelerated into a wild and furious rush, ending with a spring or a series of wild lashes on the top of the water. Whether the fish leaps clean out of the water or merely lashes it, the angler should regulate with great care the amount of strain he then puts on the fish. The proper amount varies with circumstances and can be learned only by experience, for the delicate exercise of vis major is no book-acquired art.

Care must be taken never to let the fish away at an angle, or to get too far. As he bursts away (and the natural tendency of the fish is to get away as far as possible, and into reeds if there be any near) follow him with the boat, and endeavour to keep abreast of him. A fish is always least likely to escape when he is parallel with the angler; at no time is he so likely to escape as when he runs out at an angle of 45degs. or thereby with the stern. The explanation may be that the gillie pauses and grows interested in the rush, neglects his oars, the fish jumps, the boat drifts a little, and the strain is too great just at the dangerous moment and the "hold gives." This explains, how-

ever, the danger of the "windward" rush only, for it is quite as fatal
when made to leeward, though the danger then consists not in a too
tight but in too slack a line.

Follow the fish, therefore, with the boat, and endeavour to keep it
parallel with the boat. If he bursts at the dangerous angle above
noticed, a strong stroke with the oar on the side opposite to the fish
and a few rapid strokes with both oars will restore the status quo ante
of safety. A good and willing boatman is thus quite as essential to
success as skill on the part of the angler.*

The first burst (usually a mad and irrational rush, save when the
fish is hooked near reeds) and its perils being surmounted a quieter
period ensues. The fish's efforts to be free assume a cooler and more
rational form. He moves more slowly, as a rule, and only now and then
gives a little savage swirl on the top. Now is the time to begin to make
him work for his dying. By turning him constantly, by making him,
with a gently persuasive exercise of force pursue now this direction
and now that he becomes exhausted, hope vanishes, and the anger
of despair follows.

It is now that the angler begins to feel those peculiar jerks which are
far from pleasant and intensely suggestive of near escape. These jerks
are, as a rule, caused by the fish shaking its head in savage despair—a
very moving sight to see when a gallant fish is foredone with the sore
striving of a stricken field. The fish also gets his head down and his
tail up and strikes the gut with the latter. If the water be clear and
the fish visible, the angler can, by the exercise of a little skill, avoid
the tail, and steer the gut clear.

The supreme moment of the fight is now approaching and victory

* It is scarcely necessary for me at this period to state that I totally disagree with the
opinion expressed by Sir Herbert Maxwell, M.P., in the "Outlook," that the proper
way to fish a loch is from the shore. No one can appreciate more highly than myself
the pleasure of a fish's "rush from shallow to deep," but neither on moral nor on
expedient grounds can the loch-fisher be expected to place himself voluntarily in a position
he would not voluntarily occupy in a river—a position of inability to follow his fish On
a single-handed rod with a limited supply of line a big fish cannot be followed from the
shore nor can his rush be safely checked on light tackle. If Sir Herbert Maxwell (or any
other angler) considers the boat to be the "Duffer's refuge," a big sea-trout hooked in
Lower Kildoran, South Uist, would soon undeceive him. It is a lake of many lessons.
The using of a big rod and strong tackle may make shore-fishing for large fish possible,
but it is only in a very strong breeze that it pays, while, in any case, such a method robs
loch-trouting of its special "character."

is within your grasp. With the landing net lying to your hand—and the proper way to hold it has already been explained, coax the now enfeebled fish round to windward, and work the boat stern first towards him as he lies partially inert. You thus present less surface of the boat towards the fish, if he should make a final effort and endeavour to burst under the boat, a common trick of heavy sea-trout. The net should be placed quietly under him and the fish allowed to slide into it ; it should not be jerked towards and under him, for then he may be alarmed, and a last struggle may mean his loss. On calmer days it is advisable to bring the fish to leeward and let the stern come slowly down on him, the gillie standing by the oars in readiness to pull forward should occasion arise, but care must be taken in any case not to let the shadow of the boat fall on the fish, for it may alarm him.

I have up to this point avoided any specific mention of the "circular system" of playing a fish from a boat, but it may be explained, first, that the art consists in "bluffing" the fish into a belief that he is having his own way and, second, in heading him off on each rush and working him slowly round in a circle with a long radius. This is, however, an art which the angler must necessarily reason out for himself. I may say, however, that unless it is acquired very few fish of any size will be landed in reedy lakes.

It is necessary, however, to add some observations on the general line of action with regard to both reeds and weeds which always have been and always will be, to a greater or less extent, as the angler is accustomed to them or otherwise, troublesome and dangerous to the loch fisher. Reeds are far more dangerous and fatal to the angler than weeds, and this for two reasons—the angler must at all costs keep a fish out of reeds, and so put a heavy strain and risk his tackle; while a fish once amongst strong reeds, has nine chances in his favour to one against him, provided the angler does not act promptly. On the other hand, a fish may with comparative impunity be allowed to enter a bed of bottom weeds, and there is no imperative necessity for the exercise of a dangerous amount of vis major to keep him out of it. Some lochs are quite free from these pests, if it is fair so to describe features which add to the difficulties and dangers of playing a fish. A trout "embunched" in weeds soon tires itself, and if the angler merely keeps the strain steady, and attempts no sudden jerks, etc., he will in the majority of cases land his fish safely. When he thinks the fish has had time enough he should order the boat to be rowed sufficiently far from the fish to enable him to bring his rod parallel with the water.* Putting on a gradual strain, he should pull evenly and strongly—as strongly as he thinks his tackle will admit of. Weeds are weakest vertically, and he thus has a vertical pull artificially produced. If this even steady pull, with the rod parallel with the water, does not shortly bring the fish up, foredone and embedded in weeds, the angler may either rest assured that the fish is gone or he must clear the weeds away with the oar or an iron-shod pole (carried for the purpose), or else get broken; but in nine cases out of ten the method is completely success-ful and the fish secured, if fairly well hooked initially. Even very large sea-trout can be suffered thus to " embunch ' themselves, and may be finally captured after doing so.

I have dwelt at some length upon the weed question, because more fish are lost in weeds than should be lost. Whether trout ever hold on weeds with their teeth I am not prepared to say, but if they do they must be very foolish fish, for to go clean through and out at the other side is a much better plan of escape. In Loch Lomond, Loch Leven, and many Scottish lochs of the larger class, the angler need hardly trouble himself about fish getting into weeds, but in the Hebrides—particularly the Outer Hebrides—and, speaking generally, in the majority of small lochs, he will find them a practical obstacle.

Reeds are in quite a different position. They are seen dangers, which is so far an advantage, but they are just as much more fatal as they are more apparent. In confined lochs—especially in sea-trout lochs with reeds—it is a confirmed habit of large fish to lie just beside the beds of reeds, while those which lie out and are raised and hooked in the open invariably endeavour to rush into the reeds, or to work their way near to them. When a fish rises close by a bed of reeds, the best policy is to humour him, and to coax him, if possible, away from them in the manner already outlined. If he be a wild fish and makes

---

* While these pages were in the Press, I observed in an editorial note in the " Fishing Gazette," that a somewhat similar plan was recommended by the late Francis Francis. The coincidence is instructive, and I am pleased, but not surprised, to note that I have such an authority on my side. Any angler, of ordinary intelligence, should soon make the discovery for himself. I was a very young angler when experience taught me " the trick."

a fierce rush in amongst them, the whole performance is so rapid that you have no time to stop him. More than once I have seen a large fish make such a wild rush and get one of my flies fast in the reeds. So astonished have such fish been at the sudden check that they have lain quite quiet, or nearly so, on the surface, and by prompt, but quiet action, I have had the net under them. I have never, however, secured a heavier fish than one of 5lb. after reeds have been entered, and since 1887, can only recall five occasions on which fish have reached this sanctuary. On three of these occasions I secured the fish (5lb., 4½lb., and 4¼lb.), while on both the other occasions the fish escaped with the fly. This plan of letting the fish have its own way, or nearly so, once it is amongst the reeds, and then going quietly down on him with the net ready for quick but deliberate use, may succeed, if carefully executed, on three occasions out of five. In any view it is the angler's only chance. Should you get into a fish, however, which begins quietly, you may succeed in coaxing him gently along outside the reeds for a bit, endeavouring at the same time to get the boat quietly into them. If you succeed in doing so without raising his latent ire, you may then put on the strain. The fish will probably rush outwards; if so let him have a good rush, but follow him as fast as you can lest he turn and come towards you and the reeds. Once you have him safely away from the reeds, play him in the manner already described. A fish hooked out in the clear water away from the reeds and making a mad rush for them must of course be checked. It is quite impossible to suddenly check the rush of that gamest and most active of all fish, a fresh-run 4lb. sea-trout (by far the most awkward of his tribe to tackle); but as the rush is really a mad rush, and more or less blind in its purpose, it can be done gradually. When a sufficient quantity of line has been run out consistent with safety, and the chance of renewing control (and the more line is out the easier it is to stop the rush), the rod must be brought slowly over the left shoulder and the butt moved away from the body. This can be done principally by the left hand, while the right is ready to wind in. This is the proper way to check a rush, and what is of more importance, when the fish has got near reeds, it will turn him in the right direction, and make him move in a line at an angle of about 45 degs. to the line of his original rush.

I confess frankly that this didactic tone is forced upon me by the necessities of the situation. It is necessary to the completeness at which I have endeavoured to aim in treating the subject. My methods may lack purpose. Possibly there are other and better methods. I can at least claim for them that they are the results of lessons learned on the field of battle, and may, therefore, illustrate the truism that nothing trains for war save war.*

* It savours strongly of the egotistical to say that by playing big sea-trout in the manner described, I have been fortunate enough to be broken only five times in my angling career, and only once in the open. In vindicating the efficacy of methods, one s, however, forced to quote the facts of personal experience.

CHAPTER XXX.

Loch Fishing in a Calm.

The "sugh of a boding wind" may be the only music which can console the salmon angler standing by some West Highland river drinking in the bitter poison of dwindled waters and longing for the rain that is to flash in the whirling pools of his chosen Simois. His position may, indeed, be one of hopeless despair so long as the wind sits and the sky is hard. With the streams at the heads of pools reduced to mere shallows, purling over the scarcely hidden stones and the "lies" and holding spots covered with a foot of clear water that boasts no current, and the deeper pools simply stagnant dubs in which the fish obstinately sulk and show no desire to feed and very little to play, the river which might seem, with a brown spate rolling down, alive with fish and full of life, is a dull and sullen Cocytus—a river of angling woe—a Dead Sea over which no fly can float with the expectation that is the life of angling success—a smooth-sliding Mincius whose reeds can but pipe despair, whose rocks are not harder than its irresponsive mood—a Lethe, whose tide is fatal to the happy memories of the past, kills all the zeal of effort for the present and obliterates all hopes for the future. If you search the history of despairing moods, on earth at least, since even Dantes Infernos owe something to the play of fearful fancy on the unknown, you will scarcely find a situation that will match that of the salmon angler under the conditions outlined. Yet just as life holds few pictures, whose colours are all borrowed from the pessimistic pallet that revels in the sombre hues of its night-side, so even under such hopeless conditions the salmon angler can still find consolation in Nature as one of her children, and in the larger air as a commoner of inalienable rights in her heritage. He may not, perhaps, with the beggared bohemianism of Burns be able to make music which will console his frustrated hopes out of the babbling of a river reduced to the dimen-

sions of a brook, but there is an inspiring optimism in the clear outline of a hill even against the cold blue of a non-angling sky, and a
whole world of wondrously soothing hope in the music of even an
autumnal east wind piping a dirge that is only sad when "angling"
thinking makes it so amongst the rustling reeds of a "riseless" pool.

Yet to be quite frank these consolations come with the aftermath of
thoughts by the fireside when the hills are seen through the mists of
an evening pipe, and the music of the reeds waits upon the digestion
of a dinner that has inspired. By the riverside the cold east wind, the
hard sky, the ruffled unyielding surface of the pools unbroken by the
rise of a single fish, the hopelessness that is a rival element of air and
water, and is almost the only constituent of the atmosphere of your
little angling world bounded by the single stream of your present ambition—these seem to make, in all the strength of an infernal unity of
impatient suffering and sickened hope, that "monopoly of hell" sung of
by the poet held in bondage of despair. Perhaps if we could glide
back down the long ascent of time, up which the lingering train
of laborious years have toiled, "grey with the eld" of immemorial centuries, we might find a stream in which the first angler cast his line
with success under such grievous conditions, and the remote ancestors
of our present salmon rose to a fly dressed with the feathers of a pterodactyl, the fur of the mastodon, and ribbed with primeval silver. A
priori angling, however, neither fills the basket nor lifts the heart bowed
down, and the splendid triumphs of the quasi-historical fancy in the
virgin waters of the comparatively new-created world, if magnificent to
dream about, offer but poor compensation for the disturbance of mind
caused by the sad realities of a day whose crowded evil is sufficient not
only for itself but for a whole calender of days that are angling dies
irae.

The angler situated as I have described has truly some reason for
allowing the iron to enter his soul and for turning to nature for those
compensations of Cocytus that make it not a river of woe, but a river of
joy even in its most unyielding mood. There is, however, no parallel
to his case in loch fishing, though scarcely an article is penned on the
subject which does not chronicle the falling away of the breeze as putting
an end to the possibility of sport, justifying the cessation of effort and
affording a substantial reason for an indulgence during the sleep of the

winds in a glorious dream with the head pillowed on the very lap of nature.*

Procul esti profani, but surely angling man can choose another hour for his day dreams, than that which will tax his greatest skill and make the conditions of the fight favour the fish. In the loch angler's dictionary there are no such words as "hopeless condition," though there may be and indeed are conditions under which the killing of good fish is a matter of such extreme difficulty that one triumph won against desperate odds gives greater pleasure than a series of victories cheaply won, and, therefore, lightly esteemed. "Sport," that word which bids all definition defiance, may no doubt be personal to the individual from the point of view of enjoyment, but what constitutes successful and satisfying sport depends upon the circumstances and conditions under which the sport is obtained. The youthful angler who wanders rod in hand amidst the dark hill-fed burns of the north, or the brooks of southern localities, or penetrates on slaughter bent to some remote hill tarn cradled away up in the silence of the hills, is content with the capture of the small and accommodating fish that haunt the stream or lake of his fancy. His standard of comfort in angling is not a high one, and so long as he is contented he has his sport. Good sport to him is a bag of these small fish. So too there are men who will sit or stand by canal banks hour after hour, day after day, almost season after season, and catch nothing but gudgeon and occasional small roach. To them the capture of a little eel is an event, the death of a half-pound roach brings joy untold, and the landing of a bream or chub is ecstasy. Those who have breathed what one might term the rarer atmosphere of the angling world would say that these men do not know what sport means, but in this they would err, for they would regard and define sport in terms of their standard of comfort in angling, and deny to these humbler brethren of the angle a similar right to measure sport from the personal point of view.

Good sport, however, from the impersonal aspect, may be said to depend upon the quality of the water fished, and the conditions under

* The earliest advice on this point in angling literature, is put by Franck into the mouth of Aquilla standing by the shores of Loch Lomond. "But this pace I perceive won't carry on my design, nor are complaints proper engines or suitable instruments to surprize fish." "How pitifully it looks," continues the contemporary of Cromwell, "for the angler to lie puling, whilst fish, like allegators are pulling all in pieces, let any man judg that's destinated to be undone."

which it is fished. A basket with which we would be more than
pleased in some waters would afford us but meagre satisfaction in
others; while what we would esteem good sport under unfavourable,
or what we consider unfavourable (and here the personal again intrudes)
conditions of weather and water, would be regarded as the very opposite
if the conditions of weather and water were all that
could be desired. Suppose one sets forth to fish
some carefully preserved sea-trout loch teeming with
fish that are but little disturbed, and in which 30lb. to 50lb. of sea-
trout can reasonably be expected on a good or even a fair fishing day,
and we return with a poor 20lbs., are we satisfied with our sport?
Assuredly not, because our anticipations have not been even approximately realised. Let us take it from the other point of view. Perhaps
the very day before we set forth to fish some "hotel" loch with hopes
of a few sea-trout, and have returned with 20lb. of these fish. Which
day has given most sport? Most certainly the day on the second water,
because anticipation has been more than realised. If any angler sub-
mits himself to a process of self-analysis, he will find this to be true—
that good sport is directly proportioned to the more or less approximate
realisation of the anticipations of it which the fame and nature of the
water fished have warranted him in forming. Sport is thus not only
dependent upon the number of the slain, but also upon the number to be
slain and their willingness to be slaughtered operating through our
fancy and upon the difficulties to be overcome. One trout killed under
unfavourable conditions of weather and water is worth half a dozen
willing victims that spring almost obsequious to the fly.

And so is it with the loch-fisher who sees in a calm not the hour for
dreaming but the hour of his prospective triumph—not an excuse for
idleness, but the spur of ambition that will urge him on to greater,
higher, more purposeful and reasoned exertion. This "purposeful and
reasoned" exertion is justified by more considerations than the were
desire to overcome difficulties and secure a greater measure of sport in
the overcoming. The habits of the quarry are, in the first place, not
such as impose a barrier on the use of the fly as a lure for its capture;
nor, in the second place, is it impossible to place that lure in such a way
before the fish that he will not see in it something to alarm him which
will change desire to dread. In a river the wet fly fisher would not by rea-

son of the scanty tide or the stillness of pools, unkissed by even a zephyr, hang rod and line in idle trophy until the amber floods came as allies to his skill or the ripple by the reed gave to his martial fly the uniform of nature and concealed the dagger beneath. What is true of the wet fly angler is doubly true of the dry fly exponent who would welcome those very conditions which the average loch fisher hails not only as the harbingers of his season of despair, but also as a reasonable excuse for hours of idleness, during which he can pray to Saint Antonio for a capful of wind and keep his ears open for the first sounds of the prologue to the omen coming on. Yet so far from a calm loch being water in which an angler may cast his flies with less hope than in a river, a loch is the very water one might design, if the object desired were the production of a water in which sport was at all times possible, and angling under no conditions was hopeless.

I was educated in the older faith; the faith that sits by the shores of old romance, when it is imaginative and has the root of the matter, and anathematizes the breezes that do not blow, when it is prosaic, and matter of fact and treats angling as a business. I was told that to fish in calm, still water was as vain a task as that of Simple Simon angling in his pail, and I accepted the traditional faith, until experience proved it not only a weak-kneed belief without moral basis, but also a poor policy on those very grounds of selfish expediency on which it was supposed to rest. I first awoke to the light on the river. Fishing one July day in a dwindled river and under a cloudless sky, I killed a few but not many trout in a long still reach that was practically a loch in so far as there was no current in it and it was artificially dammed. Wherever I saw a feeding fish or wherever I thought a fish might be—and I am writing of a day that joined the past 21 years ago—I dropped my fly as lightly and as gently as I could. I met with my reward, not merely in the form of fish, but in the form of a lesson, whose value I immediately tested on a neighbouring mill-pond. It stood the test of that experience and was entered on the tablets. Some years elapsed before it was utilised in practice owing to the drift of angling circumstance, but the day came, when I remembered it and first vindiated to the complete satisfaction of a sceptic the possibility of securing not merely an occasional fish, but even a large basket on a loch innocent of ripple from shore to shore. In an hour and a half I killed by casting over, as it happened, rising fish, 28 sea-trout weighing 36lbs. From that time forward the words "hopeless condition" were erased from my dictionary of loch fishing phrases.

Fate is sometimes kind to the sceptic who finds it easier to doubt than to examine, and convinces him in spite of himself that certain things are possible which he deems to be impossible. A genial example of the doubter, some short time after my faith had been firmly established, made a chance cast on the glassy surface of a lake which is the most hopeless sea-trout loch in a dead calm in which I ever angled. He rose, hooked, and killed the largest sea-trout that ever fell to his rod. He never, so far as I am aware followed up this chance lesson or studied the subject with a view to discovering the theory underlying it and of evolving a system in terms of the principles thus discovered. Fortune favoured experiment in my case, as I happened to have permission to fish certain most admirable sea-trout lochs, in which there were so many fish, and in which one could kill such good baskets that the variety a calm afforded was not only a welcome relief from the monotony of constant and, on the whole, easily won victories over the trout, but also necessitated the devising of methods for their capture and hence of studying the problem in all its aspects. When fish were on the move, whether at flies on the water or merely for some occult reason, one naturally succeeded in tempting a greater number to their doom than when the lake appeared tenantless save for the occasional leap and sounding splash of some mighty specimen. On the first occasion on which I set myself to a study of the problem a high tide was conjoined with a low loch, and the majority of the fish were therefore not only fresh from the rich tables of the deep, but had located themselves some distance from the shore, near which the water had become rather shallow and clear. They were rising freely as sea-trout will when fresh-run into a loch. I commenced operations purposely with the tackle and flies I would have used in a strong breeze—tackle, that is to say, whose strength was proportioned to the size of the fish and the conditions of a fair fight. I soon discovered that many of the fish came short in the various ways already described. I, therefore, put on finer tackle but retained the same size of flies. I then found that all the fish which appeared likely takers from their rise, could by the exercise of care and a little ingenuity be made to take, and that the percentage of fish hooked to fish moved markedly increased. I had thus established as a first principle that as in a river so in a lake the fineness of one's tackle, on mere grounds of expediency and leaving ethical considerations out of account, must vary with the degree of ease with which it may be made visible to the trout. I then tried smaller flies, but did not find that the number of fish killed appreciably increased, so long, that is to say, as they kept rising, and I cast over them with a long line, allowed my flies to sink and drew them towards me with an even motion. I, therefore, came to the conclusion that the mere size of the fly had less to do with success than the fineness of the gut. As it so happened the conclusion in the matter of flies was indeterminate for the flies I used even in a gale were relatively small to the flies which the fish might have taken in a good fishing breeze. I, therefore, tried them with larger flies on the same gut and at once they betrayed an appreciation of the difference in the size of the lure and a corresponding diffidence in it as something alarming them they knew not why. A return to the original gut and the "large" flies did not, indeed, put an end to my sport, but it caused a relative decrease in the casualty roll. The question of education could not possibly arise in this loch. The fish were migratory and had come straight from the sea, yet they were just as easily alarmed by an improper size of fly as the so called "educated trout" are said to be by an improper colour in an imitation only to be detected under the magnifying glass.*

It was clear, however, that there were certain limitations in the matter of tackle and flies. Flies beyond a certain size and gut beyond a certain thickness could not be employed with any hope of success, and the angler using them was really in the hopeless position in which tradition had placed him, and in which he, in terms of that tradition, believed himself to be. These points being settled, the rest of my self-imposed task was easy. The fixing of the extreme limits of both fly and gut was a mere matter of calculation, and I found Nos. 11 and 12 (on the old scale) small enough on grounds of expediency—though often using No. 13 of choice on moral grounds, whilst I used the finest gut that met all the requirements of the situation, gut, that is to say, with which one could deliver

---

* Mr. Smurthwaite accounts for short rising on this singular ground in an admirable essay on the subject of colour in flies in the cheap edition of Mr. Halford's "Dry Fly Fishing."

2 A

a light cast and which hit the golden mean between expediency and
morality. So far as the mere playing of a fish was concerned, I soon
discovered that it was possible to use finer gut in a calm than in a
breeze, for the boat was more easily worked and responded more quickly
to a movement of the oars, while the fish was in no way aided by that
bellying of the line frequent after a rush in a breeze or by the roll of
the wave when travelling high. Lastly his movements actual and
threatened could be more easily judged and anticipated. The great
difficulty was the persuading of the fish to take; but once that was
accomplished the crowning mercy of capture, if longer delayed, was certainly more easily accomplished.

. The pattern of fly, if of less moment than its size and the fineness of
the gut was, however, a factor in success which could not be overlooked.
After trying various flies possessed of some "characteristic colour," I
came to the conclusion that a small "Woodcock and Red " was the best
fly for sea-trout in a calm during the heat and brightness of the day and
that a small "Red Stuart," was the best evening fly. When fish were
rising with any degree of freedom, it was, of course, a comparatively
easy matter to cast the fly across their rise, sink it well and draw it
evenly and gently through the water. The art consisted in timing the
strike. In the case of "rising" fish, this was moderately easy, though
in some instances when a fish came somewhat short and hesitated in
the manner already described, it was a matter of considerable difficulty
to increase the motion without causing him alarm. It was when fish
were not rising that the process of persuading them to "take" became
an extremely difficult and trying operation. The process itself differed
with the lake and was much simpler, though far less effective in shore
lochs where the fish lay near rocks than in lochs in which they lay in
the open. In the former the only plan that was feasible was to cast a
long, light line on to the rocks and suffer the fly to slip off them on to
the water, or alternatively, to cast a long line in such a way that the fly
lighted just by the rocks. The fish for which one was angling when
using this method were feeding fish. In consequence the rise was not
delayed and was either immediate, in which case it took the form of a
mere bubble and suck, or occurred before the fly had travelled very far,
in which case one might or might not see a slight wave, but would assuredly feel a tightening of the line. This is the simplest form which

loch fishing in a calm assumes. Nevertheless, it is very pretty fishing and obviously necessitates considerable mechanical skill, and the exercise of not a little patience for one may search a good deal of water without reward, and with but little encouragement. The third method which one may have to adopt in fishing for sea-trout in a calm, when the fish are not rising, is by far the most difficult of all, and it was only after trying a variety of ways and giving the problem some very serious consideration that I at last evolved a plan of campaign, which, when put in practice yielded not a few good baskets and many large fish, under conditions which were as nearly hopeless, not only as conditions can appear to be, but also as they actually are when any other method is employed. It is true that an occasional large sea-trout even in a loch in which they lie in the open is killed in a dead calm and under a bright sun and clear sky by promiscuous casting on the ordinary plan. That is not the point at issue. What is desired is a method which will secure not one, but many fish under these conditions. Anglers without a coward conscience, who trail the flies behind the boat know that by this means trout can be killed in the most glassy of calms, and those who have essayed the same method in sea-trout lochs know that it is often as effective in such waters as in trout lakes. It was this fact which gave me the first clue to the solution of the problem. That clue once gained, the rest was easy and the method stood revealed. I ordered my gillie to keep the boat moving steadily but very slowly ahead. I then cast a long line as lightly as possible to a point to the right of the stern, allowed my flies to sink and then aided by the way on the boat worked them evenly and gently round until they were almost parallel with the stern. This, of course, requires merely mechanical skill, but the first fish I rose soon showed me that the method was not only an effective and sporting means of raising fish, but also that in nine cases out of ten the rise secured was the most difficult of all rises obtained in lochs to time. Nay more. After experiencing several such rises I came to the unavoidable conclusion that I was face to face with a mechanical difficulty which by reason of the intrusion of the psychological was the most difficult to overcome in the whole realm of practical sport.

The most brilliant of one-handed catches low down in the slips, the killing of a woodcock flashing like a sheet of brown lightning down a corrie when the season nears its end, the shot at an oblique angle that nearly bursts the net and leaves the toe as a ball breaks from the cannon, these and similar feats have an element of the unconscious in their masterly doing; and even the hooking of a trout taken after a successful stalk off clear sand under the scanty tide of a sun-dried, sun-kissed river is little more than a mere tightening of the line, for the fish hooks himself. The raising is everything; the hooking is practically nothing; it is an ensured consequence of the rise. In the case of big sea-trout angled for as above, the opposite obtains. The rise is nothing; the hooking is everything, for this is what usually happens. The fish will come to the fly out of nothingness, and will follow it in precisely the same way as a dace follows the fly. The effect, however, is very different and it is at this point that the psychological intrudes. Even a "specimen" dace will scarcely set the angler's heart thumping against his ribs, as if the fate of empires depended upon his maintaining a resolute calm—a tenacity of reasoned purpose not to be shaken from its seat though the tail of Leviathan himself should show in wide-spreading majesty by his fly. And if you would be a man of blood, you must first be a man of iron. The fish you have persuaded to rise from the vasty deep of your hopes is not a taking fish in the strict sense of the phrase. He is a fish who may take provided nothing occurs to alarm him and you can keep your head cool and your hand steady, waiting for the lure to operate on his appetite and create the taking mood by its suggestive presence. Moreover you must be sufficiently collected to be able to judge perhaps intuitively and by a sort of personal telepathy, which is a gift, the proper moment to give a slightly increased way to the fly with a view not only to avoiding too close an inspection but also to creating that desire for things whose value is only appreciated when they are lost, common alike to men and fish. All that I have described takes only a second to happen, but the second is so crowded that a whole life of angling seems compressed into a single beat of the pulse. Any relaxation of vigilance, however temporary, the least yielding to natural impulse, the display, in a word, of the slightest knowledge of his presence, will startle the fish; he will cease to dimple after your fly and with an alarmed boil below the surface similar to that made by a fish which having risen once, comes again but comes short, he will vanish into the brown mystery of the lake from whence he came. I am not describing with such minuteness of detail what is imaginary or remembered only through the joys of the "haec olims" as fancy paints them on the canvas of life. I am describing what has actually been my experience, on many occasions, what was my experience on the very last occasion on which I put this method in practice.

After a quiet day on a certain loch the keeper chanced to meet me on its shores in the act of taking down my rod. The lake was a glassy calm; every rock and stone, each hill and crofter's wigwam on its banks had its double in the mirror. Not a rise broke its surface from shore to shore, though now and then some great sea-trout would leap from the water and come down with a splash; the only other sounds that broke the hush in which nature slept was the roar of the Atlantic on a western beach and the rattle of an occasional cart on the public road coming on the ear as a displeasing discord amidst the solemn music of the tireless sea. It was the beau ideal of a day not only inviting but justifying an indulgence in the dolce far niente, the smoking of the pipe of peace amongst the rocks. I had ceased fishing not because I had failed to kill fish, but because my time was limited. The keeper made some remark upon the impossibility of killing fish on such a day in such a loch, and we fell, as men will, into an argument. At length, having failed to persuade him that his contention was wrong, I determined to give ocular proof, which he could scarcely combat. Within a quarter of an hour I succeeded, as luck would have it, in securing a dimpling offer from a good fish, and keeping cool and collected, hooked and duly landed him, a trout of close on 5lbs. Elated by this success I tried again and by the irony of fate a giant of his race gave me the same sort of rise as the first—the rise that I have described. I was, however, unequal to the occasion. I misjudged the fish; " a little shaking of mine elbow" and he disappeared with the usual boil. Ten minutes afterwards on the scene of my failure, he sprang from the water in derision and sent wavelets to lap with laughter, which mocked my misery, the furthest shore.

To attempt to catch sea-trout in a loch in a calm is thus not to essay the impossible, but only the difficult, terms that are, as in the wider sphere of life, too often confounded with one another by the angler. As a mechanical art, the skill and perseverance necessary to success

vary with the lake and the angling conditions of the day. When fish
are rising, it is comparatively easy to hook them; in a shore loch light
casting is the only essential if one ignores all qualities that are not
special to the occasion; when, however, fish are not rising, have to
be persuaded to rise and come, as they usually do, in the way described,
the difficulty of hooking them is admittedly so great and the skill required so much a matter of temperament and of determination to cultivate an artificial kind of indifference, that very few anglers can acquire
it even after they have drunk deep of the strong wine of angling. It
is this personal aspect of the last of these three methods which makes
it less efficacious in some lochs than in others, even if one ignores the
fact that in some lochs, however skilfully done, the method is not so
productive of fish as in others. In a lake in which moderate baskets are
the rule and big fish the exception, the difficulty of self-control naturally
increases with the greatness of the occasion, and on precisely the same
principle underlying the fact that an angler not used to hooking big fish
will be too nervously anxious when one is thus risen, to keep methodically
cool and display the masterly inactivity necessary to success. Nor are two
of these methods, for we can ignore the third which, ex hypothesi, presupposes rising fish, equally efficacious in all lochs even when the
personal aspect does not intrude. Such lochs as yield poor sport even
in a breeze can scarcely be expected to change their character in a
calm, and as even the best of lochs yield proportionately fewer fish
under "unfavourable" or, at least difficult, conditions than when the
conditions are favourable and comparatively easy, it is possible that on
some lakes the putting of these methods in practice may be labour in
vain. There can, however, from a sporting point of view be no doubt
that fish killed under such conditions give more pleasure, and, on the
last analysis, "better sport" than hecatombs slaughtered when the
angling wind sits fair. On the same principle a single sea-trout killed
in an indifferent loch is the greatest triumph of all—a fact which warrants no man in lying "puling" even when the fish are not in the
alligator mood referred to by Franck.

The art of fishing in a calm for loch trout is not quite similar in all
its aspects. In the first place loch trout, as we have already seen, are
somewhat different in their habits to sea-trout. For example, in a
shore loch a trout will either be found feeding in his special habitat

or ranging up and down a bit of shore near his habitat. In the former case he should be angled for just as one would angle for a river trout. If he is feeding and rising one would put a fly over him in a river, and it is in such a case that the dry fly may with advantage be used in a loch, if, that is to say the angler desires to introduce a little variety into his methods. The "dry fly" is not necessary, however, unless the fish be feeding on a particular fly, as noted in the chapter on "Moods." If he is, a "floating fly" imitating the insect of his meal may alone tempt him to his doom. In the second case, when a fish is ranging and feeding, I have found no fly more effective than the "Red and Teal." Fished far and fine, and cast, if possible, across the probable line of his march—which may often be judged by the wave he makes as he moves to and fro, this fly will persuade him to rise if any fly can do so. His capture may occupy a long time, but so long as he is feeding there is hope. Sometimes the fish is clearly visible. You can follow his ghostly outline and can, therefore, judge his position with greater accuracy. When this is so, loch fishing becomes to all intents and purposes the same as river fishing, save that you are not compelled to conceal yourself and need only keep still. When no fish are rising, then as in the sea-trout lake you have to adopt the plan of casting in likely places and of searching the shore water—a system which every wet fly fisher and a few dry fly men adopt on a river. When fishing in the open water the plan utilized in the sea-trout loch, when fish are not rising need not be rigidly adhered to, but it is equally efficacious and loch trout are not nearly so difficult to hook as sea-trout. As a rule they rise slowly and take quietly and below the water a mere bubble marking the rise. There is generally nothing exceptional in the rise, and ordinary rules apply for the difficulties to be overcome are of an ordinary character. Sometimes, however, the opposite obtains and loch trout of a large size will rise in precisely the same long-drawn-out style as do big sea-trout. In fact the accuracy of the generalisation as stated may be said to depend upon the size of the fish. In lakes holding comparatively small trout the long-drawn-out rise is practically unknown; in lakes holding large fish it is fairly common. In my list of noted cases occur examples of days on which 50 per cent. of the trout killed have so risen, while cases in which the ratio has been 33 per cent are fairly common. As a rule the cause producing this effect is individual to the fish; it is rarely the product of a mood displayed universally by all the trout which are raised. It is no doubt akin to "smutting" in character and is certainly the rise of a not over keen or specially hungry fish. That it has a purely sensational origin, whether in the individual fish or in the conditions or both, is in any case absolutely certain.

Fine tackle is, of course, essential, while the patterns of flies need not, save under the exceptional condition of a special pre-disposing cause, differ from those employed in a breeze with success.

For my own part, though rejoicing as all anglers do in killing large baskets, I confess that I have derived more pleasure from loch fishing in a calm than from loch fishing under the most so-called favourable conditions. On a bright calm day with nature looking her loveliest, there is an infinite restfulness, different from the rough work by the stream, in casting far and fine under the trees or by the rocks and in studying with the zeal of interest the life of lakeland while the world sleeps.

LOWER KILDONAN, SOUTH UIST: DISTANT VIEW OF "THE RUSTLING SANCTUARY.

ON A FAMOUS SEA TROUT LOCH: THE BREEZE AND SPOT FOR A SEVEN-POUNDER.

CHAPTER XXXI.

ON "SPORTING" LOCHS AND KINDRED WATERS.

Each in his own dub, we are all "kindly tenants" of the same great King. The rights of citizenship are not of the chalk-stream nor the canal nor the salmon river nor the upland tarn nor even the wide sea, but wherever a rod gleams and a fish swims, and the Great Brotherhood boasts a single commoner of the larger air, coming salt or fresh on the lips amidst the weary spaces of life, the Great Charter writ on many waters grants equality and liberty conditioned only by a love of "all things both great and small" and a due observance of the golden rule of all honest men and honest sportsmen, that the law of the game is the art of the "good and fair," to live honestly, injure no man and render to each fish and all fishers their due.

I may, therefore, in this broad spirit of toleration throw special pleading to the winds. Whether, therefore, the purist is right or wrong in claiming for his trout a meaure of that same brain muscularity which Shakespeare and Socrates possessed only in a higher degree, he is justified in maintaining that the ordinary loch trout is more easily killed under normal conditions than is the trout of the river, especially that acutely sensitive, and reputedly suspicious dweller in the clear and limpid chalk-streams of the south, whose sentinel-watch for the tit-bits of Nature's fly-spread table is held in spots that bid seen danger defiance, and challenge the ambushed guile of his circumventor.

Nevertheless, it is as just as true that there are lochs and lochs, as it is that there are rivers and rivers. In some of the larger lakes, such as Loch Lomond, the "chuck and chance it" method is, no doubt, characteristic of the mode of angling, for it takes no great wind to send big waves rolling over the surface of their spreading waters, and all, therefore, the angler can do is to fish patiently and not miss the chances that come his way in his too great haste to be "into" a rising fish. Who, however, dares to say that in some reed-begirt and weed-hampered loch of the Hebrides no skill is required in handling on light tackle and a single-handed rod some mammoth sea-trout, rejoicing in his ocean-strength and superabundant activity, borrowed from the salt wash of estuary life and the rich tables of the kindly deep? In a gale his wild rushes require a mastery of the vis major to control; in a calm his long-drawn out rise is difficult to time, and whatever way he be regarded, his killing and his undoing are essentially sporting.

Moreover, amongst the many lakes of this country there occur some waters which even the ultra dry fly man would appreciate because they would tax his skill, perhaps exhaust his patience—a dubious quality in the angler who angles only where a feeding fish is—and are not to be conquered and robbed of their spoil without a combined attack of those best allies, cunning and strength—the mental power to conceive a plan of action and the physical power to put it in force.

Take a typical water of this kind in Southern Argyleshire to which I have frequently referred. It is a lovely lake that lies embosomed in hills whose rocky and wood-clad sides rise steep from its margin and throughout whose whole length the branches weep and wave over the shore waters. Far under the boughs where the broken sunlight streams and the flies dance in countless thousands, and swirl in those endless mazes of giddy purpose that the ephemerid alone can match, the great trout love to lurk. Sunken rocks and deep abiding places are everywhere to be found in its waters of swift descent from shallow to deep, and it is only for the most part in these feeding places of narrow confines that trout are to be taken at all. As a consequence, feeding fish alone rise to the fly, save on those rare days when a big move is on, and all the many fish in the lake seem bent on surface feeding. Once a month—perhaps once in an angling life-time, so far as the individual is concerned—the fish will depart from their immemorial custom and rise like the common herd of their fellows, the greedy trout of some upland tarn, whose optimistic appetite sees good and fears naught in everything that carries feather, fur and tinsel.

The "duffer" in this lake will cast, as a rule, in vain, though sometimes he will stumble across one of fortune's many paths and be surprised by a swirling rise that will set his heart beating. A master of the arts of such a loch is worth watching. He prefers a calm still day, when the wind sits in the west and gentle airs just dimple here and there the lake. Gusty days with squalls from "'a the airts" are his abomination, for he wants to cast far and clean and not to have his line caught in middle air by a wayward and sudden blast just as his flies are speeding fair with a graceful swirl to light in glistening softness where a bubble denotes a feeding fish, close by the rocks and far under the boughs, where sunshine and shadow are francifully fretted beyond the power of imitation.

Place a lover of such a lake twenty-five yards from the shore just opposite the feeding ground of a lusty fish that keeps watch and ward over its chosen domain, and ranges up and down with ceaseless vigilance, now sucking in a fly, now giving a merry little dash as though challenging intrusion from his fellows, and he is happy. Gradually lengthening his line and making it perform all manner of graceful gyrations, he will at length send the fly on its way to fall with graceful, quivering sweep that leaves no ripple to mark its lighting just in front of where the trout will be in the course of his stately faring to and fro. There is a bubble merely, the line grows taut, the rod bends, and the battle has quietly begun to be noisily continued as the reel sings and the fish at the close of a humming rush throws himself clean from the water, his yellow sides gleaming in the sunshine. The combat is an Homeric one. The fish is not, perhaps, a monster. As a rule he is only a fish of 2 to 2½lbs., but he has fed on rich and dainty fare, and' the aristocratic blood in his shapely person only yields in death. He fights then as becomes his gentle race to do or die; and he fights under fair conditions, for the gut is fine, the rod light, the supply of line limited, and on all hands lurk those allies, the great, tall, strong reeds, amidst which he played hide and seek in his fishy infancy, or dashed for safety from some giant cannibal of his race, forgetful of its lofty traditions. Soon, however, the end comes. High courage and well-nurtured strength can do no more. His rush grows feebler, and finally broad-gleaming in the glory of a well-won death, he sinks within the fatal meshes of the eager net Such a fish is worth killing, such an experience is worth waiting for. It is sport in the best and highest sense of the word.

On fine gut—and this is an essential to successful raising—a hard or unskilful angler would when a fish rose find it by no means easy to time the quiet, perhaps, long-drawn-out rise, and there would be every risk of a too sharp and hard strike sending Master Trout away to ruminate on the deceitfulness of man with a strand hanging from his mouth. If he overcame this initial difficulty and tyro and trout were linked in that sweetest of unions between fish and man of which sporting gear in rod, line and cast are the outward and visible symbols, even then the lusty twopounder would lead him an anxious dance, if in one of his wild evolutions he did not succeed in jumping free from the noxious curb or dashing into the friendly deeps or boring down until some lusty ally in the person of a stout and friendly reed came to his aid and enabled him to taste once more his old freedom as a commoner of water.

The day may come and often does come, when the conditions alter. Such a day fell to my lot on a recent occasion and its joys, if not quite the same, were equally great. Overhead lazy-pacing white clouds moved with the languorous speed that becomes summer skies in the pride of June; a fine, gentle west wind came sighing off the Atlantic, and rid itself of the salt sea on its wings by kissing into countless laughter the sunlit waters of the lake; the Mayflies, keenly alive to seizing the day were everywhere bursting from the surface and sailing away in the fluttering fulness of a life that is all sunshine and knows nothing of those gates of death, the jaws that lurk below the water and the beaks that gape in the air; thousands of smaller flies were on the wing, and above and beyond all as a sign of hope the trout were rising here, there and everywhere with a flopping persistency that argued keen-set appetites and a heavy basket for the homeward bound angler.

For an hour these conditions may prevail on such red letter days and during that hour the skilful reaper will reap his harvest—as well he may—with a clear conscience if he fishes fair and "plays the game."

So, too, when a South-wester arises and goes roaring down the loch, churning its waters into foam-crested waves, the tyro may regain his paradise in the kindly curl of surge and yeast and the trout pass to a dishonoured doom. On such a day in such a loch the true coarse fisher may issue forth with a light heart and return with a heavy creel. He may mount salmon gut and he may adorn it with largish flies. He may cast anyhow and strike as hard and bear as hard on his rising and hooked fish as he will, for death to trout even in such a loch sometimes rides on the wings of a south-westerly gale. Then I resign the paradise to those who think that under such conditions with no difficulties to be overcome it retains its paradisaic character. I do so, however, with one proviso. Even under such favourable conditions the basket of the skilled angler will far outweigh that of the unskilled. The latter may kill fish in the storm, when he failed in the calm or the light air; the former will kill more fish in a gale than he did in the still water, but their capture will not afford him nearly the same satisfaction. The reason for this is not far to seek; on the last analysis, sport, whether amongst fin, fur, or feather, does not consist in the number slain, but in the difficulties overcome, so that two trout killed after the exercise of cunning and skill and actually beguiled to their doom are worth a thousand willing and obsequious victims, just as one carefully stalked and circumvented wild goose may outweigh in sporting value a hundred fast-travelling "rocketers" that have come on straight, to be killed clean and true, or a perfect hecatomb of driven grouse that have taken every dip in the course of a low-pitched and fast-winged flight towards the fatal butts.*

It is clearly not on such days that the sporting loch of this type reaches its ideal. That is attained from the point of view of pure angling when only an occasional fish is killed under a bright sun and nature sleeps and all her children respect the solemn hush lest they disturb the slumber of the Great Mother. The supreme hour may come with the evening, and with it the reward of laborious hours so crowded with interest that the toil has been a pleasure. The evening rise on such a lake on a calm June night, with only the sound of feeding fish swirling in madness or sucking in with assurance and many a satisfied tail-flop, the great moth-like things that evening brings to flutter at the gates of death, is a source of joy untold, when far and fine is the rule and each fish is fairly and specially angled for in the knowledge that the harvest was sown by the reaper with laborious care when the sun was high and is the meet reward of virtue. If there be high treason to scientific ang-

* I trust I may escape the charge of hypocritical asceticism to which this may lay me open. It is not the shooting of, but the getting of a shot at, the wild goose which places the killing of that bird above the killing of "rocketers" and of low-flying grouse, birds which, with the exception of a late woodcock in a February corrie, afford the most difficult and most sporting of shots.

ling in such sport as this, a blunt axe and a big block by the nearest chalk stream be my doom!

Away in the further West, where the Hebrides "forget the main" and the weird moors seem still in the grey of evening to be the home of Picts of pattering feet sounding with fleshlike eeriness in the silence, and the great Kelpie, fabled dweller in all lakes dangerous to the lily-hunting child, may rise to greet you with his roar, lie lakes that may fairly claim a place amongst the "sporting" waters—lakes whose brown-trout if scarcely so hard to beguile, nevertheless are harder to play and kill than even the trout of the ideal sporting loch.

Nor do sea-trout and mixed lochs fail to divide themselves naturally into "sporting" and less "sporting" waters. Loch Lomond, Loch Maree, Loch Shiel and large lakes cannot when the wind sits fair and the waves roar shorewards be called sporting lochs in the true sense of the phrase, for a sporting loch is either one in which fish are difficult to raise or one in which, if easy to raise, they are extremely difficult to play and land on "sporting" tackle owing to the presence of weeds and reeds and their own strength.

The last consideration is the rub, and though in the great lakes the fish have few allies, and the killing and landing of heavy fish is only a matter of time and assuredly a feat demanding less skill and cunning than in the confined reed-girt waters of the small lochs of the west, yet even the great lakes may become sporting waters when the wind falls. Nay more. When it still ruffians it and speaks aloud, if, scorning the temptation to use great flies, stout gut, and a rod fit to enter the lists against Leviathan, the angler adheres to the golden rule of sporting morality and uses only such gear as his conscience tells him gives his quarry "law" and removes the reproach of the "big battalions," they must enter the sacred circle.

The true "sporting" loch, however, is the lake that is always "sporting," the lake that in a gale of wind does not suffer the conscientious angler to depart from his virtue; and that is so beset with seen and unseen allies of the fish that even the strongest tackle is of no avail unless aided by the cool head and the steady, skilful hand. In such a lake a single combat with one big fish is worth a hundred battles with foes met in open water, for there is just as much difference between the conditions of the two contests as there is between a fight, man

against man and a general melee, or between waging guerilla warfare in
a country of fastnesses and the conversion of the plain of Omdurman
into a stricken field by a hail of lead.   Nor do such lochs lose, but
gain in sporting character when the wind falls and the fish are more
easily " played " to their doom.   Another and greater difficulty takes
the vacant place and the raising and hooking of fish becomes the
standard by which the character of the loch is judged.   Moreover, even
if the wind has fallen, our tackle must be proportionately finer in the
calm than in the kindly curl, so that whether the wind blows high or no
zephyr shakes the reeds, such lochs retain their " sporting " character
and are ever within the pale.

For their mastery there is no worse school than the lake of wide-
spreading free-waters.   I remember watching a master of the free lake
fishing one of these reed-girt sporting waters.   He had killed a few
fish of a decent size and was in the very highest feather and yearning
for the blood of a giant.   Presently the giant gratified his desire.   He
rose some twenty yards to leeward of a bed of reeds and some forty
yards to windward of another bed.   I saw the white gleam of his rise
and caught just a glimpse of the steely blue of his back; I saw the
fourteen foot rod bend—the free water angler affects such weapons—and
heard the scream of the reel, but the sound had scarcely reached my
ears when the fish was in the furthest reed bed.   There was a white
boil, a faint sound as of an angry man, and the boat came towards where
I was sitting, an interested spectator.   Presently the discomfitted angler, whiter far as to the gills than the fish he had lost, came ashore and
acknowledged in the most " sporting " fashion that he was a mere tyro
in the art of angling for such fish in such water, finishing up his modestly
expressed excuses for his defeat with the unassailable dictum that " he
had never seen such a fish and did not know what loch fishing meant
until he felt his own helplessness before that rush for the reeds."   In
the " open water " loch he might not have encountered such a fish, and
if he had done so, he could have survived the rush.   Three other equally
convincing experiences are recalled by this episode in the life of a sea-
trout in a sporting loch.   The first brings back to me a more glorious
fishing evening than my recollection can parallel.   A soft and balmy
wind from the west ruffled into an even, gentle ripple the waters of the
lake ; overhead a grey dome, without a covert threat of rain, stretched

from horizon to horizon ; above and beyond these signs of promise, the sea-trout seemed to have gone mad, and only giants were on the war path. They were rising everywhere. Out on the loch were two anglers, dry fly men both, and the harvest was about to be reaped. One of them was a parson. Presently through the evening air came the sharp scream of a reel, then silence, broken after a second by an uncanonical exclamation. And so for the rest of the evening I could tell which angler had risen, struck and been broken by a big fish from the superior theological flavour of the mild expletives, sent like Colonel Everard's " one and only " across the water, when the parson did not let " I dare not " wait upon " I shall." The second experience was afforded by a confident slayer of Tay salmon, who acknowledged defeat like a man, and the third by two anglers who had waded knee-deep in slaughter in the Tweed and who left the lake and the island in disgust, threatening to return and take dire vengeance with 19 feet rods and tackle to correspond.

Let me pass, however, from the tales of woe to the more joyful chronicles of the sporting lakes.

In the districts where lie the true sporting lochs calm succeeds storm, and storm comes sweeping into the hush of calm with a rapidity that gives infinite variety. Amongst the many days of chance and change graven on the tablets of the " haec olims," four stand out with a vividness to which time is forced to be gentle. On the first the wind " ruffianed it " to such purpose " by land and sea " that the waters of a small reed-girt lake were white with the fury of racing waves. To keep the boat from flying before the gale was all my gillie could do. To make headway was at some periods impossible, at others, and even in the lulls, a matter of the utmost difficulty. Yet, strange to say, the few fish that rose, and they were all large sea-trout, came up from the churn of the yellow loch at a small red fly. One great fish rose with majestic calm clean across a wave in whose roll he essayed to come down on the fly, but which swept it from him as a Cape pigeon is rolled on the crest of a Horn sea. One battle with a fish of 5 lbs. was as exciting a combat as the heart of angling man could desire and was worth " ten years of peaceful life." He came up with a high rolling rise when the gale was at its fiercest, and dashed when he felt the steel and the strain straight up to windward, where it was impossible to fol-

low him, travelling high through the waves towards the sanctuary of
the bending reeds rustling in the gale. Luckily he
hung for a moment or two, restrained by the butt and
finally came across and down wind, and I was able to get on terms
with him at the expense of not a few brown seas. When at length I
got parallel with him, he was led a merry circling dance down and across
wind and though the reeds were never far away the strain was so steady
and my gillie guided the boat with such skill on the "circular sailing"
plan, that the fish was fairly outwitted and finally died a sporting death
in the very centre of the lake. The final moment was the very crisis in
his fate for to attempt to hold the boat when he was foredone to windward was to risk dragging, and to land him to leeward was to run the
equal peril of a sudden squall that might blow us on to the top of him.
He was, therefore, landed with the boat broadside to the wind, just to
leeward of the stern. The fight recalled another experience on a similar
day on a more open, but still a sporting lake, when on a nine foot rod
carrying twenty yards of line I allowed myself the glorious luxury of
following through a mile of water a fresh-run sea-trout of 6½lbs., which
charitably rushed down wind. These memories crowd thick, yet each
is a separate picture deep-graven in the tablets. Vivid and clear, they
grow not old and on them ever falls the "memorial gleam." But let
the full tale tell why "forgetfulness cannot lay them to sleep." The
next morning the fury of the gale increased and I fished for half-an-hour
from the rocks in a "shore" loch, killing a 6lb. sea-trout with such ease
on a 14ft. rod, that the experience was sufficient to make me abjure for
ever and a day such a weapon, as unworthy of the chivalrous contest of
such lakes. Nevertheless had I not continued to use the same rod for
half-an-hour in the evening, I would have missed one of those thrilling
experiences, born of the mystery of the lake. Darkness was creeping over the weird land and away under the shadows of the bens it
was already almost night; the loch itself was wrapt in gloom and across
its vexed surface spindrift was flying thick, when I made a chance cast—
again with that fatal fly of red—close by a rock. I saw nothing and felt
only the electric shock of seizure. Then suddenly my rod bent, and the
reel screamed as a fish with a speed to which the circumstances lent an
uncanny velocity sped away into the lake. Spurting high through the
waves, without a fin showing, his "phit phit" came to the ear of my

fancy through the howling of the gale, as he rushed away into the hurly
burly of the gloom just as night closed over the storm-tost waters and
a fiercer blast, as if saluting the hooking of the demon trout, came roaring
up the glen below and swept with the fury of concentrated venom over
moor and lake, speaking with a voice that found a thousand muttering
echoes amongst the hills. It was weird, eerie, awe-inspiring—one of
those crowded minutes of glorious life in which one drinks deep not
only of the joy of angling but of the mystery of a thousand fables born
of the grey moors and the lone waters, the silence that may soothe or
madden, steep in sleepy content or terrify into hysterical fear of the
unknown, haunting the last kingdom left by the onward march. My
line, a black curve for a few yards, was soon lost in the gloom. My
gillie oppressed by the weirdness of the situation and yet not wholly
oblivious to the utilitarian glory that would be his, were the fish finally
led to the net for doom, invoked at one moment all the saints in Gaelic,
the next cursed all the devils in English, and with one breath bade me
be careful, and with the next implored me to check the wild career of
the demon fish. But I said never a word. It is not every day, much
less every night, that ideals are realised and the lake gives of its
mystery with so free a hand, and with that bountiful measure eyes
gazing into the blackness of its depth have often visioned. Look upon
the picture. One hundred yards or more away and still urging on his
mad career through the impenetrable gloom was a fish, great surely
beyond the dreams of waking ambition, the very demon trout said to
haunt every lake and once every century doomed to seize a fly and give
to one of the enemies of his race the sport of a magic fish before, unseen, he vanishes into the mystery from whence he came, once more
resumes his watch and ward by the treasure houses of the undiscover-
able, and gains a second immortality in an angler's tale. But even the
rush of such a demon fish of fancy or reality must have an end. And
the end of the rush of this fish came. A few seconds only had elapsed
from his hooking, when I ventured to check his career and, strange to
say, he turned, turned and came back, not with the fury that had characterised his going, but with a slow, a stately, a deliberate motion that
was almost more weird and uncanny. Yard after yard of line was
slowly reeled in. Nearer and nearer he came and thinner and thinner
grew the thread of the spell. The gillie silent, alert, obedient as a

soldier in the crisis of a battle, the supreme moment when the tide of war turns, stands at the burn mouth on a rocky point, myself on its further bank. But still the demon does not show. Presently he is within ten yards—five—three—above the net and the red fly flashes its danger signal from the expiring wave of a broad tail, above a brown wrist, and comes away as the fish sinks in the net. The spell is broken. A close finish, truly, and a marvellous realisation of an ideal, for the relaxation of the strain was sufficient to at once release the hook, whose hold in the skin *above the tail* had been of the slighest. And what of the demon, this child of the mystery of the lake, that should never have been caught, but left to adorn a tale told over the fifth tumbler when the lights wax low and mortals sleep and spectres rise and the dead alone are wakeful? The prose of his mystery told only a tale of 5¾lbs., but he should never have been weighed in any scale, and have escaped to find no record in black and white, in pounds and ounces; his only chronicle should have been a legend of the loch.

Next morning a strange change had come over the scene. The gale had died, as all gales die, and nature slept to the soothing music of a gentle breeze and the lapping of wavelets amongst the rocks. The sun "lit up the morn," and in the light of garish day, the loch was once more merely a Highland lake, yielding of its spoil with a frankness that was commonplace. The hour of the demon trout and the mystery of the lake were gone. On the fourth day I was again afloat on the reed-girt lake, and in its "drumlie" waters one could read the only traces of the gale. Scarcely a ripple stirred from shore to shore, and the water lay in unbroken calm save for an occasional baby zephyr that would kiss the surface with its sun-warmed lips. The sun blazed from a cloudless sky. All day I cast over rising fish, killing only three and all day the silence would be broken by the sound of leaping fish which gave promise of sport when the shadows came and with them the evening rise. It is long delayed, but presently when the west is still blushing with the last kiss of the sun and just as the shy young moon peeps over the shoulder of a hoary ben and sends a long shaft of quivering silver across the lake, the first gleam of a rising fish greets from the water the silver signal from the sky. A long light cast, a steady movement of the flies, and a fish is dimpling, dimpling after the red fly and finally takes it with a wavy dash and I am playing

a lusty five pounder in the pale and uncertain light of a silvered loch.
He is fresh from the salt wash and his strength is immense, while turn
him as I may, I cannot escape the myriad moons that dance everywhere
on the lake and always across and between the fish and myself.   Here,
there, everywhere always striving for the sanctuary of the weeds that
fish leads me. His jump in which he rivals in silvery splendour the
beams of the moon caught and reflected from his gleaming sides, the
glistening spume of his recoil in the calm water form a picture on
which memory lingers.   But at length he succumbs and joins the
immortals that have died, as all good fish must hope to die, in fair
fight "with their feet to the foe."   Before we finally abandon the loch,
six more fish of smaller size join him in death, and who can say that
ten fish thus taken do not vindicate the claim of the sporting loch to
a place in the waters of the angling paradise, judged from every point
of view, and even by the standard of the stern and captious " moralist "?
And what of the other kindred sporting lakes or waters that partake of
the character of lakes?   Amongst them—after their own sort—even
the " ditches " may claim a place, provided the golden rule of proportion
in tackle be observed, while there is no opposing the claim of the salt
water river to rank amongst the chosen few.   Consider only the variety
of its fish, the opportunities it affords of diversified sport.   Occasional
salmon sail in majesty up and down its waters in quest of a change from
the diet of the estuary proper and the open sea.   Sea-trout abound,
and nowhere do they attain higher weights.   Wandered yellow and
brown trout with their kindred ally, the slob or tidal trout, haunt
its waters in varying number.   Grey mullet, most shy and difficult to
tempt of all sea-fish to their undoing by the angler's guile, invade its
channel ; lythe, saithe, and cod are regular denizens, while in its
stiller portions flounders flit their uncanny way over such sandy patches
as the weeds have spared, and of crustacean and minute forms of salt-
water life there is no end.   Angling for sea-trout with the fly in such
a river is as nerve-thrilling sport as any mortal can hope to enjoy.   The
gleam of a salmon near the fly in the dark waters of the Findhorn or the
Awe, the electric thrill of a new-hooked fish, the first plunge in the
dubious strife, rank high amongst the emotions of sport, but they must
yield pride of place to the dash of a sea-trout amongst the green and
swirling depths of a salt-water river with all its attendant dangers of

trailing weeds and perils of waving tangle. With his ocean-fed strength unimpaired, his activity still that of a trained athlete, champion sprinter of the salt ways, and his acrobatic agility as restless as the sea itself, he will urge his mad career without pause at such a desperate pace, throw himself with such sudden force from the water in a succession of bewildering leaps, that almost before the sound of the first has reached your ears, he has ended another rush and turned another summersault. The last you see of him as he vanishes for ever is either the white boil which is his scornful farewell or the momentary vision of a bright and dripping form, gleaming silver above the blue, as full fifty yards from where you stand amazed, your spirit overcrowed, your admiration aglow, your ambition rivalling your regret in intensity, he leaps from the surge and thunder of the waters and is once more free of the sea.

What then is the true criterion, the standard that admits each and all of these waters within the sphere of the " sporting," the moral order of field and moor and loch and river? Only one answer can be returned to such a question, and it has already been indicated. The criterion is that the 'greater the difficulties to be overcome, the greater is the victory and the higher on the sporting scale rises the water conquered.

Waters and days which tax and exhaust skill and ingenuity are always on the last analysis the best waters and the best angling days. I have had days on sea-trout and other lochs when a steady breeze curled the water all day, when clear skies, save for fleecy clouds, and a bracing atmosphere gave the best promise of sport, and when the fish, responding to the conditions, rose with an almost montonous persistency which reduced angling to the mechanical art of casting, striking, playing and landing, fish after fish coming obsequious to the doom of steel and feather. It is true that on such days the quick eye acting in unison with the ready hand enables the angler of experienced skill to basket three fish for every one creeled by the tyro or by the impatient. But the higher lesson is lost in the treading of the smooth and easy path to success. No demand is made upon the store of optimistic energy, the unwearied, though but ill-rewarded patience, which rise superior to the frowns of immediate fortune, and by the inspiration of effort and the consciousness that success has been merited, though not com-

manded, teach the most useful of the lessons of angling to all warriors
in the battle of life, that "Nil Desperandum" is the best blazon for
those who toil on the sunless side of the great and thorny hedge.

THE END

CPSIA information can be obtained
at www.ICGtesting.com
Printed in the USA
LVHW091349170619
621471LV00001B/179/P